C by Dissection

The Essentials of C Programming

SECOND EDITION

Al Kelley & Ira Pohl

The Benjamin/Cummings Publishing Company, Inc.
Redwood City, California ● Menlo Park, California
Reading, Massachusetts ● New York ● Don Mills, Ontario ● Wokingham, U.K.
Amsterdam ● Bonn ● Sydney ● Singapore ● Tokyo ● Madrid ● San Juan

TO OUR WIVES

Sponsoring Editor: Dan Joraanstad
Cover Designer: John Martucci
Copy Editor: Nick Murray
Proofreader: Christine Sabooni
Production: Alyssa Weiner
Composition: G & S Typesetters, Inc.

Library of Congress Cataloging-in-Publication Data
Kelley, Al.
        C by dissection : the essentials of C programming / Al Kelley &
Ira Pohl.—2nd ed.
            p.   cm
        Includes index.
        ISBN 0-8053-3140-9
        1. C (Computer program language)   I. Pohl, Ira.   II. Title.
    QA76.73.C15K45   1992
    005.13'3—dc20   91-38278
                                                                        CIP

ISBN 0-8053-3140-9
1 2 3 4 5 6 7 8 9 10–DO–95 94 93 92

The Benjamin/Cummings Publishing Company, Inc.
390 Bridge Parkway
Redwood City, California 94065

SELECTED TITLES FROM THE BENJAMIN/CUMMINGS SERIES IN COMPUTER SCIENCE

G. Booch
Object Oriented Design with Applications (1991)

G. Brookshear
Computer Science: An Overview, Third Edition (1991)

D. M. Etter
FORTRAN 77 with Numerical Methods for Scientists and Engineers (1992)

C. N. Fischer and R. J. LeBlanc
Crafting a Compiler with C (1991)

P. Helman, R. Veroff, and F. Carrano
Intermediate Problem Solving and Data Structures: Walls and Mirrors, Second Edition (1991)

D. W. Gonzalez
Ada Programmer's Handbook with LRM (1991)

A. Kelley and I. Pohl
A Book on C: Programming in C, Second Edition (1990)

A. Kelley and I. Pohl
C by Dissection: Essentials of C Programming, Second Edition (1992)

I. Pohl
C++ for C Programmers (1990)

I. Pohl
C++ for Pascal Programmers (1990)

I. Pohl
Turbo C++ (1991)

W. J. Savitch
Pascal: An Introduction to the Art and Science of Programming, Third Edition (1990)

W. J. Savitch
Turbo Pascal 6.0: An Introduction to the Art and Science of Programming, Third Edition (1992)

M. Sobell
A Practical Guide to the UNIX System, Second Edition (1989)

M. Sobell
A Practical Guide to UNIX System V, Release 4 (1991)

M. Weiss
Data Structures and Algorithm Analysis (1991)

CONTENTS

PREFACE   xiii

1. WRITING AN ANSI C PROGRAM   2
   1.1   GETTING READY TO PROGRAM   4
   1.2   A FIRST PROGRAM   5
   1.3   VARIABLES, EXPRESSIONS, AND ASSIGNMENT   8
   1.4   INITIALIZATION   14
   1.5   THE USE OF #define   15
   1.6   THE USE OF printf() AND scanf()   16
         THE USE OF printf()   17
         THE USE OF scanf()   19
   1.7   THE while STATEMENT   22
   1.8   PROBLEM SOLVING: COMPUTING SUMS   24
   1.9   STYLE   27
   1.10 COMMON PROGRAMMING ERRORS   28
   1.11 SYSTEM CONSIDERATIONS   29
         WRITING AND RUNNING A C PROGRAM   29
         INTERRUPTING A PROGRAM   32
         TYPING AN END-OF-FILE SIGNAL   32
         REDIRECTION OF THE INPUT AND THE OUTPUT   32
   1.12 SUMMARY   33
   1.13 EXERCISES   34

2. LEXICAL ELEMENTS, OPERATORS, AND THE C SYSTEM   44

2.1	CHARACTERS AND LEXICAL ELEMENTS	46
2.2	COMMENTS	49
2.3	KEYWORDS	50
2.4	IDENTIFIERS	51
2.5	CONSTANTS	52
2.6	STRING CONSTANTS	53
2.7	OPERATORS AND PUNCTUATORS	54
2.8	PRECEDENCE AND ASSOCIATIVITY OF OPERATORS	55
2.9	INCREMENT AND DECREMENT OPERATORS	57
2.10	ASSIGNMENT OPERATORS	59
2.11	AN EXAMPLE: COMPUTING POWERS OF TWO	62
2.12	THE C SYSTEM	63
	THE PREPROCESSOR	64
	THE STANDARD LIBRARY	65
2.13	STYLE	68
2.14	COMMON PROGRAMMING ERRORS	70
2.15	SYSTEM CONSIDERATIONS	72
2.16	SUMMARY	73
2.17	EXERCISES	74

3. FLOW OF CONTROL   80

3.1	RELATIONAL, EQUALITY, AND LOGICAL OPERATORS	82
3.2	RELATIONAL OPERATORS AND EXPRESSIONS	83
3.3	EQUALITY OPERATORS AND EXPRESSIONS	84
3.4	LOGICAL OPERATORS AND EXPRESSIONS	85
	SHORT-CIRCUIT EVALUATION	88
3.5	THE COMPOUND STATEMENT	89
3.6	THE EMPTY STATEMENT	89
3.7	THE if AND THE if-else STATEMENTS	90
3.8	THE while STATEMENT	95
3.9	PROBLEM SOLVING: FINDING MAXIMUM VALUES	96
3.10	THE for STATEMENT	99
3.11	PROBLEM SOLVING: COMBINATORICS	101
3.12	PROBLEM SOLVING: BOOLEAN VARIABLES	103
3.13	THE COMMA OPERATOR	104
3.14	THE do STATEMENT	106
3.15	THE goto STATEMENT	107
3.16	THE break AND continue STATEMENTS	108
3.17	THE switch STATEMENT	110
3.18	NESTED FLOW OF CONTROL	111

3.19	THE CONDITIONAL OPERATOR	112
3.20	STYLE	114
3.21	COMMON PROGRAMMING ERRORS	115
3.22	SYSTEM CONSIDERATIONS	119
3.23	SUMMARY	120
3.24	EXERCISES	121

4. FUNCTIONS AND STRUCTURED PROGRAMMING — 128

4.1	FUNCTION INVOCATION	130
4.2	FUNCTION DEFINITION	130
4.3	THE return STATEMENT	133
4.4	FUNCTION PROTOTYPES	136
4.5	TOP-DOWN DESIGN	138
4.6	PROBLEM SOLVING: RANDOM NUMBERS	143
4.7	A SIMULATION: THE GAME OF HEADS OR TAILS	146
4.8	INVOCATION AND CALL-BY-VALUE	149
4.9	STYLE	150
4.10	COMMON PROGRAMMING ERRORS	150
4.11	SYSTEM CONSIDERATIONS	152
4.12	SUMMARY	154
4.13	EXERCISES	155

5. CHARACTER PROCESSING — 160

5.1	THE DATA TYPE char	162
5.2	THE USE OF getchar() AND putchar()	164
5.3	AN EXAMPLE: CAPITALIZE	167
5.4	THE MACROS IN ctype.h	171
5.5	PROBLEM SOLVING: REPEATING CHARACTERS	172
5.6	PROBLEM SOLVING: COUNTING WORDS	174
5.7	STYLE	177
5.8	COMMON PROGRAMMING ERRORS	178
5.9	SYSTEM CONSIDERATIONS	180
5.10	SUMMARY	182
5.11	EXERCISES	182

6. THE FUNDAMENTAL DATA TYPES — 186

6.1	DECLARATIONS AND EXPRESSIONS	187
6.2	THE FUNDAMENTAL DATA TYPES	188
6.3	CHARACTERS AND THE DATA TYPE char	189

6.4	THE DATA TYPE int	191
6.5	THE INTEGRAL TYPES short, long, AND unsigned	193
6.6	THE FLOATING TYPES	194
6.7	THE sizeof OPERATOR	197
6.8	MATHEMATICAL FUNCTIONS	198
6.9	CONVERSIONS AND CASTS	201
	THE INTEGRAL PROMOTIONS	201
	THE USUAL ARITHMETIC CONVERSIONS	202
	CASTS	203
6.10	PROBLEM SOLVING: COMPUTING INTEREST	204
6.11	STYLE	209
6.12	COMMON PROGRAMMING ERRORS	210
6.13	SYSTEM CONSIDERATIONS	212
6.14	SUMMARY	213
6.15	EXERCISES	214

7. ENUMERATION TYPES, typedef, AND BITWISE OPERATORS — 224

7.1	ENUMERATION TYPES	225
7.2	THE USE OF typedef	227
7.3	AN EXAMPLE: THE GAME OF PAPER, ROCK, SCISSORS	230
7.4	BITWISE OPERATORS AND EXPRESSIONS	236
	BITWISE COMPLEMENT	237
	TWO'S COMPLEMENT	238
	BITWISE BINARY LOGICAL OPERATORS	239
	LEFT AND RIGHT SHIFT OPERATORS	239
7.5	MASKS	241
7.6	SOFTWARE TOOLS: PRINTING AN int BITWISE	242
7.7	PACKING AND UNPACKING	245
	MULTICHARACTER CHARACTER CONSTANTS	248
7.8	STYLE	249
7.9	COMMON PROGRAMMING ERRORS	250
7.10	SYSTEM CONSIDERATIONS	252
7.11	SUMMARY	252
7.12	EXERCISES	254

8. FUNCTIONS, POINTERS, AND STORAGE CLASSES — 262

8.1	POINTER DECLARATION AND ASSIGNMENT	264
8.2	ADDRESSING AND DEREFERENCING	264
8.3	POINTERS TO void	270
8.4	CALL-BY-REFERENCE	271

8.5	SCOPE RULES	273
8.6	STORAGE CLASSES	274
	THE STORAGE CLASS auto	274
	THE STORAGE CLASS extern	275
	THE STORAGE CLASS register	277
	THE STORAGE CLASS static	278
8.7	STATIC EXTERNAL VARIABLES	279
8.8	DEFAULT INITIALIZATION	281
8.9	AN EXAMPLE: PROCESSING CHARACTERS	281
8.10	FUNCTION DECLARATIONS AND DEFINITIONS	286
8.11	THE TYPE QUALIFIERS const AND volatile	287
8.12	STYLE	288
8.13	COMMON PROGRAMMING ERRORS	290
8.14	SYSTEM CONSIDERATIONS	291
8.15	SUMMARY	292
8.16	EXERCISES	294

9.	**ARRAYS AND POINTERS**	**300**
9.1	ONE-DIMENSIONAL ARRAYS	301
	INITIALIZATION	303
	SUBSCRIPTING	304
9.2	AN EXAMPLE: COUNTING EACH LETTER SEPARATELY	304
9.3	THE RELATIONSHIP BETWEEN ARRAYS AND POINTERS	307
9.4	POINTER ARITHMETIC AND ELEMENT SIZE	308
9.5	PASSING ARRAYS TO FUNCTIONS	309
9.6	A SORTING ALGORITHM: BUBBLE SORT	310
9.7	MULTIDIMENSIONAL ARRAYS	312
	TWO-DIMENSIONAL ARRAYS	312
	TWO-DIMENSIONAL ARRAYS AND FUNCTIONS	314
	THREE-DIMENSIONAL ARRAYS	315
	INITIALIZATION	316
9.8	DYNAMIC MEMORY ALLOCATION	316
9.9	STYLE	318
9.10	COMMON PROGRAMMING ERRORS	322
9.11	SYSTEM CONSIDERATIONS	322
9.12	SUMMARY	323
9.13	EXERCISES	324

10.	**STRINGS AND POINTERS**	**330**
10.1	THE END-OF-STRING SENTINEL \0	332
10.2	INITIALIZATION OF STRINGS	333
10.3	AN EXAMPLE: HAVE A NICE DAY	334

10.4	USING POINTERS TO PROCESS A STRING	337
10.5	PROBLEM SOLVING: COUNTING WORDS	342
10.6	PASSING ARGUMENTS TO main()	342
10.7	STRING HANDLING FUNCTIONS IN THE STANDARD LIBRARY	344
10.8	STYLE	346
10.9	COMMON PROGRAMMING ERRORS	347
10.10	SYSTEM CONSIDERATIONS	347
10.11	SUMMARY	348
10.12	EXERCISES	349

11.	**THE PREPROCESSOR AND SOFTWARE METHODOLOGY**	**352**
11.1	THE USE OF #include	354
11.2	THE USE OF #define	354
	SYNTACTIC SUGAR	355
11.3	MACROS WITH ARGUMENTS	356
11.4	THE TYPE DEFINITIONS AND MACROS IN *stddef.h*	358
11.5	PROBLEM SOLVING: SORTING WITH qsort()	359
11.6	AN EXAMPLE: MACROS WITH ARGUMENTS	364
11.7	CONDITIONAL COMPILATION	369
11.8	PREDEFINED MACROS	372
11.9	THE OPERATORS # AND ##	372
11.10	THE assert() MACRO	374
11.11	THE USE OF #error AND #pragma	375
11.12	LINE NUMBERS	375
11.13	CORRESPONDING FUNCTIONS	376
11.14	SOFTWARE METHODOLOGY	376
11.15	DEVELOPING A LARGE PROGRAM	377
11.16	AN EXAMPLE: PRINTING IN COLUMNS	377
11.17	STYLE	387
11.18	COMMON PROGRAMMING ERRORS	388
11.19	SYSTEM CONSIDERATIONS	390
11.20	SUMMARY	391
11.21	EXERCISES	393

12.	**RECURSION**	**402**
12.1	RECURSIVE PROBLEM SOLVING	404
12.2	AN EXAMPLE: DRAWING PATTERNS ON THE SCREEN	410
12.3	STRING HANDLING USING RECURSION	411
12.4	THE DIVIDE-AND-CONQUER METHODOLOGY	412
12.5	STYLE	415

12.6	COMMON PROGRAMMING ERRORS	416
12.7	SYSTEM CONSIDERATIONS	418
12.8	SUMMARY	419
12.9	EXERCISES	420

13. STRUCTURES AND LINKED LISTS — 428

13.1	DECLARING STRUCTURES	430
13.2	ACCESSING A MEMBER	432
13.3	OPERATOR PRECEDENCE AND ASSOCIATIVITY: A FINAL LOOK	436
13.4	STRUCTURES, FUNCTIONS, AND ASSIGNMENT	437
13.5	PROBLEM SOLVING: STUDENT RECORDS	440
13.6	INITIALIZATION OF STRUCTURES	443
13.7	THE USE OF typedef	444
13.8	SELF-REFERENTIAL STRUCTURES	446
13.9	LINEAR LINKED LISTS	448
	DYNAMIC STORAGE ALLOCATION	449
13.10	LIST OPERATIONS	450
13.11	COUNTING AND LOOKUP	452
13.12	INSERTION AND DELETION	453
13.13	STYLE	456
13.14	COMMON PROGRAMMING ERRORS	457
13.15	SYSTEM CONSIDERATIONS	458
13.16	SUMMARY	458
13.17	EXERCISES	459

14. INPUT/OUTPUT AND FILES — 464

14.1	THE OUTPUT FUNCTION printf()	465
14.2	THE INPUT FUNCTION scanf()	471
	DIRECTIVES IN THE CONTROL STRING	471
	ORDINARY CHARACTERS	472
	WHITE SPACE CHARACTERS	472
	CONVERSION SPECIFICATIONS	473
	FLOATING NUMBERS IN THE INPUT STREAM	475
	USING THE SCAN SET	475
	THE RETURN VALUE	477
	A scanf() EXAMPLE	477
14.3	THE FUNCTIONS sprintf() AND sscanf()	478
14.4	THE FUNCTIONS fprintf() AND fscanf()	479
14.5	ACCESSING FILES	480
14.6	AN EXAMPLE: DOUBLE-SPACING A FILE	482
14.7	USING TEMPORARY FILES AND GRACEFUL FUNCTIONS	486

14.8   ACCESSING A FILE RANDOMLY   490
14.9   STYLE   491
14.10 COMMON PROGRAMMING ERRORS   492
       THE FUNCTION sscanf() IS DIFFERENT   494
14.11 SYSTEM CONSIDERATIONS   494
14.12 SUMMARY   495
14.13 EXERCISES   496

15. SOFTWARE TOOLS   506
15.1   EXECUTING COMMANDS FROM WITHIN A C PROGRAM   508
15.2   ENVIRONMENT VARIABLES   509
15.3   THE C COMPILER   511
15.4   CREATING A LIBRARY   513
15.5   USING THE PROFILER   515
15.6   HOW TO TIME C CODE   519
15.7   THE USE OF *dbx*   523
15.8   THE USE OF *make*   525
15.9   THE USE OF *touch*   531
15.10 OTHER USEFUL TOOLS   531
15.11 STYLE   532
15.12 COMMON PROGRAMMING ERRORS   533
15.13 SYSTEM CONSIDERATIONS   533
15.14 SUMMARY   534
15.15 EXERCISES   535

16. FROM C TO C++   540
16.1   OUTPUT   542
16.2   INPUT   543
16.3   CLASSES AND ABSTRACT DATA TYPES   546
16.4   OVERLOADING   549
16.5   CONSTRUCTORS AND DESTRUCTORS   552
16.6   OBJECT-ORIENTED PROGRAMMING AND INHERITANCE 554
16.7   STYLE   557
16.8   COMMON PROGRAMMING ERRORS   558
16.9   SYSTEM CONSIDERATIONS   559
16.10 SUMMARY   559
16.11 EXERCISES   561

APPENDIX A   THE STANDARD LIBRARY   564
A.1   DIAGNOSTICS: <assert.h>   566
A.2   CHARACTER HANDLING: <ctype.h>   566

A.3   ERRORS: <errno.h>   567
A.4   FLOATING LIMITS: <float.h>   568
A.5   INTEGRAL LIMITS: <limits.h>   569
A.6   LOCALIZATION: <locale.h>   569
A.7   MATHEMATICS: <math.h>   570
A.8   NONLOCAL JUMPS: <setjmp.h>   573
A.9   SIGNAL HANDLING: <signal.h>   574
A.10   VARIABLE ARGUMENTS: <stdarg.h>   575
A.11   COMMON DEFINITIONS: <stddef.h>   576
A.12   INPUT/OUTPUT: <stdio.h>   577
A.13   GENERAL UTILITIES: <stdlib.h>   586
A.14   MEMORY AND STRING HANDLING: <string.h>   594
A.15   DATE AND TIME: <time.h>   598
A.16   MISCELLANEOUS   603

APPENDIX B   DIFFERENCES: ANSI C COMPARED TO TRADITIONAL C

                                                               606
B.1   TYPES   607
B.2   CONSTANTS   608
B.3   DECLARATIONS   609
B.4   INITIALIZATIONS   609
B.5   EXPRESSIONS   609
B.6   FUNCTIONS   610
B.7   CONVERSIONS   611
B.8   ARRAY POINTERS   612
B.9   STRUCTURES AND UNIONS   612
B.10   PREPROCESSOR   613
B.11   HEADER FILES   613
B.12   MISCELLANEOUS   614

APPENDIX C   ASCII CHARACTER CODES

                                                               616

APPENDIX D   OPERATOR PRECEDENCE AND ASSOCIATIVITY

                                                               618

INDEX

                                                               619

PREFACE

This book assumes that the reader has no programming background, and it can be used by students and first-time computer users. For student use, it is intended for a first course in programming. Each chapter presents a number of carefully explained programs, which lead the student in a holistic manner to ever-improving programming skills. The student is introduced to complete programs right from the start.

ANSI C is the language of computer professionals and is rapidly becoming the language of choice for programming and computer science instruction. A key reason for this is that ANSI C remedies a number of deficiencies found in traditional C, such as weak typing rules. These improvements make ANSI C a logical choice as a first instructional language. This book, by carefully developing working C programs, using the method of dissection, presents a thorough introduction to the programming process.

Dissection is a unique explanatory tool first developed by the authors in *A Book on C* (The Benjamin/Cummings Publishing Company, Inc., Redwood City, CA, 1984). It is similar to a structured walk-through of the code, and its intention is to explain to the reader newly encountered programming elements and idioms. Dissections are also used to illuminate key features of working code. Working programs are explained in an easy-to-follow, step-by-step manner. Many key ideas are reinforced through use in different contexts.

This book can be used as a one-semester text for an introduction to programming. Chapters 1 through 10 cover the C programming language through the use of pointers, strings, and arrays. A second-semester course can be devoted to more advanced data types, file processing, and software methodology as covered in Chapters 11 through 16. The instructor can also use this text in conjunction with other computer science courses that require the student to know the C language.

Although intended for the beginning programmer, *C by Dissection: The Essentials of C Programming* is a friendly introduction to the entire language for the experienced programmer as well. In conjunction with *A Book on C, Second Edition* by Al Kelley and Ira Pohl (The Benjamin/Cummings Publishing Company, Inc., Redwood City, CA, 1990), the computer professional will gain a comprehensive understanding of the language, including key points concerning its use under MS-DOS and UNIX. As a package, the two books offer an integrated treatment of the C programming language and its use that is unavailable elsewhere. Furthermore, in conjunction with *C++ for C Programmers* by Ira Pohl (The Benjamin/Cummings Publishing Company, Inc., Redwood City, CA, 1990), the student or professional is also given an integrated treatment of the object-oriented language C++.

WHAT'S NEW

C by Dissection: The Essentials of C Programming, Second Edition is now up-to-date with all code and examples written in ANSI C and with a balanced presentation of UNIX and PC environments. To address the growing number of first programming courses taught in C, the second edition has been modified to include more coverage of CS1 concerns such as top-down design, modularity, and structured programming.

CHAPTER FEATURES

Each chapter contains the following pedagogical elements:

Systems Considerations. C is available on almost any computer and under most operating systems, but there are occasional differences in behavior from system to system. This book conforms explicitly to ANSI C and explains the differences between traditional C and ANSI C. All programs have been tested, and emphasis on portability has been maintained.

Programming Style. A consistent and proper coding style is adopted from the beginning with careful explanation as to its importance and rationale. The style standard used is one chosen by professionals in the working C community. C supports function prototypes and strong type checking. This is adhered to throughout.

Common Programming Errors. Many typical programming bugs, along with techniques for avoiding them, are described. Much of the frustration of learning a language is caused by encountering obscure errors. Most books discuss correct code but leave the reader to a trial-and-error process for finding out about bugs. This book explains how typical errors in C are made and corrected.

Holistic Approach. Right from the start the student is introduced to full working programs. Excessive detail is avoided in explaining the larger elements of writing working code. The student is introduced to writing functions at an early point in the text as a major feature of structured programming.

Programming Methodology. Programming style and methodology is stressed throughout. Chapter 3 shows how the `goto` statement can be avoided with structured branching statements and nested flow of control. Chapter 4 introduces the concept of top-down design and structured programming. Chapter 8 carefully explains how call-by-reference can be implemented. Chapter 11 treats modularity and shows how to use the preprocessor to improve the portability and readability of code. Chapter 12 describes the importance of recursion. It develops the divide-and-conquer methodology for solving problems. Finally, Chapter 15 describes a number of C utilities for writing code.

Summary. A succinct list of points covered in the chapter are reiterated as helpful review.

Exercises. The exercises test the student's knowledge of the language. Many exercises are intended to be done interactively while reading the text. This encourages self-paced instruction by the reader. The exercises frequently extend the reader's knowledge to an advanced area of use.

ANSI C STANDARD

ANSI (American National Standards Institute) is involved in setting standards for many kinds of systems, including programming languages. In particular, ANSI Committee X3J11 is responsible for setting the standard for the programming language C. During the 1980s the committee created draft standards for what is known as "ANSI C" or "standard C." The standard was finally approved in 1989. The standard specifies the form of programs written in C and establishes how these programs are to be interpreted. The purpose of the standard is to promote portability, reliability, maintainability, and efficient execution of C language programs on a variety of machines. Almost all recent C compilers follow the ANSI C standard.

ACKNOWLEDGMENTS

Our special thanks go to Debra Dolsberry, Cottage Consultants, Aptos, California, who acted as the chief technical editor for some of this material. Her careful reading of the working code often led to important improvements. Robert Field, University of California, Santa Cruz, acted as the technical editor for the first edition. He provided many useful insights on programming practice and methodology. Others who provided helpful suggestions include:

Paul Andersen	Purdue University, Indiana
Michael Beeson	San Jose State University, California
John Berry	Foothill College, California
John Carroll	San Diego State University
A! Conrad	University of California, Santa Cruz
Albert Crawford	Southern Illinois University
John de Pillis	University of California, Riverside
Dan Drew	Texas A & M University, College Station
Rex Gantenbein	University of Wyoming
Arthur Geis	College of DuPage, Illinois
William Giles	San Jose State University, California
Susan Graham	University of California, Berkeley
Paul Higbee	University of North Florida
Rex Hurst	Utah State University
Ann Mitchell	Purdue University, Indiana
Jay Munyer	University of California, Santa Cruz
Tom Poston	Postech, Korea
Dain Smith	Mt. Hood Community College, Oregon
Dennie Van Tassel	University of California, Santa Cruz

In addition, we would like to thank our sponsoring editor, Dan Joraanstad, for his encouragement and constant support, and Alyssa Weiner for her excellent work on the production of this text.

Al Kelley   Ira Pohl
University of California, Santa Cruz

1

WRITING AN ANSI C PROGRAM

1.1   GETTING READY TO PROGRAM

1.2   A FIRST PROGRAM

1.3   VARIABLES, EXPRESSIONS, AND ASSIGNMENT

1.4   INITIALIZATION

1.5   THE USE OF #define

1.6   THE USE OF printf() AND scanf()

   THE USE OF printf()

   THE USE OF scanf()

1.7   THE while STATEMENT

1.8   PROBLEM SOLVING: COMPUTING SUMS

1.9   STYLE

1.10   COMMON PROGRAMMING ERRORS

1.11   SYSTEM CONSIDERATIONS

   WRITING AND RUNNING A C PROGRAM

   INTERRUPTING A PROGRAM

   TYPING AN END-OF-FILE SIGNAL

   REDIRECTION OF THE INPUT AND THE OUTPUT

1.12   SUMMARY

1.13   EXERCISES

This chapter introduces the reader to the ANSI C programming world. Some general ideas on programming are discussed, and a number of elementary programs are thoroughly explained. The basic ideas presented here become the foundation for more complete explanations that occur in later chapters. An emphasis is placed on the basic input/output functions of C. Getting information into and out of a machine is the first fundamental task to be mastered in any programming language.

C uses the functions `printf()` and `scanf()` extensively for output and input, respectively. The use of both of these functions is explained. Other topics discussed in this chapter include the use of variables to store values, and the use of expressions and assignment to change the value of a variable. The chapter also includes a discussion of the `while` statement. An example is presented to show how a `while` statement provides for repetitive action.

Throughout this chapter and throughout the text many examples are given. Included are many complete programs, and often they are dissected. This allows the reader to see in detail how each construct works. Topics that are introduced in this chapter are seen again in later chapters, with more detailed explanation where appropriate. This spiral approach to learning emphasizes ideas and techniques essential for the C programmer.

1.1 GETTING READY TO PROGRAM

Programs are written to instruct machines to carry out specific tasks, or to solve specific problems. A step-by-step procedure that will accomplish a desired task is called an *algorithm*. Thus programming is the activity of communicating algorithms to computers. We are all used to giving instructions to someone in English and having that person carry out the instructions. The programming process is analogous, except that machines have no tolerance for ambiguity and must have all steps specified in a precise language and in tedious detail.

The programming process

1 Specify the task.
2 Discover an algorithm for its solution.
3 Code the algorithm in C.
4 Test the code.

A computer is a digital electronic machine composed of three main components: processor, memory, and input/output devices. The processor is also called the *central processing unit*, or *CPU*. The processor carries out instructions that are stored in the memory. Along with the instructions, data is also stored in memory. The processor typically is instructed to manipulate the data in some desired fashion. Input/output devices take information from agents external to the machine and provide information to those agents. Input devices are typically terminal keyboards, disk drives, and tape drives. Output devices are typically terminal screens, printers, disk drives, and tape drives. The physical makeup of a machine can be quite complicated, but the user need not be concerned with the details. The operating system on a machine looks after the coordination of machine resources.

The *operating system* consists of a collection of special programs and has two main purposes. First, the operating system oversees and coordinates the resources of the machine as a whole. For example, when a file is created on a disk, the operating system takes care of the details of locating it in an appropriate place and keeping track of its name, size, and date of creation. Second, the operating system provides tools to users, many of which are useful to the C programmer. Two of these tools are of paramount importance: a text editor and the C compiler.

We assume that the reader is capable of using a text editor to create and modify files containing C code. C code is also called *source code*, and a file containing source code is called a *source file*. After a file containing source code (a program) has been created, the C compiler is invoked. The actual process of doing this is system-dependent. (We discuss this in more detail in Section 1.11, "System Considerations.") For example, on some systems we can invoke the compiler with the command

cc pgm.c

where *pgm.c* is the name of a file that contains a program. If there are no errors in *pgm.c*, this command produces an *executable file*, one that can be run, or executed. Although we think of this as "compiling the program," what actually happens is more complicated.

In Chapter 15, "Software Tools," we discuss the compilation process in more detail. Here, we just want to mention the basics. When we compile a simple program, three separate actions occur: first the preprocessor is invoked, then the compiler, and finally the loader. The preprocessor modifies a copy of the source code by including other files and by making other changes. (Later in this chapter we will discuss the preprocessor further.) The compiler then translates this into *object code* that the loader then uses to produce the final executable file. A file that contains object code is called an *object file*. Object files, unlike source files, usually are not read by humans. When we speak of "compiling a program," we really mean invoking the preprocessor, the compiler, and the loader. For a simple program this all gets done with a single command.

After a programmer writes a program, it has to be compiled and tested. If modifications are needed, then the source code has to be edited again. Thus part of the programming process consists of the cycle

When the programmer is satisfied with the performance of the program, the cycle ends.

1.2   A FIRST PROGRAM

A first task for anyone learning to program is to get the machine to print on the screen. Let us begin by writing a program that prints the phrase "she sells sea shells" on the screen. The complete program is

```
#include <stdio.h>

main()
{
    printf("she sells sea shells\n");
}
```

Using the text editor, the programmer types this into a file ending in *.c*. The choice of a file name should be mnemonic. Let us suppose that *sea.c* is the name of the file in which the program has been written. When this program is compiled and executed, it prints on the screen

```
she sells sea shells
```

DISSECTION OF THE *sea* PROGRAM

■ `#include <stdio.h>`

Lines that begin with a `#` are called *preprocessing directives*. They communicate with the preprocessor. This `#include` directive causes the preprocessor to include a copy of the standard header file *stdio.h* at this point in the code. This header file is provided by the C system. The angle brackets around `<stdio.h>` indicate that this file is to be found in the "usual place," which is system-dependent. We have included this file because it contains information about the `printf()` function.

■ `main()`

Every program has a function named `main`, where execution begins. The parentheses following `main` indicate to the compiler that it is a function.

■ `{`

A left brace begins the body of each function. A corresponding right brace must end the function. Our style will be to place these braces on separate lines in column 1. Braces are also used to group statements together.

■ `printf()`

The C system contains a standard library of functions that can be used in programs. This is a function from the library that prints on the screen. We included the header file *stdio.h* because it provides certain information to the compiler about the function `printf()`, namely, its function prototype. (Function prototypes will be discussed in later chapters.)

■ `"she sells sea shells\n"`

A string constant in C is a series of characters surrounded by double quotes. This string is an argument to the function `printf()`, which controls what is to be printed.

The two characters \n at the end of the string (read "backslash n") represent a single character called *newline*. It is a nonprinting character. Its effect is to advance the cursor on the screen to the beginning of the next line.

■ `printf("she sells sea shells\n");`

This is the function `printf()` being called, or *invoked*, with a single argument, namely, the string

   `"she sells sea shells\n"`

Even though a string may contain many characters, the string itself should be thought of as a single quantity. Notice that this line ends with a semicolon. All declarations and statements in C end with a semicolon.

■ `}`

This right brace matches the left brace above and ends the function `main()`.

The function `printf()` acts to continuously print across the screen. It moves to a new line when a newline character is read. The screen is a two-dimensional display that prints from left to right and top to bottom. To be readable, output must appear properly spaced on the screen.

Let us rewrite our program to make use of two `printf()` statements. Although the program looks different, its output is the same.

```
#include <stdio.h>

main()
{
   printf("she sells ");
   printf("sea shells\n");
}
```

Notice that the string used as an argument to the first `printf()` statement ends with a blank character. If the blank were not there, then the words `sells` and `sea` would have no space between them in the output.

As a final variation to this program, let us add the phrase "by the seashore" and print on three lines.

```
#include <stdio.h>

main()
{
    printf("she sells\n");
    printf("sea shells\n");
    printf("by the seashore\n");
}
```

When we execute this program, the following appears on the screen:

```
she sells
sea shells
by the seashore
```

Notice that the three printf() statements in the body of main() could be replaced by the single statement

```
printf("she sells\nsea shells\nby the seashore\n");
```

The availability of useful functions such as printf() in the standard library is a powerful feature of C. Although technically the standard library is not part of the C language, it is part of the C system. Because the functions in the standard library are available wherever a C system is found, programmers routinely use them.

1.3   VARIABLES, EXPRESSIONS, AND ASSIGNMENT

Our first program illustrated the use of printf() for output. In our next program we want to illustrate the use of variables to manipulate integer values. Variables are used to store values. Since different kinds of variables are used to store different kinds of data, the type of each variable must be specified. To illustrate our ideas, we will write a program based on the wreck of the *Hesperus*, a calamity at sea made famous in a poem by Henry Wadsworth Longfellow. The wreck occurred off the reef of Norman's Woe near Gloucester, Massachusetts, in 1839. The waters off the reef are about 7 fathoms deep. In the program we will convert this depth to other units of measure. Here is the algorithm that our program implements:

1   Assign the number of fathoms to a variable.
2   Convert fathoms to feet and store in a variable.
3   Convert feet to inches and store in a variable.
4   Print the different units of measure neatly on the screen.

In writing the C code, we have to choose an appropriate set of variables. In this case, integer variables are a natural choice. We have to make sure that our conversion expressions use the right constants. Finally, the output must be convenient to read.

```c
#include <stdio.h>

main()
{
    int    inches, feet, fathoms;

    fathoms = 7;
    feet = 6 * fathoms;
    inches = 12 * feet;
    printf("Wreck of the Hesperus:\n");
    printf("Its depth at sea in different units:\n");
    printf("    %d fathoms\n", fathoms);
    printf("    %d feet\n", feet);
    printf("    %d inches\n", inches);
}
```

When we compile this program and run it, here is what appears on the screen:

```
Wreck of the Hesperus:
Its depth at sea in different units:
    7 fathoms
    42 feet
    504 inches
```

DISSECTION OF THE *depth* PROGRAM

■ `#include <stdio.h>`

In any program that uses `printf()` we include the standard header file *stdio.h*. We will see later why the compiler wants this file.

■ `main()`
`{`
`    int    inches, feet, fathoms;`

The first line within the body of the function `main()` is a declaration. The variables `inches`, `feet`, and `fathoms` are declared to be of type `int`, one of the fundamental types in C. A variable of type `int` can take on integer values. All variables in a program must be declared before they can be used. Declarations, as well as statements, end with a semicolon.

■ `fathoms = 7;`

This is an assignment statement. The equal sign = is the basic assignment operator in C. The value of the expression on the right side of the = symbol is assigned to the variable on the left side. Here, the expression on the right side is the constant expression 7. That value is assigned to the variable `fathoms`.

■ `feet = 6 * fathoms;`
`  inches = 12 * feet;`

These are assignment statements. Since 1 fathom is equal to 6 feet, to convert a given number of fathoms to an equivalent number of feet, we must multiply by 6. The symbol * is the multiplication operator. The value of the expression 6 * `fathoms` is assigned to the variable `feet`. Since the current value of the variable `fathoms` is 7, the expression 6 * `fathoms` has the value 42, and this value is assigned to `feet`. To convert feet to inches, we must multiply by 12. The value of the expression 12 * `feet` is assigned to the variable `inches`.

■ `printf("   %d fathoms\n", fathoms);`

This `printf()` statement has two arguments

`   "   %d fathoms\n"`   and   `fathoms`

Note that they are separated by a comma. The first argument in a `printf()` function is always a string, called the *control string*. In this example the control string contains the conversion specification `%d`. A conversion specification is also called a *format*. The format `%d` causes the value of the expression in the second argument, in this case the variable `fathoms`, to be printed in the format of a decimal integer. Ordinary characters in a control string, that is, characters not comprising a format, are simply printed on the screen. Notice that the control string in this example begins with three blank spaces, causing the line being printed to be indented. The remaining `printf()` statements in the program are similar to this one.

In C, all variables must be declared before they are used in expressions and statements. The general form of a simple program is

preprocessing directives

```
main()
{
      declarations
      statements
}
```

At the top of the file we might have preprocessing directives, such as `#include` lines. In the body of `main()` the declarations must come before the statements. The declarations tell the compiler what kind of data can be stored in each of the variables. This enables the compiler to set aside the appropriate amount of memory to hold the data. We have already seen the use of integer data. Shortly we will discuss character data and floating data. The statements in the program carry out the desired computations and display information on the screen.

A variable name, also called an *identifier*, consists of a sequence of letters, digits, and underscores, but may not begin with a digit. Identifiers should be chosen to reflect their use in the program. In this way they serve as documentation, making the program more readable. After variables have been declared, they can be assigned values and used in expressions.

Certain keywords, also called *reserved words*, cannot be used by the programmer as names of variables. Examples of keywords are `char`, `int`, and `float`. In Chapter 2 we will present a table of all the keywords. Other names are known to the C system and normally would not be redefined by the programmer. The name `printf` is an example. Since `printf` is the name of a function in the standard library, it usually is not used as the name of a variable.

Expressions typically are found on the right side of assignment operators and as arguments to functions. The simplest expressions are just constants, such as 6 and 12, which were both used in the previous program. The name of a variable alone can be considered an expression, and meaningful combinations of operators with variables and constants are also expressions.

Among the many operators in C are the binary arithmetic operators,

```
+    -    *    /    %
```

used for addition, subtraction, multiplication, division, and modulus, respectively. These are called *binary* operators because they act on two operands, as in the expression

```
a + b
```

Here, the operator + is acting on the two operands a and b. An expression such as this has a value that depends on the values of a and b. For example, if a has value 1 and b has value 2, then the expression a + b has value 3.

In C, an integer expression divided by another integer expression yields an integer value. Any fractional part is discarded. Thus 1 / 2 has value 0, 7 / 2 has value 3, 18 / 4 has value 4, and 29 / 5 has value 5. Division by zero is not allowed. If a and b are int variables and one (or both) of them is negative, then the value of a / b is system-dependent (see exercise 5).

Most beginning programmers are not familiar with the modulus operator, %. As we shall see, it has many uses in programming. The expression a % b yields the remainder after a is divided by b. For example, since 5 divided by 3 is 1 with a remainder of 2, the expression 5 % 3 has value 2. In a similar fashion 7 % 4 has value 3, 12 % 6 has value 0, 19 % 5 has value 4, and 33 % 7 has value 5. In the expression a % b the value of b cannot be zero, since this would lead to division by zero. The modulus operator can act only on integer expressions, whereas all the other arithmetic operators can act on both integer and floating expressions. As with the division operator, if either operand of the modulus operator is negative, then the value of the operation is system-dependent (see exercise 5).

The keyword char stands for "character." Variables and constants of type char are used to manipulate characters. Constants of type char are written within single quotes, as in 'A' and '1' and '+'. As a simple example consider the following program:

```
#include <stdio.h>

main()
{
    char    c;

    c = 'A';
    printf("%c\n", c);      /* the letter A is printed */
}
```

The output of this program is the letter A followed by a newline character. First the variable c is declared to be of type char. Then c is assigned the value 'A'. Finally, the printf() statement causes printing to occur. Notice that the control string in the argument list for printf() contains the format %c. This causes the variable c in the second argument to be printed in the format of a character.

In ANSI C, there are three floating types, float, double, and long double. They are used to manipulate real numbers, also called *floating* numbers or *floating point* numbers. Floating constants such as 1.069, 0.003, and 7.0 are all of type double, not float. We express this idea by saying that double is the *working floating type* in C. A constant of type float is created by adding an F suffix, as in 1.069F. Similarly, a constant of type long double is created by adding an L suffix, as in -7.0L. Note carefully that the floating constant 7.0 and the int constant 7 are different. Although their conceptual values are the same, their types are different, causing them to be stored differently in a machine. The technical details concerning float and double will be discussed in Chapter 6.

Let us next give a simple illustration of the use of floating point constants and variables in a program.

```
#include <stdio.h>

main()
{
    float   x, y;

    x = 1.0;
    y = 2.0;
    printf("The sum of x and y is %f.\n", x + y);
}
```

The output of this program is

```
The sum of x and y is 3.000000.
```

First the variables x and y are declared to be of type float. Then x and y are assigned the floating values 1.0 and 2.0, respectively. Although these constants are of type double and the variables are of type float, there is no difficulty. Floating types can be freely mixed in expressions and assignments. The control string in the first argument to printf() contains the format %f. This causes the value of the expression x + y in the second argument to be printed in the format of a floating number with six digits to the right of the decimal point.

The division of floating values works as expected. For example, the floating expression 7.0 / 2.0 has 3.5 for its value. In contrast to this, the int expression 7 / 2 has the value 3, since with integer division, any remainder is discarded. In a floating expression division by zero is either disallowed or results in a value that is not a number (see exercise 11).

The modulus operator % works with integer expressions only. If x and y are variables of type float or double, then an expression such as x % y is not allowed.

Typically, an assignment statement is composed of a variable on the left side followed by an = followed by an expression on the right side. The expression can be simple or complicated and can contain function calls. Constants and ordinary expressions are not allowed on the left side of an = . We can write

```
a = b + c;
```

but not

```
a + b = c;      /* assignment to this expression is not allowed */
2 = c;          /* assignment to a constant is not allowed */
```

1.4   INITIALIZATION

When variables are declared, they may also be initialized. As an example of this, consider the declarations

```
char    c = 'A';
int     i = 1;
```

The variable c is declared to be of type char, and its value is initialized to 'A'. The variable i is declared to be of type int, and its value is initialized to 1. As another example of initialization, the *depth* program can be rewritten as follows:

```
#include <stdio.h>

main()
{
    int    inches, feet, fathoms = 7;

    feet = 6 * fathoms;
    . . . . .
```

Whether a variable is initialized depends on its intended use in a program. Typically, constants or constant expressions are used to initialize a variable. We could have written

```
    int    inches, feet, fathoms = 3 + 4;
```

but not

```
    int    inches, feet = 6 * fathoms, fathoms = 7;
```

The variable fathoms cannot be used before it has been declared; the C language does not have look-ahead capability. In exercise 6 at the end of the chapter we will point out a situation where it makes sense to use a constant expression as an initializer.

1.5 THE USE OF #define

When the C compiler is invoked, the preprocessor does its work first. Just before compilation takes place, the preprocessor modifies the source code being passed to the compiler. For example, files may be included, and specified character strings in the source code may be changed into other specified strings. The lines in a program that give commands to the preprocessor are called *preprocessing directives*, and they begin with a #. In traditional C the # must occur in column 1; in ANSI C it can be preceded on the line by white space. A common programming style is to write the # in column 1. Some examples of #define directives are

```
#define    LIMIT    100
#define    PI       3.14159
```

If these preprocessing directives occur at the top of a file that is being compiled, the preprocessor first changes all occurrences of the identifier LIMIT to 100 and all occurrences of the identifier PI to 3.14159. Whatever is in a string constant remains unchanged. Thus the preprocessor changes

```
printf("PI = %f\n", PI);          to          printf("PI = %f", 3.14159);
```

Since the identifier PI will be replaced everywhere by 3.14159, it is called a *symbolic constant*.

The use of symbolic constants in a program makes it more readable. More importantly, if a constant has been defined symbolically by the #define facility and then used throughout a program, it is easy to change it later, if necessary. For example, if we write

```
#define   LIMIT   100
```

and then use LIMIT throughout thousands of lines of code to symbolically represent the constant 100, it will be easy to change the code later. If we want to redefine the symbolic constant LIMIT from 100 to 10000, all we have to do is to change the preprocessing directive to

```
#define   LIMIT   10000
```

This automatically updates all the code; to update the executable file produced by the program, we have to recompile it.

A #define line can occur anywhere in a program. It affects only those lines in the file that come after it. Normally, all #define directives are placed at the beginning of the file, just after any #include directives. By convention, identifiers that are to be changed by the preprocessor are written in capital letters.

We will illustrate the use of a symbolic constant in the program that computes area in the next section.

1.6   THE USE OF printf() AND scanf()

The function printf() is used for printing formatted output. In an analogous fashion the function scanf() is used for reading formatted input. These functions are in the standard library and are available for use wherever a C system resides. Both printf() and scanf() are passed a list of arguments that can be thought of as

control_string   and   *other_arguments*

where *control_string* is a string that may contain conversion specifications, or formats. A conversion specification begins with a % character and ends with a conversion character. For example, in the format %d the letter d is the conversion character.

THE USE OF printf()

As we have already seen, the format %d is used to print the value of an expression as a decimal integer. In a similar fashion %c is used to print the value of an expression as a character, %f is used to print the value of a floating expression, and %s is used to print a string. The formats in a control string are used to determine how the other arguments are to be printed. Formats that are appropriate for the arguments should be used. Consider

```
printf("Get set: %s %d %f %c%c\n", "one", 2, 3.33, 'G' 'O');
```

The arguments to printf() are separated by commas. In this example there are six arguments:

```
"Get set: %s %d %f %c%c\n"    "one"    2    3.33    'G'    'O'
```

The first argument is the control string. The formats in the control string are matched with the other arguments. In this example the %s corresponds to "one", the %d corresponds to 2, the %f corresponds to 3.33, the first %c corresponds to 'G', and the second %c corresponds to 'O'. Each format in a control string specifies how the value of its corresponding argument is to be printed. When executed, the above printf() statement causes

```
Get set: one 2 3.330000 GO
```

to be printed. Sometimes it is convenient to write a long printf() statement on more than one line. Here is an example that illustrates how we can do this:

```
printf("%s%s\n",
    "This statement will print ",
    "just one very long line of text on the screen.");
```

The following table describes how the conversion characters in formats affect their corresponding arguments.

printf()	
Conversion character	**How the corresponding argument is printed**
c	as a character
d	as a decimal integer
e	as a floating point number in scientific notation
f	as a floating point number
g	in the e-format or f-format, whichever is shorter
s	as a string

When an argument is printed, the *place* where it is printed is called its *field* and the number of characters in its field is called its *field width*. The field width can be specified in a format as an integer occurring between the % and the conversion character. Thus the statement

```
printf("%c%3c%7c\n", 'A', 'B', 'C');
```

will print

```
A B      C
```

First the letter A is printed. Then the letter B is printed in a field of three characters. Since the letter B requires only one space, the other two spaces are blanks. Then the letter C is printed in a field of seven characters. Since the letter C requires only one space, the other six spaces are blanks.

For floating values, we can control the *precision*, as well as the field width. The precision is the number of decimal digits printed to the right of the decimal point. In a format of the form %$m.n$f the field width is specified by m, and the precision is specified by n. With a format of the form %mf only the field width is specified. With a format of the form %$.n$f only the precision is specified. The following statements illustrate these ideas:

```
printf("Some numbers: %.1f %.2f %.3f\n", 1.0, 2.0, 3.0);
printf("More numbers:%7.1f%7.2f%7.3f\n", 4.0, 5.0, 6.0);
```

Here is the output:

```
Some numbers: 1.0 2.00 3.000
More numbers:    4.0   5.00  6.000
```

To understand the output, you have to count the spaces carefully. The printf() function gives the programmer the ability to print neatly on the screen. Nonetheless, getting printout to "look right" can be very tedious.

THE USE OF scanf()

The function scanf() is analogous to the function printf(), but is used for input rather than output. Its first argument is a control string having formats corresponding to the various ways the characters in the input stream are to be interpreted. After the control string, the other arguments are *addresses*. The address of a variable is the place in memory where that variable is stored. (Addresses and pointers are explained in detail in later chapters.) The symbol & represents the *address operator*. In the example

```
scanf("%d", &x);
```

the format %d causes input characters typed at the keyboard to be interpreted as a decimal integer, and causes the value of the decimal integer to be stored at the address of x.

When the keyboard is used to input values into a program, a sequence of characters is typed, and a sequence of characters is received by the program. This sequence is called the *input stream*. If "123" is typed, the person typing it may think of it as a decimal integer, but the program receives it as a sequence of characters. The scanf() function can be used to convert strings of decimal digits, such as 123, into integer values and store them in the appropriate place.

The following table describes the effects of the conversion characters in formats used with the function scanf().

scanf()	
Conversion character	*What characters in the input stream are converted to*
c	to a character
d	to a decimal integer
f	to a floating point number (float)
lf	to a floating point number (double)
Lf	to a floating point number (long double)
s	to a string

Caution: With printf() a %f is used to print either a float or a double. With scanf() a %f is used to read in a float, and a %lf is used to read in a double. (We will warn you again about this in Section 1.10, "Common Programming Errors.")

Let us write a program in which the user is prompted to input her initials followed by her age. We will use the scanf() function to read the input characters typed on the keyboard, to convert them to appropriate values, and to store the values at specified addresses.

```
#include <stdio.h>

main()
{
    char    first, middle, last;
    int     age;

    printf("Input your three initials and your age:  ");
    scanf("%c%c%c%d", &first, &middle, &last, &age);
    printf("\nGreetings %c.%c.%c.  %s %d.\n",
        first, middle, last,
        "Next year your age will be", age + 1);
}
```

Notice carefully that the arguments passed to scanf() are

    "%c%c%c%d"   &first   &middle   &last   &age

The first argument is the control string. Each format in the control string corresponds to one of the remaining arguments. More explicitly, the first format is a %c, and it corresponds to &first, which is the first argument following the control string; the second format is a %c, and it corresponds to &middle, which is the second argument following the control string; and so forth. After the control string, all the arguments passed to scanf() must be addresses. The address operator & applied to a variable yields its address.

Suppose that we execute the above program and input CBD and 19 when prompted. Here is what appears on the screen:

```
Input your three initials and your age:  CBD  19

Greetings C.B.D.  Next year your age will be 20.
```

When reading in numbers, scanf() will skip white space (blanks, newlines, and tabs), but when reading in a character, white space is *not* skipped. Thus the program will not run correctly with the input CB D. Instead, the third character will be read in as a blank, a perfectly good character, and then scanf() will attempt to interpret the character D as a decimal integer. This will cause the program to misbehave.

The above program is not robust. After all, if the user is asked to type in initials, the program should accept white space between them. This can easily be done in C with the help of string variables, a topic that we will cover in Chapter 10.

In our next program we use a #define preprocessing directive to define a symbolic constant. Then we use scanf() to read in a value from the keyboard and printf() to print on the screen. In this program we are particularly concerned with the %lf and %f formats.

```
#include <stdio.h>

#define    PI    3.141592653589793

main()
{
    double    radius;

    printf("\n%s\n\n%s",
        "This program computes the area of a circle.",
        "Input the radius:  ");
    scanf("%lf", &radius);
    printf("\n%s\n%s%.2f%.2f%s%.2f\n%s%.5f\n\n",
        "Area = PI * radius * radius",
        "     = ", PI, " * ", radius, " * ", radius,
        "     = ", PI * radius * radius);
}
```

Suppose that we execute this program and input 2.333 when prompted. Then the following appears on the screen:

```
This program computes the area of a circle.

Input the radius:  2.333

Area = PI * radius * radius
     = 3.14 * 2.33 * 2.33
     = 17.09934
```

A hand calculation shows that $3.14 \times 2.33 \times 2.33$ is the number 17.046746, which does not agree with the result printed by our program. The reason for this is that PI and radius are printed with only two digits to the right of the decimal point, whereas their values in memory have more precision.

Note carefully that we used a %lf format in the control string used in the call to scanf() to read in a double. If we change the type of the variable radius from double to float, then we must change the %lf to %f. No change would be necessary in the control string used in the call to printf(). The lf in the format %lf stands for "long float." In traditional C, the type long float was synonymous with double. In ANSI C, the type long float does not exist, although some implementations will still accept it.

Another difference between printf() and scanf() concerns the int value returned by each of these functions. When printf() is called, the number of characters printed is returned, whereas when scanf() is called, the number of successful conversions is returned. In Section 1.8 we will illustrate a typical use of the value returned by scanf(). Although many programmers rarely use the value returned by printf(), it certainly is easy to do so (see exercise 18).

For complete details concerning printf(), scanf(), and related functions, see Chapter 14.

1.7   THE while STATEMENT

Statements in a program are normally executed one after another. This is called *sequential flow of control*. C provides the while statement to perform a repetitive action instead of a sequential flow of control.

Counting, adding, searching, sorting, and other tasks often involve doing something over and over. In this section we illustrate how a while statement can be used to perform a repetitive action. In so doing, we will also illustrate many of the other ideas already presented in this chapter.

The following program uses a while statement to add the consecutive integers from 1 to 10. In the dissection that follows we will explain how a while statement works.

```
#include <stdio.h>

main()
{
    int   i = 1, sum = 0;

    while (i <= 10){
        sum = sum + i;
        i = i + 1;
    }
    printf("Sum = %d\n", sum);
}
```

DISSECTION OF THE *add_ten* PROGRAM

■ int   i = 1, sum = 0;

The variables i and sum are declared to be of type int and are initialized to 1 and 0, respectively.

■ while (i <= 10) {
      sum = sum + i;
      i = i + 1;
   }

This whole construct is a while statement, or while loop. First the expression i <= 10 is evaluated. One reads this as "i is less than or equal to 10." Since the current value of i is 1, the expression is *true*, causing the statements between the braces { and } to be executed. The variable sum is assigned the old value of sum plus the value of i. Since the old value of sum is 0 and i is 1, sum is assigned the value 1. The variable i is assigned the old value of i plus 1. Since the old value of i is 1, i is assigned the value 2. At this point we have gone through the loop once. Now the program goes back and evaluates the expression i <= 10 again. Since i has the value 2, the expression is still *true*, causing the body of the loop to be executed again. At the end of the second time through the loop, the value of sum is 1 + 2, and the value of i is 3. Since the expression i <= 10 is still *true*, the body of the loop is executed again. At the end of the third time through the loop, the value of sum is 1 + 2 + 3, and the value of i is 4.

This process continues until i has the value 11, which causes the expression i <= 10 to be *false*. When this happens, the body of the loop is skipped, and the next statement after the while statement is executed.

■ printf("Sum = %d\n", sum);

This printf() statement causes the line

    Sum = 55

to be printed.

A while loop has the general form

    while (*expression*)
        statement

where *statement* can be a single statement or a group of statements enclosed between the braces { and }. A group of statements enclosed in braces is called a *compound statement*. In C, a compound statement can go anywhere that a statement can go.

1.8   PROBLEM SOLVING: COMPUTING SUMS

Programming is problem solving with the help of a computer. Many problems require the use of a particular problem-solving pattern, or technique, to arrive at their solution. In the following program we use *iteration* to solve our problem. Iteration is repeated action. Computers are champion iterators, readily performing tens of millions of repetitions in reliable and rapid fashion.

We want to write a program that repeatedly adds numbers that are typed in by the user. Here is our algorithm to accomplish this:

1   Initialize the two variables cnt and sum.

2   Prompt the user for input.

3   Repeatedly read in data, increment cnt, and add to sum.

4   Finally, print the values of cnt and sum.

The while statement is one of three kinds of constructs provided in C to perform iterative actions. In our solution, we use the value returned by scanf() to control the action of a while statement. This allows the user of the program to type in an arbitrary amount of data. In the dissection that follows, we will explain the mechanisms in detail.

```c
/* Sums are computed. */

#include <stdio.h>

main()
{
    int     cnt = 0;
    float   sum = 0.0, x;

    printf("The sum of your numbers will be computed.\n\n");
    printf("Input some numbers:  ");
    while (scanf("%f", &x) == 1){
        cnt = cnt + 1;
        sum = sum + x;
    }
    printf("\n%s%5d\n%s%12f\n\n",
        "Count:", cnt,
        "  Sum:", sum);
}
```

DISSECTION OF THE *find_sum* PROGRAM

■ scanf("%f", &x) == 1

The symbols == represent the equals operator. An expression such as a == b tests to see if the value of a is equal to the value of b. If it is, then the expression is *true*; if not, then the expression is *false*. For example, 1 == 1 is *true*, and 2 == 3 is *false*. The scanf() function is being used to read in characters typed by the user, to convert those characters to a value of type float, and to place the value at the address of x. If scanf() is successful in doing this, then one successful conversion has been made, and the value 1 is returned by the function. If for some reason the conversion process fails, then the value 0 is returned; if no more data is available, then the value −1 is returned. Thus the expression

```
scanf("%f", &x) == 1
```

tests to see whether scanf() succeeded in its task. If it did, then the expression is *true*; otherwise it is *false*.

■ ```
while (scanf("%f", &x) == 1) {
    cnt = cnt + 1;
    sum = sum + x;
}
```

We can think of this as

```
while (scanf() succeeds in making a conversion)  {
    . . . . .
```

As long as the expression scanf("%f", &x) == 1 is *true*, the body of the while loop is repeatedly executed. Each time through the loop, scanf() reads in characters, converts them to a number, and places the value of the number at the address of x. Then cnt is assigned the old value of cnt plus 1, and sum is assigned the old value of sum plus x. Thus cnt keeps a count of the numbers entered so far, and sum keeps a running total of those numbers. When does the process stop? Well, there are two typical things that can happen. First, the user may type in something that cannot be converted to a float. Suppose, for example, a letter is typed instead of a digit. Then scanf(), failing to make a successful conversion, will return the value 0, which in turn will cause the expression

```
scanf("%f", &x) == 1
```

to be *false*. Another way to stop the process is for the user to indicate to the program that all the data has been entered. To do this, the user must type an end-of-file signal. What must be typed to effect an end-of-file signal is system-dependent. In UNIX, a carriage return followed by a control-d is the typical way to effect an end-of-file signal. In MS-DOS a control-z must be typed instead.

■ ```
printf("\n%s%5d\n%s%12f\n\n",
    "Count:", cnt,
    " Sum:", sum);
```

Suppose this program is executed and the numbers

```
1.1  2.02  3.003  4.0004  5.00005
```

are entered, followed by a newline and a control-d (or whatever is required to effect an end-of-file signal). Here is what appears on the screen:

```
The sum of your numbers will be computed.

Input some numbers: 1.1 2.02 3.003 4.0004 5.00005

Count: 5
  Sum: 15.123449
```

If you carefully count spaces, you will see that the value of cnt has been printed in a field of 5 characters, and that sum has been printed in a field of 12 characters. This was caused by the %5d and %12f formats. Notice that the digits printed for the sum are wrong beyond the third decimal place. See exercise 17 for a discussion of this.

1.9   STYLE

A good coding style is essential to the art of programming. It facilitates the reading, writing, and maintenance of programs. A good style will use white space and comments so that the code is more easily read and understood, and is visually attractive. The proper use of indentation is crucial, as it indicates to the reader the intended flow of control. For example, in the construct

```
while (expression)
    statement
```

the indentation of *statement* indicates that its execution is under the control of the while loop. Another important stylistic point is to choose names for variables that convey their use in the program. This is a further aid to understanding. A good style will avoid error-prone coding habits.

In this text we are following the "Bell Labs industrial programming style." We place #include's, #define's, main(), and the braces { and } that begin and end the body of main() all in column 1.

```
#include <stdio.h>
#include <stdlib.h>

#define   GO   "Let's get started."

main()
{
   .....
}
```

The declarations and statements in the body of main() are indented 3 spaces. This visually highlights the beginning and end of the function body. There is one blank line following the #include's, there is one blank line following the #define's, and there is one blank line between the declarations and statements in the body of main().

An indentation of 2, 3, 4, 5, or 8 spaces is common. We use 3 spaces. Whatever is chosen as an indentation should be used consistently. To heighten readability, we put a blank space on each side of the binary operators. Some programmers do not bother with this, but it is part of the Bell Labs style.

There is no single agreed-upon "good style." As we proceed in this text, we will often point out alternate styles. Once a style has been chosen, it should be used consistently. Good habits reinforce good programming. *Caution:* Beginning programmers sometimes think they should dream up their own distinctive coding style. This should be avoided. The preferred strategy is to choose a style that is already in common use.

1.10   COMMON PROGRAMMING ERRORS

When you first start programming you will make many frustrating simple errors. One such error is to leave off a closing double quote character to mark the end of a string. When the compiler sees the first " , it starts collecting all the characters that follow as a string. If the closing " is not present, then the string continues to the next line, causing the compiler to complain. Error messages vary from one compiler to another. Here is one possibility:

```
Unterminated string or character constant
```

Another common error is to misspell a variable name, or to forget to declare it. Compilers readily catch this kind of error and properly inform you of what is wrong. However, if you misspell the name of a function, such as prinf() instead of printf(), the compiler will inform you that the function cannot be found. If you do not notice that the error message refers to `prinf` instead of `printf`, you may be quite mystified (see exercise 4).

Even elementary errors, such as forgetting to place a semicolon at the end of a statement or leaving off a closing brace, can result in rather mystifying error messages from compilers. As you become more experienced, some of the error messages produced by your compiler will begin to make sense. Exercise 4 at the end of this chapter suggests some programming errors you may want to introduce on purpose in order to experiment with the error-message capability of the compiler.

Both `printf()` and `scanf()` use a control string that can contain conversion specifications, or formats. The `%f` format is used with `printf()` to print either a `float` or a `double`. But with `scanf()`, a `%f` is used to read in a `float`, and a `%lf` is used to read in a `double`. It is a common programming error to forget to use `%lf` when using `scanf()` to read in a `double`. Most compilers cannot catch this error. All that happens is that your program produces wrong results.

Another common programming error is to forget that a format in a `printf()` statement of the form `%m.nf` uses *m* to specify the field width. For example, to specify two decimal digits to the left of the decimal point and three to the right, do *not* use `%2.3f`. Instead, use `%6.3` to account for all the digits plus the decimal point itself.

Perhaps the most common error of all when using `scanf()` is to omit the address operator `&`. If you write

```
scanf("%d%d", a, b);      instead of      scanf("%d%d", &a, &b);
```

your compiler probably will not catch the error. Instead, you are more likely get a run-time error that is difficult to debug.

1.11 SYSTEM CONSIDERATIONS

In this section we discuss a number of topics that are system-dependent. We begin with the mechanics of writing and running a C program.

WRITING AND RUNNING A C PROGRAM

The precise steps that have to be followed to create a file containing C code and to compile and execute it depend on three things: the operating system, the text editor, and the compiler. However, in all cases the general procedure is the same. We first describe in some detail how it is done in a UNIX environment. Then we discuss how it is done in an MS-DOS environment.

In the discussion that follows we will be using the *cc* command to invoke the C compiler. In reality, however, the command depends on the compiler that is being used. For example, if we were using the command-line version of the Turbo C compiler from Borland, then we would use the command *tcc* instead of *cc*. (For a list of C compilers, see the table in Section 15.3, "The C Compiler," in Chapter 15.)

Steps to be followed in writing and running a C program

1   Using an editor, create a text file, say *pgm.c*, that contains a C program. The name of the file must end with *.c*, indicating that the file contains C source code. For example, to use the *vi* editor on a UNIX system, we would give the command

  vi pgm.c

To use an editor, the programmer must know the appropriate commands for inserting and modifying text.

2   Compile the program. This can be done with the command

  cc pgm.c

The *cc* command invokes in turn the preprocessor, the compiler, and the loader. The preprocessor modifies a copy of the source code according to the preprocessing directives and produces what is called a *translation unit*. The compiler translates the translation unit into object code. If there are errors, then the programmer must start again at step 1 with the editing of the source file. Errors that occur at this stage are called *syntax errors* or *compile-time errors*. If there are no errors, then the loader uses the object code produced by the compiler, along with object code obtained from various libraries provided by the system, to create the executable file *a.out*. The program is now ready to be executed.

3   Execute the program. This is done with the command

  a.out

Typically, the program will complete execution, and a system prompt will reappear on the screen. Any errors that occur during execution are called *run-time* errors. If for some reason the program needs to be changed, the programmer must start again at step 1.

If we compile a different program, then the file *a.out* will be overwritten, and its previous contents lost. If the contents of the executable file *a.out* are to be saved, then the file must be moved, or renamed. Suppose that we give the command *cc sea.c*

This causes executable code to be written automatically into *a.out*. To save this file, we can give the command

mv a.out sea

This causes *a.out* to be moved to *sea*. Now the program can be executed by giving the command

sea

In UNIX, it is common practice to give the executable file the same name as the corresponding source file, except to drop the *.c* suffix. If we wish, we can use the *-o* option to direct the output of the *cc* command. For example, the command

cc −o sea sea.c

causes the executable output from *cc* to be written directly into *sea*, leaving intact whatever is in *a.out*.

Different kinds of errors can occur in a program. Syntax errors are caught by the compiler, whereas run-time errors manifest themselves only during program execution. For example, if an attempt to divide by zero is encoded into a program, a run-time error may occur when the program is executed (see exercises 10 and 11). Usually, an error message produced by a run-time error is not very helpful for finding the trouble.

Let us now consider an MS-DOS environment. Here, some other text editor would most likely be used. Some C systems, such as Turbo C, have both a command line environment and an integrated environment. The integrated environment includes both the text editor and the compiler. (Consult the Turbo C manuals for details.) In MS-DOS, the executable output produced by a C compiler is written to a file having the same name as the source file, but with the extension *.exe* instead of *.c*. Suppose, for example, that we are using the command line environment in Turbo C. If we give the command

tcc sea.c

then the executable code will be written to *sea.exe*. To execute the program, we give the command

sea.exe   or equivalently   *sea*

To invoke the program, we do not need to type the *.exe* extension. If we wish to rename this file, we can use the *rename* command.

INTERRUPTING A PROGRAM

When running a program, the user may want to interrupt, or kill, the program. For example, the program may be in an infinite loop. (In an interactive environment it is not necessarily wrong to use an infinite loop in a program.) Throughout this text we assume that the user knows how to interrupt a program. In MS-DOS and in UNIX, a control-c is commonly used to effect an interrupt. On some systems a special key, such as *delete* or *rubout* is used. Make sure that you know how to interrupt a program on your system.

TYPING AN END-OF-FILE SIGNAL

When a program is taking its input from the keyboard, it may be necessary to type an end-of-file signal for the program to work properly. In UNIX, this is done by typing a carriage return followed by a control-d. In MS-DOS, a control-z is typed instead. For further discussion see exercise 19.

REDIRECTION OF THE INPUT AND THE OUTPUT

Many operating systems, including MS-DOS and UNIX, can redirect the input and the output. To understand how this works, first consider the UNIX command

   ls

This command causes a list of files and directories to be written to the screen. (The comparable command in MS-DOS is *dir*.) Now consider the command

   ls > temp

The symbol > causes the operating system to redirect the output of the command to the file *temp*. (In MS-DOS, the file name needs an extension.) What was written to the screen before is now written to the file *temp*.

Our next program is called *dbl_out*. It can be used with redirection of both the input and the output. The program reads characters from the standard input file, which is normally connected to the keyboard, and writes each character twice to the standard output file, which is normally connected to the screen.

```
#include <stdio.h>

main()
{
    char    c;

    while (scanf("%c", &c) == 1) {
        printf("%c", c);
        printf("%c", c);
    }
}
```

If we compile the program and put the executable code in the file *dbl_out*, then using redirection, we can invoke this program in four ways:

dbl_out
dbl_out < *infile*
dbl_out > *outfile*
dbl_out < *infile* > *outfile*

Used in this context, the symbols < and > can be thought of as arrows. See exercise 19 for further discussion.

Some commands are not meant to be used with redirection. For example, the *ls* command does not read characters from the keyboard. Therefore, it makes no sense to redirect the input to the *ls* command; since it does not take keyboard input, there is nothing to redirect.

1.12   SUMMARY

1   An algorithm is a computational procedure consisting of elementary steps. Programming is the art of communicating algorithms to computers.

2   A simple program consists of preprocessing directives and the function main(). The body of the function is made up of declarations and statements written between the braces { and }. All variables must be declared. The declarations must occur before the statements.

3   The simplest expressions consist of just a constant, a variable, or a function call. In general, expressions consist of combinations of operators and other expressions. Most expressions have values. The assignment operator = is used to assign the value of an expression to a variable.

4   When a variable is declared, it may also be initialized. Typically, constants or constant expressions are used as initializers.

5   When source code is compiled, the preprocessor does its work first. Lines that begin with a # are called *preprocessing directives*. The programmer uses preprocessing directives to give commands to the preprocessor. Typically, the #include and #define directives are placed at the top of the file. A #define directive affects only the lines in the file that occur after it.

6   A preprocessing directive of the form

> #define   *identifier*   *replacement_string*

causes the preprocessor to change every occurrence of *identifier* to *replacement_string* before compilation takes place.

7   In traditional C, the # that begins a preprocessing directive must begin in column 1. In ANSI C, the # can be preceded by blanks and tabs.

8   The printf() function in the standard library is used for output. The arguments to this function consist of a control string followed by other arguments. The control string consists of ordinary text intermixed with conversion specifications, or formats. The ordinary text is simply printed, whereas a format causes the value of an associated argument to be printed according to the instructions embodied in the format. A format begins with a % and ends with a conversion character.

9   The scanf() function in the standard library is used for input. It is analogous to printf(). Both functions take a variable number of arguments, the first one being a control string. For printf() the other arguments are expressions; for scanf() they are addresses. The expression &v has as its value the address of v.

10   Statements are ordinarily executed sequentially. The special flow-of-control statements, such as a while statement, can alter the sequential execution of a program.

1.13   EXERCISES

1   Write on the screen the words

    she sells sea shells by the seashore

(a) all on one line, (b) on seven lines, (c) inside a box.

2   Here is part of a program that begins by asking the user to input three integers:

```
#include <stdio.h>

main()
{
    int    a, b, c, sum;

    printf("Input three integers:  ");
    . . . . .
```

Complete the program so that when the user executes it and types in 2, 3, and 7, this is what appears on the screen:

```
Input three integers:  2  3  7

Twice the sum of your integers plus 7 is 29  --  bye!
```

3   The following program writes a large letter *I* on the screen:

```
#include <stdio.h>

#define   HEIGHT    17

main()
{
    int    i = 0;

    printf("\n\nIIIIIIII\n");
    while (i < HEIGHT){
        printf("   III\n");
        i = i + 1;
    }
    printf("IIIIIIII\n\n\n");
}
```

Execute this program so you understand its effect. Write a similar program that prints a large letter *C* on the screen.

4   The purpose of this exercise is to help you become familiar with some of the error messages produced by your compiler. You can expect some error messages to be helpful and others to be less so. First check to see that the following program compiles with no error messages.

```
#include <stdio.h>

main()
{
    int   a = 1, b = 2, c = 3;

    printf("Some output:  %d %d %d\n", a, b, c);
}
```

Now introduce each of the following programming errors in turn, compile the program, and record the error messages generated:

Change the first comma in the declaration to a semicolon.

Change `printf` to `prinf`.

Remove the second " in the control string.

Replace the list `a, b, c` by `a, b, c, c`.

Remove the semicolon at the end of the `printf()` statement.

Remove the closing brace.

5   In this exercise we want to investigate how the operators / and % work with negative integer operands. If a and b are of type `int` and either a or b is negative, then the value of a / b is system-dependent. For example, 7 / −2 has value −3 on some machines and it has value −4 on others. Also, the sign of a % b is system-dependent, but on all ANSI C systems it is guaranteed that

$$(a / b) * b + a \% b \qquad \text{has the value} \qquad a$$

What happens on your system? Write an interactive program that contains the following code:

```
int   a, b;

printf("Input two nonzero integers:  ");
scanf("%d%d", &a, &b);
printf("%s%4d\n%s%4d\n%s%4d\n%s%4d\n%s%4d\n",
    "         a =", a,
    "         b =", b,
    "     a / b =", a / b,
    "     a % b =", a % b,
    "ANSI check =", (a / b) * b  +  a % b  -  a);
```

6   Write an interactive program that asks the user to input the length and width of a rectangular lawn. The dimensions should be in yards. Your program should compute the area of the lawn in square yards, square feet, and square inches (and in square meters, too, if you are ambitious). Print all the information neatly on the screen. Use the following declaration:

```
int   cv_factor = 36 * 36;     /* conversion factor: sq in per sq yrd */
```

An equivalent declaration is

```
int   cv_factor = 1296;        /* conversion factor: sq in per sq yrd */
```

but since most people know that there are 36 inches in a yard, the first declaration is preferable. One can tell at a glance that the right conversion factor is being used. *Caution:* If your lawn is large and you are working on a small machine, you may not get the right number of square inches, even though you wrote a correct program. There are limitations on the size of an integer that can be stored in an int (see Chapter 6).

7   Here is part of an interactive program that computes the value of some coins. The user is asked to input the number of half dollars, quarters, dimes, etc.

```
#include <stdio.h>

main()
{
    int    h,      /* number of half dollars */
           q,      /* number of quarters     */
           d,      /* number of dimes        */
           n,      /* number of nickels      */
           p;      /* number of pennies      */
    .....

    printf("The value of your change will be computed.\n\n");
    printf("How many half dollars do you have?  ");
    scanf("%d", &h);
    printf("How many quarters do you have?  ");
    scanf("%d", &q);
    .....
```

Complete the program, causing it to print out relevant information. For example, you may want to create output that looks like this:

```
You entered:     0 half dollars
                 3 quarters
                 2 dimes
                17 nickels
                 1 pennies
```

```
The value of your 23 coins is equivalent to 181 pennies.
```

Notice that pennies is plural, not singular as it should be. After you learn about the if-else statement in Chapter 3, you will be able to modify your program so that its output is grammatically correct.

8 Modify the program that you wrote in exercise 7 so that the last line of the output looks like this:

```
The value of your 23 coins is $1.81
```

Hint: Declare value to be a variable of type float, and use the format %.2f in your printf() statement.

9 The function scanf() returns the number of successful conversions as an int. Consider the statement

```
printf("%d\n", scanf("%d%d%d", &a, &b, &c));
```

When this statement is executed, an integer will be printed. What are the possible values for the integer? Explain. *Hint:* Write a test program and execute it using redirection. If you do not use redirection, then input and output can be intermixed on the screen in such a way as to cause confusion. When scanf() receives an end-of-file signal, the value −1 is returned.

10 The purpose of this exercise is to find out what happens on your system when a run-time error occurs. Try the following code:

```
int    a = 1, b = 0;

printf("Division by zero: %d\n", a / b);
```

On a UNIX system you might get a "core dump." That is, the system might create a file named *core* that contains information about the state of your program just before it ended abnormally. This file is not meant to be read by humans. A debugger can use the core dump to give you information about what your program was doing when it aborted. (Do not leave core dumps lying around. Since they are rather large, they eat up valuable disk space.)

11 On some systems, dividing by a floating zero does not result in a run-time error. On others it does. Try the following code:

```
double    x = 1.0, y = -1.0, z = 0.0;

printf("Division by zero: %f %f\n", x / z, y / z);
```

What happens on your system? If Inf or NaN gets printed, you can think of the value as "infinity" or as "not a number."

12 Except for a printf() statement, the following program is complete. It uses integer division and the modulus operator to convert seconds to minutes and seconds.

```
/* Convert seconds to minutes and seconds. */

#include <stdio.h>

main()
{
    int    input_value, minutes, seconds;

    printf("Input the number of seconds:   ");
    scanf("%d", &input_value);
    minutes = input_value / 60;
    seconds = input_value % 60;
    printf(...);
}
```

Complete the program by writing an appropriate printf() statement. For example, if 123 is entered after the prompt, the program might print the line

```
123 seconds is equivalent to 2 minutes and 3 seconds
```

13 Modify the program that you completed in exercise 12 so that seconds are converted to hours, minutes, and seconds. For example, if 7384 is entered after the prompt, your program might print the line

```
7384 seconds is equivalent to 2 hours, 3 minutes, and 4 seconds
```

14 Repetitive action is essential to most programs. Therefore a programmer must know precisely how a while loop works. Study the following code in detail, writing down what you think gets printed. Then write a test program to check your answer.

```
int   i = 1, sum = 0;

while (i < 10) {
    sum = sum + i;
    i = i + 1;
    printf("sum = %d   i = %d\n", sum, i);
}
```

15 Do two variations of the program that you wrote in exercise 14. For the first variation the line

```
sum = sum + i;
```

should be replaced by

```
sum = sum + 2 + i;
```

For the second variation the line should be replaced by

```
sum = (sum / 3) + (i * i);
```

16 How is an end-of-file signal entered at the keyboard on your system? Experiment with the *find_sum* program to see that the program terminates when either an inappropriate character is typed or an end-of-file signal is typed. What happens when the program is executed and no numbers are entered?

17 Unlike integer arithmetic, floating arithmetic need not be exact. Very small errors can occur in computations with floating data. Moreover, the errors are system-dependent. Often this is of no concern to the user. With the data that we used as input for the *find_sum* program, the sum had an error in the sixth decimal place. Modify the program so that the variable sum is a double instead of a float. Since a double usually (but not always; see Chapter 6) represents real numbers more accurately than a float does, the result may be more accurate with the same input. Check to see if this is the case on your machine.

18 In ANSI C the printf() function returns the number of characters printed as an int. To see how this works, write a small program containing the following lines:

```
int    cnt;

cnt = printf("abc\n");
printf("%d\n", cnt);
```

What integer gets printed? Replace the string `"abc\n"` by the following string:

```
"\tMontana!\n\n\tIt really is big sky country!\n\n"
```

Now what integer gets printed? Write down your answer, then run your program to verify it. *Hint:* Do not forget that newlines and tabs get counted too.

19 Redirection, like many new ideas, is best understood with experimentation. Write the program *dbl_out* that we presented in Section 1.11, "System Considerations," in a file named *dbl_out.c*. After you have compiled and executed the program so that you understand its effects, try the following commands:

> *dbl_out < dbl_out.c*
> *dbl_out < dbl_out.c > temp*

The following command is of special interest:

> *dbl_out > temp*

This command causes characters that are typed in at the keyboard to be written to the file *temp*, provided that you type an end-of-file signal when you are finished. What happens if instead of typing an end-of-file signal, you type a control-c to kill the program?

20 In this exercise we want to use the *dbl_out* program that you used in exercise 19. First give the command

> *dbl_out*

and then type in abc followed by a carriage return. What gets printed on the screen depends on how your operating system is configured. Normally, the operating system waits for a complete line to be typed in before processing the characters. If this is the case, then you will see aabbcc printed on the next line on the screen. If UNIX is available to you, give the command

> *stty cbreak*

Now the operating system will read each character as it is typed. Try the command *dbl_out* again, and type in abc followed by a carriage return. What appears on the screen? Explain. *Hint:* Characters typed on the keyboard are normally echoed on the screen. You may want to experiment further by giving the command

   stty −echo

which turns off the echoing. When you are finished with this exercise, you should give the command

   stty −cbreak echo

to return the operating system to its normal state. *Caution:* With echoing turned off you cannot see what you are doing!

2

LEXICAL ELEMENTS, OPERATORS, AND THE C SYSTEM

2.1   CHARACTERS AND LEXICAL ELEMENTS

2.2   COMMENTS

2.3   KEYWORDS

2.4   IDENTIFIERS

2.5   CONSTANTS

2.6   STRING CONSTANTS

2.7   OPERATORS AND PUNCTUATORS

2.8   PRECEDENCE AND ASSOCIATIVITY OF OPERATORS

2.9   INCREMENT AND DECREMENT OPERATORS

2.10   ASSIGNMENT OPERATORS

2.11   AN EXAMPLE: COMPUTING POWERS OF 2

2.12   THE C SYSTEM
       THE PREPROCESSOR
       THE STANDARD LIBRARY

2.13   STYLE

2.14   COMMON PROGRAMMING ERRORS

2.15   SYSTEM CONSIDERATIONS

2.16   SUMMARY

2.17   EXERCISES

In this chapter we explain the lexical elements of the C programming language. C is a language. Like other languages, it has an alphabet and rules for putting together words and punctuation to make correct, or legal, programs. These rules are the *syntax* of the language. The program that checks on the legality of C code is called the *compiler*. If there are errors, then the compiler will print error messages and stop. If there are no errors, then the source code is legal, and the compiler translates it into object code, which in turn gets used by the loader to produce an executable file.

When the compiler is invoked, the preprocessor does its work first. For that reason we can think of the preprocessor as being built into the compiler. On some systems this is actually the case, whereas on others the preprocessor is separate. This is not of concern to us in this chapter. We have to be aware, however, that we can get error messages from the preprocessor as well as from the compiler (see exercise 24). Throughout this chapter, we use the term *compiler* in the sense that, conceptually, the preprocessor is built into the compiler.

A C program is a sequence of characters that will be converted by a C compiler to object code, which in turn gets converted to a target language on a particular machine. On most systems the target language will be a form of machine language that can be run or interpreted. For this to happen the program must be syntactically correct. The compiler first collects the characters of the program into *tokens*, which can be thought of as the basic vocabulary of the language.

In ANSI C there are six kinds of tokens: keywords, identifiers, constants, string constants, operators, and punctuators. The compiler checks that the tokens can be formed into legal strings according to the syntax of the language. Most compilers are very precise in their requirements. Unlike human readers of English, who are able to understand the meaning of a sentence with an extra punctuation mark or a misspelled word, a C compiler will fail to provide a translation of a syntactically incorrect program, no matter how trivial the error. Hence the programmer must learn to be precise in writing code.

The programmer should strive to write understandable code. A key part of this is to produce well-commented code with meaningful identifier names. In this chapter we illustrate these important concepts.

The compilation process

C program $\rightarrow$ group characters into tokens

$\rightarrow$ translate to target code

2.1 CHARACTERS AND LEXICAL ELEMENTS

A C program is first constructed by the programmer as a sequence of characters. Among the characters that can be used in a program are the following:

lowercase letters	a b c ... z
uppercase letters	A B C ... Z
digits	0 1 2 3 4 5 6 7 8 9
other characters	d f * / = ( ) { } [ ] < > ' "
	! @ # $ % & _ | ^ ~ \ . , ; : ?

white space characters such as *blank, newline,* and *tab*

These characters are collected by the compiler into syntactic units called *tokens*. Let us look at a simple program and informally pick out some of its tokens before we go on to a strict definition of C syntax.

```
/* Read in two integers and print their sum. */

#include <stdio.h>

main()
{
   int   a, b, sum;

   printf("Input two integers:  ");
   scanf("%d%d", &a, &b);
   sum = a + b;
   printf("%d + %d = %d\n", a, b, sum);
}
```

LEXICAL DISSECTION OF THE *sum* PROGRAM

■ `/* Read in two integers and print their sum. */`

Comments are delimited by `/*` and `*/` . The compiler first replaces each comment by a single blank. Thereafter, the compiler either disregards white space or uses it to separate tokens.

■ `#include <stdio.h>`

This is a preprocessing directive that causes the standard header file *stdio.h* to be included. We have included it because it contains the function prototypes for `printf()` and `scanf()`. A function prototype is a kind of declaration. The compiler needs function prototypes to do its work.

■ `main()`
   `{`
      `int   a, b, sum;`

The compiler groups these characters into four kinds of tokens. The function name `main` is an identifier, and the parentheses `()` immediately following `main` are an operator. They tell the compiler that `main` is a function. The characters "`{`", "`,`", and "`;`" are punctuators; `int` is a keyword; `a`, `b`, and `sum` are identifiers.

■ `int   a, b, sum;`

The compiler uses the white space between `int` and `a` to distinguish the two tokens. We cannot write

```
inta, b, sum;      /* wrong: white space is necessary */
```

On the other hand, the white space following a comma is superfluous. We could have written

```
int  a,b,sum;    but not    int   absum;
```

The compiler would consider `absum` to be an identifier.

■ `printf("Input two integers:  ");`
  `scanf("%d%d", &a, &b);`

The names `printf` and `scanf` are identifiers, and the parentheses following them tell the compiler that they are functions. After the compiler has translated the C code, the loader will attempt to create an executable file. If the code for `printf()` and `scanf()` has not been supplied by the programmer, it will be taken from the standard library. A programmer would not normally redefine these identifiers.

■ `"Input two integers:  "`

A series of characters enclosed in double quotes is a string constant. The compiler treats this as a single token. The compiler also provides space in memory to store the string.

■ `&a, &b`

The character `&` is the address operator. The compiler treats it as a token. Even though the characters `&` and `a` are adjacent to each other, the compiler treats each of them as a separate token. We could have written

```
&  a  ,  &  b    or    &a,&b
```

but not

```
&a &b        /* the comma is missing */
a&, &b       /* & requires its operand to be on the right */
```

The comma is a punctuator.

■ `sum = a + b;`

The characters = and + are operators. White space here will be ignored, so we could have written

```
    sum=a+b;            or           sum  =  a  +  b  ;
```

but not

```
    s u m = a + b;
```

If we had done so, then each letter on this line would be treated by the compiler as a separate identifier. Since not all of these identifiers have been declared, the compiler would complain. Even if they were declared, the expression s u is not legal.

The compiler either ignores white space or uses it to separate elements of the language. The programmer uses white space to provide more legible code. To the compiler, program text is implicitly a single stream of characters, but to the human reader it is a two-dimensional tableau.

2.2 COMMENTS

Comments are arbitrary strings of symbols placed between the delimiters /* and */ . Comments are not tokens. The compiler changes each comment into a single blank character. Thus comments are not part of the executable program. We have already seen examples such as

```
    /* a comment */   /*** another comment ***/   /*****/
```

Another example is

```
    /*
     *   A comment can be written in this fashion
     *   to set it off from the surrounding code.
     */
```

The following illustrates one of many styles that can be used to give prominence to comments:

```
/******************************
*    If you wish, you can      *
*    put comments in a box.    *
*****************************/
```

Comments are used by the programmer as a documentation aid. The aim of documentation is to explain clearly how the program works and how it is to be used. Sometimes a comment contains an informal argument demonstrating the correctness of the program.

Comments should be written simultaneously with program text. Although some programmers insert comments as a last step, there are two problems with this. The first is that once the program is running, the tendency is either to omit or abbreviate the comments. The second is that ideally the comments should serve as running commentary, indicating program structure and contributing to program clarity and correctness. They cannot serve this purpose if they are inserted after the coding is finished.

2.3   KEYWORDS

Keywords are explicitly reserved words that have a strict meaning as individual tokens in C. They cannot be redefined or used in other contexts.

Keywords

auto	do	goto	signed	unsigned
break	double	if	sizeof	void
case	else	int	static	volatile
char	enum	long	struct	while
const	extern	register	switch	
continue	float	return	typedef	
default	for	short	union	

Some implementations may have additional keywords. These will vary from one implementation, or system, to another. As an example, here are some of the additional keywords in Turbo C:

asm	cdecl	far	huge	interrupt	near	pascal

Compared to other major languages, C has only a small number of keywords. Ada, for example, has 62 keywords. It is a characteristic of C that it does a lot with relatively few special symbols and keywords.

2.4   IDENTIFIERS

An identifier is a token that is composed of a sequence of letters, digits, and the special character _, which is called an *underscore*. A letter or underscore must be the first character of an identifier. In most implementations of C the lower- and uppercase letters are treated as distinct. It is good programming practice to choose identifiers that have mnemonic significance so that they contribute to the readability and documentation of the program. Some examples of identifiers are

```
k
_id
iamanidentifier2
so_am_i
```

but not

```
not#me        /* special character # not allowed */
101_south     /* must not start with a digit */
-plus         /* do not mistake - for _ */
```

Identifiers are created to give unique names to various objects in a program. Keywords can be thought of as identifiers that are reserved to have special meaning in the C language. Identifiers such as scanf and printf are already known to the C system as input/output functions in the standard library. These names would not normally be redefined. The identifier main is special, in that C programs always begin execution at the function called main.

One major difference among operating systems and C compilers is the length of discriminated identifiers. On some older systems, an identifier with more than 8 characters will be accepted, but only the first 8 characters will be used. The remaining characters are simply disregarded. On such a system, for example, the variable names

```
i_am_an_identifier    and    i_am_an_elephant
```

will be considered the same.

In ANSI C, at least the first 31 characters of an identifier are discriminated. Many C systems discriminate more. (See Section 2.15, "System Considerations," for further discussion.)

Good programming style requires the programmer to choose names that are meaningful. If you were to write a program to figure out various taxes, you might have identifiers such as tax_rate, price, and tax, so that the statement

```
tax = price * tax_rate;
```

would have an obvious meaning. The underscore is used to create a single identifier from what would normally be a string of words separated by spaces. Meaningfulness and avoiding confusion go hand in hand with readability to constitute the main guidelines for a good programming style.

Caution: Identifiers that begin with an underscore can conflict with system names. Only systems programmers should use such identifiers. As an example, consider the identifier _iob, which is often defined as the name of an array of structures in *stdio.h.* If a programmer tries to use _iob for some other purpose, the compiler may complain, or the program may misbehave. Applications programmers are best advised to use identifiers that do not begin with an underscore.

2.5   CONSTANTS

As we have seen in some simple introductory programs, C manipulates various kinds of values. Numbers such as 0 and 17 are examples of integer constants, and numbers such as 1.0 and 3.14159 are examples of floating constants. Like most languages, C treats integer and floating constants differently. In Chapter 6 we will discuss in detail how C understands numbers. Also, there are character constants such as 'a', 'b', and '+'. Character constants are written between single quotes, and as we shall see in Chapter 6, they are closely related to integers. Some character constants are of a special kind, such as the newline character, written '\n'. The backslash is the escape character, and we think of \n as "escaping the usual meaning of n." Even though \n is written with the two characters \ and n, it represents a single character called *newline.*

In addition to the constants that we have already discussed, there are enumeration constants in C. We will discuss these along with the keyword enum in Chapter 7. Integer constants, floating constants, character constants, and enumeration constants are all collected by the compiler as tokens. Because of implementation limits, constants that are syntactically expressible may not be available on a particular machine. For example, an integer may be too large to be stored in a machine word.

Decimal integers are finite strings of decimal digits. Because C provides octal and hexadecimal integers as well as decimal integers, we have to be careful to distinguish between the different kinds of integers. For example, 17 is a decimal integer constant, 017 is an octal integer constant, and 0x17 is a hexadecimal integer constant. (See Chapter 6 for further discussion.) Also, negative constant integers such as -33 are considered constant expressions. Some examples of constant decimal integers are

```
0
77
123456789000          /* too large for the machine? */
```

but not

```
0123                   /* an octal integer */
-49                    /* a constant expression */
123.0                  /* a floating constant */
```

While we have already used integer constants such as 144 and floating constants such as 39.7, their meaning in terms of type, along with details concerning memory requirements and machine accuracy, is complicated enough to require a thorough discussion. We do this in Chapter 6.

2.6 STRING CONSTANTS

A sequence of characters enclosed in a pair of double quote marks, such as "abc", is a string constant, or a string literal. It is collected by the compiler as a single token. In Chapter 10 we will see that string constants are stored by the compiler as arrays of characters. String constants are always treated differently from character constants. For example, "a" and 'a' are not the same.

Note that a double quote mark " is just one character, not two. If the character " itself is to occur in a string constant, it must be preceded by a backslash character \ . If the character \ is to occur in a string constant, it too must be preceded by a backslash. Some examples of string constants are

```
"a string of text"
""                                     /* the null string */
"       "                              /* a string of blank characters */
"   a = b + c;   "                     /* nothing is executed */
"   /* this is not a comment */   "
"a string with double quotes \" within"
"a single backslash \\ is in this string"
```

but not

```
/* "this is not a string" */
"and
neither is this"
```

Character sequences that would have meaning if outside a string constant are just a sequence of characters when surrounded by double quotes. In the previous examples one string contains what appears to be the statement a = b + c;, but since it occurs surrounded by double quotes, it is explicitly this sequence of characters.

Two string constants that are separated only by white space are concatenated by the compiler into a single string. Thus

"abc" "def"   is equivalent to   "abcdef"

This is a new feature of the language available in ANSI C. It is not available in traditional C.

String constants are treated by the compiler as tokens. As with other constants, the compiler provides the space in memory to store string constants. We will emphasize this point again in Chapter 10 when we discuss strings and pointers.

2.7 OPERATORS AND PUNCTUATORS

In C, there are many special characters with particular meanings. Examples include the arithmetic operators

       +   –   *   /   %

which stand for the usual arithmetic operations of addition, subtraction, multiplication, division, and modulus, respectively. Recall that in mathematics the value of a modulus b is obtained by taking the remainder after dividing a by b. Thus, for example, 5 % 3 has the value 2, and 7 % 2 has the value 1. (For a discussion of % with negative operands, see exercise 5 in Chapter 1.)

In a program, operators can be used to separate identifiers. Although typically we put white space around binary operators to heighten readability, this is not required.

```
a+b        /* this is the expression a plus b */
a_b        /* this is a 3-character identifier */
```

Some symbols have meanings that depend on context. As an example of this, consider the % symbol in the two statements

```
printf("%d", a);        and          a = b % 7;
```

The first % symbol is the start of a conversion specification, or format, whereas the second % symbol represents the modulus operator.

Examples of punctuators include parentheses, braces, commas, and semicolons. Consider the following code:

```
main()
{
    int   a, b = 2, c = 3;

    a = 17 * (b + c);
    . . . . .
```

The parentheses immediately following main are treated as an operator. They tell the compiler that main is the name of a function. After this, the symbols "{", ",", ";", "(", and ")" are punctuators. Both operators and punctuators are collected by the compiler as tokens, and along with white space, they serve to separate language elements.

Some special characters are used in many different contexts, and the context itself can determine which use is intended. For example, parentheses are sometimes used to indicate a function name; at other times they are used as punctuators. Another example is given by the expressions

```
a + b    ++a    a += b
```

They all use + as a character, but ++ is a single operator, as is +=. Having the meaning of a symbol depend on context makes for a small symbol set and a terse language.

2.8 PRECEDENCE AND ASSOCIATIVITY OF OPERATORS

Operators have rules of *precedence* and *associativity* that determine precisely how expressions are evaluated. Since expressions inside parentheses are evaluated first, parentheses can be used to clarify or change the order in which operations are performed. Consider the expression

```
1 + 2 * 3
```

In C, the operator * has higher precedence than +, causing the multiplication to be performed first, followed by the addition. Hence the value of the expression is 7. An equivalent expression is

```
1 + (2 * 3)
```

On the other hand, since expressions inside parentheses are evaluated first, the expression

```
(1 + 2) * 3
```

is different; its value is 9. Now consider the expression

```
1 + 2 - 3 + 4 - 5
```

Because the binary operators + and - have the same precedence, the associativity rule "left to right" is used to determine how it is evaluated. The "left to right" rule means that the operations are performed from left to right. Thus

```
(((1 + 2) - 3) + 4) - 5
```

is an equivalent expression.

The following table gives the rules of precedence and associativity for some of the operators of C. In addition to the operators we have already seen, the table includes operators that will be discussed later in this chapter.

Operators	Associativity
() ++ (*postfix*) -- (*postfix*)	left to right
+ (*unary*) - (*unary*) ++ (*prefix*) -- (*prefix*)	right to left
* / %	left to right
+ -	left to right
= += -= *= /= *etc.*	right to left

All the operators on a given line, such as *, /, and %, have equal precedence with respect to each other, but have higher precedence than all the operators that occur on the lines below them. The associativity rule for all the operators on a given line appears on the right side of the table. Whenever we introduce new operators, we will give their rules of precedence and associativity, and often we will encapsulate the information by augmenting the above table. These rules are essential information for every C programmer.

In addition to the binary plus, which represents addition, there is a unary plus, and both these operators are represented by a plus sign. Similar remarks hold for the minus sign. Note carefully that the unary plus was introduced with ANSI C. There is no unary plus in traditional C, only unary minus.

From the above table we see that the unary operators have higher precedence than binary plus and minus. In the expression

```
- a * b - c
```

the first minus sign is unary, and the second binary. Using the rules of precedence, we see that

```
((- a) * b) - c
```

is an equivalent expression.

2.9 INCREMENT AND DECREMENT OPERATORS

The increment operator ++ and decrement operator -- are unary operators with the same precedence as the unary plus and minus, and they associate from right to left. Both ++ and -- can be applied to variables, but not to constants or ordinary expressions. Moreover, the operators can occur in either prefix or postfix position, and different effects may occur. Some examples are

```
++i
cnt--
```

but not

```
777++            /* constants cannot be incremented */
++(a * b - 1)    /* ordinary expressions cannot be incremented */
```

Each of the expressions ++i and i++ has a value; moreover, each causes the stored value of i in memory to be incremented by 1. The expression ++i causes the stored value of i to be incremented first, with the expression then taking as its value the new stored value of i. In contrast, the expression i++ has as its value the current value of i; then the stored value of i is incremented. The following code illustrates the situation:

```
int   a, b, c = 0;

a = ++c;
b = c++;
printf("%d %d %d\n", a, b, ++c);        /* 1 1 3 is printed */
```

In a similar fashion --i causes the stored value of i in memory to be decremented by 1 first, with the expression then taking this new stored value as its value, but with i-- the value of the expression is the current value of i; then the stored value of i in memory is decremented by 1.

Note carefully that ++ and -- cause the value of a variable in memory to be changed. The operator +, for example, does not do this. An expression such as a + b has a value, which when evaluated leaves the values of the variables a and b unchanged. These ideas are expressed by saying that the operators ++ and -- have a *side effect*; not only do these operators yield a value, they also change the stored value of a variable in memory (see exercise 20).

In some cases we can use ++ in either prefix or postfix position, with both uses producing equivalent results. For example, each of the two statements

```
++i;      and      i++;
```

is equivalent to

```
i = i + 1;
```

In simple situations one can consider ++ and -- as operators that provide concise notation for the incrementing and decrementing of a variable. In other situations, careful attention must be paid as to whether prefix or postfix position is desired.

Declarations and initializations		
`int   a = 1, b = 2, c = 3, d = 4;`		
Expression	*Equivalent expression*	*Value*
`a * b / c`	`(a * b) / c`	0
`a * b % c + 1`	`((a * b) % c) + 1`	3
`++ a * b - c --`	`((++ a) * b) - (c --)`	1
`7 - - b * ++ d`	`7 - ((- b) * (++ d))`	17

2.10   ASSIGNMENT OPERATORS

To change the value of a variable, we have already made use of assignment statements such as

```
a = b + c;
```

Unlike other languages, C treats = as an operator. Its precedence is lower than all the operators we have discussed so far, and its associativity is right to left. In this section we explain in detail the significance of this.

To understand = as an operator, let us first consider + for the sake of comparison. The binary operator + takes two operands, as in the expression a + b. The value of the expression is the sum of the values of a and b. By comparison, a simple assignment expression is of the form

variable = right_side

where *right_side* is itself an expression. Notice that a semicolon placed at the end would have made this an assignment statement. The assignment operator = has the two operands *variable* and *right_side*. The value of *right_side* is assigned to *variable*, and that value becomes the value of the assignment expression as a whole. To illustrate this, consider the statements

```
b = 2;
c = 3;
a = b + c;
```

where the variables are all of type int. By making use of assignment expressions, we can condense this to

```
a = (b = 2) + (c = 3);
```

The assignment expression b = 2 assigns the value 2 to the variable b, and the assignment expression itself takes on this value. Similarly, the assignment expression c = 3 assigns the value 3 to the variable c, and the assignment expression itself takes on this value. Finally, the values of the two assignment expressions are added, and the resulting value is assigned to a.

Although this example is artificial, there are many situations where assignment occurs naturally as part of an expression. A frequently occurring situation is multiple assignment. Consider the statement

```
a = b = c = 0;
```

Since the operator = associates from right to left, an equivalent statement is

```
a = (b = (c = 0));
```

First, c is assigned the value 0, and the expression c = 0 has value 0. Then b is assigned the value 0, and the expression b = (c = 0) has value 0. Finally, a is assigned the value 0, and the expression a = (b = (c = 0)) has value 0. Many languages do not use assignment in such an elaborate way. In this respect C is different.

In addition to =, there are other assignment operators, such as += and -=. An expression such as

```
k = k + 2
```

will add 2 to the old value of k and assign the result to k, and the expression as a whole will have that value. The expression

```
k += 2
```

accomplishes the same task. The following list contains all the assignment operators.

Assignment Operators
_____

| = | += | -= | *= | /= | %= | >>= | <<= | &= | ^= | \|= |

All these operators have the same precedence, and they all have right-to-left associativity. The semantics is specified by

variable op= expression

which is equivalent to

variable = variable op (expression)

with the exception that if *variable* is itself an expression, it is evaluated only once. When dealing with arrays, this is an important technical point (see exercise 15 in Chapter 9). Note carefully that an assignment expression such as

```
j *= k + 3          is equivalent to          j = j * (k + 3)
```

rather than

```
j = j * k + 3
```

The following table illustrates how assignment expressions are evaluated.

Declarations and initializations			
`int i = 1, j = 2, k = 3, m = 4;`			
Expression	*Equivalent expression*	*Equivalent expression*	*Value*
`i += j + k`	`i += (j + k)`	`i = (i + (j+ k))`	6
`j *= k = m + 5`	`j *= (k = (m + 5))`	`j = (j * (k = (m + 5)))`	18

Even though assignment statements sometimes resemble mathematical equations, the two notions are distinct and should not be confused. The mathematical equation

$$x + 2 = 0$$

does not become an assignment statement by typing

```
x + 2 = 0;      /* wrong */
```

The left side of the equal sign is an expression, not a variable, and this expression may not be assigned a value. Now consider the assignment statement

```
x = x + 1;
```

The current value of x is assigned the old value of x plus 1. If the old value of x is 2, then the value of x after execution of the statement will be 3. Observe that as a mathematical equation,

$$x = x + 1$$

is meaningless; after subtracting x from both sides of the equation, we obtain

$$0 = 1$$

Although they look alike, the assignment operator in C and the equal sign in mathematics are not comparable.

2.11   AN EXAMPLE: COMPUTING POWERS OF 2

To illustrate some of the ideas presented in this chapter, we will write a program that prints on a line some powers of 2. Here is the program:

```
/* Some powers of 2 are printed. */

#include <stdio.h>

main()
{
   int   i = 0, power = 1;

   while (++i <= 10)
      printf("%6d", power *= 2);
   printf("\n");
}
```

The output of the program is

```
   2    4    8   16   32   64   128   256   512   1024
```

DISSECTION OF THE *pow_of_2* PROGRAM

■ /* Some powers of 2 are printed. */

Programs often begin with a comment that explains the intent or the use of the program. If the program is large, the comment may be extensive. The compiler treats comments as white space.

■ #include <stdio.h>

The header file *stdio.h* contains the function prototype for the printf() function. This is a kind of declaration for printf(). The compiler needs it to do its work correctly. (See Section 2.12, "The C System," for further details.)

■ `int   i = 0, power = 1;`

The variables i and power are declared to be of type int. They are initialized to 0 and 1, respectively.

■ `while (++i <= 10)`

As long as the value of the expression ++i is less than or equal to 10, the body of the while loop is executed. The first time through the loop the expression ++i has the value 1; the second time through the loop ++i has the value 2; and so forth. Thus the body of the loop is executed 10 times.

■ `printf("%6d", power *= 2);`

The body of the while loop consists of this statement. The string constant "%6d" is passed as the first argument to the printf() function. The string contains the format %6d, which indicates that the value of the expression power *= 2 is to be printed as a decimal with field length 6.

■ `power *= 2`

This assignment expression is equivalent to

```
power = power * 2
```

which causes the old value of power to be multiplied by 2 and the resulting value to be assigned to power. The value assigned to power is the value of the assignment expression as a whole. The first time through the loop, the old value of power is 1, and the new value is 2; the second time through the loop, the old value of power is 2, and the new value is 4, and so forth.

2.12   THE C SYSTEM

The C system consists of the C language, the preprocessor, the compiler, the library, and other tools useful to the programmer, such as editors and debuggers. In this section we discuss the preprocessor and the library. For further details about the preprocessor, see Chapter 11. For details about functions in the standard library, see Appendix A.

THE PREPROCESSOR

Lines that begin with a *#* are called *preprocessing directives*. These lines communicate with the preprocessor. In traditional C, preprocessing directives were required to begin in column 1. In ANSI C this restriction has been removed. Although a *#* may be preceded on a line by white space, it is still a common programming style to start preprocessing directives in column 1.

We have already made use of preprocessing directives such as

```
#include <stdio.h>          and          #define PI 3.14159
```

Another form of the *#include* facility is given by

```
#include "filename"
```

This causes the preprocessor to replace the line with a copy of the contents of the named file. A search for the file is made first in the current directory and then in other system-dependent places. With a preprocessing directive of the form

```
#include <filename>
```

the preprocessor looks for the file only in the "other places" and not in the current directory.

Since *#include* directives commonly occur at the beginning of the program, the include files that they refer to are called *header files*, and a .h is used to end the file name. This is a convention; the preprocessor does not require this. There is no restriction on what an include file can contain. In particular, it can contain other preprocessing directives that will be expanded by the preprocessor in turn. Although files of any type may be included, it is considered poor programming style to include files that contain the code for function definitions (see Chapter 5).

On UNIX systems the standard header files such as *stdio.h* are typically found in the directory */usr/include*. On Turbo C systems they might be found in the directory *tc**include* or *bc**include*. In general, the location of the standard *#include* files is system-dependent. All of these files are readable, and programmers, for a variety of reasons, have occasion to read them.

One of the primary uses of header files is to provide function prototypes. For example, in *stdio.h* the following lines are found:

```
int   printf(const char *format, . . . );
int   scanf(const char *format, . . . );
```

These are the function prototypes for the `printf()` and `scanf()` functions in the standard library. Roughly speaking, a function prototype tells the compiler the types of the arguments that get passed to the function and the type of the value that gets returned by the function. Before we can understand the function prototypes for `printf()` and `scanf()`, we need to learn about the function definition mechanism, pointers, and type qualifiers. These ideas are presented in later chapters. The main point that we are making here is that header files are often included because they contain the function prototypes of functions that are being used. The compiler needs the function prototypes to do its work correctly.

THE STANDARD LIBRARY

The standard library contains many useful functions that add considerable power and flexibility to the C system. Many of the functions are used extensively by all C programmers, whereas other functions are used more selectively. Most programmers become acquainted with functions in the standard library on a need-to-know basis.

Programmers are not usually concerned about the location on the system of the standard library, since it contains compiled code that is unreadable to humans. It can happen that the standard library is made up of more than one file. The mathematics library, for example, is conceptually part of the standard library, but it typically exists in a separate file. Whatever the case, the system knows where to find the code that corresponds to functions from the standard library, such as `printf()` and `scanf()`, that the programmer has used. However, even though the system provides the code, *it is the responsibility of the programmer to provide the function prototype*. This is usually accomplished by including appropriate header files.

Caution: Do not mistake header files for the libraries themselves. The standard library contains object code of functions that have already been compiled. The standard header files do not contain compiled code.

As an illustration of the use of a function in the standard library, let us show how `rand()` can be used to generate some randomly distributed integers. In later chapters we will have occasion to use `rand()` to fill arrays and strings for testing purposes. Here, we use it to print some integers on the screen.

```
#include <stdio.h>
#include <stdlib.h>

main()
{
   int   i, n;

   printf("\n%s\n%s",
      "Some randomly distributed integers will be printed.",
      "How many do you want to see?  ");
   scanf("%d", &n);
   for (i = 0; i < n; ++i){
      if (i % 6 == 0)
         printf("\n");
      printf("%12d", rand());
   }
   printf("\n");
}
```

Suppose that we execute the program and type 11 when prompted. Here is what appears on the screen:

```
Some randomly distributed integers will be printed.
How many do you want to see?  11

        16838        5758       10113       17515       31051        5627
        23010        7419       16212        4086        2749
```

DISSECTION OF THE *prn_rand* PROGRAM

■ `#include <stdio.h>`
  `#include <stdlib.h>`

These header files are included because of the function prototypes they contain. In particular, the function prototype

```
   int   rand(void);
```

is in *stdlib.h*. It tells the compiler that rand() is a function that takes no arguments and returns an int value. Rather than include *stdlib.h*, we could just as well supply this line ourselves, either at the top of the file or as a declaration inside main().

■
```
printf("\n%s\n%s",
    "Some randomly distributed integers will be printed.",
    "How many do you want to see?  ");
scanf("%d", &n);
```

A prompt to the user is printed on the screen. The characters typed in by the user are received by scanf(), converted in the format of a decimal integer, and placed at the address of n.

■
```
for (i = 0; i < n; ++i) {
    .....
}
```

This is a for loop. It is equivalent to

```
i = 0;
while (i < n) {
    .....
    ++i;
}
```

Another way to write this program would be to initialize i to be zero and then use the construct

```
while (i++ < n) {
    .....
}
```

Note carefully that i++ < n is different from ++i < n (see exercise 10).

■
```
if (i % 6 == 0)
    printf("\n");
printf("%12d", rand());
```

The operator == is the "is equal to" operator. If *expr1* and *expr2* are two expressions having the same value, then the expression *expr1* == *expr2* will be *true*; otherwise it will be *false*. In Chapter 4 we will see that == has lower precedence than %. Thus i % 6 == 0   is equivalent to   (i % 6) == 0

The effect of this is that starting with the first time through the loop, and every sixth time thereafter, the expression as a whole is *true*. Whenever the expression is *true*, a newline character is printed.

■ `printf("%12d", rand());`

Every time through the loop, the value returned by the call to rand() is printed in the format of a decimal integer. The width of the field where the integer gets printed is 12.

2.13   STYLE

Each of the statements

    ++i;   and   i++;

has the effect of incrementing the stored value of i in memory by 1. No use is made of the value of the expression; only the side effect of the operator ++ is being used. In this simple example, it is a matter of personal taste whether ++i or i++ is used. As part of a more complicated expression, only one of ++i or i++ may be appropriate. The two expressions do not have the same value.

A correct style strives for code that is readable. Although the statement

    x = (y = 2) + (z = 3);

is both correct and concise, it is not as readable as

    y = 2;
    z = 3;
    x = y + z;

It is important not to condense code just for the sake of using less space. Readability is an attribute that should not be sacrificed.

If we want to add 7 to the variable a, we can write either

    a += 7;   or   a = a + 7;

Although the choice is largely a matter of taste, professional programmers definitely favor the first.

Commenting style is crucial to program readability. There is no one correct style. Comments, properly used, give an arbitrary reader of the code the ability to understand both what the program does and how it works. One should adopt and consistently stay with a given commenting style. This is true both for individuals and organizations. Style becomes habit, and good habits reinforce good programming practice.

Comments should occur at the top of the program and at the head of major structural groupings within the source code. Short comments should occur to the right of individual statements when the effect of the statement is not obvious.

The lead comment should be visually set off and should include information such as the name of the organization, the programmer's name, the date, and the purpose of the program.

```
/*
 *   Organization:  SOCRATIC SOLUTIONS (Trade Mark)
 *   Programmer:    Constance B. Diligent
 *   Date:          19 April 1993
 *
 *   Purpose:       Birthday greetings
 */

#include <stdio.h>

main()
{
    printf("\nHAPPY BIRTHDAY TO YOU!\n\n");
}
```

While in practice the overcommenting of code almost never occurs, comments, nevertheless, should not clutter the program. Comments should illuminate what the program is doing. For example,

```
tax = price * rate;     /* sales tax formula */
```

gives insight into the program, but

```
tax = price * rate;     /* multiply price by rate */
```

is redundant, and therefore useless. It is very important to choose identifiers that describe their own use and thereby avoid extraneous commenting.

2.14   COMMON PROGRAMMING ERRORS

The programming errors discussed in this section are chiefly syntactic. These errors are caught by the compiler, and in general they keep the compiler from producing an executable output file.

Consider the following code contained in the file *exmpl_1.c*. Since the code is not syntactically correct, error and warning messages will be produced when we compile it. The exact form of the messages will vary from one compiler to another, but in general the content of the messages is similar.

```
#include <stdio.h>

main()
{
    int   a = 1, b = 2, c = 3;

    x = a + b;
    printf("x = %d\n", x);
}
```

Suppose that we compile this program on a Turbo C system, using either the *tcc* or *tc* command. Here are some of the messages that are produced:

```
Error EXMPL_1.C 7: Undefined symbol 'x' in function main
Warning EXMPL_1.C 9: 'c' is assigned a value that is never used
Warning EXMPL_1.C 9: 'b' is assigned a value that is never used
. . . . .
```

The name of the file containing the code is listed, along with the line number in which the error occurs. The integrated environment *tc* highlights the line the error occurs in, so that the programmer can immediately use the editor to correct that line. The error is easily understood; namely, x is used but not declared. The first warning message is appropriate, but the second is not. It is a spurious warning that is the result of an earlier problem; namely, x being undeclared.

Let us consider another example. Unless you are an experienced programmer, you will not see the errors at first glance.

```
#include <stdio.h>

main()
{
   int   a, b = 2, c = 3;   /* a, b, and c will be used
                               to illustrate arithmetic /

   a = (4 * b + 5 * c) / 6
   printf("a = %d   b = %d   c = %d\n", a, b, c);
)
```

Again, a raft of messages are produced by the compiler, some of them spurious.

```
Error EXMPL_2 12: Unexpected end of file in comment started
                  on line 5 in function main
Error EXMPL_2 13: Compound statement missing } in function main
Warning EXMPL_2 13: 'c' is assigned a value that is never used
                    in function main
. . . . .
```

What has happened is that the comment starting on line 5 is never closed. The first error message indicates this. Note that since the compiler was unable to find a closing } to end the program, the line numbering in the messages is spurious. Also, a spurious warning about c is produced. Compilers frequently produce this type of misleading advice. Automatic error detection by the compiler is no substitute for great care in program preparation.

After the programmer fixes one error, the compiler may uncover others. This would happen in the above program, because there is a semicolon missing at the end of the line preceding the printf() statement.

Most compilers have options that specify the kind of warnings they will produce. As a general rule, the warning level should be set as high as possible. Consider the following code:

```
#include <stdio.h>

main()
{
   printf("Try me!\n");
}
```

Since the option *-w* sets the highest warning level for the Turbo C compiler, we give the command

    tcc −w try_me.c

The following warning is produced:

    `Warning TRY_ME.C 6: Function should return a value in function main`

This warning will disappear if we change

    `main()`   `to`   `void main(void)`

This tells the compiler that `main()` is a function that takes no arguments and returns no values. The Turbo C compiler is happy with this, but for technical reasons a lot of other compilers will still complain. We will discuss this issue in more detail in Section 4.10, "Common Programming Errors," in Chapter 4. *Warning:* The *-w* option on some compilers will turn all warnings off! The kinds of options and how they are invoked vary from one compiler to another.

2.15 SYSTEM CONSIDERATIONS

ANSI C has both a unary minus and unary plus, but traditional C has only a unary minus. If you are writing portable code that has to run on a traditional compiler as well as an ANSI C compiler, then you should not use the unary plus operator.

The floating type `long double` is not available in traditional C. Since the type is new to ANSI C, many compilers treat a `double` and a `long double` the same. With time, we expect this to change.

One major difference among operating systems and C compilers is the length of discriminated identifiers, both internal and external. Examples of internal identifiers are macro names and ordinary variables. On some systems an internal identifier with more than 8 characters will be accepted, but only the first 8 characters will be used. The remaining characters are simply disregarded. On such a system, for example, the variable names

    `cafeteria_1`   `and`   `cafeteria_2`

will be considered the same.

Typical examples of external identifiers are the names of functions in the standard library, such as `printf` and `scanf`, and the names of files. In MS-DOS, file names are restricted to 8 characters plus a 3-letter extension. On a given system a programmer learns the length of discriminated identifiers by experimenting, reading the local manual, or asking someone. This is not a problem. On the other hand, if a programmer is writing C code to run on a spectrum of systems, then the limitations of all the systems must be known and respected. In ANSI C, the compiler must discriminate at least 31 characters of an internal identifier, and the system as a whole must discriminate at least 6 characters of an external identifier. Many systems discriminate more.

2.16 SUMMARY

1   Tokens are the basic syntactic units of C. They include keywords, identifiers, constants, string constants, operators, and punctuators. White space, along with operators and punctuators, can serve to separate tokens. For this reason, white space, operators, and punctuators are collectively called *separators*. White space, other than serving to separate tokens, is ignored by the compiler.

2   Comments are enclosed by the bracket pair `/*` and `*/` and are treated as white space by the compiler. They are critical for good program documentation. Comments should assist the reader to both use and understand the program.

3   A keyword, also called a *reserved word*, has a strict meaning. There are 32 keywords in C. They cannot be redefined.

4   Identifiers are tokens that the programmer uses chiefly to name variables and functions. They begin with a letter or underscore and are chosen to be meaningful to the human reader.

5   Some identifiers are already known to the system because they are the names of functions in the standard library. These include the input / output functions `scanf()` and `printf()`, and mathematical functions such as `sqrt()`, `sin()`, `cos()`, and `tan()`.

6   Constants include various kinds of integer and floating constants, character constants such as `'a'` and `'#'`, and string constants such as `"abc"`. All constants are collected by the compiler as tokens.

7   String constants such as `"deep blue sea"` are arbitrary sequences of characters, including white space characters, that are placed inside double quotes. A string constant is stored as an array of characters, but it is collected by the compiler as a single token. The compiler provides the space in memory needed to store a string constant. Character constants and string constants are treated differently. For example, `'x'` and `"x"` are not the same.

8   Operators and punctuators are numerous in C. The parentheses following main()
    are an operator; they tell the compiler that main is a function. The parentheses in the
    expression a * (b + c) are punctuators. The operations inside the parentheses are
    done first.

9   In C, the rules of precedence and associativity for operators determine how an ex-
    pression gets evaluated. The programmer needs to know them.

10 The increment operator ++ and the decrement operator -- have a side effect. In addi-
    tion to having a value, an expression such as ++i causes the stored value of i in
    memory to be incremented by 1.

11 The operators ++ and -- can be used in both prefix and postfix position, possibly
    with different effects. The expression ++i causes i to be incremented in memory,
    and the new value of i is the value of the expression. The expression i++ has as its
    value the current value of i, and then i is incremented in memory.

12 In C, the assignment symbol is an operator. An expression such as a = b + c assigns
    the value of b + c to a, and the expression as a whole takes on this value. Although
    the assignment operator in C and the equal sign in mathematics look alike, they are
    not comparable.

13 Many useful functions are available in the standard library. When a library function
    is used, the corresponding function prototype can be obtained by including the ap-
    propriate standard header file.

2.17   EXERCISES

1   Is main a keyword? Explain.

2   List five keywords and explain their use.

3   Give examples of three types of tokens.

4   Which of the following are not identifiers and why?

3id	_yes	o_no_o_no	00_go	star*it
1_i_am	one_i_aren't	me_to-2	xYshouldI	int

5   Design a standard form of introductory comment that will give a reader informa-
    tion about who wrote the program and why.

6   Take a symbol such as + and illustrate the different ways it can be used in a
    program.

7 ANSI C does not provide for the nesting of comments, although many compilers provide an option for this. Try the following line on your compiler and see what happens.

```
/* This is an attempt /* to nest */ a comment. */
```

8 Write an interactive program that converts pounds and ounces to kilograms and grams. Use symbolic constants that are defined before `main()`.

9 This question illustrates one place where white space around operators is important. Since both + and ++ are operators, the expression a+++b can be interpreted as either

```
a++ + b            or        a + ++b
```

depending on how the plus symbols are grouped. Normally, the first two plusses would be grouped and passed to the compiler to see if this were syntactically correct. Write a short program to see which interpretation is made by your compiler.

10 For the *pow_of_2* program, explain what the effect would be if the expression ++i were changed to i++ .

11 Study the following code and write down what you think gets printed. Then write a test program to check your answers.

```
int   a, b = 0, c = 0;

a = ++b + ++c;
printf("%d %d %d\n", a, b, c);
a = b++ + c++;
printf("%d %d %d\n", a, b, c);
a = ++b + c++;
printf("%d %d %d\n", a, b, c);
a = b-- + --c;
printf("%d %d %d\n", a, b, c);
```

12 What is the effect in the following statement if some, or all, of the parentheses are removed? Explain.

```
x = (y = 2) + (z = 3);
```

13   First complete the entries in the table that follows. After you have done this, write a program to check that the values you entered are correct.

Declarations and initializations		
int a = 2, b = -3, c = 5, d = -7, e = 11;		
Expression	*Equivalent expression*	*Value*
a / b / c	(a / b) / c	0
7 + c * -- d / e	7 + ((c * (-- d)) / e)	
2 * a % - b + c + 1		
39 / - ++ e - + 29 % c		
a += b += c += 1 + 2		
7 - + ++ a % (3 + b)		/* error, why? */

14   Consider the following code:

```
int   a = 1, b = 2, c = 3;

a += b += c += 7;
```

Write an equivalent statement that is fully parenthesized. What are the values of the variables a, b, and c? First write down your answer. Then write a test program to check your answer.

15   A good programming style is crucial to the human reader, even though the compiler sees only a stream of characters. Consider the following program:

```
main()
) {float qx,
zz,
tt;printf("gimme 3"
);scanf
(   "%f%f       %f",&qx,&zz

,&tt);printf("averageis=%f", (qx+tt+zz)/3.0);}
```

Although the code is not very readable, it should compile and execute. Test it to see if that is true. Then completely rewrite the program. Use white space and comments to make it more readable and well documented. *Hint:* Include a header file and choose new identifiers to replace qx, zz, and tt.

16 The integers produced by the function rand() all fall within the interval [0, *n*], where *n* is system-dependent. In ANSI C, the value for *n* is given by the symbolic constant RAND_MAX, which is defined in the standard header file *stdlib.h*. Of course, an incomplete ANSI C system may fail to make this symbolic constant available. Is it available on your system? Write a small program to find out.

17 The function rand() returns values in the interval [0, RAND_MAX] (see exercise 16). If we declare the variable median and initialize it to have the value RAND_MAX / 2, then rand() will return a value that is sometimes larger than median and sometimes smaller. On average, however, there should be as many values that are larger as there are values that are smaller. Test this hypothesis. Write a program that calls rand(), say 500 times, inside a for loop, increments the variable plus_cnt every time rand() returns a value larger than median, and increments the variable minus_cnt every time rand() returns a value less than median. Each time through the for loop, print out the value of the difference of plus_cnt and minus_cnt. This difference should oscillate about 0. Does it?

18 Rewrite the *prn_rand* program so that the integers printed are in the interval [0, 100]. *Hint:* Use the modulus operator. How many numbers do you have to print before you see the value 100? (If you do not see it, you have done something wrong.)

19 Rewrite the *prn_rand* program to make use of the construct

```
while (i++ < n) {
    . . . . .
}
```

After you get your program running and understand its effects, rewrite the program, changing

```
i++ < n      to      ++i < n
```

Now the program will behave differently. To compensate for this, rewrite the body of the while loop so that the program behaves exactly as it did in the beginning.

20 The value of an expression such as ++a + a++ is system-dependent. This is because the side effects of the increment operator ++ can take place at different times. This is both a strength and a weakness of C. On the one hand, compilers can do what is natural at the machine level. On the other hand, because such an expression is

system-dependent, the expression will have different values on different machines. Experienced C programmers recognize expressions such as this to be potentially dangerous and do not use them. Experiment with your machine to see what value is produced by ++a + a++ after a has been initialized to 0. Does your compiler warn you that the expression is dangerous?

21   Libraries on a UNIX system typically end in *.a*, which is mnemonic for "archive." Libraries in MS-DOS typically end in *.lib*. See if you can find the standard C libraries on your system. These libraries are not readable. On a UNIX system you can give a command such as

ar   t   /lib/libc.a

to see all the titles (names) of the objects in the library.

22   In both ANSI C and traditional C, a backslash at the end of a line in a string constant has the effect of continuing it to the next line. Here is an example of this:

```
"by using a backslash at the end of the line \
a string can be extended from one line to the next"
```

Write a program that uses this construct. Many screens have 80 characters per line. What happens if you try to print a string with more than 80 characters?

23   In ANSI C, a backslash at the end of *any* line is supposed to have the effect of continuing it to the next line. This can be expected to work in string constants and macro definitions on any C compiler, either ANSI or traditional (see exercise 22). However, not all ANSI C compilers support this in a more general way. After all, except in macro definitions, this construct gets little use. Does your C compiler support this in a general way? Try the following:

```
#\
include <stdio.h>

mai\
n()
{
    print\
f("Will this \
work?\n");
}
```

24 When you invoke the compiler, the system first invokes the preprocessor. In this exercise we want to deliberately make a preprocessing error, just to see what happens. Try the following program:

```
#incl <stdixx.h>

main()
{
    printf("Try me.\n");
}
```

What happens if you change #incl to #include?

25 If Turbo C is available to you, try the following program:

```
#include <stdio.h>

main()
{
    int    _ss = 1;       /* leading underscore, danger! */

    printf("_ss = %d\n", _ss);
}
```

It so happens that _ss is an additional keyword in Turbo C, and this program misuses it. Do you find the error message produced by the compiler helpful? *Remember:* The programmer can avoid problems by not using variable names that begin with an underscore.

3

FLOW OF CONTROL

3.1   RELATIONAL, EQUALITY,
      AND LOGICAL OPERATORS

3.2   RELATIONAL OPERATORS
      AND EXPRESSIONS

3.3   EQUALITY OPERATORS
      AND EXPRESSIONS

3.4   LOGICAL OPERATORS
      AND EXPRESSIONS
         SHORT-CIRCUIT
         EVALUATION

3.5   THE COMPOUND
      STATEMENT

3.6   THE EMPTY STATEMENT

3.7   THE if AND THE if-else
      STATEMENTS

3.8   THE while STATEMENT

3.9   PROBLEM SOLVING: FINDING
      MAXIMUM VALUES

3.10 THE for STATEMENT

3.11 PROBLEM SOLVING:
      COMBINATORICS

3.12 PROBLEM SOLVING:
      BOOLEAN VARIABLES

3.13 THE COMMA OPERATOR

3.14 THE do STATEMENT

3.15 THE goto STATEMENT

3.16 THE break AND continue
      STATEMENTS

3.17 THE switch STATEMENT

3.18 NESTED FLOW OF CONTROL

3.19 THE CONDITIONAL
      OPERATOR

3.20 STYLE

3.21 COMMON PROGRAMMING
      ERRORS

3.22 SYSTEM CONSIDERATIONS

3.23 SUMMARY

3.24 EXERCISES

Statements in a program are normally executed one after another. This is called *sequential flow of control*. Often we want to alter the sequential flow of control to provide for a choice of action, or a repetition of action. We can use `if`, `if-else`, and `switch` statements to select among alternative actions, and we can use `while`, `for`, and `do` statements to achieve iterative actions. We explain these flow-of-control constructs in this chapter.

Since the relational, equality, and logical operators are heavily used in flow-of-control constructs, we begin with a thorough discussion of them. These operators are used in expressions that we think of as being *true* or *false*. We explain how *true* and *false* are implemented in C. We also discuss the compound statement, which is used to group together statements that are to be treated as a unit.

3.1 RELATIONAL, EQUALITY, AND LOGICAL OPERATORS

The following table contains the operators that are most often used to affect flow of control:

Relational, Equality, and Logical Operators

Relational operators:	less than:	‹
	greater than:	›
	less than or equal to:	‹=
	greater than or equal to:	›=
Equality operators:	equal to:	==
	not equal to:	!=
Logical operators:	(unary) negation:	!
	logical and:	&&
	logical or:	||

Just like other operators, the relational, equality, and logical operators have rules of precedence and associativity that determine precisely how expressions involving these operators are evaluated.

Operators	Associativity
() ++ (*postfix*) -- (*postfix*)	left to right
+ (*unary*) - (*unary*) ++ (*prefix*) -- (*prefix*)	right to left
* / %	left to right
+ -	left to right
‹ ‹= › ›=	left to right
== !=	left to right
&&	left to right
||	left to right
?:	right to left
= += -= *= /= etc	right to left
, (*comma operator*)	left to right

The ! operator is unary. All the other relational, equality, and logical operators are binary. They all operate on expressions and yield either the int value 0 or the int value 1.

The reason for this is that in the C language *false* is represented by any zero value, and *true* is represented by any nonzero value. Some examples of expressions that can be used to represent *false* are an `int` expression having value 0, a floating expression having value 0.0, the null character `'\0'` (see Chapter 5), and the `NULL` pointer (see Chapter 9). Similarly, any expression with a nonzero value can be used to represent *true*. Intuitively, an expression such as `a < b` is either *true* or *false*. In C, this expression will yield the `int` value 1 if it is *true* or the `int` value 0 if it is *false*.

3.2   RELATIONAL OPERATORS AND EXPRESSIONS

The relational operators

```
<     >     <=     >=
```

are all binary. They each take two expressions as operands and yield either the `int` value 0 or the `int` value 1. Some examples are

```
a < 3
a > b
-1.1 >= (2.2 * x + 3.3)
a < b < c                        /* syntactically correct, but confusing */
```

but not

```
a =< b       /* out of order */
a < = b      /* space not allowed */
a >> b       /* this is a shift expression */
```

Consider a relational expression such as `a < b`. If `a` is less than `b`, then the expression has the `int` value 1, which we think of as being *true*. If `a` is not less than `b`, then the expression has the `int` value 0, which we think of as *false*. Observe that the value of `a < b` is the same as the value of `a - b < 0`. Because the precedence of the relational operators is less than that of the arithmetic operators, the expression

```
a - b < 0     is equivalent to     (a - b) < 0
```

On most machines, an expression such as `a < b` is implemented as `a - b < 0`, which is equivalent. The usual arithmetic conversions occur in relational expressions (see Chapter 6).

Let *e1* and *e2* be arbitrary arithmetic expressions. The following table shows how the value of *e1* − *e2* determines the values of relational expressions:

Values of: e1 − e2	e1 < e2	e1 > e2	e1 <= e2	e1 >= e2
positive	0	1	0	1
zero	0	0	1	1
negative	1	0	1	0

The following table illustrates the use of the rules of precedence and associativity to evaluate relational expressions.

Declarations and initializations		
int i = 1, j = 2, k = 3; double x = 5.5, y = 7.7;		
Expression	**Equivalent expression**	**Value**
i < j - k	i < (j - k)	0
- i + 5 * j >= k + 1	((- i) + (5 * j)) >= (k + 1)	1
x - y <= j - k - 1	(x - y) <= ((j - k) - 1)	1
x + k + 7 < y / k	((x + k) + 7) < (y / k)	0

3.3   EQUALITY OPERATORS AND EXPRESSIONS

The equality operators == and != are binary operators that act on expressions. They yield either the int value 0 or the int value 1. Some examples are

```
c == 'A'
k != -2
x + y == 2 * z - 5
```

but not

```
a = b            /* an assignment expression */
a = = b - 1      /* space not allowed */
(x + y) =! 44    /* syntax error: equivalent to (x + y) = (!44) */
```

Intuitively, an equality expression such as a == b is either *true* or *false*. More precisely, if a is equal to b, then a == b yields the int value 1 (*true*); otherwise it yields the int value 0 (*false*). Note that an equivalent expression is a - b == 0. This is what is implemented at the machine level.

The expression a != b illustrates the use of the "not equal to" operator. It is evaluated in a similar fashion, except that the test here is for inequality rather than for equality. The operator semantics is given by the following table.

Values of: expr1 - expr2	*expr1 == expr2*	*expr1 != expr2*
zero	1	0
nonzero	0	1

The next table shows how the rules of precedence and associativity are used to evaluate some expressions with equality operators:

Declarations and initializations		
int i = 1, j = 2, k = 3;		
Expression	**Equivalent expression**	**Value**
i == j	j == i	0
i != j	j != i	1
i + j + k == - 2 * - k	((i + j) + k) == ((- 2) * (- k))	1

3.4 LOGICAL OPERATORS AND EXPRESSIONS

The logical operator ! is unary, and the logical operators && and || are binary. Each of these operators when applied to expressions yields either the int value 0 or the int value 1.

Logical negation can be applied to an expression of arithmetic or pointer type. If an expression has value zero, then its negation will yield the int value 1. If the expression has a nonzero value, then its negation will yield the int value 0. Some examples are

```
!a
!(x + 7.7)
!(a < b || c < d)
```

but not

```
a!        /* out of order */
a != b    /* != is the token for the "not equal" operator */
```

The following table gives the semantics of the ! operator.

Values of:	
expr	*!expr*
zero	1
nonzero	0

While logical negation is a very simple operator, there is one subtlety. The operator !
in C is unlike the *not* operator in ordinary logic. If *s* is a logical statement, then

not (*not s*) = *s*

whereas in C the value of !!5, for example, is 1. Since ! associates from right to left,
the same as all other unary operators, the expression

!!5   is equivalent to   !(!5)

and !(!5) is equivalent to !(0), which has value 1. The following table shows how
some expressions with logical negation are evaluated.

Declarations and initializations		
int i = 7, j = 7; double x = 0.0, y = 999.9;		
Expression	**Equivalent expression**	**Value**
! (i - j) + 1	(! (i - j)) + 1	2
! i - j + 1	((! i) - j) + 1	−6
! ! (x + 3.3)	! (! (x + 3.3))	1
! x * ! ! y	(! x) * (!(! y))	1

The binary logical operators && and || also act on expressions and yield either the int value 0 or the int value 1. Some examples are

```
a && b
a || b
!(a < b) && c
3 && (-2 * a + 7)
```

but not

```
a &&         /* one operand missing */
a | | b      /* extra space not allowed */
a & b        /* this is a bitwise operation */
&b           /* the address of b */
```

The operator semantics is given by the following table.

Values of: *expr1*	*expr2*	*expr1 && expr2*	*expr1 || expr2*
zero	zero	0	0
zero	nonzero	0	1
nonzero	zero	0	1
nonzero	nonzero	1	1

This table, although completely accurate, does not reflect the way that programmers usually think when dealing with logical expressions. Even experienced programmers think in terms of truth values.

Values of: *expr1*	*expr2*	*expr1 && expr2*	*expr1 || expr2*
F	F	F	F
F	T	F	T
T	F	F	T
T	T	T	T

The precedence of && is higher than ||, but both operators are of lower precedence than all unary, arithmetic, and relational operators. Their associativity is left to right. The next table shows how the rules of precedence and associativity are used to compute the value of some logical expressions.

Declarations and initializations		
int i = 3, j = 3, k = 3; double x = 0.0, y = 2.3;		
Expression	**Equivalent expression**	**Value**
i && j && k	(i && j) && k	1
x || i && j - 3	x || (i && (j - 3))	0
i < j && x < y	(i < j) && (x < y)	0
i < j || x < y	(i < j) || (x < y)	1

SHORT-CIRCUIT EVALUATION

In the evaluation of expressions that are the operands of && and ||, the evaluation process stops as soon as the outcome *true* or *false* is known. This is called *short-circuit* evaluation. It is an important property of these operators. Suppose that *expr1* and *expr2* are expressions and that *expr1* has value zero. In the evaluation of the logical expression

    expr1 && *expr2*

the evaluation of *expr2* will not occur, because the value of the logical expression as a whole is already determined to be 0. Similarly, if *expr1* has a nonzero value, then in the evaluation of

    expr1 || *expr2*

the evaluation of *expr2* will not occur, because the value of the logical expression as a whole is already determined to be 1. The following code illustrates short-circuit evaluation.

```
int   i, j;

i = 2 && (j = 2);
printf("%d  %d\n", i, j);      /* 1  2 is printed */
(i = 0) && (j = 3);
printf("%d  %d\n", i, j);      /* 0  2 is printed */
i = 0 || (j = 4);
printf("%d  %d\n", i, j);      /* 1  4 is printed */
(i = 2) || (j = 5);
printf("%d  %d\n", i, j);      /* 2  4 is printed */
```

Here is a simple example of how short-circuit evaluation might be used. Suppose that we want to do a calculation that depends on certain conditions:

```
if (x >= 0.0 && sqrt(x) <= 7.7) {
    .....                        /* do something */
```

If the value of x is negative, then the square root of x will not be taken. See exercise 19 for further discussion.

3.5   THE COMPOUND STATEMENT

A compound statement is a series of declarations and statements surrounded by braces. The chief use of the compound statement is to group statements into an executable unit. When declarations come at the beginning of a compound statement, it is called a *block* (see Chapter 8). In C, wherever it is syntactically correct to place a statement, it is also syntactically correct to place a compound statement. *A compound statement is itself a statement.* An example of a compound statement is

```
{
    a = 1;
    {
        b = 2;
        c = 3;
    }
}
```

Note that in this example there is a compound statement within a compound statement. An important use of the compound statement is to achieve the desired flow of control in if, if-else, while, for, do, and switch statements.

3.6   THE EMPTY STATEMENT

The empty statement is written as a single semicolon. It is useful where a statement is needed syntactically, but no action is required semantically. As we shall see, this is sometimes useful in flow-of-control constructs such as if-else statements and for statements.

An expression followed by a semicolon is called an *expression statement*. The empty statement is a special case of the expression statement. Some examples of expression statements are

```
a = b;              /* an assignment statement */
a + b + c;          /* legal, but no useful work gets done */
;                   /* an empty statement */
printf("%d\n", a);  /* a function call */
```

3.7   THE if AND THE if-else STATEMENTS

The general form of an if statement is

if (*expr*)
    statement

If *expr* is nonzero (*true*), then *statement* is executed; otherwise *statement* is skipped, and control passes to the next statement. In the example

```
if (grade >= 90)
    printf("Congratulations!\n");
printf("Your grade is %d.\n", grade);
```

a congratulatory message is printed only when the value of grade is greater than or equal to 90. The second printf() is always executed.

Usually, the expression in an if statement is a relational, equality, or logical expression, but an expression from any domain is permissible. Some other examples of if statements are

```
if (y != 0.0)
    x /= y;

if (a < b && b < c) {
    d = a + b + c;
    printf("Everything is in order.\n");
}
```

but not

```
if  b == a            /* parentheses missing */
    area = a * a;
```

Where appropriate, compound statements should be used to group a series of state-ments under the control of a single if expression. The following code consists of two if statements:

```
if (j < k)
    min = j;
if (j < k)
    printf("j is smaller than k\n");
```

The code can be written in a more efficient and more understandable way by using a single if statement with a compound statement for its body:

```
if (j < k) {
    min = j;
    printf("j is smaller than k\n");
}
```

The if-else statement is closely related to the if statement. It has a general form given by

```
if (expr)
    statement1
else
    statement2
```

If *expr* is nonzero, then *statement1* is executed and *statement2* is skipped; if *expr* is zero, then *statement1* is skipped, and *statement2* is executed. In both cases control then passes to the next statement. Consider the code

```
if (x < y)
    min = x;
else
    min = y;
printf("Min value = %d\n", min);
```

If x < y is *true*, then min will be assigned the value of x, and if it is *false*, then min will be assigned the value of y. Control then passes to the printf() statement. Here is another example of an if-else construct:

```
if (c >= 'a' && c <= 'z')
    ++lc_cnt;
else {
    ++other_cnt;
    printf("%c is not a lowercase letter\n", c);
}
```

but not

```
if (a != b) {
    a += 1;
    b += 2;
} ;
else            /* syntax error */
    c *= 3;
```

The syntax error occurs because the semicolon following the right brace creates an empty statement, and consequently the else has nowhere to attach.

Since an if statement is itself a statement, it can be used as the statement part of another if statement. Consider the code

```
if (a == 1)
    if (b == 2)
        printf("***\n");
```

This is of the form

```
if (a == 1)
    statement
```

where *statement* is the following if statement

```
if (b == 2)
    printf("***\n");
```

In a similar fashion, an if-else statement can be used as the statement part of another if statement. Consider, for example,

```
if (a == 1)
    if (b == 2)
        printf("***\n");
    else
        printf("###\n");
```

Now we are faced with a semantic difficulty. This code illustrates the "dangling else" problem: it is not clear what the else part is associated with. Do not be fooled by the format of the code. As far as the machine is concerned, the following code is equivalent:

```
if (a == 1)
    if (b == 2)
        printf("***\n");
else
    printf("###\n");
```

The rule is that an else attaches to the nearest if. Thus the code is correctly formatted as we first gave it. It has the form

```
if (a == 1)
    statement
```

where *statement* is the if-else statement

```
if (b == 2)
    printf("***\n");
else
    printf("###\n");
```

To illustrate the use of the if and if-else statements, we will write an interactive program that finds the minimum of three values entered at the keyboard.

```
/* Find the minimum of three values. */

#include <stdio.h>

main()
{
    int    x, y, z, min;
```

```
    printf("Input three integers:   ");
    scanf("%d%d%d", &x, &y, &z);
    if (x < y)
        min = x;
    else
        min = y;
    if (z < min)
        min = z;
    printf("The minimum value is %d\n", min);
}
```

DISSECTION OF THE *find_min* PROGRAM

■ #include <stdio.h>

The header file *stdio.h* is supplied by the system. We have included it because it contains the function prototypes for printf() and scanf().

■ printf("Input three integers: ");

In an interactive environment, the program must prompt the user for input data.

■ scanf("%d%d%d", &x, &y, &z);

The library function scanf() is used to read in three integer values that are stored at the address of x, the address of y, and the address of z, respectively.

■ if (x < y)
    min = x;
  else
    min = y;

This whole construct is a single if-else statement. The values of x and y are compared. If x is less than y, then min is assigned the value of x; if x is not less than y, then min is assigned the value of y.

■ if (z < min)
    min = z;

This is an if statement. A check is made to see if the value of z is less than the value of min. If it is, then min is assigned the value of z; otherwise the value of min is left unchanged.

3.8 THE while STATEMENT

Repetition of action is one reason we rely on computers. When there are large amounts of data, it is very convenient to have control mechanisms that repeatedly execute specific statements. In C, the while, for, and do statements provide for repetitive action.

Although we have already used the while statement, or while loop, in many examples, we now want to explain precisely how this iterative mechanism works. Consider a construction of the form

```
while (expr)
    statement
next statement
```

First *expr* is evaluated. If it is nonzero (*true*), then *statement* is executed, and control is passed back to the beginning of the while loop. The effect of this is that the body of the while loop, namely *statement*, is executed repeatedly until *expr* is zero (*false*). At that point control passes to *next statement*.

An example of a while statement is

```
while (i <= 10) {
    sum += i;
    ++i;
}
```

Assume that just before this loop the value of i is 1 and the value of sum is 0. Then the effect of the loop is to repeatedly increment the value of sum by the current value of i and then to increment i by 1.

Number of times through the loop	Value of sum
first	0 + 1
second	0 + 1 + 2
third	0 + 1 + 2 + 3
. . . . .	

After the body of the loop has been executed ten times, the value of i is 11, and the value of the expression i <= 10 is 0 (*false*). Thus the body of the loop is not executed, and control passes to the next statement. When the while loop is exited, the value of sum is 55. Note again that a compound statement is used to group statements together, with the compound statement itself syntactically representing a single statement.

3.9   PROBLEM SOLVING: FINDING MAXIMUM VALUES

A task that programmers often encounter is to find an item having a particular property from among a given collection of items. We will illustrate such a task by finding the maximum value of some real numbers entered interactively at the keyboard. Our program will make use of if and while statements to do this.

```c
/* Find the maximum of n real values. */

#include <stdio.h>

main()
{
    int     cnt = 0, n;
    float   max, x;

    printf("The maximum value will be computed.\n");
    printf("How many numbers do you wish to enter?  ");
    scanf("%d", &n);
    while (n <= 0)  {
        printf("\nERROR: A positive integer is required.\n\n");
        printf("How many numbers do you wish to enter?  ");
        scanf("%d", &n);
    }
    printf("\nEnter %d real numbers:  ", n);
    scanf("%f", &x);
    max = x;
    while (++cnt < n) {
        scanf("%f", &x);
        if (max < x)
            max = x;
    }
    printf("\nMaximum value:  %g\n", max);
}
```

Let us suppose that we execute this program and enter 5 after the first prompt. If after the second prompt we enter the numbers 1.01, −3, 2.2, 7.07000, and 5, here is what appears on the screen:

```
The maximum value will be computed.
How many numbers do you wish to enter?  5

Enter 5 real numbers:  1.01  -3  2.2  7.07000  5

Maximum value:  7.07
```

DISSECTION OF THE *find_max* PROGRAM

- ```
  int     cnt = 0, n;
  float   max, x;
  ```

  The variables cnt and n are declared to be of type int, and the variables max and x are declared to be of type float. We will use cnt as a counter.

- ```
  printf("The maximum value will be computed.\n");
  ```

  A line of text is printed explaining the purpose of the program. This is an important documentation aid. The program in effect is self-documenting in its own output. This is good programming style.

- ```
  printf("How many numbers do you wish to enter?  ");
  scanf("%d", &n);
  ```

  The user is prompted to input an integer. Then the function scanf() is used to store the value of the integer entered by the user at the address of n.

- ```
  while (n <= 0) {
      printf("\nERROR: A positive integer is required.\n\n");
      printf("How many numbers do you wish to enter?  ");
      scanf("%d", &n);
  }
  ```

  If n is negative or zero, then the value of the expression n <= 0 is 1 (*true*), causing the body of the while loop to be executed. An error message and another prompt are printed, and a new value is stored at the address of n. As long as the user enters nonpositive numbers, the body of the loop is repeatedly executed. This while loop provides the program with some input error-correction capability. Other input errors, such as typing the letter a instead of a digit, still cause the program to fail. For more robust error correction, we need to look at the actual characters typed by the user. To do this we need character processing tools and strings (see Chapters 5 and 10).

■
```
printf("\nEnter %d real numbers:  ", n);
scanf("%f", &x);
max = x;
```

The user is prompted to input n real numbers. The scanf() function uses the format %f to convert the characters in the input stream to a floating point number and to store its value at the address of x. The variable max is assigned the value of x.

■
```
while (++cnt < n) {
    scanf("%f", &x);
    if (max < x)
        max = x;
}
```

Before we enter this loop, we have already picked up one value for x. We count it by incrementing cnt as we enter the loop. The first time through the loop, the expression ++cnt has value 1, the variable n has value 5, and the expression ++cnt < n has value 1 (*true*). Each time through the loop, we pick up another value for x, test to see if it is larger than the current value for max, and if it is, we assign x to max. Control then passes back to the top of the loop, where cnt gets incremented and a test is made to see if we need to get more values. The body of a while statement is a single statement, in this case a compound statement. The compound statement aids flow of control by grouping several statements to be executed as a unit.

■
```
printf("\nMaximum value:  %g\n", max);
```

We print the value of max with the %g format. Notice that 7.07000 was entered at the keyboard, but 7.07 was printed. With the %g format extraneous zeros are not printed.

3.10   THE for STATEMENT

The for statement, like the while statement, is used to execute code iteratively. We can explain its action in terms of the while statement. The construction

> for (*expr1*; *expr2*; *expr3*)
>   *statement*
> *next statement*

is semantically equivalent to

> *expr1*;
> while (*expr2*) {
>   *statement*
>   *expr3*;
> }
> *next statement*

provided that *expr2* is present, and provided that a continue statement is not in the body of the for loop. From our understanding of the while statement, we see that the semantics of the for statement is the following. First *expr1* is evaluated. Typically, *expr1* is used to initialize the loop. Then *expr2* is evaluated. If it is nonzero (*true*), then *statement* is executed, *expr3* is evaluated, and control passes back to the beginning of the for loop again, except that evaluation of *expr1* is skipped. Typically, *expr2* is a logical expression controlling the iteration. This process continues until *expr2* is zero (*false*), at which point control passes to *next statement*.

Some examples of for loops, or for statements, are

```
for (i = 1; i <= n; ++i)
   factorial *= i;

for (j = 2; k % j == 0; ++j) {
   printf("%d is a divisor of %d\n", j, k);
   sum += j;
}
```

but not

```
for (i = 0, i < n, i += 3)     /* semicolons are needed */
   sum += i;
```

Any or all of the expressions in a for statement can be missing, but the two semicolons must remain. If *expr1* is missing, then no initialization step is performed as part of the for loop. The code

```
i = 1;
sum = 0;
for ( ; i <= 10; ++i)
    sum += i;
```

computes the sum of the integers from 1 to 10, and so does the code

```
i = 1;
sum = 0;
for ( ; i <= 10 ; )
    sum += i++;
```

When *expr2* is missing, the rule is that the test is always *true*. Thus the for loop in the code

```
i = 1;
sum = 0;
for ( ; ; ) {
    sum += i++;
    printf("%d\n", sum);
}
```

is an infinite loop.

A for statement can be used as the statement part of an if, if-else, while, or another for statement. Consider, for example, the construction

```
for (...)
    for (...)
        for (...)
            statement
```

This construction as a whole is a single for statement. Its statement part is another for statement, which in turn has as its statement part yet another for statement.

In many situations, program control can be accomplished by using either a while or a for statement; the choice is often a matter of taste. One major advantage of a for loop is that control and indexing can both be kept right at the top. When loops are nested, this can facilitate the reading of the code. The program in the next section illustrates this.

3.11   PROBLEM SOLVING: COMBINATORICS

We want to consider a problem that comes from the domain of combinatorics, the art of enumerating combinations and permutations. The problem is to list all triples of non-negative integers that add up to a given number. For example, suppose they add up to 7. Here is a program that does this.

```
/* Find triples of integers that add up to N. */

#include <stdio.h>

#define  N   7

main()
{
    int   cnt = 0, i, j, k, n;

    for (i = 0; i <= N; ++i)
       for (j = 0; j <= N; ++j)
          for (k = 0; k <= N; ++k)
             if (i + j + k == N) {
                ++cnt;
                printf("%3d%3d%3d\n", i, j, k);
             }
    printf("\nCount: %d\n", cnt);
}
```

When we execute this program, here is some of the output that appears on the screen:

```
  0  0  7
  0  1  6
  0  2  5
  0  3  4
  . . . . .
  6  0  1
  6  1  0
  7  0  0

Count: 36
```

DISSECTION OF THE *add_to_N* PROGRAM

■ `#define   N   7`

We use the symbolic constant N so that we can easily experiment with the program.

■ `for (i = 0; i <= N; ++i)`
   `. . . . .`

The outermost for loop has for its statement part a for loop, which in turn has for its statement part another for loop. Notice that we could have written

```
for (i = 0; i <= N; ++i) {
   . . . . .
}
```

However, since the body of this for statement is another for statement, the braces are not necessary.

■ `for (j = 0; j <= N; ++j)`
   `for (k = 0; k <= N; ++k)`
      `. . . . .`

This is the statement part, or body, of the outermost for loop. For each outermost value of i, all values of j within the inner loop get cycled through. For each value of j, all values of k within the innermost loop get cycled through. This is similar to an odometer, where the lower digits are first cycled through before a higher digit is changed.

■ `if (i + j + k == N) {`
   `++cnt;`
   `printf("%3d%3d%3d\n", i, j, k);`
   `}`

This is the body of the innermost loop. A check is made to see if i plus j plus k add up to N. If they do, cnt is incremented, and the triple of integers is printed.

3.12 PROBLEM SOLVING: BOOLEAN VARIABLES

Boolean algebra plays a major role in the design of computer circuits. In this algebra all variables have only the values 0 or 1. Transistors and memory technologies implement zero-one value schemes with currents, voltages, and magnetic orientations. Frequently the circuit designer has a function in mind and needs to check whether for all possible zero-one inputs the output has the desired behavior.

We will use int variables b1, b2, . . . , b5 to represent five boolean variables. They will be allowed to take on only the values 0 and 1. A boolean function of these variables is one that returns only 0 or 1. A typical example of a boolean function is the majority function; it returns 1 if a majority of the variables have value 1, and 0 otherwise. We want to create a table of values for the functions

        b1 || b3 || b5   and   b1 && b2 || b4 && b5

and the majority function. Recall that logical expressions always have the int value 0 or 1.

```
/* Print a table of values for some boolean functions. */

#include <stdio.h>

main()
{
    int    b1, b2, b3, b4, b5;              /* boolean variables */
    int    cnt = 0;

    printf("\n%5s%5s%5s%5s%5s%5s%7s%7s%11s\n\n",   /* headings */
        "Cnt", "b1", "b2", "b3", "b4", "b5",
        "fct1", "fct2", "majority");

    for (b1 = 0; b1 <= 1; ++b1)
        for (b2 = 0; b2 <= 1; ++b2)
            for (b3 = 0; b3 <= 1; ++b3)
                for (b4 = 0; b4 <= 1; ++b4)
                    for (b5 = 0; b5 <= 1; ++b5)
                        printf("%5d%5d%5d%5d%5d%5d%6d%7d%9d\n",
                            ++cnt, b1, b2, b3, b4, b5,
                            b1 || b3 || b5, b1 && b2 || b4 && b5,
                            b1 + b2 + b3 + b4 + b5 >= 3);
    printf("\n");
}
```

The program illustrates a typical use of nested for loops. The output of the program is a table of values for all possible inputs and their corresponding outputs. The circuit designer can use the table to check that the boolean functions are behaving in the required fashion. Here is some of the output of the program:

Cnt	b1	b2	b3	b4	b5	fct1	fct2	majority
1	0	0	0	0	0	0	0	0
2	0	0	0	0	1	1	0	0
3	0	0	0	1	0	0	0	0

. . . . .

3.13   THE COMMA OPERATOR

The comma operator has the lowest precedence of all the operators in C. It is a binary operator with expressions as operands, and it associates from left to right. In a comma expression of the form

expr1 , expr2

expr1 is evaluated first, and then *expr2*. The comma expression as a whole has the value and type of its right operand. An example is

```
a = 0, b = 1
```

If b has been declared an int, then this comma expression has value 1 and type int. The comma operator is sometimes used in for statements. It allows multiple initializations and multiple processing of indices. For example, the code

```
for (sum = 0, i = 1; i <= n; ++i)
    sum += i;
```

can be used to compute the sum of the integers from 1 to *n*. Carrying this idea further, we can stuff the entire body of the for loop inside the for parentheses. The previous code could be rewritten as

```
for (sum = 0, i = 1; i <= n; sum += i, ++i)
    ;
```

but not as

```
for (sum = 0, i = 1; i <= n; ++i, sum += i)
    ;
```

In the comma expression

```
++i, sum += i
```

the expression ++i is evaluated first, and this will cause sum to have a different value.

The comma operator should be used only in situations where it fits naturally. So far, we have given examples to illustrate its use, but none of the code is natural. In Chapter 13, where we discuss linked lists, we will have occasion to keep track of an index and a pointer at the same time. The comma operator can be used in a natural way to do this by writing

```
for (i = 0, p = head; p != NULL; ++i, p = p -> next)
    . . . . .
```

Some examples of comma expressions are given in the following table:

Declarations and initializations		
`int      i, j, k = 3;` `double   x = 3.3;`		
Expression	*Equivalent expression*	*Value*
`i = 1, j = 2, ++ k + 1`	`((i = 1), (j = 2)), ((++ k) + 1)`	5
`k != 7, ++ x * 2.0 + 1`	`(k != 7), (((++ x) * 2.0) + 1)`	9.6

Most commas in programs do not represent comma operators. For example, the commas used to separate expressions in argument lists of functions or within initializer lists are not comma operators. If a comma operator is to be used in these places, the comma expression in which it occurs must be enclosed in parentheses.

3.14 THE do STATEMENT

The do statement can be considered a variant of the while statement. Instead of making its test at the top of the loop, it makes it at the bottom. An example is

```
do {
    sum += i;
    scanf("%d", &i);
} while (i > 0);
```

Consider a construction of the form

```
do
    statement
while (expr);
next statement
```

First *statement* is executed, and *expr* is evaluated. If the value of *expr* is nonzero (*true*), then control passes back to the beginning of the do statement, and the process repeats itself. When *expr* is zero (*false*), then control passes to *next statement*.

As an example, suppose that we want to read in a positive integer and we want to insist that the integer be positive. The following code will do the job:

```
do {
    printf("Input a positive integer: ");
    scanf("%d", &n);
    if (error = (n <= 0))
        printf("\nERROR: Negative value not allowed!\n\n");
} while (error);
```

As long as a nonpositive integer is entered, the user will be notified with a request for a positive integer. Control will exit the loop only after a positive integer has been entered.

3.15   THE goto STATEMENT

The goto statement is considered a harmful construct in most accounts of modern programming methodology. It causes an unconditional jump to a labeled statement somewhere in the current function. Thus it can undermine all the useful structure provided by other flow-of-control mechanisms (if, if-else, for, while, do, switch).

Since a goto jumps to a labeled statement, we need to discuss this construct first. A labeled statement is of the form

label : *statement*

where *label* is an identifier. Some examples of labeled statements are

```
bye: exit(1);
L444: a = b + c;
bug1: bug2: bug3: printf("bug found\n");     /* multiple labels */
```

but not

```
333: a = b + c;     /* 333 is not an identifier */
```

Label identifiers have their own name space. This means that the same identifier can be used both for a label and a variable. This practice, however, is considered bad programming style and should be avoided.

Control can be unconditionally transferred to a labeled statement by executing a goto statement of the form

```
goto label;
```

An example would be

```
goto error;
.....
error: {
   printf("An error has occurred - bye!\n");
   exit(1);
}
```

Both the goto statement and its corresponding labeled statement must be in the body of the same function. Here is a more specific piece of code that makes use of a goto:

```
while (scanf("%lf", &x) == 1) {
   if (x < 0.0)
      goto negative_alert;
   printf("%f  %f  %f\n", x, sqrt(x), sqrt(2 * x));
}
negative_alert:
   if (x < 0.0)
      printf("Negative value encountered!\n");
```

This code can be rewritten in a number of different ways without using a goto. Here is one way to accomplish the task:

```
while (scanf("%lf", &x) == 1 && x >= 0.0)
   printf("%f  %f  %f\n", x, sqrt(x), sqrt(2 * x));
if (x < 0.0)
   printf("Negative value encountered!\n");
```

In general, the goto should be avoided. The goto is a primitive method of altering the flow of control, which, in a richly structured language, is unnecessary. Labeled statements and goto's are the hallmark of incremental patchwork program design. A programmer who modifies a program by adding goto's to additional code fragments soon makes the program incomprehensible.

When should a goto be used? A simple answer is never. Indeed, one cannot go wrong by following this advice. In some rare instances, however, which should be carefully documented, a goto can make the program significantly more efficient. In other cases it can simplify the flow of control. This may occur, for example, if we are in a deeply nested inner loop and we want program control to jump to the outermost level of the function.

3.16   THE break AND continue STATEMENTS

Two special statements,

```
break;           and           continue;
```

interrupt the normal flow of control. The break statement causes an exit from the inner-most enclosing loop or switch statement. (We discuss the switch statement in the next section.) In the following example, a test for a negative argument is made, and if the test is true, then a break statement is used to pass control to the statement immediately following the loop.

```
while (1) {
   scanf("%lf", &x);
   if (x < 0.0)
      break;                    /* exit loop if x is negative */
   printf("%f\n", sqrt(x));
}
/* break jumps to here */
```

This is a typical use of break. What would otherwise be an infinite loop is made to terminate upon a given condition tested by the if expression.

The continue statement causes the current iteration of a loop to stop and causes the next iteration of the loop to begin immediately.

```
while (cnt < n) {
   scanf("%lf", &x);
   if (x > -0.01 && x < +0.01)
      continue;                 /* disregard small values */
   ++cnt;
   sum += x;
/* continue transfers control to here to begin next iteration */
}
```

The continue statement may only occur inside for, while, and do loops. As the ex-amples show, continue transfers control to the end of the current iteration, whereas break terminates the loop.

In the presence of a continue statement, a for loop of the form

```
for (expr1; expr2; expr3) {
   statements
   continue;
   more statements
}
```

is equivalent to

```
expr1;
while (expr2) {
    statements
    goto next;
    more statements
next:
    expr3;
}
```

which is different from

```
expr1;
while (expr2) {
    statements
    continue;
    more statements
    expr3;
}
```

See exercise 23 for a convenient way to test this.

3.17   THE switch STATEMENT

The switch is a multiway conditional statement generalizing the if-else statement. The following is a typical example of a switch statement:

```
switch (val) {
case 1:
    ++a_cnt;
    break;
case 2:
case 3:
    ++b_cnt;
    break;
default:
    ++other_cnt;
}
```

Notice that the body of the switch statement in the example is a compound statement. This will be so in all but the most degenerate situations. The controlling expression in the parentheses following the keyword switch must be of integral type (see Chapter 6). In the example, it is just the int variable val. After the expression is evaluated, control jumps to the appropriate case label. The constant integral expressions following the case labels must all be unique. Typically, the last statement before the next case or default label is a break statement. If there is no break statement, then execution "falls through" to the next statement in the succeeding case. Missing break statements are a frequent cause of error in switch statements. There may be at most one default label in a switch. Typically, it occurs last, although it can occur anywhere. The keywords case and default cannot occur outside of a switch.

The effect of a switch

---

1   Evaluate the switch expression.

2   Go to the case label having a constant value that matches the value of the expression found in step 1; or, if a match is not found, go to the default label; or, if there is no default label, terminate the switch.

3   Terminate the switch when a break statement is encountered, or terminate the switch by "falling off the end."

Let us review the various kinds of jump constructs that are available to us. These include the goto, break, continue, and return. The goto is unrestricted in its use and should be avoided as a dangerous construct. The break statement may be used in loops and is important to the proper structuring of the switch statement. The continue statement must be used within loops and is often unnecessary. The return statement must be used in functions that return values. It will be discussed in Chapter 4.

3.18   NESTED FLOW OF CONTROL

Flow-of-control statements such as if, for, while, and switch statements can be nested within themselves and within each other. Although such nested control constructs can be quite complicated, some have a regular structure and are easily understood.

One of the more common nested flow-of-control constructs makes repeated use of if-else statements. Its general form is given by

```
if (expr1)
    statement1
else if (expr2)
    statement2
else if (expr3)
    statement3
. . . . .
else if (exprN)
    statementN
else
    default statement
next statement
```

This whole giant construction, except for *next statement*, is a single if-else statement. Suppose, for example, that *expr1* and *expr2* are both zero (*false*) and that *expr3* is nonzero (*true*). Then *statement1* and *statement2* will be skipped, and *statement3* will be executed; then control will pass to *next statement*. No other intervening statement will be executed. If we suppose that all of the expressions are zero, then only *default statement* will be executed. In some circumstances the execution of a default statement is not wanted. In this case a construction such as the above would be used, except that the two lines

```
else
    default statement
```

would not appear. *Programming tip:* If you place the more likely cases at the top of this giant if-else construct, then your code will be more efficient, because fewer expressions will be computed before control passes beyond the construct.

3.19   THE CONDITIONAL OPERATOR

The conditional operator ?: is unusual because it is a ternary operator. It takes as operands three expressions. The general form of a conditional expression is

expr1 ? expr2 : expr3

First, *expr1* is evaluated. If it is nonzero (*true*), then *expr2* is evaluated, and that is the value of the conditional expression as a whole. If *expr1* is zero (*false*), then *expr3* is evaluated, and that is the value of the conditional expression as a whole. Thus a conditional expression can be used to do the work of an `if-else` statement. Consider, for example, the code

```
if (y < z)
    x = y;
else
    x = z;
```

The effect of the code is to assign to x the minimum of y and z. This also can be accomplished by writing

```
x = (y < z) ? y : z;
```

The parentheses are not necessary because the precedence of the conditional operator is just above assignment. Nonetheless, they help to make clear what is being tested for.

The type of the conditional expression

expr1 ? expr2 : expr3

is determined by both *expr2* and *expr3*. If they are of different types, then the usual conversion rules are applied (see Chapter 6). Note carefully that the type of the conditional expression does not depend on which of the two expressions, *expr2* or *expr3*, is evaluated.

The conditional operator ?: has precedence just above the assignment operators, and it associates from right to left. The next table illustrates how conditional expressions are evaluated.

Declarations and initializations			
`int      a = 1, b = 2;` `double    x = 7.07;`			
Expression	*Equivalent expression*	*Value*	*Type*
`a == b ? a - 1 : b + 1`	`(a == b) ? (a - 1) : (b + 1)`	3	`int`
`a - b < 0 ? x : a + b`	`((a - b) < 0) ? x : (a + b)`	7.07	`double`
`a - b > 0 ? x : a + b`	`((a - b) > 0) ? x : (a + b)`	3.0	`double`

3.20 STYLE

Throughout this text we use the "Bell Labs industrial programming style." This style embodies four key features:

1   Follow the normal rules of English, where possible, such as putting a space after a comma.

2   Put one space on each side of a binary operator to heighten readability.

3   Indent code in a consistent fashion to indicate the flow of control.

4   Place braces as indicated in the following example:

```
for (i = 0; i < n; ++i) {
    . . . . .
}
```

The placement of braces to reflect flow of control is crucial to good programming style. The statements in the body of the loop are indented 3 spaces, and the closing brace } is lined up directly under the for. The indentation serves to visually set off those statements making up the body of the loop. The placement of the for and the } one above the other in the same column serves to visually mark the beginning and end, respectively, of the loop. A variation of this style would be to choose a different indentation, such as 2, 4, 5, or 8 spaces.

Another programming style altogether is to place beginning and ending braces in the same column. Here is an example:

```
while (i < 10)
{
    . . . . .
}
```

This is sometimes called *student style*. Which style is used is a matter of taste, and (to some extent) the power of the editor being used. Programmers who use the Bell Labs style tend to use a powerful editor; one that can easily find matching braces or parentheses, can indent multiple lines of code as a unit, has an autoindent feature, and so forth. For example, the *emacs* and *vi* editors in UNIX have these features.

If the body of a loop is a single statement, braces are not necessary. Nonetheless, as a matter of style, some programmers *always* use braces:

```
while (i < 10) {
    a single statement
}
```

This is an acceptable practice. The executable code produced by the compiler will be just as efficient with or without the extraneous braces.

Since in C only a small percentage of loops tend to be do loops, it is considered good programming style to use braces even when they are not needed. The braces in the construct

```
do {
    a single statement
} while (...);
```

make it easier for the reader to realize that this is a do statement rather than a while statement followed by an empty statement.

In many situations either a while loop or a for loop can be used. However, if it makes sense to keep control and indexing visible at the top, then a for loop should be used. Otherwise, the choice is a matter of personal taste.

The following style for nested if-else statements is not recommended and, in fact, is seldom used:

```
if (expr1)              /* wrong style */
    statement1
else if (expr2)
        statement2
    else if (expr3)
            statement3
        else if (expr3)
                statement3
            . . . . .
```

Any variation of this style that causes the nested if-else statements to march across the screen is unacceptable, because long chains will run out of space. The horizontal space across the screen is a scarce resource.

3.21 COMMON PROGRAMMING ERRORS

We will discuss a number of common programming errors. The first one concerns the confusion between the two expressions

```
a == b          and          a = b
```

Although they are *visually* similar, they are radically different in function. The expression a == b is a test for equality, whereas a = b is an assignment expression. One of the more common programming mistakes is to code something like

```
if (k = 1)
    . . . . .
```

instead of

```
if (k == 1)
    . . . . .
```

Because its value is 1, the assignment expression k = 1 is always *true*. Some compilers will give a warning about this; others will not. Without a warning, such an error can be quite difficult to find. Note that if we write

```
if (1 = k)
    . . . . .
```

then the compiler will certainly warn us about the error. It is not legal to assign a value to a constant. For this reason, some programmers routinely write tests of the form

constant == *expr*

This guards against the error of writing = instead of ==. A disadvantage of this style is that it does not conform to the way we ordinarily think, namely, "if k is equal to 1, . . ."

The second common programming error occurs when an expression that controls an iterative statement causes an unwanted infinite loop. Care should be taken to avoid this difficulty. As an example, consider the code

```
printf("Input an integer: ");
scanf("%d", &n);
while (--n) {
    . . . . .
}
```

The intent is for a positive integer to be entered, its value to be stored at the address of n, and the body of the while loop to be executed repeatedly until the value of the expression --n is eventually zero. However, if a negative integer is assigned to n inadvertently, then the loop will be infinite. To guard against this possibility, the programmer should code instead

```
while (--n > 0) {
    . . . . .
}
```

A third common programming error involves the use of an unwanted semicolon after an if, while, or for. Consider as an example the following code:

```
for (i = 1; i <= 10; ++i);
    sum += i;
```

It does not behave as expected because the semicolon at the end of the first line creates an unwanted null statement. The code is equivalent to

```
for (i = 1; i <= 10; ++i)
    ;
sum += i;
```

which clearly is not what the programmer intended. This type of bug can be very difficult to find.

Next, we want to discuss how the misuse of relational operators can lead to an unexpected result. Recall that in mathematics the expression $2 < k < 7$ means that k is greater than 2 and less than 7. We can also consider this as an assertion about k that is either *true* or *false*, depending on the value of k. For example, if k is 8, then the assertion is *false*. In contrast to this, consider the following code:

```
int   k = 8;

if (2 < k < 7)
    printf("true");         /* true gets printed! */
else
    printf("false");
```

The reason that the expression is *true* is straightforward. Since relational operators associate from left to right,

```
2 < k < 7          is equivalent to          (2 < k) < 7
```

Since 2 < k is *true*, its value is 1. Thus

```
(2 < k) < 7          is equivalent to          1 < 7
```

which is obviously *true*. The correct way to write a test for both 2 < k and k < 7 is

2 < k && k < 7   which is equivalent to   (2 < k) && (k < 7)

because < has higher precedence than &&. The expression as a whole is *true* if and only if both operands of && are *true*.

Our final common programming error involves a test for equality that is beyond the accuracy of most machines. Here is a program that illustrates the problem:

```
/* An equality test that fails. */

#include <stdio.h>

main()
{
    int     cnt = 0;
    double  sum = 0.0, x;

    for (x = 0.0; x != 9.9; x += 0.1) {        /* trouble! */
        sum += x;
        printf("cnt = %5d\n", ++cnt);
    }
    printf("sum = %f\n", sum);
}
```

Mathematically, if x starts at zero and gets incremented by 0.1 repeatedly, it will eventually take on the value 9.9. The intent of the programmer is for program control to exit the for loop when that happens. However, if the test x == 9.9 is beyond the accuracy of the machine, the expression x != 9.9 will always be *true*, and the program will go into an infinite loop. The programmer must remember that on any machine, floating arithmetic, unlike integer arithmetic, is not exact. To fix the problem, we can write x <= 9.9 rather than x != 9.9 (see exercise 25).

A good programming style is to use a relational expression, if appropriate, rather than an equality expression to control a loop or an if or if-else statement. In general, this style produces code that is more robust.

3.22   SYSTEM CONSIDERATIONS

Both the machine and its operating system determine how numbers are represented in the machine. We want to discuss a problem that arises because floating numbers are not representable with infinite precision. Sometimes this can cause unexpected results. In mathematics, the relation

$$x < x + y \qquad \text{is equivalent to} \qquad 0 < y$$

Mathematically, if y is positive, then both of these relations are logically true. Computationally, if x is a floating variable with a large value, such as 7×10^{33}, and y is a floating variable with a small value, such as 0.001, then the relational expression

```
x < x + y
```

may be *false*, even though mathematically it is true. An equivalent expression is

```
(x - (x + y)) < 0.0
```

and it is this expression that the machine implements. If in terms of machine accuracy the values of x and x + y are equal, the expression will yield the int value 0 (see exercise 6).

Next, we want to discuss infinite loops. They sometimes occur inadvertently, but in an interactive environment, the programmer may want to deliberately use an infinite loop. If so, then the user will have to interrupt the program to stop it. What must be typed to interrupt a program is system-dependent. In both MS-DOS and UNIX, a control-c is typically used to terminate a program. However, other operating systems may do it differently. Two conventional styles for an infinite loop are

```
while (1) {
    .....
}
```

and

```
for ( ; ; ) {
    .....
}
```

Let us suppose that a programmer wishes to experiment. Rather than running a program over and over, it may be more convenient to put the essential code into an infinite loop. Here is an example:

```
printf("Sums from 1 to n will be computed.\n\n");
for ( ; ; ) {
    printf("Input n:  ");
    scanf("%d", &n);
    sum = 0;
    for (i = 1; i <= n; ++i)
        sum += i;
    printf("sum = %d\n\n", sum);
}
```

3.23 SUMMARY

1 Relational, equality, and logical expressions have the int value 0 or 1. These expressions are used chiefly to test data to affect flow of control.

2 The relational, equality, and logical operators are binary, except the negation operator !, which is unary. A negation expression such as !a has the int value 0 or 1. Usually, the values of !!a and a are different.

3 The grouping construct { ... } is a compound statement. It allows enclosed statements to be treated as a single unit.

4 An if statement provides a means of choosing whether or not to execute a statement. An if-else statement provides a means of choosing which of two statements gets executed. The else part of an if-else statement associates with the nearest available if. This resolves the "dangling else" problem.

5 One reason we use computers is to repeatedly perform certain actions. The while, for, and do statements provide looping mechanisms in C. The body of a while or for statement is executed zero or more times. The body of a do statement is executed one or more times.

6 The programmer often has to choose between the use of a for or a while statement. In situations where clarity dictates that both the control and the indexing be kept visible at the top of the loop, the for statement is the natural choice.

7 The comma operator is occasionally useful in for statements. Of all the operators in C, it has the lowest priority.

8 The four statement types

    goto   break   continue   return

cause an unconditional transfer of the flow of control. Except for the use of break statements in a switch, their use should be minimized.

9 goto's are considered harmful to good programming. Avoid them.

10 The switch statement provides a multiway conditional branch. It is useful when dealing with a large number of special cases. Typically, the break statement is needed for the proper functioning of a switch.

3.24 EXERCISES

1 Give equivalent logical expressions without using negation.

```
!(a > b)                    !(a <= b && c <= d)
!(a + 1 == b + 1)           !(a < 1 || b < 2 && c < 3)
```

2 Complete the following table:

Declarations and initializations		
int a = 1, b = 2, c = 3; double x = 1.0;		
Expression	*Equivalent expression*	*Value*
a > b && c < d		
a < ! b || ! ! a		
a + b < ! c + c		
a - x || b * c && b / a		

3 Write a program that contains the loop

```
while (scanf("lf", &salary) == 1) {
    .....
}
```

Within the body of the loop compute a 23% federal withholding tax and a 7% state withholding tax and print these values along with the corresponding salary. Accumulate the sums of all salaries and taxes printed. Print these sums after the program exits the while loop.

4 What gets printed?

```
int     a = 1, b = 2, c = 3;
float   x = 3.3, y = 5.5;

printf("%d %d\n", !  a+b/c, !a + b / c);
printf("%d %d\n", a == -b + c, a * b > c == a);
printf("%d %d\n", !!x < a + b + c, !!x + !!!y);
printf("%d %d\n", a || b == x && y, !(x || !y));
```

5 Suppose that a programmer is working on a problem that requires special action if the int variable k has value 7. Consider the following code:

```
while (k = 7) {
    .....               /* do something */
    k = 0;              /* finished, exit the loop */
}
```

Contrast this with the following code:

```
if (k = 7) {
    .....               /* do something */
}
```

Both pieces of code are logically wrong. The run-time effect of one of them is so striking that the error is easy to spot, whereas the other piece of wrong code has a subtle effect that is much harder to spot. Explain.

6 The following code is system-dependent. Nonetheless, most machines produce an answer that is logically incorrect. First explain what logically should be printed. Then test the code on your machine to see what actually gets printed.

```
double   x = 1e+33, y = 0.001;

printf("%d\n", x + y > x - y);
```

What happens if you assign the value 1000 to y? Or 1 million? The point of this exercise is to emphasize that floating point arithmetic need not approximate mathematics very well.

7 What gets printed? Explain.

```
int   i = 7, j = 7;

if (i == 1)
   if (j == 2)
      printf("%d\n", i = i + j);
else
   printf("%d\n", i = i - j);
printf("%d\n", i);
```

8 The syntax error in the following piece of code does not really show up on the line indicated. Run a test program with this piece of code in it to find out which line is flagged with a syntax error. Explain why.

```
while (++i < LIMIT) do {     /* syntax error */
   j = 2 * i + 3;
   printf("j = %d\n", j);
}
   /* Many other languages require "do", but not C. */
```

9 In the following code assume that the values of i and j are not changed in the body of the loop. Can the code ever lead to an infinite loop? Explain.

```
printf("Input two integers: ");
scanf("%d%d", &i, &j);
while (i * j < 0 && ++i != 7 && j++ != 9) {
   .....       /* do something */
}
```

10 Write a program that reads in an integer value for n and then sums the integers from n to 2 * n if n is nonnegative, or from 2 * n to n if n is negative. Write the code in two versions: one using only for loops and the other using only while loops.

11 Until interrupted, the following code prints True forever! on the screen repeatedly. (In MS-DOS and UNIX, type a control-c to effect an interrupt.)

```
while (1)
    printf(" True forever! ");
```

Write a simple program that accomplishes the same thing, but instead of a while statement, use a for statement that has as its body an empty statement.

12 We have already explained that

```
while (1) {
    . . . . .
}
```

is an infinite loop. What does the following code do? If you are not quite sure, try it. That is, create a program containing these lines and run it.

```
while (-33.777)
    printf("run forever, if you can");
```

13 Let *e1* and *e2* be arithmetic expressions. We want to establish that

$e1 \text{ != } e2$ is equivalent to $!(e1 == e2)$

Do this by completing the following table:

Values of:			
e1 – e2	*e1 != e2*	*e1 == e2*	*!(e1 == e2)*
zero			
nonzero			

14 Run the program *find_max* and enter 1 when first prompted. Then you will see on the screen

```
Enter 1 real numbers:
```

This is, of course, improper English. Change the program so that number is printed if n has the value 1, and numbers is printed otherwise.

15 Suppose that you detest even integers but love odd ones. Modify the *find_max* program so that all variables are of type int and only odd integers are processed. Of course, you will have to explain all of this to the user via appropriate printf() statements.

16 What happens when you run the following code on your system? If it does not run correctly, change it so that it does.

```
double   sum = 0.0, x;

printf("%5s%15s\n", "Value", "Running sum");
printf("%5s%15s\n", "-----", "-----------");
for (x = 0.0; x != 9.9; x += 0.1) {              /* test not robust */
   sum += x;
    printf("%5.1f%15.1f\n", x, sum);
}
```

17 Beginning programmers sometimes mix up the order of the expressions used to control a for loop. In the following code an attempt is being made to sum the integers from 1 to 5. What is the effect of mixing up the expressions? First, hand-simulate what happens, and then write a test program to find out if you were correct.

```
int   i, sum = 0;

for (i = 1; ++i; i <= 5)
   printf("i = %d   sum = %d\n", i, sum += i);
```

18 Write an interactive program that asks the user to supply three integers *k*, *m*, and *n*, with *k* being greater than 1. Your program should compute the sum of all the integers between *m* and *n* that are divisible by *k*.

19 This exercise gives you practice with short-circuit evaluation.

```
int   a = 0, b = 0, x;

x = 0 && (a = b = 777);
printf("%d %d %d\n", a, b, x);
x = 777 || (a = ++b);
printf("%d %d %d\n", a, b, x);
```

What gets printed? First write down your answers; then write a test program to check them.

20 Complete the following table:

Declarations and initializations		
int a = 1, b = 2, c = 3;		
Expression	Equivalent expression	Value
a && b && c	(a && b) && c	
a && b || c		
a || b && c		
a || ! b && ! ! c + 4		
a += ! b && c == ! 5		

21 The semantics of logical expressions imply that the order of evaluation is critical in some computations. Which of the following two alternate expressions is most likely to be the correct one? Explain.

    (a)   if ((x != 0.0) && ((z - x) / x * x < 2.0))

            . . . . .

    (b)   if (((z - x) / x * x < 2.0) && (x != 0.0))

            . . . . .

22 A *truth table* for a boolean function is a table consisting of all possible values for its variables and the corresponding values of the boolean function itself. In Section 3.12, "Problem Solving: Boolean Variables," we created a truth table for the majority function and two other functions. Create separate truth tables for the following boolean functions:

     b1 \|\| b2 \|\| b3 \|\| b4   !(!b1 \|\| b2) && (!b3 \|\| b4)

Use the letters T and F in your truth tables to represent *true* and *false*, respectively. *Hint:* Use a #define preprocessing directive to define a BOOLEX. Then write your program to operate on an arbitrary BOOLEX.

23 Here is a simple way to test the effect of a continue statement in the body of a for loop. What gets printed?

```
for (putchar('1'); putchar('2'); putchar('3')) {
    putchar('4');
    continue;
    putchar('5');
}
```

24 The mathematical operation min(x, y) can be represented by the conditional expression

```
(x < y) ? x : y
```

In a similar fashion, using only conditional expressions, describe the mathematical operations

```
min(x, y, z)            and            max(x, y, z, w)
```

25 Does the nonrobust program given in Section 3.21 (the equality test) result in an infinite loop on your machine? If so, then modify the program as suggested and execute it. Does it produce an answer that is close to being mathematically correct? After all, if x == 9.9 is never *true* as x gets incremented in the loop, then perhaps the answer is off by an amount approximately equal to 0.1.

4

FUNCTIONS AND STRUCTURED PROGRAMMING

4.1   FUNCTION INVOCATION
4.2   FUNCTION DEFINITION
4.3   THE return STATEMENT
4.4   FUNCTION PROTOTYPES
4.5   TOP-DOWN DESIGN
4.6   PROBLEM SOLVING: RANDOM NUMBERS
4.7   A SIMULATION: THE GAME OF HEADS OR TAILS
4.8   INVOCATION AND CALL-BY-VALUE
4.9   STYLE
4.10 COMMON PROGRAMMING ERRORS
4.11 SYSTEM CONSIDERATIONS
4.12 SUMMARY
4.13 EXERCISES

Structured programming is a problem solving strategy and a programming methodology that includes the following two guidelines:

1   The flow of control in a program should be as simple as possible.
2   The construction of a program should embody top-down design.

Top-down design, also referred to as *stepwise refinement*, consists of repeatedly decomposing a problem into smaller problems. Eventually, one has a collection of small problems or tasks, each of which can be easily coded.

The function construct in C is used to write code for the small and hopefully simple problems that result from this decomposition. These functions are combined into other functions and ultimately used in main() to solve the original problem. The function mechanism is provided in C to perform distinct programming tasks. Some functions, such as printf() and scanf(), are provided by the system; others can be written by the programmer.

We will illustrate structured programming and top-down design in this chapter, but first we want to describe the function mechanism.

4.1   FUNCTION INVOCATION

A program is made up of one or more functions, one of them being main(). Program execution always begins with main(). When program control encounters a function name, the function is *called*, or *invoked*. This means that program control passes to the function. After the function does its work, program control is passed back to the calling environment, which then continues with its work. As a simple example, consider the following program, which prints a message.

```
#include <stdio.h>

void prn_message(void)
{
    printf("Message for you:  ");
    printf("Have a nice day!\n");
}

main()
{
    prn_message();
}
```

Execution begins in main(). When program control encounters prn_message(), the function is invoked, and program control is passed to it. After the two printf() statements in prn_message() have been executed, program control passes back to the calling environment, which in this example is main(). Since there is no more work to be done in main(), the program ends.

4.2   FUNCTION DEFINITION

The C code that describes what a function does is called the *function definition*. It has the following general form:

type function_name(parameter list)
{
    declarations
    statements
}

Everything before the first brace comprises the *header* of the function definition, and everything between the braces comprises the *body* of the function definition. In the function definition for prn_message() above, the parameter list is empty. This empty list is designated by the keyword void. The body of the function consists of two printf() statements. Since the function does not return a value, the type of the function was void. This type is used to specify that no value may be returned.

The *type* of a function depends on the type of the value that the function returns, if any. The return mechanism is fully explained in Section 4.3.

Parameters are syntactically a comma-separated list, with each item a type declaration followed by an identifier. The identifiers can be used within the body of the function. Sometimes the parameters in a function definition are called *formal parameters* to emphasize their role as placeholders for actual values that are passed to the function when it is called. Upon function invocation, the value of the argument corresponding to a formal parameter is used within the body of the executing function.

To illustrate these ideas, let us rewrite the above program so that prn_message() has a formal parameter. The parameter will be used to specify how many times the message is printed.

```
#include <stdio.h>

void prn_message(int k)
{
    int    i;

    printf("Message for you:\n");
    for (i = 0; i < k; ++i)
        printf("   Have a nice day!\n");
}

main()
{
    int    n;
    printf("Input a small positive integer:   ");
    scanf("%d", &n);
    prn_message(n);
}
```

DISSECTION OF THE *message* PROGRAM

■ main()
```
  {
    int   n;

    printf("Input a small positive integer:  ");
    scanf("%d", &n);
```

The variable n is declared to be an int. The function printf() is used to prompt the user for a small integer. The function scanf() is used to store the value typed in by the user in the variable n.

■ prn_message(n);

This statement causes the function prn_message() to be called. The value of n is passed as an argument to the function.

■ void prn_message(int k)

This is the header of the function definition for prn_message(). The identifier k is a parameter that is declared to be of type int. One can think of the parameter k as representing the value of the actual argument that is passed to the function when it is called. A call to this function occurred in main() in the statement

```
    prn_message(n);
```

In main(), suppose that the value of n is 2. Then when program control passes to prn_message(), the variable k will have the value 2. Since no value is returned by the function, we specify void as the function type.

```
■ {
    int   i;

    printf("Message for you:\n");
    for (i = 0; i < k; ++i)
        printf("   Have a nice day!\n");
}
```

This is the body of the function definition for prn_message(). If we think of k as having the value 2, then the message is printed twice. When program control reaches the end of the function, control is passed back to the calling environment.

Notice that parameters and local variables used in one function definition have no relation to those in another. For example, if the variable i had been used in main(), it would have had no relationship to the variable i used in prn_message().

4.3   THE return STATEMENT

The return statement is used for two purposes. When a return statement is executed, program control is immediately passed back to the calling environment. In addition, if an expression follows the keyword return, then the value of the expression is returned to the calling environment as well. This value will be converted, if necessary, to the type specified in the function definition header. A return statement has one of the following two forms:

```
return;
return expression;
```

Some examples are

```
return 3;
return (a + b);
```

The expression being returned can be enclosed in parentheses, but this is not required. If the expression is something other than a simple constant or variable, it is considered good programming style to enclose it in parentheses.

As an example, let us write a program that computes the minimum of two integers.

```
#include <stdio.h>

int min(int x, int y)
{
   if (x < y)
      return x;
   else
      return y;
}

main()
{
   int   j, k, m;

   printf("Input two integers:  ");
   scanf("%d%d", &j, &k);
   m = min(j, k);
   printf("\n%d is the minimum of %d and %d\n\n", m, j, k);
}
```

DISSECTION OF THE *minimum* PROGRAM

■ main()
```
{
   int   j, k, m;

   printf("Input two integers:  ");
   scanf("%d%d", &j, &k);
```

The variables j, k, and m are declared to be of type int. The user is asked to input two integers. The function scanf() is used to store the values in j and k.

■ m = min(j, k);

The values of j and k are passed as arguments to min(). The function min() is expected to return a value, and that value is assigned to m.

■ printf("\n%d is the minimum of %d and %d\n\n", m, j, k);

The values of m, j, and k are printed out.

■ `int min(int x, int y)`

This is the header of the function definition for `min()`. The parameter list consists of x and y. They are declared to be of type `int`. The return type is `int`. This means that the value that is returned from within the function will be converted to an `int` before it is returned to the calling environment.

■
```
{
    if (x < y)
        return x;
    else
        return y;
}
```

This is the body of the function definition for `min()`. If the value of x is less than the value of y, then the value of x is returned to the calling environment; otherwise the value of y is returned.

Even a small function such as `min()` provides useful structuring to the code. If we now want to write a function `max()` that computes the maximum of two values, then we can copy `min()` and modify it slightly. Let us write that function as well.

```
int max(int x, int y)
{
    if (x > y)
        return x;
    else
        return y;
}
```

We have designed `min()` and `max()` to work with integer values. If we want these functions to work with values of type `double`, then we must rewrite the functions. We will rewrite `min()` and leave the rewriting of `max()` as an exercise.

```
double min(double x, double y)
{
    if (x < y)
        return x;
    else
        return y;
}
```

Before the compiler sees a call to a function, it wants to know the number and type of its parameters and the type of the value returned by the function. Since we placed the function definitions of min() and max() above main(), the compiler is able to get this information. The function prototype mechanism provides another way of supplying this information to the compiler.

4.4   FUNCTION PROTOTYPES

In C, a function call can appear before the function is defined. The function can be defined later in the same file, or in another file, or it can come from a library. When this happens in traditional C, the compiler does not know the number and types of the parameters to the function. This leads to error prone code. In ANSI C, the *function prototype* remedies the problem by explicitly providing the number and types of parameters required by the function. The function prototype also provides the type returned by the function.

The function prototype has the following general form:

type function_name (parameter type list) ;

The *type* is the type of the value returned by the function. The *parameter type list* is a comma-separated list of types. Each type in the *parameter type list* can be followed by an identifier that represents the parameter itself, but this is optional. If a function has no parameters, then the keyword void is used. The information provided by the function prototype allows the compiler to enforce type compatibility. When a function is called, its arguments are converted, where possible, to the appropriate types. As an example of how function prototyping is used, let us recode the *message* program. The difference is that the function definition for prn_message() appears after main(), instead of before. The function prototype inside main() is a type declaration that must be consistent with the function definition.

```
#include <stdio.h>

main()
{
    int    n;
    void   prn_message(int);

    printf("Input a small positive integer:  ");
    scanf("%d", &n);
    prn_message(n);
}

void prn_message(k)
{

    . . . . .
```

The function prototype declaration

```
void   prn_message(int);
```

informs the compiler that the function, when called, is to be passed a single argument of type int, and that the function does not return a value.

A function prototype can be placed in the body of a function definition where other declarations go, or it can be placed at the top of the file, typically above any function definitions but below #include's and #define's.

```
#include <stdio.h>

void   prn_message(int);

main()
{

    . . . . .
```

This gives the function prototype *file visibility,* meaning that it is known throughout the file. In a large coding project, this is the preferred style.

In the last section in the *minimum* program, we used the function min(x, y). The prototype for this function would be

```
int    min(int, int);
```

Both the function type and the parameter-list types are explicitly mentioned. The function definition of min() that occurs later in the file must match this declaration. The function prototype can also include the identifier names of parameters. For example, we could write

```
int   min(int x, int y);
```

This is an alternate style. The compiler ignores the parameters x and y; they are meant to serve as further documentation for the human reader.

4.5 TOP-DOWN DESIGN

Imagine that we have the problem of analyzing some company data that is represented by a file of integers. As we read each integer, we want to print out the count, the integer, the sum of all the integers seen up to this point, the minimum integer seen up to this point, and the maximum integer seen up to this point. In addition to this, suppose that a banner should be printed at the top of the page, and that all the information should be neatly printed in columns under appropriate headings. To construct this program, we will use a top-down design.

We can decompose the problem into the following subproblems:

1   Print a banner.

2   Print the headings over the columns.

3   Read the data and print it neatly in columns.

Each of these subproblems can be coded directly as functions. Then these functions can be used in main() to solve the overall problem. Note that by designing the code this way, we can add further functions analyzing the data without affecting the program structure.

```
#include <stdio.h>

main()
{
    void    prn_banner(void);
    void    prn_headings(void);
    void    read_and_prn_data(void);

    prn_banner();
    prn_headings();
    read_and_prn_data();
}
```

This illustrates in a very simple way the idea of top-down design. The programmer
thinks of the tasks to be performed and codes each task as a function. If a particular task
is complicated, then that task in turn can be subdivided into other tasks, each coded as a
function. A further benefit of this is that the program as a whole is more readable and
self-documenting.

Coding the individual functions is straightforward. The first function contains a
single printf() statement.

```
void prn_banner(void)
{
    printf("\n%s%s%s\n",
        "**********************************************\n",
        "*       RUNNING SUMS, MINIMUMS, AND MAXIMUMS      *\n",
        "**********************************************\n");
}
```

The next function writes headings over columns. The format %5s is used to print a string
in 5 spaces. The format %12s is used four times to print four strings, each in 12 spaces.

```
void prn_headings(void)
{
    printf("%5s%12s%12s%12s%12s\n\n",
        "Count", "Item", "Sum", "Minimum", "Maximum");
}
```

Most of the work is done in read_and_prn_data(). We will dissect this program below to show in detail how it works.

```
void read_and_prn_data(void)
{
    int   cnt = 0, item, sum, smallest, biggest;
    int   min(int, int), max(int, int);

    if (scanf("%d", &item) == 1) {
        ++cnt;
        sum = smallest = biggest = item;
        printf("%5d%12d%12d%12d%12d\n",
            cnt, item, sum, smallest, biggest);
        while (scanf("%d", &item) == 1) {
            ++cnt;
            sum += item;
            smallest = min(item, smallest);
            biggest = max(item, biggest);
            printf("%5d%12d%12d%12d%12d\n",
                cnt, item, sum, smallest, biggest);
        }
    }
    else
        printf("No data was input - BYE.\n\n");
}
```

Suppose that this program is compiled and that the executable code is put into the file named *run_sums*. If we execute the program and enter data directly from the keyboard, we get the echoing of input characters and the output of the program intermixed on the screen (see exercise 12). To prevent this problem, we create a file called *data* containing the following integers:

    19   23   -7   29   -11   17

Now, we give the command

run_sums < *data*

This causes the input to the program to be redirected from the keyboard to the file. Here is what gets printed on the screen:

```
***********************************************
*     RUNNING SUMS, MINIMUMS, AND MAXIMUMS     *
***********************************************
```

Count	Item	Sum	Minimum	Maximum
1	19	19	19	19
2	23	42	19	23
3	-7	35	-7	23
4	29	64	-7	29
5	-11	53	-11	29
6	17	70	-11	29

DISSECTION OF THE *read_and_prn_data()* FUNCTION

■ ```
void read_and_prn_data(void)
{
    int   cnt = 0, item, sum, smallest, biggest;
    int   min(int, int), max(int, int);
```

The header of the function definition is the single line before the brace. Since the function does not return a value, its type is void. The parameter list is empty. In the body of the function definition, the local variables cnt, item, sum, smallest, and biggest are declared to be of type int. The variable cnt is initialized to zero. The value of the variable item will be taken from the input stream. The values of the variables sum, smallest, and biggest are to be computed. The function prototypes for min() and max() have been supplied.

■ ```
if (scanf("%d", &item) == 1) {
    ++cnt;
    sum = smallest = biggest = item;
    printf("%5d%12d%12d%12d%12d\n",
        cnt, item, sum, smallest, biggest);
    .....
}
else
    printf("No data was input - BYE.\n\n");
```

The function scanf() returns the number of successful conversions made. Here scanf() is attempting to read characters from the standard input stream (keyboard), to convert them to a decimal integer, and to store the result at the address of item. If this conversion process is successful, then the expression

```
scanf("%d", &item) == 1
```

will be *true*, and the body of the if statement will be executed. That is, cnt will be incremented, and the variables sum, smallest, and biggest will be assigned the value of item, and these values will be printed out in appropriate columns. Notice that the formats in the printf() statement are similar to those found in prn_headings(). If scanf() is unsuccessful in its conversion attempt, then the else part of the if-else statement will be executed. The conversion process can fail for two reasons. First, there might be an inappropriate character, for example a letter x, before any digits occur in the input stream. Since scanf() cannot convert the character x to a decimal integer, the value returned by scanf() would be 0. Second, there may be no characters at all in the input stream, or only white space characters. Since scanf() skips white space, it would come to the end of the file. When the end-of-file mark is read, then scanf() returns the value EOF. This value, although system-dependent, is typically -1.

■ while (scanf("%d", &item) == 1) {
```
    ++cnt;
    sum += item;
    smallest = min(item, smallest);
    biggest = max(item, biggest);
    printf("%5d%12d%12d%12d%12d\n",
        cnt, item, sum, smallest, biggest);
}
```

After the first integer has been obtained from the input stream, we use scanf() in this while loop to find others. Each time a successful conversion is made by scanf(), the body of this while loop is executed. This causes cnt to be incremented by 1, sum to be incremented by the current value of item, smallest to be assigned the minimum of the current values of item and smallest, biggest to be assigned the maximum of the current values of item and biggest, and all these values to be printed in appropriate columns. Eventually, scanf() will encounter an inappropriate character in the input stream or encounter the end-of-file mark. In either case scanf() will return a value different from 1, causing program control to exit from the while loop.

4.6   PROBLEM SOLVING: RANDOM NUMBERS

Random numbers have many uses on computers. One use is to serve as data to test code; another use is to simulate a real-world event that involves a probability. The method of simulation is an important problem solving technique. Programs that use random number functions to generate probabilities are called *Monte Carlo* simulations. This technique can be applied to many problems that otherwise would have no possibility of solution.

A random number generator is a function that returns integers that appear to be randomly distributed in some interval 0 to *n*, where *n* is system-dependent. The function rand() in the standard library is provided to do this. Let us begin to write a program that displays some random numbers generated by rand().

```
#include <stdio.h>

main()
{
    int     n;
    void    prn_random_numbers(int);

    printf("Some random numbers are to be printed.\n");
    printf("How many would you like to see?  ");
    scanf("%d", &n);
    prn_random_numbers(n);
}
```

The user is asked how many random numbers are wanted. The function scanf() is used to convert the characters typed at the keyboard to a decimal integer and to store the value at the address of n. The value of n is passed as an argument to the function prn_random_numbers().

```
void prn_random_numbers(int k)      /* print k random numbers */
{
   int   i, r, smallest, biggest;
   int   min(int, int),  max(int, int), rand(void);

   r = smallest = biggest = rand();
   printf("\n%12d", r);
   for (i = 1; i < k; ++i) {
      if (i % 5 == 0)
         printf("\n");
      r = rand();
      smallest = min(r, smallest);
      biggest = max(r, biggest);
      printf("%12d", r);
   }
   printf("\n\n%d random numbers printed.\n", k);
   printf("Minimum:%7d\nMaximum:%7d\n\n", smallest, biggest);
}
```

We want to dissect this function definition, but before we do so, let us show what the output of the program looks like. Suppose we run this program and input 19 when prompted. Here is what appears on the screen.

```
Some random numbers are to be printed.
How many would you like to see?  19

       346        130      10982       1090      11656
      7117      17595       6415      22948      31126
      9004      14558       3571      22879      18492
      1360       5412      26721      22463

19 random numbers printed.
Minimum:    130
Maximum:  31126
```

DISSECTION OF THE *prn_random_numbers()* FUNCTION

■ ```
void prn_random_numbers(int k)
{
    int   i, r, smallest, biggest;
```

The variable k is a parameter that is declared to be an int. The local variables i, r, smallest, and biggest are all declared to be of type int.

■ ```
r = smallest = biggest = rand();
printf("\n%12d", r);
```

The function rand() from the standard library is used to generate a random number. That number is assigned to the variables r, smallest, and biggest. The function printf() is used to print the value of r in 12 spaces as a decimal integer.

■ ```
for (i = 1; i < k; ++i) {
    if (i % 5 == 0)
        printf("\n");
    r = rand();
    . . . . .
}
```

This for loop is used to print the remaining random numbers. Because one random number has already been printed, the variable i at the top of the loop is initialized to 1 rather than 0. Whenever i is divisible by 5 (the values 5, 10, 15, . . . ), the expression

```
i % 5 == 0
```

controlling the if statement is *true*, causing a newline to be printed. The effect of this is to print at most five random numbers on each line.
```

4.7   A SIMULATION: THE GAME OF HEADS OR TAILS

To provide a further example of the use of functions, we wish to implement a computer game that simulates the children's game of calling heads or tails. In this game the first child tosses a coin, and the second child calls heads or tails. If the second child guesses the outcome correctly, then he wins; otherwise he loses. The game can be played repeatedly with a count kept of the number of wins and losses.

The machine will use rand() to simulate tossing a coin. As mentioned in the previous section, this is a simple form of Monte Carlo simulation. If the integer returned by rand() is even, it will be considered heads, and if it is odd, it will be considered tails. The program begins by printing instructions to the player. These instructions contain some of the design considerations for the program. After each toss of the coin, a report of the outcome is printed. At the conclusion of the program a final report is printed.

Top-down design reveals the need for a number of different functions. Each function is short, making the overall program easy to read.

```c
#include <stdio.h>
#include <stdlib.h>     /* for prototype of rand() */

main()
{
    int     n;
    void    prn_instructions(void), play(int);

    prn_instructions();
    printf("How many times do you want to play?  ");
    scanf("%d", &n);
    play(n);
}

void prn_instructions(void)
{
    printf("\n%s\n%s\n%s\n%s\n%s\n\n",
        "This is the game of calling heads or tails.",
        "I will flip a coin; you call it.",
        "If you call it correctly, you win; otherwise, I win.",
        "To call heads, type 0; to call tails, type 1.",
        "As I toss my coin I will tell you to \"call it\".");
}
```

```c
void play(int n)      /* machine does the tossing, user does the calling */
{
   int    coin, i, lose = 0, win = 0;
   int    toss(void), get_call_from_user(void);
   void   report_a_win(int), report_a_loss(int);
   void   prn_final_report(int, int, int);

   for (i = 0; i < n; ++i) {
      printf("Call it:  ");
      coin = toss();
      if (get_call_from_user() == coin) {
         ++win;
         report_a_win(coin);
      }
      else {
         ++lose;
         report_a_loss(coin);
      }
   }
   prn_final_report(win, lose, n);
}


int toss(void)      /* return 0 for heads and 1 for tails */
{
   return (rand() % 2);
}


int get_call_from_user(void)      /* return 0 for heads and 1 for tails */
{
   int    guess;

   scanf("%d", &guess);
   while (guess != 0 && guess != 1) {
      printf("ERROR: type 0 for heads and 1 for tails\n");
      scanf("%d", &guess);
   }
   return guess;
}
```

```
void report_a_win(int coin)
{
   if (coin == 0)
      printf("I have heads, you win.\n");
   else
      printf("I have tails, you win.\n");
}

void report_a_loss(int coin)
{
   if (coin == 0)
      printf("I have heads, you lose.\n");
   else
      printf("I have tails, you lose.\n");
}

void prn_final_report(int win, int lose, int n)
{
   printf("\n%s\n%s%3d\n%s%3d\n%s%3d\n\n",
      "Final report:",
      "   Number of games that you won:    ", win,
      "   Number of games that you lost:   ", lose,
      "   Total number of games:           ", n);
}
```

There are only a few new ideas in this program. In prn_instructions(), the format %s is used a number of times in the printf() statement to print strings. Notice that the last string contains \"call it\" as part of the string. When a double quote is contained as a character within a string, then it must be preceded by the escape character \ to prevent the string from ending prematurely. In the next chapter we will see other examples of the escape mechanism.

The body of the function toss() consists of a single statement. The value being returned is the value of the expression

```
rand() % 2
```

Recall that a modulus expression of the form a % b has the value of the remainder after b is divided into a. For example, 4 % 2 has the value 0, and 5 % 2 has the value 1. Thus rand() % 2 has the value 0 if the integer returned by rand() is even, and it has the value 1 if the integer returned by rand() is odd.

The user of this program has to type 0 for heads and 1 for tails. A better strategy would be to type the letter *h* for heads and the letter *t* for tails, but we need the ideas presented in Chapter 5 to do this. Thus we leave this change to an exercise at the end of that chapter.

4.8 INVOCATION AND CALL-BY-VALUE

A function is invoked by writing its name and an appropriate list of arguments within parentheses. Typically these arguments will match in number and type the parameters in the parameter list in the function definition. All arguments are passed *call-by-value*. This means that each argument is evaluated, and its value is used locally in place of the corresponding formal parameter. Thus if a variable is passed to a function, the stored value of that variable in the calling environment will not be changed.

Here is a simple example that clearly illustrates the concept of call-by-value.

```
#include <stdio.h>

main()
{
    int   n = 3, sum, compute_sum(int);

    printf("%d\n", n);        /* 3 is printed */
    sum = compute_sum(n);
    printf("%d\n", n);        /* 3 is printed */
    printf("%d\n", sum);      /* 6 is printed */
}

int compute_sum(int n)      /* sum the integers from 1 to n */
{
    int   sum = 0;
    for ( ; n > 0; --n)       /* n gets changed here, but not in main() */
        sum += n;
    printf("%d\n", n);        /* 0 is printed */
    return sum;
}
```

Even though n is passed to compute_sum(), and the value of n in the body of that function is changed, the value of n in the calling environment remains unchanged.

In Chapter 8, we will explain how to accomplish the effect of call-by-reference. It is a way to pass addresses (references) of variables to a function that then allows the body of the function to make changes to the values of variables in the calling environment.

4.9 STYLE

Breaking a problem into small subproblems that are then coded as functions is critical to good programming style. So as to be easily readable, a function should be at most a page of code. Where it is not transparent from a choice of identifier names, functions should be commented as to their purpose. Furthermore, each parameter should be an identifier that clearly indicates its own purpose, or else a comment as to its purpose is needed.

The order in which function definitions occur in a file is not important. It is usually a matter of taste whether one writes main() followed by the other function definitions, or vice versa. If a function is invoked and its definition occurs in another file, or later in the same file, then its function prototype should occur before the function invocation. If one is doing a top-down development, however, it is natural to start with main(). Of course, for large projects a good deal of program organization might be done on paper first, so even in a top-down development effort, the coding of the functions can occur first.

It is considered good programming style to have only a few return statements in a given function. If there are many return statements, then the logic of the code may be difficult to follow.

The names read, write, and print are commonly used as parts of names for system functions. For example, printf() uses print in its name. To clearly distinguish our names from system names, we often use prn and wrt as parts of names. Even though we could write a function named print(), it would be confusing to do so. The name print is visually too close to printf.

Whenever something is being counted inside a loop, it is a good idea to count it as soon as it is possible to do so. This rule is followed in the incrementing of cnt in the function definition for read_and_prn_data().

4.10 COMMON PROGRAMMING ERRORS

A common error is to mistakenly assume that a function is changing the value of a variable. Since the function mechanism in C is strictly call-by-value, it is not possible to change the value of a variable in the calling environment by invoking a function with the variable as an argument. If f() is a function and v is a variable, then the statement

```
f(v);
```

cannot change the value of v in the calling environment. However, in contrast to this, if f() returns a value, then the statement

```
v = f(v);
```

can change the value of v.

In ANSI C, main() is supposed to return an int value. This can be done with either

```
return expr;          or          exit(expr);
```

In main(), these two statements are equivalent, but in any other function their effects are different. A call to exit() from within any function causes the program to terminate and a value to be returned to the host environment. The value returned is called the *exit status*. By convention, a zero exit status indicates successful program termination, whereas a nonzero exit status indicates an abnormal situation.

If your compiler complains about main() not returning a value, you can write

```
int main(void)
{
   . . . . .
   return 0;
}
```

With some compilers you can write

```
void main(void)
{
   . . . . .
```

and omit any return statement or call to exit(). Although the compiler is happy with this, it is technically wrong, and this style will not be acceptable to other ANSI C compilers.

The lack of function prototypes can cause hard-to-detect run-time errors. Traditional C was considered unsuitable for novice programmers because the function parameter mechanism did not provide the safety of type checking. Consider the following program:

```
/* Print a table of square roots. */

double   sqrt();                      /* traditional C style */

main()
{
   int   i;

   for (i = 1; i < 20; ++i)
      printf("%d%12.3f\n", i, sqrt(i));
}
```

Here is some of the output from the program:

```
1        0.000
2        0.000
3        0.000
. . . . .
```

In this example, when the int value i is passed to the sqrt() function, it does not get converted to a double, which is what the function expects. This causes incorrect values to be printed. In ANSI C, the function prototype for sqrt() is provided in *math.h* as

```
double   sqrt(double);
```

If we use this prototype in place of the traditional C declaration, then the value of any integer expression passed as an argument to sqrt() will be converted to a double. Many C practitioners consider this improvement in type safety of the parameter-passing mechanism to be the single most important advantage of ANSI C over traditional C.

4.11   SYSTEM CONSIDERATIONS

The function rand() is in the standard library, and its prototype is in *stdlib.h*. This function must be tested carefully to see if its use is appropriate in a particular application. In some cases rand() may generate repetitive patterns that undermine a particular use. Many systems provide random() or other random number generators that are more statistically reliable.

The function rand() returns integers in the range from 0 to RAND_MAX, where the macro RAND_MAX is given in *stdlib.h*. Often, RAND_MAX is the largest int available on the system, but this is not always the case. For example, on a Sun workstation, a Silicon Graphics workstation, and a Cray supercomputer, we find the following line in *stdlib.h*:

```
#define    RAND_MAX 32767
```

This is certainly not the largest int available on these systems (see Chapter 6). For serious work, these systems provide other random number generators.

It is important to configure your compiler so that all warnings are turned on. Suppose that we are using the command-line version of Turbo C in an MS-DOS environment. When we give the command

   tcc −w pgm.c

the option −w turns on all warnings. In particular, if *pgm.c* is missing one or more function prototypes, the compiler will tell us. We can configure *tcc* so that it will be invoked automatically with the −w option by placing −w in the file *turboc.cfg* in the directory where *tcc.exe* exists. Similarly, the integrated environment for Turbo C can be configured so that all warnings are automatically turned on (see the Turbo C manuals). To understand the value of having warnings, try the following program:

```
#include <stdio.h>

main()
{
   printf("%d\n", f(2));         /* 7 is printed */
   printf("%d\n", f(2.0));       /* 1 is printed */
}

int f(int n)
{
   return (3 * n + 1);
}
```

What gets printed by this program is system-dependent. We have shown what gets printed on our Turbo C system.

ANSI C is compatible with traditional C. Since traditional C does not have function prototyping, if we write a program without prototypes on an ANSI C system, then actual arguments get passed into functions "as is," which means without type checking or conversion. In the above program, when the constant 2.0, which is a double, is passed to f(), no conversion takes place. This causes an error, because inside f() an int is expected. If we place the function prototype

```
int    f(int);
```

just above main(), then the compiler will convert the value of any arithmetic expression passed to f() to an int.

The type safety feature of function prototyping in ANSI C is very powerful, but the programmer must consistently use prototypes to reap the benefits.

4.12   SUMMARY

1 Structured programming is a problem-solving strategy and a programming methodology that strives for simple flow of control and uses top-down design.

2 Top-down design, also referred to as *stepwise refinement*, consists of repeatedly decomposing a problem into smaller problems.

3 A long program should be written as a collection of functions, each one being no longer than, say, a page in length. Each function should capture some small task of the overall problem.

4 In the body of a function the compiler recognizes a name followed by parentheses, such as prn_message() or min(x, y), as a call to a function.

5 A programmer creates a function by writing a function definition, which consists of a header and a body. The header consists of the type returned by the function, the function name, and a comma-separated list of declarations of parameters enclosed by parentheses. The body consists of declarations and statements enclosed by braces.

6 When a function is called, program control is passed to the function. When a return statement is executed, or the end of the function is reached, control is passed back to the calling environment. If a return statement contains an expression, the value of the expression is passed back to the calling environment as well.

7 The function prototype mechanism exists in ANSI C, but not in traditional C. A function prototype has the following general form:

type function_name (parameter type list) ;

The *type* is the type returned by the function. The *parameter type list* is typically a comma-separated list of types. If a function has no parameters, then the keyword void is used. A function prototype allows the compiler to enforce type compatibility when the function is called.

8 In a function prototype an identifier may follow each of the types in the *parameter type list*. For example, the two function prototypes

```
    int f(int a, float b);          and          int f(int, float);
```

are equivalent. The compiler does not need the parameter identifiers, only the types of the parameters. However, the parameters themselves may provide further documentation for the human reader.

9 In C, all arguments are passed call-by-value. This means that when a variable is passed as an argument to a function, its value remains unchanged in the calling environment.

10 All C systems provide the function rand(); however, for serious work other random number generators may be more appropriate.

4.13   EXERCISES

1 Rewrite the *message* program so that the output looks like the following:

```
Message for you:  Have a nice day!
                  Have a nice day!
                  Have a nice day!
                  .....
```

2 Write a function square() that will take an integer and return its square. Write another function cube() that will take an integer and return its cube.

3 Using the functions written in exercise 2, write a program to produce a neatly printed table containing a list of integers, their squares, and their cubes. The integers should run from 1 to 25.

4 The program *prn_rand* does not work right if the user types in 0 when asked for the number of random numbers desired. Correct the program so that it works correctly for this case.

5 Consider the `for` loop in the function `prn_random_numbers()` that begins

```
for (i = 1; i < k; ++i) {
   if (i % 5 == 0)
      printf("\n");
      .....
```

Suppose that we rewrite the first line as follows:

```
for (i = 2; i <= k; ++i) {
```

Will the same number of random numbers be printed? This modification causes the format of the output to change. Try it and see. Make a further program modification in the body of the `for` loop to get the output formatted correctly.

6 Run the program that prints random numbers. Notice that each time the program is executed, the same sequence of numbers is printed. The function `srand()` in the standard library can be used to supply a seed to the random number generator, causing a different sequence of numbers to be printed. The following program illustrates the use of `srand()`:

```
#include <stdio.h>
#include <stdlib.h>

main()
{
   int   seed = 13579;

   srand(seed);
   printf("%d   %d   %d\n", rand(), rand(), rand());
}
```

Different values for `seed` will result in the random number generator starting in a different place. Modify the program that prints random numbers so that the user supplies a seed first.

7 Investigate how to write your own random number generator. There are many ways to write one. If you are not concerned with statistical reliability, then the task is easy (but you have to look it up). Understanding the theory of a random number generator can be much more difficult than writing the code for it.

8 In Section 4.3 we wrote an interactive program that computes the minimum of two integers. Rewrite the code to work with type `double`. After you have tested your

program and are satisfied that it works correctly, modify the program so that it finds the minimum of four numbers.

9 Let n_0 be a given positive integer. For $i = 0, 1, 2, \ldots$, define

$$n_{i+1} = \begin{cases} n_i/2 & \text{if } n_i \text{ is even} \\ 3n + 1 & \text{if } n_i \text{ is odd} \end{cases}$$

The sequence stops whenever n_i has the value 1. Numbers that are generated this way are called "hailstones." Write a program that generates some hailstones. The function

```
void hailstones(int n)
{
    .....
```

should be used to compute and print the sequence generated by n. The output of your program might look as follows:

```
Hailstones generated by 77:

        77       232       116        58        29        88
        44        22        11        34        17        52
        26        13        40        20        10         5
        16         8         4         2         1

Number of hailstones generated:   23
```

You will find that all the sequences you generate are finite. Whether this is true in general is still an open question. *Hint:* Use variables of type long instead of int if the program misbehaves (see Chapter 6).

10 (Advanced) There is a famous conjecture, called the Goldbach conjecture, that every even integer n greater than 2 has the property that it is the sum of two prime numbers. With the help of machines, this conjecture has been tested extensively. No counterexample has ever been found. Write a program that will prove that the conjecture is true for all the even integers between the symbolic constants START and FINISH. For example, if you write

```
#define   START   700
#define   FINISH  1100
```

then the output of your program might look like this:

```
Every even number greater than 2 is the sum of two primes:

      700 = 17 + 683
      702 = 11 + 691
      704 =  3 + 701
      . . . . .
     1098 =  5 + 1093
     1100 =  3 + 1097
```

Hint: Write a function definition for is_prime(n). The function should return the int value 1 or 0, depending on whether n is prime or not.

11 In this exercise we want to use the random number generator rand() to simulate tossing a coin repeatedly. Try the following program:

```c
#include <stdio.h>
#include <stdlib.h>

#define   MY_LUCKY_NUMBER   1337
#define   N                 55

main()
{
   int   i;

   srand(MY_LUCKY_NUMBER);      /* seed the random number generator */
   for (i = 0; i < N; ++i) {
      if (i % 7 == 0)
         printf("\n");
      printf("%10s", (rand() % 2 == 1) ? "heads" : "tails");
   }
   printf("\n");
}
```

Note the use of the conditional operator ?: (see Section 3.19 in Chapter 3). Also, note that the format %10s is used to print a string in a field of 10 characters. What happens if you change the format to %15s? What happens if you move the call to srand() so that it is the first statement in the body of the for loop? After you have finished experimenting, return the code to its original state. Observe that repeated executions of the program produce the same output. For many applications, this is undesirable. Replace the call to srand() with

```
srand(time(NULL))
```

The function time() is in the standard library. On most systems the call time(NULL) returns the number of seconds that have elapsed since 1 January 1970 (see Chapter 15). Since the function prototype is in *time.h*, you should include that file, too. With these changes, your program should behave differently each time it is invoked. Does it? *Caution:* It is quite easy to get the machine to simulate tossing a coin. It is quite another matter to test whether the simulation is reasonable or not.

12 Consider the following function:

```
void report_a_win(int coin)
{
    if (coin == 0)
        printf("I have heads, you win.\n");
    else
        printf("I have tails, you win.\n");
}
```

Rewrite the function, replacing the if-else construct by a single printf() statement. *Hint:* Use the ideas presented in exercise 11.

13 Execute the program *run_sums* and enter data directly from the keyboard. When you are finished entering data, you should type an end-of-file signal (see Section 1.11, "System Considerations," in Chapter 1). What happens if you enter a letter instead of a number?

5

CHARACTER PROCESSING

5.1 THE DATA TYPE char
5.2 THE USE OF getchar() AND putchar()
5.3 AN EXAMPLE: CAPITALIZE
5.4 THE MACROS IN *ctype.h*
5.5 PROBLEM SOLVING: REPEATING CHARACTERS
5.6 PROBLEM SOLVING: COUNTING WORDS
5.7 STYLE
5.8 COMMON PROGRAMMING ERRORS
5.9 SYSTEM CONSIDERATIONS
5.10 SUMMARY
5.11 EXERCISES

In this chapter we will introduce some of the basic ideas involved in character processing. We want to discuss how characters are stored and manipulated in a machine, how characters can be treated as small integers, and how use is made of certain standard header files. To illustrate the ideas, we present simple character processing programs that accomplish useful work. These example programs make use of the character input/output macros getchar() and putchar(). For anyone trying to master a new language, getting data into and out of a machine is a skill that has to be developed early.

A number of important concepts are covered in this chapter. The use of the symbolic constant EOF is explained. When getchar() detects an end-of-file mark, it returns the value EOF, which makes it possible for the programmer to detect when the end of a file has been reached. The use of the header file *ctype.h* is explained. This file provides the programmer with a set of macros that can be used to process character data. Programmers use macros in the same manner as functions. The use of system header files such as *ctype.h* allows the programmer to write portable code. The programs, such as *caps*, presented in this chapter are quite simple, but we are able to use them to explain the essential ideas of character processing.

5.1   THE DATA TYPE char

The type char is one of the fundamental types of the C language. Constants and variables of this type are used to represent characters. Each character is stored in a machine in 1 byte. We will assume throughout that a byte is composed of 8 bits. A byte composed of 8 bits is capable of storing 2^8, or 256, distinct values.

When a character is stored in a byte, the contents of that byte can be thought of as either a character or as a small integer. Although 256 distinct values can be stored in a byte, only a subset of these values represents actual printing characters. These include the lowercase letters, uppercase letters, digits, punctuation, and special characters such as +, *, and %. The character set also includes the white space characters blank, tab, and newline. Examples of nonprinting characters are newline and the alert character, or bell. We will illustrate the use of the bell in this chapter.

A character constant is written between single quotes, as in 'a', 'b', or 'c'. A typical declaration for a variable of type char is

```
char   c;
```

Character variables can be initialized as in the example

```
char   c1 = 'A', c2 = 'B', c3 = '*';
```

A character is stored in memory in 1 byte according to a specific encoding. Most machines use either ASCII or EBCDIC character codes. In the discussion that follows we will be using the ASCII code. For any other code, the numbers will be different, but the ideas are analogous. A table of the ASCII code appears in an appendix.

In C, a character is considered to have the integer value corresponding to its ASCII encoding. Some examples are given in the following table:

Some character constants and their corresponding integer values

Character constants:	'a'	'b'	'c'	$\cdots$	'z'
Corresponding values:	97	98	99	$\cdots$	112
Character constants:	'A'	'B'	'C'	$\cdots$	'Z'
Corresponding values:	65	66	67	$\cdots$	90
Character constants:	'0'	'1'	'2'	$\cdots$	'9'
Corresponding values:	48	49	50	$\cdots$	57
Character constants:	'&'	'*'	'+'		
Corresponding values:	38	42	43		

Observe that there is no particular relationship between the value of the character constant representing a digit and the digit's intrinsic integer value. That is, the value of '7' is *not* 7. The fact that the values of 'a', 'b', 'c', and so forth, occur in order is an important property that facilitates the sorting of characters, words, lines, etc., into lexicographical order.

In the functions printf() and scanf(), a %c is used to designate the character format. For example, the statement

```
printf("%c", 'a');    /* a is printed */
```

causes the character constant 'a' to be printed in the format of a character. Similarly,

```
printf("%c%c%c", 'A', 'B', 'C');    /* ABC is printed */
```

causes ABC to be printed.

Constants and variables of type char can be treated as small integers. The statement

```
printf("%d", 'a');    /* 97 is printed */
```

causes the value of the character constant 'a' to be printed in the format of a decimal integer. Thus 97 is printed. On the other hand, the statement

```
printf("%c", 97);    /* a is printed */
```

causes the value of the decimal integer constant 97 to be printed in the format of a character; thus a is printed.

Some nonprinting and hard-to-print characters require an *escape sequence*. For example, the newline character is written as '\n' in a program, and even though it is being described by the two characters \ and n, it represents a single ASCII character. The backslash character \ is also called the *escape character*; it is used to "escape" the usual meaning of the character that follows it. The following table contains some nonprinting and hard-to-print characters:

Name of character	*Written in C*	*Integer value*
alert	\a	7
backslash	\\	92
backspace	\b	8
carriage return	\r	13
double quote	\"	34
formfeed	\f	12
horizontal tab	\t	9
newline	\n	10
null character	\0	0
single quote	\'	39
vertical tab	\v	11

The double quote character " has to be escaped if it is used as a character in a string. Otherwise it would prematurely terminate the string. An example is

```
printf("\"ABC\"");   /* "ABC" is printed */
```

However, inside single quotes one could write '"', although '\"' is also accepted. In general, escaping an ordinary character has no effect. Inside a string, the single quote is just an ordinary character:

```
printf("'ABC'");   /* 'ABC' is printed */
```

Another way to write a character constant is by means of a one-, two-, or three-octal-digit escape sequence, as in '\007'. This is the alert character \a, or the audible bell. It can be written also as '\07' or '\7', but it cannot be written as '7'.

5.2   THE USE OF getchar() AND putchar()

The system provides getchar() and putchar() for the input and output of characters. These are macros defined in *stdio.h*. To read a character from the keyboard, getchar() is used; to write a character to the screen, putchar() is used. For example, a program that prints the line

```
She sells sea shells by the seashore.
```

on the screen can be written as follows:

```
#include <stdio.h>

main()
{
    putchar('S');
    putchar('h');
    putchar('e');
    putchar(' ');
    .....
    putchar('e');
    putchar('.');
    putchar('\n');
}
```

Of course, this is a tedious way to accomplish the task; using a printf() statement would be much easier.

In the next program getchar() gets a character from the input stream (keyboard) and assigns it to the variable c. Then putchar() is used to print the character twice on the screen.

```
#include <stdio.h>

main()
{
   char    c;

   while (1) {
      c = getchar();
      putchar(c);
      putchar(c);
   }
}
```

Note that the variable c is of type char. In the next version of this program we will change this. Also, because 1 is nonzero, as an expression it is always *true*. Thus the construct

```
while (1) {
   .....
}
```

is an infinite loop. The only way to stop this program is with an interrupt, which on our system is effected by typing a control-c.

For a number of reasons, the above program is not really acceptable. Let us rewrite the program and call the new version *dbl_out*.

```
#include <stdio.h>

main()
{
   int    c;

   while ((c = getchar()) != EOF) {
      putchar(c);
      putchar(c);
   }
}
```

DISSECTION OF THE *dbl_out* PROGRAM

■ `#include <stdio.h>`

Lines that begin with a # are preprocessing directives. These lines communicate with the preprocessor. A preprocessing directive of the form

```
#include <filename>
```

causes the preprocessor to include a copy of the named file into the source code at that point before passing the code to the compiler. The angle brackets around stdio.h tell the system to look for this file in the "usual place." The location of this place is system-dependent. The file *stdio.h* is a standard header file supplied with C systems and is typically included in functions that make use of certain standard input/output constructs. One line of this header file is

```
#define   EOF   (-1)
```

The identifier EOF is mnemonic for "end-of-file." What is actually used to signal an end-of-file mark is system-dependent. Although the int value −1 is often used, different systems can have different values. By including the file *stdio.h* and using the symbolic constant EOF, we have made the program portable. This means that the source file can be moved to a different system and run with no changes.

■ `int   c;`

The variable c has been declared in the program as an int rather than a char. Whatever is used to signal the end of a file, it cannot be a value that represents a character. Since c is an int, it can hold all possible character values as well as the special value EOF. Although one usually thinks of a char as a very short int type, one can also think of an int as a very long char type.

■ `while ((c = getchar()) != EOF) {`

The expression

```
(c = getchar()) != EOF
```

is composed of two parts. The subexpression

```
c = getchar()
```

gets a value from the keyboard and assigns it to the variable c, and the value of the subexpression takes on that value as well. The symbols != represent the "not equal to" operator. As long as the value of the subexpression c = getchar() is not equal to EOF, the body of the while loop is executed. To exit the loop, we have to enter an end-of-file signal at the keyboard. The operating system then tells getchar() that the end of the file has been reached, which in turn causes getchar() to return EOF. The user cannot enter the value EOF directly at the keyboard. How an end-of-file value is entered at the keyboard is system-dependent. In UNIX, it is usually entered by typing a carriage return followed by a control-d. In MS-DOS, one types a control-z instead.

■ (c = getchar()) != EOF

The parentheses around the subexpression c = getchar() are necessary. Suppose that we had typed

```
c = getchar() != EOF
```

Because of operator precedence, this is equivalent to

```
c = (getchar() != EOF)
```

This has the effect of getting a character from the input stream, testing to see if it is not equal to EOF, and assigning the result of the test (either 0 or 1) to the variable c (see exercise 10).

5.3   AN EXAMPLE: CAPITALIZE

Characters have an underlying integer-valued representation that on most C systems is the numeric value of their 7-bit ASCII representation. For example, the character constant 'a' has value 97. If one thinks of characters as small integers, then arithmetic on characters makes sense. Since the values of the letters in both the lower- and uppercase alphabet occur in order, the expression 'a' + 1 has the value 'b', the expression 'b' + 1 has the value 'c', and the expression 'Z' - 'A' has the value 25. Moreover, 'A' - 'a' has a value that is the same as 'B' - 'b', which is the same as 'C' - 'c', etc. Because of this, if the variable c has the value of a lowercase letter, then the expression c + 'A' - 'a' has the value of the corresponding uppercase letter. These ideas are incorporated into the next program, which capitalizes all lowercase letters and doubles the newline characters.

```
/* Capitalize lowercase letters and double space. */

#include <stdio.h>

main()
{
    int    c;
    while ((c = getchar()) != EOF)
        if ('a' <= c && c <= 'z')
            putchar(c + 'A' - 'a');
        else if (c == '\n') {
            putchar('\n');
            putchar('\n');
        }
        else
            putchar(c);
}
```

DISSECTION OF THE *caps* PROGRAM

■ while ((c = getchar()) != EOF)

The macro getchar() gets a character and assigns it to the variable c. As long as the value of c is not EOF, the body of the while loop is executed.

■ if ('a' <= c && c <= 'z')
        putchar(c + 'A' - 'a');

Because of operator precedence, the expressions

'a' <= c && c <= 'z'   and   ('a' <= c) && (c <= 'z') are equivalent. The symbols `<=` represent the operator "less than or equal to." The subexpression `'a' <= c` tests to see if the value `'a'` is less than or equal to the value of c. The subexpression `c <= 'z'` tests to see if the value of c is less than or equal to the value `'z'`. The symbols `&&` represent the "logical and" operator. If both subexpressions are *true*, then the expression

```
'a' <= c && c <= 'z'
```

is *true*; otherwise it is *false*. Thus the expression as a whole is *true* if and only if c is a lowercase letter. If the expression is *true*, then the statement

```
putchar(c + 'A' - 'a');
```

is executed, causing the corresponding uppercase letter to be printed.

■ `else if (c == '\n') {`
```
    putchar('\n');
    putchar('\n');
}
```

The symbols `==` represent the "is equal to" operator. If c is not a lowercase letter, a test is made to see if it is equal to a newline character. If it is, two newline characters are printed.

■ `else`
```
    putchar(c);
```

If the value of c is not a lowercase letter, and it is not a newline character, then the character corresponding to the value c is printed. An `else` is always associated with the immediately preceding `if`.

Although the *caps* program is portable to any ASCII machine, it will not work as expected on an EBCDIC machine. The reason for this is that the uppercase letters are not all contiguous in the EBCDIC code. Here is a version of the *caps* program that can be expected to work on all machines.

```
/* Capitalize lowercase letters and double space. */

#include <stdio.h>
#include <ctype.h>

main()
{
    int   c;

    while ((c = getchar()) != EOF)
        if (islower(c))
            putchar(toupper(c));
        else if (c == '\n') {
            putchar('\n');
            putchar('\n');
        }
        else
            putchar(c);
}
```

DISSECTION OF THE PORTABLE *caps* PROGRAM

■ #include <stdio.h>
  #include <ctype.h>

The file *ctype.h*, along with *stdio.h*, is a standard header file provided with the C system. This file contains macros and prototypes of functions that are often used when processing characters. A macro is code that gets expanded by the preprocessor. In Chapter 11 we will explain in detail how macros work. For the purposes of this chapter we will treat the macros in *ctype.h* just as if they were functions. Although there are technical differences between a macro and a function, both are used in a similar fashion. The program *caps* makes use of islower() and toupper(). Since *ctype.h* contains the macro definition for islower() and the function prototype for toupper(), this header file gets included.

```
■ while ((c = getchar()) != EOF)
     if (islower(c))
        putchar(toupper(c));
```

A character is read from the input stream and assigned to c. As long as the value of c is not EOF, the body of the while loop is executed. The macro islower() is defined in *ctype.h*. If c is a lowercase letter, then islower(c) has nonzero value; otherwise it has the value 0. The function prototype for toupper() is given in *ctype.h*. The function itself is provided by the standard library. If c is a lowercase letter, then toupper(c) has the value of the corresponding uppercase letter. Therefore, the if statement has the effect of testing to see whether or not c has the value of a lowercase letter. If it does, then the corresponding uppercase letter is written on the screen. Note carefully that the stored value of c itself is not changed by invoking isupper(c) or toupper(c).

A novice C programmer need not know exactly how the macros in *ctype.h* are implemented. Along with functions in the standard library, such as printf() and scanf(), these macros can be treated as a system-supplied resource. The important point to remember is that by using these functions and macros, one is writing portable code that will run in any ANSI-conforming environment.

Why learn about a construct such as c + 'A' - 'a' at all? Well, a lot of C code is written just for an ASCII environment, and even though the construct is not considered good programming practice, one commonly sees it. Since a programmer must learn to read code as well as write it, this particular construct should be mastered. In order to avoid nonportable code, it is good programming practice to use the macros in *ctype.h* wherever appropriate.

5.4   THE MACROS IN *ctype.h*

The system provides a standard header file *ctype.h*, which contains a set of macros that are used to test characters and a set of prototypes of functions that are used to convert characters. They are made accessible by the preprocessing directive

```
#include <ctype.h>
```

The macros in the following table are used to test characters. These macros all take an argument of type int, and they return an int value that is either nonzero (*true*) or zero (*false*).

Macro	*Nonzero* (**true**) *is returned if:*
isalpha(c)	c is a letter
isupper(c)	c is an uppercase letter
islower(c)	c is a lowercase letter
isdigit(c)	c is a digit
isalnum(c)	c is a letter or digit
isxdigit(c)	c is a hexadecimal digit
isspace(c)	c is a white space character
ispunct(c)	c is a punctuation character
isprint(c)	c is a printable character
isgraph(c)	c is printable, but not a space
iscntrl(c)	c is a control character
isascii(c)	c is an ASCII code

In the next table we list the functions toupper() and tolower(), which are in the standard library, and the macro toascii(). The macro and the prototypes for the two functions are in *ctype.h*. The functions and the macro each take an int and return an int. Note carefully that the value of c stored in memory does not get changed.

Function or Macro	*Effect*
toupper(c)	changes c from lowercase to uppercase
tolower(c)	changes c from uppercase to lowercase
toascii(c)	changes c to ASCII code

5.5   PROBLEM SOLVING: REPEATING CHARACTERS

The use of a function with proper parameterization is a very powerful problem solving idea. It is an aspect of *generalization*. Frequently one can solve a particular problem in a simple special case. An example might be a need to print the letter *C* three distinct times.

```
printf("%c%c%c", 'C', 'C', 'C');
```

Now, if we need to print four *C*'s or six *b*'s, then we need a different solution. By parameterizing both the character to be printed and the number of times to print it, we solve a far more general problem. We will write a function to do this:

```
void    repeat(char c, int n);
```

Once our function is written and the code is correct, we may reuse the function for many purposes. Indeed, many of the standard library functions were developed as useful general operations that commonly occur.

In the program *dbl_out*, which we presented above, we showed how every character read in can be printed out twice. Here we want to generalize that simple idea by writing a function that prints out a given character *n* times.

```
void repeat(char c, int n)
{
    int    i;

    for (i = 0; i < n; ++i)
        putchar(c);
}
```

Notice that the variable c is declared as a char, not an int. Since a test for EOF is not made in this function, there is no need to declare c an int. Suppose that we invoke the function with the statement

```
repeat('B' - 1, 2 + 3);
```

The arguments of this function call are 'B'-1 and 2+3. The respective values of these arguments are passed and associated with the formal parameters of the function. The effect of the function call is to print the letter A five times. Here is a main() function that can be used to test repeat():

```
#include <stdio.h>

main()
{
    int            i;
    const char     alert = '\a', c = 'A';
    void           repeat(char, int);

    repeat('B' - 1, 2 + 3);
    putchar(' ');
    for (i = 0; i < 10; ++i) {
        repeat(c + i, i);
        putchar(' ');
    }
    repeat(alert, 100);
    putchar('\n');
}
```

Note that we have used the type specifier const to indicate that the variables alert and c cannot be changed. When we compile the program and run it, here is what we see on the screen.

```
AAAAA B CC DDD EEEE FFFFF GGGGGG HHHHHHH IIIIIIII JJJJJJJJJ
```

The function repeat() can be used to draw simple figures on the screen. In exercise 8 we show how to use repeat() to draw a triangle and leave as an exercise the problem of drawing a diamond.

5.6 PROBLEM SOLVING: COUNTING WORDS

Many computations are repetitive, and sometimes the repetition is based on counting. An example would be a recipe that says, "stir for 5 minutes." Here we count up to 5. Sometimes the repetition waits for some condition to change. An example would be a recipe that says, "stir until turns brown." In problem solving, looking for a special characteristic that logically ends the computation is an important method. In character processing, we often look for the end-of-file condition.

Suppose that we want to count the number of words being input at the keyboard. Again, top-down design leads us to break up the problem into small pieces. To do this, we need to know the definition of a word, and we need to know when to end our task. For our purposes we will assume that words are separated by white space. Thus any word is a contiguous string of nonwhite space characters. As usual, we will end the processing of characters when we encounter the end-of-file sentinel. The heart of our program is a function that detects a word. We will explain this function in some detail.

```
#include <stdio.h>
#include <ctype.h>

main()
{
    int   word_cnt = 0;
    int   found_next_word(void);

    while (found_next_word() == 1)
        ++word_cnt;
    printf("Number of words = %d\n\n", word_cnt);
}
```

```
int found_next_word(void)
{
   int   c;

   while (isspace(c = getchar()))
       ;                    /* skip white space */
   if (c != EOF) {      /* found a word */
      while ((c = getchar()) != EOF && !isspace(c))
         ;       /* skip everything except EOF and white space */
      return 1;
   }
   return 0;
}
```

DISSECTION OF THE *word_cnt* PROGRAM

■ `int   word_cnt = 0;`

The `int` variable `word_cnt` is initialized to zero.

■ `while (found_next_word() == 1)`
    `++word_cnt;`

As long as the function `found_next_word()` returns the value 1, the body of the `while` loop is executed, causing `word_cnt` to be indexed.

■ `printf("Number of words = %d\n\n", word_cnt);`

Just before exiting the program, we print out the number of words found.

■ `int found_next_word()`
   `{`
      `int   c;`

This is the beginning of the function definition for `found_next_word()`. The function has no parameters in its parameter list. In the body of the function, the `int` variable `c` is declared. Although we are going to use `c` to take on character values, we declare `c` as an `int`, not a `char`. Eventually `c` will hold the special value `EOF`, and on some systems that value may not fit in a `char`.

■
```
while (isspace(c = getchar()))
    ;                    /* skip white space */
```

A character is read from the input stream and assigned to c. The value of the sub-expression c = getchar() takes on this value as well. As long as this value is not a white space character, the body of the while loop is executed. However, the body of the while loop is just the empty statement. Thus the effect of the while loop is to skip white space. Notice that the empty statement is clearly displayed on a line by itself. Good programming practice requires this. If we had written

```
while (isspace(c = getchar()));
```

the visibility of the empty statement would be reduced.

■
```
if (c != EOF) {      /* found a word */
    while ((c = getchar()) != EOF && !isspace(c))
        ;       /* skip everything except EOF and white space */
    return 1;
}
```

After white space has been skipped, the value of c is either EOF or the first "letter" of a word. If the value of c is not EOF, then a word has been found. The test expression in the while loop consists of three parts. First a character is read from the input stream and assigned to c, and the subexpression c = getchar() takes on the value of c as well. A test is then made to see if that value is EOF. If it is, then the body of the while loop is not executed, and control passes to the next statement. If the value is not EOF, then a test is made to see if the value is a white space character. If it is, then the body of the while loop is not executed, and control passes to the next statement. If the value is not a white space character, then the body of the while loop is executed. However, the body is just the empty statement. Thus the effect of this while loop is to skip everything except EOF and white space characters; that is, the word that has been found has now been skipped.

■
```
return 1;
```

After a word has been found and skipped, the value 1 is returned.

■
```
return 0;
```

If a word was not found, then the value 0 is returned.

5.7 STYLE

Simple character variables are often given the identifier c, or identifiers starting with c, such as c1, c2, and c3. Functions and macros that do character manipulation frequently have char as part of their name, or the name ends with the letter c. Examples are getchar() and putchar(), and as we shall see in Chapter 14, getc() and putc(). The choice of identifiers for the macros in *ctype.h* is instructive. Those macros that answer a true/false question, such as isalpha() and isupper(), all have names that start with is. Those functions with prototypes in *ctype.h* that have the sense of changing a character value, such as toupper(), all have names that start with to. The proper choice of identifier names is crucial to readability and documentation.

For character processing tasks, we can use either getchar() or scanf() to read characters. Similarly, we can use either putchar() or printf() to write characters. In many instances the choice is a matter of personal taste. However, if there is a great deal of character processing being done, then the use of getchar() and putchar() along with the standard header file *stdio.h* can result in faster code, because getchar() and putchar() are implemented as macros in *stdio.h*. As we shall see in Chapter 11, macros are a code-substitution mechanism that can be used to avoid a function call.

One difference between putchar() and printf() is that putchar() returns the value of the character written to the output stream as an int, whereas printf() returns the number of characters printed. Sometimes this dictates the use of putchar().

A common C programming idiom is to perform both an assignment and a test in the expression that controls a while or for loop. Although this is a general practice, one most often sees it in code used to process characters. As an example, the code

```
while ((c = getchar()) != EOF) {
    . . . . .
}
```

uses this idiom. In contrast to this, we could write

```
c = getchar();
while (c != EOF) {
    . . . . .
    c = getchar();
}
```

but now, if the body of the loop is long, the last statement, which affects the control of the loop, is a long way from the test expression. On the other hand, a construct such as

```
while (isspace(c = getchar()))
    ;      /* skip white space */
```

can just as well be written

```
c = getchar();
while (isspace(c))
    c = getchar();
```

Here the body of the loop is very short—so short, in fact, that if we put the control all at the top, the body of the loop is empty. Which form is used is largely a matter of taste.

5.8   COMMON PROGRAMMING ERRORS

We have already explained that if a program uses a variable to read in characters and to test for the value EOF, then that variable should be an int, not a char. This is, in part, a portability consideration. Some C systems cannot detect EOF as an end-of-file signal if the value is assigned to a variable of type char instead of int. Try the following code:

```
char   c;                         /* wrong */

while ((c = getchar()) != EOF)
    putchar(c);
```

This may or may not work on your system. Even if it does, do not use a char when testing for EOF. You may not be porting your code today, put if you keep programming, you are likely to do so in the future.

Suppose that we have text files that are double- or triple-spaced, and our task is to copy the files, except that multiple occurrences of newlines are to be reduced to a single newline. For example, we want to be able to change a double-spaced file into one that is only single-spaced. Here is a program that will do this.

```
/* Copy stdin to stdout, except single space only. */

#include <stdio.h>

main()
{
    int   c, last_c = '\0';

    while ((c = getchar()) != EOF) {
        if (c == '\n') {
            if (last_c != '\n')
                putchar('\n');
        }
        else
            putchar(c);
        last_c = c;
    }
}
```

At the start of this program the variable last_c is initialized to the null character, but thereafter, that variable holds the last character read from the input stream (keyboard). There is nothing special about the use of the null character here. We just need to initialize last_c with some character other than a newline character. There are two common errors that can be made in this program. Suppose that we had typed

```
if (c = '\n') {
```

using = instead of ==. Since the expression c = '\n' is always *true*, the else part will never get executed, and the program will fail badly. Here is another error. Suppose that we had typed

```
if (c == '\n')
    if (last_c != '\n')
        putchar(c);
else
    putchar(c);
```

The indentation shows the logic that we want, but not what we are actually getting. Because an else statement always attaches to the nearest preceding if, the above code is equivalent to

```
if (c == '\n')
   if (last_c != '\n')
      putchar(c);
   else
      putchar(c);
```

and this is clearly in error. The programmer must always remember that the compiler sees only a stream of characters.

5.9   SYSTEM CONSIDERATIONS

In Section 1.11, "System Considerations," in Chapter 1, we discussed redirecting the standard input and output. You should review that material and try redirection with the *caps* program. Create a file called *input* and put some text in it. Then try the following commands:

> *caps*
> *caps < input*
> *caps > output*
> *caps < input > output*

Most operating systems have a command that copies one file to another. In MS-DOS, the command is *copy*; in UNIX, it is *cp*. The following program can be considered a simple version of such a command.

```
#include <stdio.h>

main()
{
   int   c;

   while ((c = getchar()) != EOF)
      putchar(c);
}
```

If we compile this program and put the executable code in *my_copy*, then the command

> *my_copy < infile > outfile*

will copy the contents of *infile* to *outfile*.

If c has the value of a lowercase letter, then toupper(c) returns the value of the corresponding uppercase letter. The ANSI C standard states that if c does not have the value of a lowercase letter, then toupper(c) should return as its value the value of the argument unchanged. Thus to change all lowercase letters to uppercase, we could use the code

```
while ((c = getchar()) != EOF)
   putchar(toupper(c));
```

However, in many older C systems, toupper() is implemented as a macro, and the above code will fail badly. On those systems an explicit test of c must be made:

```
while ((c = getchar()) != EOF)   /* traditional C code */
   if (islower(c))
      putchar(toupper(c));
   else
      putchar(c);
```

Similar remarks hold for tolower().

Many C systems provide the macros _toupper() and _tolower() for more efficient character processing. These macros, if they exist, are provided in *ctype.h*. Here is an example of their use:

```
while ((c = getchar()) != EOF)
   if (_islower(c))
      putchar(_toupper(c));
   else
      putchar(c);
```

Note, however, that many C systems, both traditional and ANSI, do not support _toupper() and _tolower(). *Warning:* If you are trying to write portable code, use toupper() and tolower() cautiously. Some organizations use traditional C, some use ANSI C, and some are somewhere in between.

All compilers treat a char as a small integer. On most systems, but not all, the default range of values for a char is from -128 to 127. Many compilers provide an option to change the range of values to go from 0 to 255 instead. If we are using the command line version of the Turbo C compiler, then the $-K$ option accomplishes this:

tcc $-K$ pgm.c

(To effect this option in the *tc* integrated environment, you need to read the Turbo C manuals.) This option could be useful when trying to minimize the amount of disk space required to store a lot of data. If all your numbers are in the range 0 to 255, a program compiled with this option can manipulate the data and store it as char's instead of int's. As we will see in Chapter 6, a char is stored in less space than an int.

5.10   SUMMARY

1   A char is stored in 1 byte according to its ASCII encoding, and is considered to have the corresponding integer value. For example, the value of the character constant 'a' is 97.

2   There are nonprinting characters. Examples are the alert character, or audible bell, '\a', and the newline character '\n'. The newline character is used extensively to format output.

3   Basic input/output for characters is accomplished readily with the macros getchar() and putchar(). These macros are defined in the standard header file *stdio.h*. In most respects these macros can be treated as functions.

4   When using certain input/output constructs, the system header file *stdio.h* should be included. This is done by means of the preprocessing directive

```
#include <stdio.h>
```

5   When doing character input, it is frequently necessary to test for the end-of-file mark. This is accomplished by using the symbolic constant EOF in a program. The symbolic constant EOF is defined in the system header file *stdio.h*. On most systems, the value of EOF is −1.

6   There are a number of system-supplied macros and functions that test or convert character values. The macros and the prototypes of these functions are made available to the programmer by including the system header file *ctype.h*.

5.11   EXERCISES

1   Write a program using putchar() and getchar() that reads characters from the keyboard and writes to the screen. Every letter that is read should be written three times and followed by a newline. Any newline that is read should be disregarded. All other characters should just be copied to the screen.

2 Write a program using getchar() that reads characters from the standard input stream (keyboard) until the sentinel character # is encountered. The program should count the number of occurrences of the letters *a*, *b*, and *c*.

3 Change the program in exercise 2 so that characters are read until EOF is encountered. Use redirection to test the program.

4 Write a program that reads characters from the keyboard and writes to the screen. Write all vowels as uppercase letters, and write all nonvowels as lowercase letters. *Hint:* Write a function isvowel() that tests whether or not a character is a vowel. You will be able to reuse your code in exercise 12.

5 Which of the characters backspace, newline, space, and tab are considered printable? Take as the authority in this matter the macro isprint() in *ctype.h*.

6 Write a program that formats text files so that most lines contain approximately *N* characters. Start with the preprocessing directive

```
#define   N   30
```

Count the characters as they are written. As long as the count is less than *N*, change any newline character to a space. When the count is *N* or more, write any white space character as a newline and change the count to zero. If we assume that most words contain less than 10 characters, then the effect of the program will be to write lines containing between *N* and *N* + 10 characters. Typists usually follow such an algorithm. Compile your program and put the executable output in the file *reformat*. Use redirection to test the program by giving the command

```
    reformat < text
```

Of course, you can get different length lines by changing the value of the symbolic constant N.

7 Write a program that indents all the lines in a text file. Each line should be preceded by N blank spaces, where N is a symbolic constant.

8 The function repeat() can be used to draw simple figures on your screen. For example, the following program draws a triangle:

```
#include <stdio.h>

#define   N    33

main()
{
   char   c = 'X';
   int    i;
   void   repeat(char, int);

   for (i = 1; i < N; i += 2) {
      repeat(c, i);
      putchar('\n');
   }
}
```

Compile and run this program so that you understand its effects. Write a similar program that prints a diamond in the middle of your screen.

9 One difference between putchar() and printf() is that putchar() returns the value of the character written to the output stream as an int, whereas printf() returns the number of characters printed. What gets printed by the following code?

```
for (putchar('0'); putchar('1'); putchar('2'))
   putchar('3');
```

Does the following make sense? Explain.

```
printf("%c%c%c\n", putchar('A'), putchar('B'), putchar('C'));
```

10 To copy the standard input file to the standard output file, a programmer can make use of the following loop:

```
while ((c = getchar()) != EOF)
   putchar(c);
```

Suppose that by mistake the inner parentheses are left out, causing the loop to be written instead as

```
while (c = getchar() != EOF)
   putchar(c);
```

Write a test program to see what the effect is. If the input file has *n* characters, are *n* characters written to the output file? Explain.

11 The game of calling heads or tails that was presented in Section 4.7 in Chapter 4 requires the user to input 0 for heads and 1 for tails. Rewrite the program so that the user must input the letter *h* for heads and the letter *t* for tails. *Hint:* You can use %c with scanf() to read in characters typed by the user, but you will have to deal with white space characters, too, since the user always types in *h* or *t* followed by a newline.

12 The ancient Egyptians wrote in hieroglyphics. In this system of writing, vowel sounds are not represented, only consonants. Is written English generally understandable without vowels? To experiment, write a function isvowel() that tests whether or not a character is a vowel. Use your function in a program that reads the standard input file and writes to the standard output file, deleting all vowels. Use redirection on a file containing some English text to test your program.

13 Most operating systems provide data-compression utilities that reduce the size of text files so that they take up less room on the disk. These utilities work both ways; compressed files can be uncompressed later. Write a *crunch* program that reduces the size of C source files. Your program should remove all extraneous white space, including newline characters. Test your program as follows:

> *crunch* < *pgm.c* > *try_me.c*

The code in *try_me.c* should compile and execute with the same effects as *pgm.c*. Does it? Try your program on a number of your *.c* files. On average, what is the reduction in space achieved by *crunch*, expressed as a percent? To answer this question, write a simple routine that counts the number of characters in a file.

14 Most systems have "pretty printing" utilities that take crunched or poorly laid out C programs and transform them to be more readable. Such a utility when applied to some crunched C code that you produced in exercise 13 would print it with nice spacing. Write your own version of a "pretty printing" utility. Given a C program as input, it should add white space and newline characters to make the program more readable. Test your "pretty printer" by running it on previously crunched C code.

15 In Section 5.5 we presented the output from our program *repeat*. Here it is again:

```
AAAAA B CC DDD EEEE FFFFF GGGGGG HHHHHHH IIIIIIII JJJJJJJJJ
```

Note that there are two blanks just before the B, whereas thereafter all the blanks occur singly. Explain why.

6

THE FUNDAMENTAL DATA TYPES

6.1   DECLARATIONS AND EXPRESSIONS

6.2   THE FUNDAMENTAL DATA TYPES

6.3   CHARACTERS AND THE DATA TYPE char

6.4   THE DATA TYPE int

6.5   THE INTEGRAL TYPES short, long, AND unsigned

6.6   THE FLOATING TYPES

6.7   THE sizeof OPERATOR

6.8   MATHEMATICAL FUNCTIONS

6.9   CONVERSIONS AND CASTS
    THE INTEGRAL PROMOTIONS
    THE USUAL ARITHMETIC CONVERSIONS
    CASTS

6.10 PROBLEM SOLVING: COMPUTING INTEREST

6.11 STYLE

6.12 COMMON PROGRAMMING ERRORS

6.13 SYSTEM CONSIDERATIONS

6.14 SUMMARY

6.15 EXERCISES

We begin this chapter with a brief discussion of declarations and expressions. Then we give a detailed explanation for each of the fundamental data types, paying particular attention to how C treats characters as small integers. In expressions with operands of different types, certain implicit conversions occur. We explain the rules for conversion, including the cast operator, which forces explicit conversion.

6.1   DECLARATIONS AND EXPRESSIONS

Variables and constants are the objects that a program manipulates. In C, all variables must be declared before they can be used. Declarations serve two purposes. First, they tell the compiler to set aside an appropriate amount of space in memory to hold values associated with variables, and second, they enable the compiler to instruct the machine to perform specified operations correctly. In the expression a + b, the operator + is being applied to two variables. The addition that the machine does as a result of applying the + operator to variables of type int is different from the addition that results from applying the + operator to variables of type float. Of course, the programmer need not be concerned that the two + operations are mechanically different, but the C compiler has to recognize the difference and give the appropriate machine instructions.

Expressions are meaningful combinations of constants, variables, and function calls. Most expressions, like variables, have both *value* and *type*. In many situations, what happens depends critically on the type of the expression, which in turn depends on the types of the constants, variables, and function calls making up the expression. In the sections that follow we will discuss a number of issues that relate to the concept of type.

6.2   THE FUNDAMENTAL DATA TYPES

C provides several fundamental types, many of which we have already seen. For all of them, we need to discuss limitations on what can be stored.

Fundamental data types: long form

char	signed char	unsigned char
signed short int	signed int	signed long int
unsigned short int	unsigned int	unsigned long int
float	double	long double

These are all keywords; they may not be used as names of variables. Other data types, such as arrays and pointers, are derived from the fundamental types. They are presented in later chapters.

Usually, the keyword signed is not used. For example, signed int is equivalent to int, and since shorter names are easier to type, int is typically used. The type char, however, is special in this regard (see the next section). Also, the keywords short int, long int, and unsigned int may be, and usually are, shortened to just short, long, and unsigned, respectively. The keyword signed by itself is equivalent to int, but it is seldom used in this context. With all these conventions we obtain a new list.

Fundamental data types

char	signed char	unsigned char
short	int	long
unsigned short	unsigned	unsigned long
float	double	long double

The fundamental types can be grouped according to functionality. The integral types are those that can be used to hold integer values; the floating types are those that can be used to hold real values. They are all arithmetic types.

Fundamental types grouped by functionality

Integral types:	char	signed char	unsigned char
	short	int	long
	unsigned short	unsigned	unsigned long
Floating types:	float	double	long double

Arithmetic types:	*Integral types* + *Floating types*

These collective names are a convenience. In Chapter 9, for example, when we discuss arrays, we will explain that only integral expressions are allowed as subscripts, meaning only expressions involving integral types are allowed.

6.3   CHARACTERS AND THE DATA TYPE char

In C, variables of any integral type can be used to represent characters. In particular, both char and int variables are used for this purpose. As we saw in Chapter 5, when a variable is used to read in characters, and a test must be made for EOF, then the variable should be of type int, not char. Constants such as 'a' and '+' that we think of as characters are of type int, not of type char. There are no constants of type char.

Recall that characters are treated as small integers, and conversely, small integers are treated as characters. In particular, any integral expression can be printed either in the format of a character or in the format of an integer.

```
char   c = 'a';        /* 'a' has ASCII encoding 97 */
int    i = 65;         /* 65 is the ASCII encoding for 'A' */

printf("%c", c + 1);   /*  b is printed */
printf("%d", c + 2);   /* 99 is printed */
printf("%c", i + 3);   /*  D is printed */
```

In C, each char is stored in 1 byte of memory. On almost all machines a byte is composed of 8 bits. Let us see how a char is stored in memory at the bit level. Consider the declaration

```
char   c = 'a';
```

We can think of c stored in 1 byte of memory as

0	1	1	0	0	0	0	1
7	6	5	4	3	2	1	0

Here, each box represents a bit, and the bits are numbered beginning with the least significant bit. The bits making up a byte are either on or off, and these states are represented by 1 and 0, respectively. This leads us to think of each byte in memory as a string of 8 binary digits. Strings of binary digits are also called *bit strings*. We can think of the variable c stored in memory as the bit string

```
01100001
```

More generally, each machine word can be thought of as a string of binary digits grouped into bytes.

A string of binary digits can be interpreted as a binary number. Before we describe how this is done, we want to recall how strings of decimal digits are interpreted as decimal numbers. Consider, for example, the decimal number 10753. Its value is given by

$$1\times 10^4 + 0\times 10^3 + 7\times 10^2 + 5\times 10^1 + 3\times 10^0$$

More generally, a decimal positional number is written in the form

$$d_n d_{n-1} \ldots d_2 d_1 d_0$$

where each d_i is a decimal digit. It has the value

$$d_n\times 10^n + d_{n-1}\times 10^{n-1} + \cdots + d_2\times 10^2 + d_1\times 10^1 + d_0\times 10^0$$

A binary, or base 2, positional number is written in the form

$$b_n b_{n-1} \ldots b_2 b_1 b_0$$

where each b_i is a binary digit, either 0 or 1. It has the value

$$b_n\times 2^n + b_{n-1}\times 2^{n-1} + \cdots + b_2\times 2^2 + b_1\times 2^1 + b_0\times 2^0$$

Now let us consider the value for c again. It was stored in a byte as 01100001. This binary number has the value

$$1\times2^6 + 1\times2^5 + 0\times2^4 + 0\times2^3 + 0\times2^2 + 0\times2^1 + 1\times2^0$$

which is 64 + 32 + 1, or 97 in decimal notation.

ANSI C provides the three types char, signed char, and unsigned char. Typically, the type char is equivalent to either signed char or unsigned char, depending on the compiler. Each of the three char types is stored in 1 byte, which can hold 256 distinct values. For a signed char, the values go from −128 to 127. For an unsigned char, the values go from 0 to 255.

6.4   THE DATA TYPE int

The data type int is the principal working type of the C language. This type, along with the other integral types, such as char, short, and long, is designed for working with the integer values that are representable on a machine.

In mathematics the natural numbers are 0, 1, 2, 3, . . . , and these numbers, along with their negatives, comprise the integers. On a machine only a finite portion of these integers is representable for a given integral type.

Typically, an int is stored in a machine word. Some computers use a machine word of 2 bytes (= 16 bits); others use a machine word of 4 bytes (= 32 bits). There are other possibilities, but many machines fall within these two classes. Examples of machines with 2-byte words are personal computers. Examples of machines with 4-byte words are high-end personal computers and workstations made by Apollo, Hewlett-Packard, Next, Silicon Graphics, Sun, and others. Also, many different kinds of mainframes have 4-byte machine words. Since the word size varies from one machine to another, the number of distinct values that an int can hold is machine-dependent. Suppose that we are working on a computer that has 4-byte words. This implies that an int, since it is stored in a word with 32 bits, can take on 2^{32} distinct states. Half of these states are used to represent negative integers, and half are used to represent nonnegative integers:

$$-2^{31}, -2^{31} + 1, \ldots, -3, -2, -1, 0, 1, 2, 3, \ldots, 2^{31}-1$$

If, on the other hand, we are using a computer that has 2-byte words, then an int can only take on 2^{16} distinct states. Again, half of these states are used to represent negative integers, and half are used to represent nonnegative integers:

$$-2^{15}, -2^{15} + 1, \ldots, -3, -2, -1, 0, 1, 2, 3, \ldots, 2^{15}-1$$

Let N_{min_int} represent the smallest integer that can be stored in an int, and let N_{max_int} represent the largest integer that can be stored in an int. If i is a variable of type int, then the range of values that i can take on is given by

$$N_{min\_int} \leq i \leq N_{max\_int}$$

with the end points of the range being machine-dependent. The typical situation is as follows:

On machines with 4-byte words:

$$N_{min\_int} = -2^{31} \quad = -2147483648 \approx -2 \text{ billion}$$
$$N_{max\_int} = +2^{31} - 1 = +2147483647 \approx +2 \text{ billion}$$

On machines with 2-byte words:

$$N_{min\_int} = -2^{15} \quad = -32768 \approx -32 \text{ thousand}$$
$$N_{max\_int} = +2^{15} - 1 = +32767 \approx +32 \text{ thousand}$$

On any machine the following code is syntactically correct:

```
#define   BIG   2000000000     /* 2 billion */

main()
{
    int   a, b = BIG, c = BIG;

    a = b + c;      /* out of range? */
    . . . . .
```

However, at run time the variable a may be assigned an incorrect value. The logical value of the expression b + c is 4 billion, which probably is greater than N_{max_int}. If it is, then the addition causes what is called an *integer overflow*. Typically, when an integer overflow occurs, the program continues to run, but with logically incorrect results. For this reason the programmer must strive at all times to keep the values of integer expressions within the proper range.

In addition to decimal integer constants, there are hexadecimal integer constants, such as 0x1a, and octal integer constants, such as 0377. Many C programmers have no particular need for hexadecimal and octal numbers, but all programmers have to know that integers that begin with a leading zero are not decimal integers. For example, 11 and 011 do not have the same value.

6.5   THE INTEGRAL TYPES short, long, AND unsigned

In C, the data type int is considered the "natural" or "usual" type for working with integers. The other integral types, such as char, short, and long, are intended for more specialized use. The data type short, for example, might be used in situations where storage is a concern. The compiler may provide less storage for a short than for an int, although it is not required to do so. In a similar fashion, the type long might be used in situations where large integer values are needed. The compiler may provide more storage for a long than for an int, although it is not required to do so. Typically, a short is stored in 2 bytes, and a long is stored in 4 bytes. Thus on machines with 4-byte words, the size of an int is the same as the size of a long, and on machines with 2-byte words, the size of an int is the same as the size of a short. If s is a variable of type short, then the range of values that s can take on is given by

$$N_{min\_short} \leq s \leq N_{max\_short}$$

where typically

$$N_{min\_short} = -2^{15} = -32768 \approx -32 \text{ thousand}$$
$$N_{max\_short} = +2^{15} - 1 = +32767 \approx +32 \text{ thousand}$$

If l is a variable of type long, then the range of values that l can take on is given by

$$N_{min\_long} \leq 1 \leq N_{max\_long}$$

where typically

$$N_{min\_long} = -2^{31} = -2147483648 \approx -2 \text{ billion}$$
$$N_{max\_long} = +2^{31} - 1 = +2147483647 \approx +2 \text{ billion}$$

A variable of type unsigned is stored in the same number of bytes as an int. However, as the name implies, the integer values stored have no sign. Typically, variables of type int and unsigned are stored in a machine word. If u is a variable of type unsigned, then the range of values that u can take on is given by

$$0 \leq u \leq 2^{wordsize} - 1$$

The typical situation is as follows:

On machines with 4-byte words:

$$N_{max\_unsigned} = +2^{32} - 1 = +4294967295 \approx +4 \text{ billion}$$

On machines with 2-byte words:

$$N_{max\_unsigned} = +2^{16} - 1 = +65535 \approx +64 \text{ thousand}$$

Arithmetic on unsigned variables is performed modulo $2^{wordsize}$ (see exercise 18).

Suffixes can be appended to an integer constant to specify its type. The type of an unsuffixed integer constant is either int, long, or unsigned long. The system chooses the first of these types that can represent the value. For example, on machines with 2-byte words, the constant 32000 is of type int, but 33000 is of type long.

Suffix	Type	Example
u or U	unsigned	37U
l or L	long	37L
ul or UL	unsigned long	37UL

6.6   THE FLOATING TYPES

ANSI C provides the three floating types: float, double, and long double. Variables of this type can hold real values, such as 0.001, 2.0, and 3.14159. A suffix can be appended to a floating constant to specify its type. Any unsuffixed floating constant is of type double. Unlike other languages, the working floating type in C is double, not float.

Suffix	Type	Example
f or F	float	3.7F
l or L	long double	3.7L

Integers are representable as floating constants, but they must be written with a decimal point. For example, the constants 1.0 and 2.0 are both of type double, whereas the constant 3 is an int.

In addition to the ordinary decimal notation for floating constants, there is an exponential notation, as in the example 1.234567e5. This corresponds to the scientific notation 1.234567×10^5. Recall that

$$1.234567 \times 10^5 = 1.234567 \times 10 \times 10 \times 10 \times 10 \times 10$$
$$= 1.234567 \times 100000$$
$$= 123456.7 \ (\textit{decimal point shifted 5 places})$$

In a similar fashion, the number 1.234567e-3 calls for shifting the decimal point 3 places to the left to obtain the equivalent constant 0.001234567.

Now we want to carefully describe the exponential notation. After we give the precise rules, we will show some examples. A floating constant such as 333.77777e-22 may not contain any embedded blanks or special characters. Each part of the constant is given a name:

> 333   is the integer part
> 77777   is the fractional part
> e-22   is the exponential part

A floating constant may contain an integer part, a decimal point, a fractional part, and an exponential part. A floating constant *must* contain either a decimal point or an exponential part or both. If a decimal point is present, either an integer part or fractional part or both *must* be present. If no decimal point is present, then there must be an integer part along with an exponential part. Some examples of floating constants are

```
3.14159
314.159e-2F      /* of type float */
0e0              /* equivalent to 0.0 */
1.               /* equivalent to 1.0, but harder to read */
```

but not

```
3.14,159         /* comma not allowed */
314159           /* decimal point or exponential part needed */
.e0              /* integer part or fractional part needed */
-3.14159         /* this is a floating constant expression */
```

Typically, a C compiler will provide more storage for a variable of type double than for one of type float, although it is not required to do so. On most machines a float is stored in 4 bytes, and a double is stored in 8 bytes. The effect of this is that a float stores about 6 decimal places of accuracy, and a double stores about 15 decimal places of accuracy. An ANSI C compiler may provide more storage for a variable of type long double than for one of type double, although it is not required to do so. Many compilers, but not all of them, implement a long double as a double (see exercise 7).

The possible values that a floating type can be assigned are described in terms of attributes called *precision* and *range*. The precision describes the number of significant decimal places that a floating value carries. The range describes the limits of the largest and smallest positive floating values that can be represented in a variable of that type. A float on many machines has an approximate precision of 6 significant figures and an approximate range of 10^{-38} to 10^{+38}. This means that a positive float value is represented in the machine in the form (only approximately true)

$$0.d_1 d_2 d_3 d_4 d_5 d_6 \times 10^n$$

where each d_i is a decimal digit, the first digit, d_1, is positive, and $-38 \le n \le +38$. The representation of a float value in a machine is actually in base 2, not base 10, but the ideas as we presented them give the correct flavor.

A double on many machines has an approximate precision of 15 significant figures and an approximate range of 10^{-308} to 10^{+308}. This means that a positive double value is represented in the machine in the form (only approximately true)

$$0.d_1 d_2 \ldots d_{15} \times 10^n$$

where each d_i is a decimal digit, the first digit, d_1, is positive, and $-308 \le n \le +308$. Suppose that x is a variable of type double. Then the statement

```
x = 123.45123451234512345;   /* 20 significant digits */
```

will result in x being assigned a value that is stored in the form (only approximately true)

$$0.123451234512345 \times 10^{+3} \quad (15 \ significant \ digits)$$

The main points that one must be aware of are (1) that not all real numbers are representable, and (2) that floating arithmetic operations, unlike the integer arithmetic operations, need not be exact. For small computations this is usually of no concern. For very large computations, such as numerically solving a large system of ordinary differential equations, a good understanding of rounding effects, scaling, and so on may be necessary. This is the domain of numerical analysis.

6.7   THE sizeof OPERATOR

C provides the unary operator sizeof to find the number of bytes needed to store an object. It has the same precedence and associativity as all the other unary operators. An expression of the form

sizeof(*object*)

returns an integer that represents the number of bytes needed to store the object in memory. An object can be a type such as int or float, or it can be an expression such as a + b, or it can be an array or structure type. The following program uses this operator. On a given machine, it provides precise information about the storage requirements for the fundamental types.

```
/* Compute the size of some fundamental types. */

#include code <stdio.h>

main()
{
    printf("The size of some fundamental types is computed.\n\n");
    printf("        char:%3d byte \n", sizeof(char));
    printf("       short:%3d bytes\n", sizeof(short));
    printf("         int:%3d bytes\n", sizeof(int));
    printf("        long:%3d bytes\n", sizeof(long));
    printf("    unsigned:%3d bytes\n", sizeof(unsigned));
    printf("       float:%3d bytes\n", sizeof(float));
    printf("      double:%3d bytes\n", sizeof(double));
    printf("long double:%3d bytes\n", sizeof(long double));
}
```

Since the C language is flexible in its storage requirements for the fundamental types, the situation can vary from one machine to another. However, it is guaranteed that

```
sizeof(char) = 1
sizeof(short) ≤ sizeof(int) ≤ sizeof(long)
sizeof(signed) = sizeof(unsigned) = sizeof(int)
sizeof(float) ≤ sizeof(double) ≤ sizeof(long double)
```

Moreover, all the signed and unsigned versions of each of the integral types are guaranteed to have the same size.

Notice that we wrote sizeof(...) as if it were a function. However, this is not so—it is an operator. If sizeof is being applied to a type, then parentheses are required; otherwise they are optional. For example,

sizeof(a + b + 7.7)   and   sizeof a + b + 7.7

are equivalent expressions. The type of the value returned by the operator is typically unsigned. This is system-dependent.

6.8   MATHEMATICAL FUNCTIONS

There are no built-in mathematical functions in C. Functions such as

sqrt()   pow()   exp()   log()   sin()   cos()   tan()

are available in the mathematics library, which is conceptually part of the standard library. In traditional C systems, the mathematics library is often considered to be separate. On such systems the -lm option or some other option may be needed to compile a program that uses mathematical functions; see Section 6.13, "System Considerations."

All of the functions listed above, except the power function, pow(), take a single argument of type double and return a value of type double. The power function takes two arguments of type double and returns a value of type double. Our next program illustrates the use of sqrt() and pow(). The program asks the user to input a value for x, and then prints it out, along with the square root of x and the value of x raised to the x power.

```
#include <stdio.h>
#include <math.h>

main()
{
   double   x;

   printf("\n%s\n%s\n%s\n\n",
      "The square root of x and x raised",
      "to the x power will be computed.",
      "---");
   while (1) {                    /* do it forever */
      printf("Input x:  ");
      scanf("%lf", &x);
      if (x >= 0.0)
         printf("\n%15s%22.15e\n%15s%22.15e\n%15s%22.15e\n\n",
            "x = ", x,
            "sqrt(x) = ", sqrt(x),
            "pow(x, x) = ", pow(x, x));
      else
         printf("\nSorry, your number must be nonnegative.\n\n");
   }
}
```

If we execute the program and enter 2 when prompted, here is what appears on the screen:

```
The square root of x and x raised
to the x power will be computed.
---

Input x:  2

          x = 2.000000000000000e+000
    sqrt(x) = 1.414213562373095e+000
  pow(x, x) = 4.000000000000000e+000

Input x:
```

DISSECTION OF THE *sqrt_pow* PROGRAM

■ #include <stdio.h>
  #include <math.h>

These header files contain function prototypes. In particular, *math.h* contains the prototypes for the functions in the mathematics library. As an alternative to including *math.h*, we can supply our own function prototypes:

```
double   sqrt(double), pow(double, double);
```

This declaration can be placed in the file above main() or in the body of main() itself.

■ while (1) {   /* do it forever */
       . . . . .

Since any nonzero value is considered to be *true*, the expression 1 creates an infinite while loop. The user is expected to input values repeatedly and to interrupt the program when finished.

■ scanf("%lf", &x);

The format %lf is used in the control string because x is a double. A common error is to use %f instead of %lf. Notice that we typed 2 when we illustrated the use of this program. Equivalently, we could have typed 2.0, 2e0, or 0.2e1. The function call scanf("%lf", &x) would have converted each of these to the same double. In C source code 2 and 2.0 are different. The first is of type int, and the second is of type double. The input stream that is read by scanf() is *not* source code, so the rules for source code do not apply. When scanf() reads in a double, the number 2 is just as good as the number 2.0. For details about scanf(), see Chapter 14.

■ if (x >= 0.0)
       . . . . .

Since the square root function is defined only for nonnegative numbers, a test is made to ensure that the value of x is nonnegative. A call such as sqrt(-1.0) causes a run-time error (see exercise 20).

```
■  printf("\n%15s%22.15e\n%15s%22.15e\n%15s%22.15e\n\n",
        "x = ", x,
        "sqrt(x) = ", sqrt(x),
        "pow(x, x) = ", pow(x, x));
```

Notice that we are printing double values in the format %22.15e. This results in 1 place to the left of the decimal point and 15 places to the right, 16 significant places in all. On our machine, only *n* places are valid, where *n* is between 15 and 16. (The reason *n* is not an integer is due to the conversion from binary to decimal.) You can ask for lots of decimal places to be printed, but you should not believe all that you read.

6.9   CONVERSIONS AND CASTS

An arithmetic expression such as x + y has both a value and a type. For example, if both x and y have type int, then the expression x + y also has type int. But if both x and y have type short, then x + y is of type int, not short. This is because in any expression, a short always gets promoted, or converted, to an int. In this section we want to give the precise rules for conversions.

THE INTEGRAL PROMOTIONS

A char or short, either signed or unsigned, or an enumeration type (see Chapter 7) can be used in any expression where an int or unsigned int may be used. If all the values of the original type can be represented by an int, then the value is converted to an int; otherwise it is converted to an unsigned int. This is called an *integral promotion*. Here is an example:

```
char c = 'A';

printf("%c\n", c);
```

The char variable c occurs by itself as an argument to printf(). However, because an integral promotion takes place, the type of the expression c is int, not char.

THE USUAL ARITHMETIC CONVERSIONS

Arithmetic conversions can occur when the operands of a binary operator are evaluated. Suppose, for example, that i is an int and f is a float. In the expression i + f, the operand i gets promoted to a float and the expression i + f as a whole has type float. The rules governing this are called the *usual arithmetic conversions*:

> If either operand is of type long double, then the other operand is converted to long double.
>
> Otherwise, if either operand is of type double, the other operand is converted to double.
>
> Otherwise, if either operand is of type float, the other operand is converted to float.
>
> Otherwise, the integral promotions are performed on both operands, and the following rules are applied:
>
>> If either operand is of type unsigned long, the other operand is converted to unsigned long.
>>
>> Otherwise, if one operand has type long and the other has type unsigned, then one of two possibilities occurs:
>>
>>> If a long can represent all the values of an unsigned, then the operand of type unsigned is converted to long.
>>>
>>> If a long cannot represent all the values of an unsigned, then both of the operands are converted to unsigned long.
>>
>> Otherwise, if either operand has type long, the other operand is converted to long.
>>
>> Otherwise, if either operand has type unsigned, the other operand is converted to unsigned.
>>
>> Otherwise, both operands have type int.

This process goes under various names:

> automatic conversion
>
> implicit conversion
>
> coercion
>
> promotion
>
> widening

To illustrate the idea of automatic conversion, we first make the following declarations:

```
char c;      short s;     int i;                unsigned u;       unsigned long ul;
float f;     double d;    long double ld;
```

Now we can list a variety of mixed expressions along with their corresponding types.

Expression	Type		Expression	Type
c - s / i	int		u * 7 - i	unsigned
u * 2.0 - i	double		f * 7 - i	float
c + 3	int		7 * s * ul	unsigned long
c + 5.0	double		ld + c	long double
d + s	double		u - ul	unsigned long
2 * i / l	long		u - l	*system-dependent*

In addition to automatic conversions in mixed expressions, an automatic conversion also can occur across an assignment. For example

```
d = i
```

causes the value of i, which is an int, to be converted to a double and then assigned to d, and double is the type of the expression as a whole. A promotion or widening such as d = i will usually be well behaved, but a narrowing or demotion such as i = d can lose information. Here, the fractional part of d will be discarded. Precisely what happens in each case is system-dependent.

CASTS

In addition to implicit conversions, which can occur across assignments and in mixed expressions, there are explicit conversions called *casts*. If i is an int, then

```
(double) i
```

will cast the value of i so that the expression has type double. The variable i itself remains unchanged. Casts can be applied to expressions. Some examples are

```
(long) ('A' + 1.0)
x = (float) ((int) y + 1)
(double) (x = 77)
```

but not

```
(double) x = 77   /* equivalent to ((double) x) = 77, error */
```

The cast operator (*type*) is a unary operator having the same precedence and right-to-left associativity as other unary operators. Thus the expression

```
(float) i +3        is equivalent to        ((float) i) + 3
```

because the cast operator (*type*) has higher precedence than +.

6.10   PROBLEM SOLVING: COMPUTING INTEREST

Everyone is familiar with putting money into a savings account to earn interest. In the business world many transactions and agreements involve the borrowing and lending of money with interest. To illustrate some of the ideas presented in this chapter, we will show how interest that is compounded yearly is computed. In the exercises at the end of the chapter we indicate how to compute interest compounded quarterly and daily.

Suppose that we put P dollars into a savings account that pays 7% interest compounded yearly. At the end of the first year we have P, our original principal, plus 7% of P, the earned interest. Since 7% of P is $0.07 \times P$, we have in our savings account

$$P + 0.07 \times P \qquad \text{or equivalently} \qquad 1.07 \times P$$

At the end of every year, to find the amount in our savings account, we take the amount that we started with at the beginning of the year and multiply it by 1.07. Thus we have

at the end of the first year	$1.07 \times P$		
at the end of the second year	$1.07 \times (1.07 \times P)$	or	$1.07^2 \times P$
at the end of the third year	$1.07 \times (1.07^2 \times P)$	or	$1.07^3 \times P$
. . . . .			
at the end of the nth year	$1.07 \times (1.07^{n-1} \times P)$	or	$1.07^n \times P$

We want to use these ideas to write an interactive program to compute interest that is compounded yearly. Values corresponding to principal, interest rate, and number of years will be supplied by the user. Our top-down design of this program is to print instructions, read in values, compute the interest, and print out the results. Following this structured design, we write the program to consist of `main()` and the three functions `prn_instructions()`, `compute()`, and `prn_results()`. Let us suppose that these functions

are all in the file *interest.c.* At the top of the file we put our #include line, the function
prototypes, and main().

```
/* Compute interest compounded yearly. */

#include <stdio.h>

double   compute(double p, double r, int n);
void     prn_instructions(void);
void     prn_results(double a, double p, double r, int n);

main()
{
    double   amount;           /* principal + interest */
    double   principal;        /* beginning amount in dollars */
    double   rate;             /* example: 7% corresponds to 0.07 */
    int      nyears;           /* number of years */

    prn_instructions();
    for ( ; ; ) {
        printf("Input three items: ");
        scanf("%lf%lf%d", &principal, &rate, &nyears);
        amount = compute(principal, rate, nyears);
        prn_results(amount, principal, rate, nyears);
    }
}
```

Notice that we wrote the function prototypes near the top of the file outside of main().
Although we could have written them inside of main(), they typically get written outside, or in a *.h* file that then gets included. The remaining function definitions follow
main() in this same file.

```
void prn_instructions(void)
{
    printf("%s",
        "This program computes interest compounded yearly.\n"
        "You must input principal, interest, and no. of years.\n"
        "For $1000 at 5.5% for 17 years here is an example:\n\n"
        "Example input:  1000  5.5  17\n\n");
}
```

Before we show the code for the rest of the program, it is helpful to see what the program does. Suppose that we execute the program and input 1000.00, 7.7, and 20 when prompted. Here is what appears on the screen:

```
This program computes interest compounded yearly.
You must input principal, interest, and no. of years.
For $1000 at 5.5% for 17 years here is an example:

Example input:   1000  5.5  17

Input three items:  1000.00  7  20

Interest rate:  7%
   Time period:  20 years

Beginning principal:  1000.00
   Interest accrued:  2869.68
      Total amount:  3869.68
```

In main(), the value returned by the function call compute() is assigned to the variable amount. This value represents the principal and interest at the end of the period. The computation of this value is at the heart of the program.

```
double compute(double principal, double rate, int nyears)
{
    int      i;
    double   amount = principal;

    rate *= 0.01;                       /* example: convert 7% to 0.07 */
    for (i = 0; i < nyears; ++i)
       amount *= 1.0 + rate;
    return amount;
}
```

DISSECTION OF THE *compute()* FUNCTION

■ `double compute(double principal, double rate, int nyears)`
```
{
    int      i;
    double   amount = principal;
```

The first `double` tells the compiler that this function returns a value of that type. The parameter list contains three identifiers: two `double`'s and an `int`. In the body of the function we initialize `amount` to `principal`, the amount of money with which we begin the computation.

■ `rate *= 0.01;      /* example: convert 7% to 0.07 */`

Of the three values entered by the user, the middle one, 7, indicates that 7% is to be used in the calculation. This value gets stored as a `double` in the variable `rate` in `main()`, and then `rate` gets passed as an argument to `compute()`. This statement converts the value of `rate` to 0.07, which is what is needed in our algorithm. Note that `rate` in `main()` is not changed by this statement. It is only a copy of `rate` that gets used in `compute()`.

■ `for (i = 0; i < nyears; ++i)`
`    amount *= 1.0 + rate;`

If `rate` has value 0.07, then `1.0 + rate` has value 1.07, and every time through the loop, `amount` gets multiplied by 1.07. Since `amount` was initialized to `principal`, the first time through the loop, `amount` has the value 1.07 times the value of `principal`; the second time through the loop, its value is 1.07^2 times the value of `principal`; and so forth. At the end of the loop its value is 1.07^{nyears} times the value of `principal`.

■ `return amount;`

The value of the variable `amount` is returned to the calling environment.

Finally, back in main(), we want to print the results of our computation on the screen. We pass the relevant variables as arguments to the function prn_results() and call it:

```
void prn_results(double a, double p, double r, int n)
{
    double   interest = a - p;      /* amount - principal */

    printf("\n%s%g%c\n%s%d%s\n\n",
        "Interest rate:  ", r, '%',
        " Time period:  ", n, " years");
    printf("%s%9.2f\n%s%9.2f\n%s%9.2f\n\n",
        "Beginning principal:", p,
        "   Interest accrued:", interest,
        "       Total amount:", a);
}
```

Notice that we used the format %g to suppress the printing of extraneous zeros. Also observe that we used the format %9.2f to align numbers on the screen.

Next, we want to show how to simplify our program by making use of pow() in the mathematical library. This function takes as arguments two expressions of type double and returns a value of type double. A function call such as pow(x, y) computes the value of x raised to the y power. Here is how we modify our program. Since pow() will take the place of compute(), we discard the code making up the function definition for compute(), as well as its function prototype near the top of the file. To get the function prototype for pow(), we can add the line

```
#include <math.h>
```

Alternatively, we can supply the function prototype ourselves.

```
double   pow(double, double);
```

Finally, we replace the statement

```
amount = compute(principal, rate, nyears);
```

with the statements

```
rate *= 0.01;
amount = pow(1.0 + rate, (double) nyears) * principal;
```

THE FUNDAMENTAL DATA TYPES

Notice that nyears has been cast to a double. With the use of function prototyping, this cast is not necessary; any int value passed to pow() will automatically be converted to a double. If, however, we are using a traditional C compiler in which function prototyping is not available, then the cast is essential.

6.11 STYLE

A common programming style is to use the identifiers i, j, k, m, and n as variables of type int, and to use identifiers such as x, y, and z as floating variables. This naming convention is loosely applied in mathematics, and historically, some early programming languages assumed that a variable name beginning with i through n was an integer type by default. This style is still acceptable in simple situations, such as using i as a counter in a for or while loop. In more complicated situations, however, one should use variable names that are descriptive of their use or purpose.

Some programmers dislike the deliberate use of infinite loops. However, if a program is only meant to be used interactively, then the practice is acceptable. In our program that computes accrued interest in Section 6.10, we used the following construct:

```
for ( ; ; ) {
   printf("Input three items: ");
   scanf("%lf%lf%d", &principal, &rate, &nyears);
   . . . . .
```

The intent here is for the user to input data interactively. The user does this repeatedly until he or she is finished, at which time an interrupt signal must be typed (a control-c on our system). Advantages of this coding style are that (1) it is simple, and (2) the reader of the code sees immediately that something is being done repeatedly until an interrupt occurs. A disadvantage of this style is that on some systems, redirecting the input to the program will not work (see exercise 10). It is easy to adopt another, more conservative style. Here we can write instead

```
printf("Input three items: ");
while (scanf("%lf%lf%d", &principal, &rate, &nyears) == 3) {
   . . . . .
   printf("Input three items: ");
}
```

Now the interactive user can either interrupt the program as before, or end the program by typing an end-of-file signal at the keyboard (a control-d on our system). In addition, the program will now work with redirection.

Another stylistic issue concerns the use of floating constants in floating expressions. Suppose that x is a floating variable. Because of automatic conversion, the value of an expression such as

    x >= 0.0   is equivalent to   x >= 0

Nonetheless, the use of the first expression is considered good programming practice. The use of the floating constant 0.0 helps to remind the reader that x is a floating type. Similarly, the expression

    1.0 / 3.0   is preferable to   1 / 3.0

Again, due to automatic conversion, the values of both expressions are the same. However, since in the first expression both the numerator and denominator are of type double, the reader is more likely to recognize immediately that the expression as a whole is of type double.

6.12 COMMON PROGRAMMING ERRORS

On machines with 2-byte words, the problem of integer overflow can occur easily. It is the responsibility of the programmer to keep values within proper bounds. The type long should be used for integer values larger than 32 thousand.

In a printf() or scanf() statement, a format such as %d, which is appropriate for an int, may cause unexpected results when used with a long. If it does, the format %ld should be used. In this context the modifier l preceding the conversion character d stands for "long." Similarly, when using a short, the format %hd should be used. In this context the modifier h preceding the conversion character stands for "short." (The second letter in the word is used, not the first letter.)

Let us show a specific example that illustrates what can go wrong. We will assume that we are on a machine with 2-byte words.

```
int   a = 1, b = 1776, c = 32000;

printf("%d\n", a + b + c);     /* error: -31759 is printed */
```

The expression a + b + c is of type int, and on machines with 2-byte words the logical value 33777 is too large to be stored in an int. One way to fix this code is to write

```
int    a = 1, b = 1776, c = 32000;

printf("%ld\n", (long) a + b + c);      /* 33777 is printed */
```

Because of operator precedence, the two expressions

```
(long) a + b + c          and          (((long) a) + b) + c
```

are equivalent. First a is cast to type long. This causes the other summands to be promoted to type long, and causes the expression

```
(long) a + b + c
```

as a whole to be of type long. Finally, the %ld format is used to print the value of the expression. Note carefully that using the %d format would have caused a wrong value to be printed. In a similar fashion, when using scanf() to read values into a long, the format %ld should be used.

With printf() the programmer can use the format %f to output either a float or a double. However, with scanf() the format %f must be used to input a float, and the format %lf must be used to input a double. This dichotomy is confusing to beginning programmers. If the wrong format is used, unexpected results occur. Typically, a C system provides no indication of the error (see exercise 2).

Using integer constants in what is meant to be a floating expression can produce unintended results. Although the two expressions 1 / 2 and 1.0 / 2.0 look similar, the first is an int having value zero, whereas the second is a double having value 0.5. To minimize the chance of using the first expression in situations where the second is correct, the programmer should get into the habit of coding floating constants in floating expressions. If, for example, the variable x is a float, and it is desired to assign zero as its value, it is better to code x = 0.0 rather than x = 0.

Another common programming error is to pass an argument of the wrong type to a function. Consider, for example, the function call sqrt(4). If the programmer has provided a prototype for the sqrt() function, then the compiler will automatically convert the int value 4 to a double, and the function call will cause no difficulty. If the programmer has not provided a function prototype, then the program will run, but with logically incorrect results. Traditional C systems do not have the function prototype mechanism. On these systems, the programmer should write

```
sqrt(4.0)        or        sqrt((double) 4)
```

A good programming style is to provide prototypes for all functions. This helps the compiler to guard against the error of invoking a function with inappropriate arguments.

On machines with 2-byte words, a cast is sometimes needed to make a constant expression behave properly. Here is an example:

```
unsigned long   product = (unsigned long) 2 * 3 * 5 * 7 * 11 * 13 * 17;
```

Without the cast this initialization has unexpected behavior.

6.13   SYSTEM CONSIDERATIONS

Throughout this chapter we have explained what normally happens on machines with 2- and 4-byte words. However, the notion of a machine having either 2- or 4-byte words is somewhat difficult to pin down. Intel produces an 80386 chip that is commonly used as the CPU in personal computers. These computers are often called "386 machines." In any case, the chip has a 4-byte word, but if the operating system on the machine is MS-DOS, then it may act as if it has a 2-byte word. If this happens, then the operating system is not utilizing the full power of the CPU. The same machine with the UNIX operating system on it will act as a 4-byte machine.

The computing world has been slowly coming to agreement (more or less) on how floating values should be represented in machines. In this regard, the ANSI C committee suggests that the recommendations in the document *IEEE Standard for Binary Floating Point Arithmetic* (ANSI/IEEE Std 754-1985) be followed. On most machines that do so, a double will have an approximate precision of 15 significant figures and an approximate range of 10^{-308} to 10^{+308}. Another effect of this standard is that division by zero, or trying to deal with numbers outside the range of a double, will not necessarily result in a run-time error. Instead, a value called *not a number* is produced (see exercise 25).

If you check the size of the fundamental types on a Cray supercomputer, you will find that the size of a char is 1 and that the size of everything else is 8, except for a long double, which is 16. This means that a Cray can handle some very large integer values.

Some C systems still treat the mathematics library as separate from the standard library. On these systems, the loader may not be able to find the object code corresponding to a mathematical function such as sqrt() unless you tell it where to look. On many older UNIX systems, the option *-lm* is needed. Here is an example:

cc pgm.c −lm

Note the unusual placement of the option. This is because it is for the loader, not the compiler. Recall that the *cc* command invokes the preprocessor, then the compiler, and finally the loader.

On all C systems the types short, int, and long are equivalent to signed short, signed int, and signed long, respectively. With respect to the type char, however, the situation is system-dependent. A char can be equivalent to either a signed or unsigned char.

The type long double is a new addition to the C language. Some C systems treat it as a double; other systems provide extended precision. In Turbo C, a long double is stored in 10 bytes. On a Sun workstation, a long double is stored in 16 bytes, providing approximately 33 significant digits of precision.

The absolute value function abs() is provided in the standard library. However, it takes an int argument and returns an int value. This means it is *not* the function that corresponds to the usual mathematical operation of taking the absolute value of a real number. The correct function for this use is fabs(), the floating point absolute value function. It is in the standard library, and its function prototype is in *math.h.*

C is a general-purpose language, but at the same time it is aptly suited for writing operating system code. System programmers frequently have to deal with the explicit representation of values stored in a byte or a word. Since hexadecimal and octal integers are useful for these purposes, they were included as part of the C language. However, we will not make explicit use of them in this text.

6.14   SUMMARY

1   The compiler needs to know the type and value of constants, variables, and expressions. This information allows the compiler to set aside the right amount of space in memory to hold values, and it allows the compiler to issue the correct kind of instructions to the machine to carry out specified operations.

2   The fundamental data types are char, short, int, long, unsigned versions of these, and three floating types. The type char is a 1-byte integral type mostly used for representing characters.

3   The type int is designed to be the "natural" or "working" integral type. The other integral types such as short, long, and unsigned are provided for more specialized situations.

4   Three floating types, float, double, and long double, are provided to represent real numbers. Typically a float is stored in 4 bytes and a double in 8 bytes. Unlike integer arithmetic, floating arithmetic is not always exact. The type double, not float, is the "working" type.

5 The type long double is available in ANSI C, but not in traditional C. On some C systems, a long double is implemented as a double; on other systems, a long double will provide more precision than a double.

6 The unary operator sizeof can be used to find the number of bytes needed to store a type or the value of an expression. The expression sizeof(int) has the value 2 on machines with 2-byte words and has the value 4 on machines with 4-byte words.

7 In ANSI C, the mathematic library is conceptually part of the standard library. The mathematical library contains the usual mathematical functions, such as sin(), cos(), and tan(). The header file *math.h* is supplied by the system. It contains the function prototypes for the mathematical functions.

8 Most of the functions in the mathematical library take a single argument of type double and return a value of type double. The function pow() is an exception. It takes two arguments of type double and returns a value of type double.

9 Automatic conversions occur in mixed expressions and across an equal sign. Casts can be used to force explicit conversions.

10 Integer constants beginning with 0x and 0 designate hexadecimal and octal integers, respectively.

11 Suffixes can be used to explicitly specify the type of a constant. For example, 3U is of type unsigned and 7.0F is of type float.

6.15   EXERCISES

1 Not all real numbers are machine-representable; there are too many of them. Thus the numbers that are available on a machine have a "graininess" to them. As an example of this, the code

```
double   x = 123.45123451234512345;
double   y = 123.45123451234512300;   /* last two digits different */

printf("%.17f  %.17f\n", x, y);
```

causes two identical numbers to be printed. How many zeros must the initializer for y end with to get different numbers printed? Explain your answer.

2 If the number 3.777 is truncated to 2 decimal places, it becomes 3.77, but if it is rounded to 2 places, it becomes 3.78. Write a test program to find out whether printf() truncates or rounds when printing a float or double with a fractional part.

3 If you use a library function and do not declare it, the compiler assumes that the function returns an int value by default (these ideas were discussed in Chapter 4). Consider the following code:

```
double   cos(double), x, y;     /* sin() is not declared */

while (1) {
   printf("Input a number:   ");
   scanf("%lf", &x);
   y = sin(x) * sin(x) + cos(x) * cos(x);
   printf("\n%s%.15g\n%s%.15e\n\n",
      "x = ", x,
      "sin(x) * sin(x) + cos(x) * cos(x) = ", y);
}
```

This code, when correctly written, illustrates the mathematical fact that

$$\sin^2(x) + \cos^2(x) = 1 \qquad \text{for all } x \text{ real}$$

Note that the function prototype for sin() is missing. Execute the code, first with the correct declaration, so that you understand its proper effects. Then experiment to see what the effect is when the sin() function is not declared. Does your compiler complain? It should.

4 Using the %f format with scanf() to read in a double is a common programming error. Try the following code on your system. Note that your compiler does not complain. The only thing that happens is that logically incorrect results are printed.

```
double   x;

printf("Input a number:   ");
scanf("%f", &x);                        /* error: wrong format */
printf("\nHere it is:  %f\n", x);
```

5 Write a program that prints a table of trigonometric values for sin(), cos(), and tan(). The angles in your table should go from 0 to π in 20 steps.

6 If your machine stores an int in 2 bytes, run the following program and explain its output. If your machine stores an int in 4 bytes, change the value of the symbolic constant BIG to 2000000000 before running the program.

```
#define   BIG   32000     /* 32 thousand is big? */

main()
{
    int       i = BIG + BIG;
    unsigned  u = BIG + BIG;

    printf("\n%s%d\n%s%d\n%s%u\n%s%u\n\n",
        "i with %d format is ", i,
        "u with %d format is ", u,
        "i with %u format is ", i,
        "u with %u format is ", u);
}
```

7 The following table shows how many bytes are required on most machines to store some of the fundamental types. What are the appropriate values for your machine? Write and execute a program that allows you to complete the table.

Fundamental type	Memory required on machines with 4-byte words	Memory required on machines with 2-byte words	Memory required on your machine
char	1 byte	1 byte	
short	2 bytes	2 bytes	
int	4 bytes	2 bytes	
unsigned	4 bytes	2 bytes	
long	4 bytes	4 bytes	
float	4 bytes	4 bytes	
double	8 bytes	8 bytes	
long double	?	?	

8 Before the age of computers it was common to make tables of square roots, sines, cosines, etc. Write a program that makes a table of square roots and fourth roots of the integers from 1 to 100. Your table should look like this:

Integer	Square root	Fourth root
1	1.000000000e+00	1.000000000e+00
2	1.414213562e+00	1.189207115e+00
3	1.732050808e+00	1.316074013e+00
4	2.000000000e+00	1.414213562e+00
. . . . .		

Hint: The fourth root of a number is just the square root of the square root of the number.

9 The program in this exercise needs to be studied carefully.

```
#include <stdio.h>

main()    /* mystery? */
{
    printf("Why is 21 + 31 equal to %d?\n", 21 + 31);
}
```

Here is the output from the program:

```
Why is 21 + 31 equal to 5?
```

Can you deduce the moral?

10 A program that has an infinite loop in it may not work as expected with redirection. Put some real numbers into a file called *data*, and try the command

> *sq_roots < data*

Now modify the *sq_roots* program so that the `for` loop is replaced by a `while` loop of the form

```
while (scanf("%lf", &x) == 1) {
    . . . . .
}
```

After you get the program to work properly in an interactive mode, try redirection again.

11 Rewrite the *interest* program (Section 6.10), making use of the function pow() in the mathematical library. Does the modified program yield the same results as before? What happens if in the call to pow() the variable nyears is not cast as a double?

12 Suppose that Constance B. DeMogul has a million dollars to invest. She is thinking of investing the money at 9% compounded yearly, or at 8.75% compounded quarterly, or at 8.7% compounded daily, for a period of either 10 or 20 years. For each of these investment strategies and periods what interest will be earned? Write a program that helps you to advise her. *Hint:* Suppose that P dollars is invested at 8.75% compounded quarterly. The amount of principal and interest is given by

$(1 + 0.0875/4)^4 \times P$ at the end of the first year
$(1 + 0.0875/4)^{4\times2} \times P$ at the end of the second year
$(1 + 0.0875/4)^{4\times3} \times P$ at the end of the third year
. . . . .

For P dollars invested at 8.7% compounded daily, the formulas are similar, except that 0.0875 is replaced by 0.087, and 4 is replaced by 365. These computations can be carried out by writing a function such as

```
double find_accrued_interest(
    double    principal,
    double    rate,          /* interest rate */
    double    c_rate,        /* compounding rate: example: with
                                daily compounding, c_rate = 365.0 */
    double    period         /* in years */
)
{
    . . . . .
```

13 Try the following code:

```
unsigned long    a = -1;

printf("The biggest integer: %lu\n", a);
```

What gets printed? Explain why. It should match one or more of the numbers in the standard header file *limits.h* on your system. Does it?

14 Occasionally a programmer needs a power function for integers. Because such a function is so easy to write, it typically is not found in a mathematics library. Write

the function definition for power() so that if m and n are integers and n is non-negative, the call power(m, n) will return m raised to the nth power. *Hint:* Use the following code:

```
product = 1;
for (i = 1; i <= n; ++i)
   product *= m;
```

15 A variable of type char can be used to store small integer values. What happens if a large value is assigned to a char variable? Consider the following code:

```
char   c = 256;        /* too big! */

printf("c = %d\n", c);
```

Some compilers will warn you that the number is too big; others will not. What happens on your machine? Can you guess what gets printed?

16 The effects of a promotion can be quite unexpected. Compile and execute the following program. What gets printed? Explain.

```
#include <stdio.h>

main()
{
   unsigned short   a = 1, b = 2;
   int              c = 1, d = 2;
   float            try_me;

   try_me = a - b;                        /* a and b get promoted */
   printf("try_me = %.1f\n", try_me);
   try_me = c - d;
   printf("try_me = %.1f\n", try_me);
}
```

17 Consider the following code:

```
char   a = 1, b = 2, c = 3;

printf("sizeof(c)          = %d\n", sizeof(c));
printf("sizeof('a')        = %d\n", sizeof('a'));
printf("sizeof(c = 'a')    = %d\n", sizeof(c = 'a'));
printf("sizeof(a + b + 7.7) = %d\n", sizeof(a + b + 7.7));
```

First, write down what you think gets printed; then execute the code to check your answer.

18 On a 24-hour clock the zero hour is midnight, and the 23rd hour is 11 o'clock at night, 1 hour before midnight. On such a clock, when 1 is added to 23, we do not get 24; instead we get 0. There is no 24. In a similar fashion 22 plus 5 yields 3, because 22 plus 2 is 0, and 3 more is 3. This is an example of modular arithmetic, or more precisely, of arithmetic modulo 24. Most machines do modular arithmetic on all the integral types. This is most easily illustrated with the unsigned types. Run the following program and explain what is printed.

```
#include <stdio.h>
#include <limits.h>   /* for UINT_MAX */

main()
{
   int       i;
   unsigned  u = UINT_MAX;

   printf("The largest unsigned int is %u\n\n", u);
   for (i = 0; i < 10; ++i)
      printf("%u + %d = %u\n", u, i, u + i);
   for (i = 0; i < 10; ++i)
      printf("%u * %d = %u\n", u, i, u * i);
}
```

19 Let $N_{min\_u\_long}$ and $N_{max\_u\_long}$ represent the minimum and maximum values that can be stored in an unsigned long on your system. What are those values? *Hint:* Read the standard header file *limits.h*.

20 The function call sqrt(-1.0) causes a run-time error. Most compilers provide adequate diagnostics for this error. (Turbo C does an especially nice job.) What diagnostics does your compiler provide?

21 When the value of x is too large, the function call pow(x, x) either causes a run-time error or exhibits some other peculiar behavior. What is the least integer value for x that causes this to happen on your system? Write an interactive program that gets x from the user and then prints x and pow(x, x) on the screen.

22 What is the largest double available on your machine? What happens when you go beyond this value? Experiment by running the following program:

```
#include <stdio.h>
#include <float.h>

main()
{
   double   x = 1.0, y = -1.0, z = 0.0;

   printf("The largest double: %.3e\n", DBL_MAX);
   printf("  Add a little bit: %.3e\n", DBL_MAX + 1.0);
   printf("         Add a lot: %.3e\n", DBL_MAX + DBL_MAX);
   printf(" Division by zero: %.3e  %.3e\n", x / z, y / z);
}
```

Modify the program so that it also prints out the largest float available on your machine. Is it a lot smaller than the largest double? *Hint:* Read the header file *float.h* on your system.

23 This problem is for those readers who are familiar with hexadecimal and octal numbers. In a program, an integer written with a leading 0 is an octal number, and an integer written with a leading 0x or 0X is a hexadecimal number. For example,

```
int   i = 077, j = 0x77, k = 0xcbd;

printf("Some numbers:%7d%7d%7d\n", i, j, k);
```

causes the line

```
Some numbers:     63    119   3261
```

to be printed. Just as the conversion character d is used in a format in printf() to print a decimal integer, the conversion character x is used to print hexadecimal numbers, and the conversion character o is used to print octal numbers. Define a symbolic constant LIMIT and print a table of values containing corresponding decimal, hexadecimal, and octal integers from 1 to LIMIT. *Hint:* Print an appropriate heading, and then use

```
for (i = 0; i <= LIMIT; ++i)
    printf("%12d%12x%12o\n", i, i, i);
```

24   In mathematics the numbers e and π are well known. The number e is the base of the natural logarithms, and the number π is the ratio of the diameter of a circle to its circumference. Which of the two numbers, e^{π} and π^{e}, is larger? This is a standard problem for students in an honors calculus course. However, even if you have never heard of e and π and know nothing about calculus, you should be able to answer this question. *Hint:*

$$e \approx 2.71828182845904524 \qquad \text{and} \qquad \pi \approx 3.14159265358979324$$

25   In Section 6.13, "System Considerations," we discussed an IEEE recommendation for floating point arithmetic. Does your machine follow this standard? Try executing the following code:

```
double   x = 1e+308;            /* on the edge */

printf("x * x = %e\n", x * x);  /* too big? */
```

If Inf or NaN gets printed, you can think of the value as "infinity" or as "not a number." If this happens, it is an indication (but not a proof) that floating point arithmetic on your machine follows the IEEE recommendations.

7

ENUMERATION TYPES, typedef, AND BITWISE OPERATORS

7.1   ENUMERATION TYPES

7.2   THE USE OF typedef

7.3   AN EXAMPLE: THE GAME OF PAPER, ROCK, SCISSORS

7.4   BITWISE OPERATORS AND EXPRESSIONS
        BITWISE COMPLEMENT
        TWO'S COMPLEMENT
        BITWISE BINARY LOGICAL OPERATORS
        LEFT AND RIGHT SHIFT OPERATORS

7.5   MASKS

7.6   SOFTWARE TOOLS: PRINTING AN int BITWISE

7.7   PACKING AND UNPACKING
        MULTICHARACTER CHARACTER CONSTANTS

7.8   STYLE

7.9   COMMON PROGRAMMING ERRORS

7.10   SYSTEM CONSIDERATIONS

7.11   SUMMARY

7.12   EXERCISES

In this chapter we first discuss the enumeration types. These are user-defined types that allow the programmer to name a finite set together with its elements, which are called *enumerators*. These types are defined and used by the programmer as the need arises. Next, we discuss the typedef facility, which provides a means of giving a new name to a type. A common use of this facility is to provide shorter names for enumeration and structure types. (As we will see in Chapter 16, in C++ this renaming is done automatically.) Finally, we discuss the bit operators, with which the programmer can access the individual bits in a byte.

7.1 ENUMERATION TYPES

The keyword enum is used to declare enumeration types. It provides a means of naming a finite set, and of declaring identifiers, called *enumerators*, as elements of the set. Consider, for example, the declaration

```
enum day {sun, mon, tue, wed, thu, fri, sat};
```

This creates the user-defined type enum day. The keyword enum is followed by the tag name day. The enumerators are the identifiers sun, mon,..., sat. They are constants of type int. By default, the first one is 0, and each succeeding one has the next integer value. This declaration is an example of a type specifier, which we also think of as a *template*. No variables of type enum day have been declared yet. To do so, we can now write

```
enum day   d1, d2;
```

This declares d1 and d2 to be of type enum day. They can only take on as values the elements (enumerators) in the set. Thus

```
d1 = fri;
```

assigns the value fri to d1, and

```
if (d1 == d2)
   .....            /* do something */
```

tests whether d1 is equal to d2. Note carefully that the type is enum day; the keyword enum by itself is not a type.

The enumerators can be initialized. Also, we can declare variables along with the template, if we wish to do so. Here is an example:

```
enum suit {clubs = 1, diamonds, hearts, spades}   a, b, c;
```

Since clubs has been initialized to 1, diamonds, hearts, and spades have the values 2, 3, and 4, respectively. This declaration consists of two parts:

> *The type specifier:* enum suit {clubs = 1, diamonds, hearts, spades}
> *Variables of this type:* a, b, c;

Here is another example of initialization:

```
enum fruit {apple = 7, pear, orange = 3, lemon}   frt;
```

Since the enumerator apple has been initialized to 7, pear has value 8. Similarly, since orange has value 3, lemon has value 4. Multiple values are allowed, but the identifiers themselves must be unique.

```
enum veg {beet = 17, carrot = 17, corn = 17}   vege1, vege2;
```

The tag name need not be present. Consider, for example,

```
enum {fir, pine}   tree;
```

Since there is no tag name, no other variables of type enum {fir, pine} can be declared.

In general, one should treat enumerators as programmer-specified constants and use them to aid program clarity. If necessary, the underlying value of an enumerator can be obtained by using a cast. The variables and enumerators in a function must all have distinct identifiers.

7.2 THE USE OF typedef

C provides the typedef facility so that an identifier can be associated with a specific type. A simple example is

```
typedef   int   color;
```

This makes color a type that is synonymous with int, and it can be used in declarations just as other types are used. An example is

```
color   red, green, blue;
```

The typedef facility allows the programmer to use type names that are appropriate for a specific application. Also, the facility helps to control complexity when programmers are building complicated or lengthy user-defined types, such as enumeration types and structure types (see Chapter 13).

We will illustrate the use of the enumeration type by writing a function that computes the next day. As is commonly done, we will typedef our enumeration type.

```
/* Compute the next day. */

enum day {sun, mon, tue, wed, thu, fri, sat};

typedef   enum day   day;

day find_next_day(day d)
{
   day   next_day;

   switch (d)  {
   case sun:
      next_day = mon;
      break;
   case mon:
      next_day = tue;
      break;
   . . . . .
   case sat:
      next_day = sun;
      break;
   }
   return next_day;
}
```

DISSECTION OF THE *find_next_day()* FUNCTION

■ `enum day {sun, mon, tue, wed, thu, fri, sat};`

This declaration is an example of a type specifier, which we also think of as a *template*. It tells the compiler that `enum day` is the name of a type and that `sun, mon,...,` `sat` are the allowable values for variables of this type. No variables of this type have been declared yet. That is why we think of it as a template; it tells the compiler the shape of things to come.

■ typedef   enum day   day;

We use the typedef facility to create a new name for our type. As is commonly done, we choose for the name of our type the tag name. In ANSI C, the name space for tags is separate from other names. Thus the compiler understands the difference between the tag name day and the type day. If we remove this typedef from our program, then throughout the remainder of the code, wherever we used the identifier day, we must use enum day instead.

■ day find_next_day(day d)
    {
        day   next_day;

The header of the function definition for find_next_day() tells the compiler that this function takes a single argument of type day and returns a value of type day to the calling environment. There is a single declaration in the body of the function definition. It tells the compiler that next_day is a variable of type day.

■ switch (d) {
    case sun:
        next_day = mon;
        break;

Recall that only a constant integral expression can be used in a case label. Since enumerators are constants, they can be used in this context. Note that the value assigned to next_day is an enumerator.

■ return next_day;

The value next_day, which is of type day, is returned to the calling environment.

The following is another version of this function, which uses a cast to accomplish the same ends:

```
/* Compute the next day with a cast. */

enum day {sun, mon, tue, wed, thu, fri, sat};

typedef   enum day   day;

day find_next_day(day d)
{
    return ((day)(((int) d + 1) % 7));
}
```

Enumeration types can be used in ordinary expressions as long as type compatibility is maintained. However, if one uses them as a form of integer type and constantly accesses their implicit representation, it is better just to use integer variables instead. The importance of enumeration types is their self-documenting character, where the enumerators are themselves mnemonic. Furthermore, they force the compiler to provide programmer-defined type checking so that one does not inadvertently mix apples and diamonds.

7.3   AN EXAMPLE: THE GAME OF PAPER, ROCK, SCISSORS

We will illustrate the use of enumeration types by writing a program to play the traditional children's game called *paper, rock, scissors*. In this game each child uses her or his hand to represent one of the three objects. A flat hand held in a horizontal position represents "paper," a fist represents "rock," and two extended fingers represents "scissors." The children face each other and at the count of three display their choices. If the choices are the same, then the game is a tie. Otherwise, a win is determined by the rules:

> Paper covers the rock.
> Rock breaks the scissors.
> Scissors cut the paper.

In our header file we put #include directives, templates for our enumeration types, type definitions, and function prototypes:

In file p_r_s.h:

```
#include <ctype.h>      /* for isspace() */
#include <stdio.h>      /* for printf(), etc */
#include <stdlib.h>     /* for rand() and srand() */
#include <time.h>       /* for time() */


enum p_r_s {paper, rock, scissors,
            game, help, instructions, quit};

enum outcome {win, lose, tie, error};


typedef    enum p_r_s      p_r_s;
typedef    enum outcome    outcome;


outcome    compare(p_r_s player, p_r_s machine);
void       game_status(int win_cnt, int lose_cnt, int tie_cnt);
void       help_for_the_player(void);
void       prn_instructions(void);
p_r_s      selection_by_player(void);
p_r_s      selection_by_machine(void);
```

We can write the functions for our program in one or more files. In each file it will be necessary to include our header file *p_r_s.h* at the top. We do not usually comment our #include lines, but here we are trying to provide a cross-reference for the novice programmer.

We will assume that the rest of the code for this program is written in the file *game.c.* The file consists of a #include line and a series of function definitions. Here is the function main(), which is at the top of the file:

```
/* The game of paper, rock, scissors. */

#include "p_r_s.h"

main()
{
    int        win_cnt = 0, lose_cnt = 0, tie_cnt = 0;
    outcome    result;
    p_r_s      player, machine;
```

```
      srand(time(NULL));        /* seed the random number generator */
      prn_instructions();
      while ((player = selection_by_player()) != quit)
         switch (player) {
         case paper:
         case rock:
         case scissors:
            machine = selection_by_machine();
            result = compare(player, machine);
            if (result == win) {
               ++win_cnt;
               printf("You win.\n");
            }
            else if (result == lose) {
               ++lose_cnt;
               printf("You lose.\n");
            }
            else if (result == tie) {
               ++tie_cnt;
               printf("A tie.\n");
            }
            break;
         case game:
            game_status(win_cnt, lose_cnt, tie_cnt);
            break;
         case instructions:
            prn_instructions();
            break;
         case help:
            help_for_the_player();
            break;
         }
      game_status(win_cnt, lose_cnt, tie_cnt);
      if (win_cnt > lose_cnt)
         printf("\nCONGRATULATIONS = You won!\n\n");
   }
```

The first executable statement in main() is

```
srand(time(NULL));
```

This seeds the random number generator rand(), causing it to produce a different sequence of integers each time the program is executed. More explicitly, passing srand()
an integer value determines where rand() will start. The function call time(NULL) returns a count of the number of seconds that have elapsed since 1 January 1970 (the
approximate birthday of UNIX). Both srand() and time() are provided in the standard
library. The function prototype for srand() is in *stdlib.h*, and the function prototype for
time() is in *time.h*. Both of these header files are provided by the system. Note that we
included them in *p_r_s.h*.

The next executable statement in main() calls prn_instructions(). This provides instructions to the user. Embedded in the instructions are some of the design considerations for programming this game.

```
void prn_instructions(void)
{
   printf("\n%s%s%s%s%s%s%s%s%s%s%s%s%s%s\n",
      "PAPER, ROCK, SCISSORS:\n",
      "   In this game p is for \"paper,\" r is for \"rock,\" and s\n",
      "   is for \"scissors.\" Both the player and the machine will\n",
      "   choose one of p, r, or s.  If the two choices are the same,\n",
      "   then the game is a tie.  Otherwise:\n",
      "      \"paper covers the rock\"     (a win for paper),\n",
      "      \"rock breaks the scissors\"  (a win for rock),\n",
      "      \"scissors cut the paper\"    (a win for scissors).\n\n",
      "   There are other allowable inputs:\n",
      "      g    for game status    (the number of wins so far),\n",
      "      h    for help,\n",
      "      i    for instructions   (reprint these instructions),\n",
      "      q    for quit           (to quit the game).\n\n",
      "   This game is played repeatedly until q is entered.\n",
      "   Good luck!\n");
}
```

Our next function processes the input made by the player. White space is skipped.
All other characters input at the terminal are processed, most of them through the default case of the switch.

```
p_r_s selection_by_player(void)
{
    int     c;
    p_r_s   player;

    printf("Input p, r, or s:  ");
    while (isspace(c = getchar()))   /* skip white space */
        ;
    switch (c) {
    case 'p':
        player = paper;
        break;
    case 'r':
        player = rock;
        break;
    case 's':
        player = scissors;
        break;
    case 'g':
        player = game;
        break;
    case 'i':
        player = instructions;
        break;
    case 'q':
        player = quit;
        break;
    default:
        player = help;
        break;
    }
    return player;
}
```

The machine's selection is computed by the next function. It uses rand() % 3 to produce a randomly distributed integer between 0 and 2. Since the type of the function is p_s_r, the value returned will be converted to this type. We provided an explicit cast to make the code more self-documenting.

```
p_r_s selection_by_machine(void)
{
    return ((p_r_s) (rand() % 3));
}
```

Once the player and the machine have made a selection, we need to compare the two selections in order to determine the outcome of the game. The following function does this:

```
outcome compare(p_r_s player, p_r_s machine)
{
    outcome   result;

    if (player == machine)
        return tie;
    switch (player) {
    case paper:
        result = (machine == rock) ? win : lose;
    case rock:
        result = (machine == scissors) ? win : lose;
    case scissors:
        result = (machine == paper) ? win : lose;
    }
    return result;
}
```

If the character g is input, then game_status() is invoked; if any character other than white space or p, r, s, g, i, or q is input, then help_for_the_player() is invoked.

```
void game_status(win_cnt, lose_cnt, tie_cnt)
{
   printf("\n%s\n%s%4d\n%s%4d\n%s%4d\n%s%4d\n\n",
      "GAME STATUS:",
      "  Win:   ", win_cnt,
      "  Lose:  ", lose_cnt,
      "  Tie:   ", tie_cnt,
      "  Total: ", win_cnt + lose_cnt + tie_cnt);
}


void help_for_the_player(void)
{
   printf("\n%s\n%s\n%s\n%s\n%s\n%s\n%s\n%s\n\n",
      "The following characters can be used for input:",
      "     p   for paper",
      "     r   for rock",
      "     s   for scissors",
      "     g   to find out the game status",
      "     h   to print this list",
      "     i   to reprint the instructions for this game",
      "     q   to quit this game");
}
```

7.4 BITWISE OPERATORS AND EXPRESSIONS

The bitwise operators act on integral expressions represented as strings of binary digits. These operators are explicitly system-dependent. We will restrict our discussion to machines having 8-bit bytes, 4-byte words, the two's complement representation of integers, and ASCII character codes.

Bitwise Operators

Logical operators:	(unary) bitwise complement:
	bitwise and: &
	bitwise exclusive or: ^
	bitwise inclusive or: |
Shift operators:	left shift: <<
	right shift: >>

Like other operators, the bitwise operators have rules of precedence and associativity that determine precisely how expressions involving them are evaluated.

Operators	Associativity
() ++ (*postfix*) -- (*postfix*)	left to right
++ (*prefix*) -- (*prefix*) ! ~ ^ sizeof (*type*) + (*unary*) - (*unary*) & (*address*)	right to left
* / %	left to right
+ -	left to right
<< >>	left to right
< <= > >=	left to right
== !=	left to right
&	left to right
^	left to right
|	left to right
&&	left to right
||	left to right
?:	right to left
= += *= <<= >>= *etc*	right to left
, (*comma operator*)	left to right

The operator ~ is unary; all the other bitwise operators are binary. They operate on integral expressions. We will discuss each of the bitwise operators in detail.

BITWISE COMPLEMENT

The operator ~ is called the *complement operator*, or the *bitwise complement operator*. It inverts the bit string representation of its argument; the 0s become 1s, and the 1s become 0s. Consider, for example, the declaration

```
int a = 70707;
```

The binary representation of a is

```
00000000 00000001 00010100 00110011
```

The expression ~a is the bitwise complement of a, and this expression has the binary representation

```
11111111 11111110 11101011 11001100
```

The int value of the expression ~a is −70708.

TWO'S COMPLEMENT

The *two's complement representation* of a nonnegative integer n is the bit string obtained by writing n in base 2. If we take the bitwise complement of the bit string and add 1 to it, we obtain the two's complement representation of $-n$. The next table gives some examples. To save space, we show only the two low-order bytes.

Value of n	Binary representation	Bitwise complement	Two's complement representation of −n	Value of −n
7	00000000 00000111	11111111 11111000	11111111 11111001	−7
8	00000000 00001000	11111111 11110111	11111111 11111000	−8
9	00000000 00001001	11111111 11110110	11111111 11110111	−9
−7	11111111 11111001	00000000 00000110	00000000 00000111	7

The preceding table is read from left to right. If we start with a positive integer n, consider its binary representation, and take its bitwise complement and add 1, then we obtain the two's complement representation of $-n$. A machine that uses the two's complement representation as its binary representation in memory for integral values is called a *two's complement machine*.

On a two's complement machine, if we start with the binary representation of a negative number $-n$ and take its bitwise complement and add 1, we obtain the two's complement representation, or binary representation, of n. This is illustrated in the last line in our previous table.

The two's complement representations of both 0 and −1 are special. The value 0 has all bits off; the value −1 has all bits on. Note that if a binary string is added to its bitwise complement, then the result has all bits on, which is the two's complement representation of −1. Negative numbers are characterized by having the high bit on.

On a two's complement machine, the hardware that does addition and bitwise complementation can be used to implement subtraction. The operation a - b is the same as a + (-b), and -b is obtained by taking the bitwise complement of b and adding 1.

BITWISE BINARY LOGICAL OPERATORS

The three operators & (and), ^ (exclusive or), and | (inclusive or) are binary operators. They take integral expressions as operands. The two operands, properly widened, are operated on bit-position by bit-position. The following table shows the bitwise operators acting on 1-bit fields. The table defines the semantics of the operators.

Values of:

a	b	a & b	a ^ b	a | b
0	0	0	0	0
1	0	0	1	1
0	1	0	1	1
1	1	1	0	1

The next table contains examples of the bitwise operators acting on int variables.

Declaration and initializations		
int a = 33333, b = -77777;		
Expression	*Representation*	*Value*
a	00000000 00000000 10000010 00110101	33333
b	11111111 11111110 11010000 00101111	−77777
a & b	00000000 00000000 10000000 00100101	32805
a ^ b	11111111 11111110 01010010 00011010	−110054
a | b	11111111 11111110 11010010 00111111	−77249
~ (a | b)	00000000 00000001 00101101 11000000	77248
(~a & ~b)	00000000 00000001 00101101 11000000	77248

LEFT AND RIGHT SHIFT OPERATORS

The two operands of a shift operator must be integral expressions. The integral promotions are performed on each of the operands. The type of the expression as a whole is that of its promoted left operand. An expression of the form

   expr1 << *expr2*

causes the bit representation of *expr1* to be shifted to the left by the number of places specified by *expr2*. On the low-order end, 0s are shifted in.

Declaration and initialization		
char c = 'Z';		
Expression	**Representation**	**Action**
c	00000000 00000000 00000000 01011010	unshifted
c << 1	00000000 00000000 00000000 10110100	left-shifted 1
c << 4	00000000 00000000 00000101 10100000	left-shifted 4
c << 31	00000000 00000000 00000000 00000000	left-shifted 31

Even though c is stored in 1 byte, in an expression it gets promoted to an int. When shift expressions are evaluated, integral promotions are performed on the two operands separately, and the type of the result is that of the promoted left operand. Thus the value of an expression such as c << 1 gets stored in 4 bytes.

The right shift operator >> is not quite symmetric to the left shift operator. For unsigned integral expressions, 0s are shifted in at the high end. For the signed types, some machines shift in 0s, while others shift in sign bits (see exercise 15). The sign bit is the high-order bit; it is 0 for nonnegative integers and 1 for negative integers.

Declarations and initializations		
int a = 1 << 31; /* shift 1 to the high bit */ unsigned b = 1 << 31;		
Expression	**Representation**	**Action**
a	10000000 00000000 00000000 00000000	unshifted
a >> 3	11110000 00000000 00000000 00000000	right-shifted 3
b	10000000 00000000 00000000 00000000	unshifted
b >> 3	00010000 00000000 00000000 00000000	right-shifted 3

Note that on our machine, sign bits are shifted in with an int. On another machine, 0s might be shifted in. To avoid this difficulty, programmers often use unsigned types when using bitwise operators.

If the right operand of a shift operator is negative or has a value that equals or exceeds the number of bits used to represent the left operand, then the behavior is undefined. It is the programmer's responsibility to keep the value of the right operand within proper bounds.

Our next table illustrates the rules of precedence and associativity with respect to the shift operators. To save space, we show only the two low-order bytes.

Declaration and assignments			
unsigned a = 1, b = 2;			
Expression	*Equivalent expression*	*Representation*	*Value*
a << b >> 1	(a << b) >> 1	00000000 00000010	128
a << 1 + 2 << 3	(a << (1 + 2)) << 3	00000000 01000000	64
a + b << 12 * a >> b	((a + b) << (12 * a)) >> b	00001100 00000000	3072

7.5 MASKS

A mask is a constant or variable that is used to extract desired bits from another variable or expression. Since the int constant 1 has the bit representation

```
00000000 00000000 00000000 00000001
```

it can be used to determine the low-order bit of an int expression. The following code uses this mask and prints an alternating sequence of 0s and 1s:

```
int i, mask = 1;

for (i = 0; i < 10; ++ i)
   printf("%d", i & mask);
```

If we wish to find the value of a particular bit in an expression, we can use a mask that is 1 in that position and 0 elsewhere. For example, we can use the expression 1 << 2, as a mask for the third bit, counting from the right. The expression

```
(v & (1 << 2)) ? 1 : 0
```

has the value 1 or 0 depending on the third bit in v.

Another example of a mask is the constant value 255, which is $2^8 - 1$. It has the following bit representation:

```
00000000 00000000 00000000 11111111
```

Because only the low-order byte is turned on, the expression

```
v & 255
```

will yield a value having a bit representation with all its high-order bytes zero and its low-order byte the same as the low-order byte in v. We express this by saying, "255 is a mask for the low-order byte."

7.6 SOFTWARE TOOLS: PRINTING AN int BITWISE

Software tools are utilities that the programmer can use to write software. Most systems provide a variety of software tools. Examples are compilers, debuggers, and the *make* utility. We will discuss these in Chapter 15. Programmers often write other software tools for their own use as the need arises. The bit_print() function that we discuss in this section is a typical example. For anyone writing software that deals with the machine at the bit level, the bit_print() utility is essential; it allows the programmer to see what is happening. For the beginning programmer, exploration with bit_print() helps to provide a conceptual framework that is very useful.

Our bit_print() function uses a mask to print out the bit representation of an int. The function can be used to explore how values of expressions are represented in memory. We used it, in fact, to help create the tables in this chapter.

```
/* Bit print an int expression. */

#include <limits.h>

void bit_print(int a)
{
   int   i;
   int   n = sizeof(int) * CHAR_BIT;        /* in limits.h */
   int   mask = 1 << (n - 1);               /* mask = 100...0 */

   for (i = 1; i <= n; ++i) {
      putchar(((a & mask) == 0) ? '0' : '1');
      a <<= 1;
      if (i % CHAR_BIT == 0 && i < n)
         putchar(' ');
   }
}
```

DISSECTION OF THE *bit_print()* FUNCTION

■ `#include <limits.h>`

In ANSI C, the symbolic constant CHAR_BIT is defined in *limits.h*. In traditional C, this header file is not usually available. The value of CHAR_BIT on most systems is 8. It represents the number of bits in a char, or equivalently, the number of bits in a byte. ANSI C requires at least 8 bits in a byte.

■ `int   n = sizeof(int) * CHAR_BIT;        /* in limits.h */`

Since we want this function to work on machines having either 2- or 4-byte words, we use the variable n to represent the number of bits in a machine word. We expect the value of the expression sizeof(int) to be either 2 or 4, and we expect that the symbolic constant CHAR_BIT, which is defined in the standard header file *limits.h*, to be 8. Thus we expect n to be initialized to either 16 or 32, depending on the machine.

■ `int    mask = 1 << (n - 1);      /* mask = 100...0 */`

Because of operator precedence, the parentheses are not needed in the initialization. We put them there to make the code more readable. Since `<<` has higher precedence than `=`, the expression `1 << (n - 1);` gets evaluated first. Suppose that n has value 32. The constant 1 has only its low-order bit turned on. The expression `1 << 31` shifts that bit to the high-order end. Thus `mask` has all of its bits off except for its high-order bit (sign bit), which is on.

■ ```
for (i = 1; i <= n; ++i) {
    putchar(((a & mask) == 0) ? '0' : '1');
    a <<= 1;
    . . . . .
```

First consider the expression

```
(a & mask) == 0
```

If the high-order bit in `a` is off, then the expression `a & mask` has all its bits off, and the expression `(a & mask) == 0` is *true*. Conversely, if the high-order bit in `a` is on, then the expression `a & mask` has its high-order bit on, and the expression `(a & mask) == 0` is *false*. Now consider the expression

```
((a & mask) == 0) ? '0' : '1'
```

If the high-order bit in `a` is off, then the conditional expression has the value `'0'`; otherwise, it has the value `'1'`. Thus `putchar()` prints a 0 if the high-order bit is off and prints a 1 if it is on.

■ ```
putchar(((a & mask) == 0) ? '0' : '1');
a <<= 1;
```

After the high-order bit in `a` has been printed, we left-shift the bits in `a` by 1 and place the result back in `a`. Recall that

```
a <<= 1;          is equivalent to          a = a << 1;
```

The value of the expression `a << 1` has the same bit pattern as `a`, except that it has been left-shifted by 1. The expression by itself does not change the value of `a` in memory. In contrast to this, the expression `a <<= 1` does change the value of `a` in memory. Its effect is to bring the next bit into the high-order position, ready to be printed the next time through the loop.

■ `if (i % CHAR_BIT == 0 && i < n)`
    `putchar(' ');`

If we assume that the value of the symbolic constant `CHAR_BIT` is 8, then this code causes a blank to be printed after each group of 8 bits has been printed. It is not necessary to do this, but it certainly makes the output easier to read.

7.7   PACKING AND UNPACKING

The use of bitwise expressions allows for data compression across byte boundaries. This is useful in saving space, but it can be even more useful in saving time. On a machine with 4-byte words, each instruction cycle processes 32 bits in parallel. The following function can be used to pack four characters into an `int`. It uses shift operations to do the packing byte by byte.

```
/* Pack 4 characters into an int. */

#include <limits.h>

int pack(char a, char b, char c, char d)
{
    int   p = a;              /* p will be packed with a, b, c, d */

    p = (p << CHAR_BIT) | b;
    p = (p << CHAR_BIT) | c;
    p = (p << CHAR_BIT) | d;
    return p;
}
```

To test our function, we write a program with the lines

```
printf("abcd = ");
bit_print(pack('a', 'b', 'c', 'd'));
putchar('\n');
```

in main(). Here is the output of our test program:

```
abcd = 01100001 01100010 01100011 01100100
```

Observe that the high-order byte has value 97, or 'a', and that the values of the remaining bytes are 98, 99, and 100. Thus pack() did its work properly.

Having written pack(), we now want to be able to retrieve the characters from within the 32-bit int. Again, we can use a mask to do this.

```
/* Unpack a byte from an int. */

#include <limits.h>

char unpack(int p, int k)                /* k = 0, 1, 2, or 3 */
{
    int        n = k * CHAR_BIT;         /* n = 0, 8, 16, or 24 */
    unsigned   mask = 255;               /* low-order byte */

    mask <<= n;
    return ((p & mask) >> n);
}
```

DISSECTION OF THE unpack() FUNCTION

■ #include <limits.h>

We have included this header file because it contains the definition of the symbolic constant CHAR_BIT. It represents the number of bits in a byte. On most machines its value is 8.

■ char unpack(int p, int k)   /* k = 0, 1, 2, or 3 */
  {
      . . . . .

We think of the parameter p as a packed int with its bytes numbered 0 through 3. The parameter k will indicate which byte we want: if k has value 0, then we want the low-order byte; if k has value 1, then we want the next byte; and so forth.

■ `int        n = k * CHAR_BIT;`   `/* n = 0, 8, 16, or 24 */`

If we assume that `CHAR_BIT` is 8 and that `k` has value 0, 1, 2, or 3, then `n` will be initialized with the value 0, 8, 16, or 24.

■ `unsigned   mask = 255;`   `/* low-order byte */`

The constant 255 is special; to understand it, first consider 256. Since $256 = 2^8$, the bit representation of 256 has all bits 0 except for a 1 in the 9th bit, counting from the low-order bit. Since 255 is one less than 256, the bit representation of 255 has all bits 0, except for the first 8 bits, which are all 1 (see exercise 7). Thus the binary representation of `mask` is

```
00000000 00000000 00000000 11111111
```

■ `mask <<= n;`

Let us assume that `CHAR_BIT` is 8. If `n` has value 0, then the bits in `mask` are not changed. If `n` has value 8, then the bits in `mask` are left-shifted by 8. In this case we think of `mask` stored in memory as

```
00000000 00000000 11111111 00000000
```

If `n` has value 16, then the bits in `mask` are left-shifted by 16. In this case we think of `mask` stored in memory as

```
00000000 11111111 00000000 00000000
```

In a similar fashion, if `n` has value 24, then `mask` will have only the bits in its high-order byte turned on.

■ `(p & mask) >> n`

Parentheses are needed because `&` has lower precedence than `>>`. Suppose that `p` has value −3579753 (which we chose because it has a suitable bit pattern), and suppose that `n` has value 16. The following table illustrates what happens:

Expression	Binary representation	Value
p	11111111 11001001 01100000 10010111	−3579753
mask	00000000 11111111 00000000 00000000	16711680
p & mask	00000000 11001001 00000000 00000000	13172736
(p & mask) >> n	00000000 00000000 00000000 11001001	201

■ return ((p & mask) >> n);

Since the function type for unpack() is char, the int expression (p & mask) >> n gets converted to a char before it gets passed back to the calling environment. When an int is converted to a char, only the low-order byte is retained; the other bytes are discarded.

Imagine wanting to keep an abbreviated employee record in one integer. We will suppose that an "employee identification number" can be stored in 9 bits and that a "job type" can be stored in 6 bits, which provides for a total of up to 64 different job types. The employee's "gender" can be stored in 1 bit. These three fields will require 16 bits, which on a machine with 4-byte words is a short integer. We can think of the three bit fields as follows:

Identification	*Job type*	*Gender*
bbbbbbbbb	bbbbbb	b

The following function can be used in a program designed to enter employee data into a short. The inverse problem of reading data out of the short would be accomplished with the use of masks.

```
/* Create employee data in a short int. */

short create_employee_data(int id_no, int job_type, char gender)
{
    short   employee = 0;        /* start with all bits off */

    employee |= (gender == 'm' || gender == 'M') ? 0 : 1;
    employee |= job_type << 1;
    employee |= id_no << 7;
    return employee;
}
```

MULTICHARACTER CHARACTER CONSTANTS

Multibyte characters are allowed in ANSI C. An example is 'abc'. On a machine with 4-byte words, this causes the characters 'a', 'b', and 'c' to be packed into a single word. However, the order in which they are packed is system-dependent. Some machines will put 'a' in the low-order byte; others will put it in the high-order byte (see exercise 10).

7.8   STYLE

Since enumerators can be chosen to be mnemonic, their use tends to be self-document-ing. Thus the use of enumeration types is considered good programming style.

Rather than using 0 and 1 to distinguish between alternate choices, the programmer can easily use an enumeration type. This often makes the code more readable. A declaration such as

```
enum no_yes {no, yes};
```

tells the compiler that `enum no_yes` is a user-defined type. Since this construct declares no variables of this type, we think of it as a template. (It tells the compiler the shape of things, but does not make any of them.) It is considered good programming style to put templates in header files. (Constructs that allocate space in memory do not belong in a header file.)

Since tag names have their own name space, we can reuse a tag name as a variable or as an enumerator. For example,

```
enum veg {beet, carrot, corn}   veg;    /* poor style */
```

Although this is legal, it is not considered good programming practice. On the other hand, it is considered a good programming style to use a tag name as a type definition. (In C++ this is done automatically.) An example is

```
typedef   enum veg {beet, carrot, corn}   veg;     /* good style */
```

This tells the compiler that `veg` is a user-defined type. To declare variables of this type, we can write

```
veg    v1, v2;
```

This practice reduces clutter, especially if there are a lot of enumeration types.

Since a left shift by 1 bit is equivalent to multiplication by 2, programmers sometimes use shift operations to perform arithmetic efficiently (see exercise 20). In some special applications this is acceptable, but in most programs it is considered bad programming style, as it obscures the meaning of the program. In most programs the time saved is negligible.

7.9   COMMON PROGRAMMING ERRORS

The same type definition cannot occur more than once in a file. Suppose the following line occurs in your *.c* file and also in your header file.

```
typedef    enum {off, on}    off_on;
```

If you include the header file at the top of your *.c* file, the compiler will complain. In this regard a `typedef` is not like a `#define`. The same `#define` can occur more than once in a file.

The order in which you define enumerators in an enumeration type can lead to logical errors. Consider the following code:

```
#include <stdio.h>

typedef    enum {yes, no}    yes_no;

yes_no    is_good(void);

main()
{
   if (is_good())
      printf("Hooray! A good condition exists.\n");
   else
      printf("Rats! Another bummer.\n");
   . . . . .
```

The idea here is that the `is_good()` function checks something and returns either `yes` or `no`, depending on the situation. Let us suppose that in the above code `yes` gets returned. Since `yes` has the `int` value 0 (*false*), the string

```
Rats! Another bummer.
```

gets printed, and that is not what we intended to happen. We can guard against this kind of error by explicitly checking the value returned:

```
if (is_good() == yes)
   . . . . .
```

As an additional safeguard, it is better to rewrite the `typedef` as

```
typedef   enum {no, yes}    no_yes;
```

Now the enumerator no has value 0 (*false*), and yes has value 1 (*true*), which is a more logical state of affairs.

Another common error is caused by the programmer confusing & with && and | with ||. Like the use of = instead of ==, this kind of error is easy to make. For the most part, the resulting expressions do not lead to syntax errors, so your compiler cannot tell you that an error has been made. To illustrate these ideas, let us suppose that a, b, and c are int variables. Then each of the expressions

```
a == b && c      a == b & c      a = b & c
```

is legal and can be used, for example, to control an if statement or a loop.

When using bitwise operators, the programmer must take into account the type of the expression. Here is an innocuous-looking initialization that results in a difficult bug:

```
unsigned   lo_byte = ~0 >> 24;   /* turn the low byte on */
```

The programmer is trying to create a mask for the low-order byte. Since 0 has all bits off, the expression ~0 has all bits on. Then the bits are right-shifted by 24 with the intention of shifting in 0s at the high end. The programmer remembered that with unsigned types, 0s are always shifted in. But this initialization failed. When the bit_print() function was used to see what happened, the programmer discovered that all bits were on! The problem is that 0 is of type int, and the operations ~0 >> 24 do not change that type. The final result gets assigned to lo_byte, which is of type unsigned, but that does not help. The correct initialization is

```
unsigned   lo_byte = ~((unsigned) 0) >> 24;   /* turn the low byte on */
```

The outer parentheses are not necessary, but they make the code more readable.

On any machine, a mask of type long is acceptable. However, when we tried the following initialization on a 2-byte machine, our code did not work as expected:

```
long   mask = 1 << 31;   /* turn the high bit on */
```

We made an egregious error. The expression 1 is of type int, and therefore stored in 2 bytes. When 1 is left-shifted by 31, all bits get turned off, so that mask effectively gets assigned the value 0, which is not what was intended. Here is the correct initialization:

```
long   mask = (long) 1 << 31;    /* turn the high bit on */
```

7.10   SYSTEM CONSIDERATIONS

The fact that some machines right-shift in 0s and other machines shift in sign bits can cause trouble. Suppose that the machine you are working on always shifts in 0s. Then using an int will produce the same result as using an unsigned. If you later move the code to a machine that shifts in sign bits, then the use of an int may cause unwanted results.

In C, any expression of type char or short gets promoted to an int, and this gets done in a way that preserves values. Any unsigned char or unsigned short gets 0s padded on the left, whereas sign extension occurs on signed quantities. This means that the sign bit gets propagated. The following table illustrates the situation:

Expression	Binary representation	Value
128	00000000 00000000 00000000 10000000	128
(char) 128	11111111 11111111 11111111 10000000	−128
-1 ^ 128	11111111 11111111 11111111 01111111	−129
(char) (-1 ^ 128)	00000000 00000000 00000000 01111111	127
255	00000000 00000000 00000000 11111111	255
(unsigned char) 255	00000000 00000000 00000000 11111111	255

On our system, a plain char is implemented as a signed char. When an int gets cast to a char, only the low-order byte gets retained; all the other bytes are discarded. But then the expression as a whole gets promoted to an int. For signed quantities, the 8th bit (sign bit) in the char determines what gets padded to the left. In contrast to this, an unsigned char gets padded with 0s irrespective of the sign bit.

The ideas of promotion and sign extension explain why using a char to test against EOF can fail on some systems (see exercise 25).

The programmer has to be cautious when using multicharacter character constants. On most systems, constants such as 'ab' can be used, but how the bytes actually get stored in a word is system-dependent.

7.11   SUMMARY

1   The keyword enum allows the programmer to define enumeration types. Consider the declaration

```
enum no_yes {no, yes};
```

This tells the compiler that `enum no_yes` is a user-defined type. The word `enum` by itself is not a type. A declaration such as

`enum no_yes    answer;`

defines the variable `answer` to be of type `enum no_yes`. It can take as values members of the set {no, yes}. The members are called *enumerators*. They are constants and have integer values. By default, the compiler assigns 0 to the first enumerator, 1 to the second enumerator, and so forth.

2   Enumerators are distinct identifiers chosen for their mnemonic significance. Their use provides a type-checking constraint for the programmer, as well as self-documentation for the program.

3   Since enumerators are constants of type `int`, they can be used in `case` labels in a `switch`. A cast can be used to resolve type conflicts.

4   The bitwise operators provide the programmer with a means of accessing the bits in an integral expression. Typically, we think of the operands of these operators as bit strings.

5   The use of bitwise expressions allows for data compression across byte boundaries. This capability is useful in saving space, but it can be even more useful in saving time. On a machine with 4-byte words, each instruction cycle processes 32 bits in parallel.

6   Most machines use the two's complement representation for integers. In this representation the high-order bit is the sign bit. It is 1 for negative integers and 0 for nonnegative integers.

7   Bitwise operations are explicitly system-dependent. A left shift causes 0s to be shifted in. The situation for a right shift is more complicated. If the integral expression is `unsigned`, then 0s are shifted in. If the expression is one of the signed types, then what gets shifted in is system-dependent. Some machines shift in sign bits. This means that if the sign bit is 0, then 0s are shifted in, and if the sign bit is 1, then 1s are shifted in. Some machines shift in 0s in all cases.

8   Masks are particular values that typically get used with the | operator to set a series of bits, and with the & operator to extract a series of bits.

9   Packing is the act of placing a number of distinct values into various subfields of a given variable. Unpacking extracts these values.

10   The function `bit_print()` is a software tool. The programmer can use it to see what is happening in memory at the bit level.

7.12   EXERCISES

1 Write a function called `previous_month()` that returns the previous month. Start with the code

```
enum month {jan, feb, . . ., dec};

typedef  enum month   month;
```

If `dec` is passed as an argument to the function, then `jan` should be returned. Write another function that prints the name of a month. More explicitly, if the enumerator `jan` is passed as an argument, then `January` should be printed. Write `main()` so that it calls your functions and produces a table of all twelve months, each one listed next to its predecessor month. *Caution:* When `printf()` is used, a variable of an enumeration type is printed as its implicit integer value. That is,

```
printf("%d\n", jan);
```

prints `0`, not `jan`.

2 Write a next-day program for a particular year. The program should take as input two integers, say 17 and 5, which represent 17 May, and it should print as output 18 May, which is the next day. Use enumeration types in the program. Pay particular attention to the problem of crossing from one month to the next.

3 Write a roulette program. The roulette (machine) will select a number between 0 and 35 at random. The player can place an odd/even bet, or can place a bet on a particular number. A winning odd/even bet is paid off at 2 to 1, except that all odd/even bets lose if the roulette selects 0. If the player places a bet on a particular number, and the roulette selects it, then the player is paid off at 35 to 1. If you play this game and make one-dollar bets, how long can you play before you lose 10 dollars?

4 (Balanced Meal Program) Use enumeration types to define five basic food groups: fish, fruits, grains, meats, and vegetables. For example:

```
enum fish {bass, salmon, shrimp, trout};
enum fruit {apple, peach, pear};
   . . . . .
```

Use a random number generator to select an item from each food group. Write a function meal() that picks an item from each of the five groups and prints out this menu. Print twenty menus. How many different menus are available?

5 In the game of paper, rock, scissors, an outcome that is not a tie is conveyed to the player by printing

```
You win.     or     You lose.
```

Rewrite the program so that messages like the following are printed:

```
You chose paper and I chose rock. You win.
```

6 Boolean types are automatically available in Pascal; in C, the programmer must explicitly provide them. Here are two ways of doing it:

```
typedef   enum {true, false}   boolean;
typedef   enum {false, true}   boolean;
```

Which one of these two typedefs is preferable? Explain.

7 Use the bit_print() function to create a table containing n, the binary representation 2^n, the binary representation for $2^n - 1$, for $n = 0, 1, 2, \ldots, 32$. If your machine has 2-byte words, then the output of your program should look like this:

```
 0:  00000000 00000001    00000000 00000000
 1:  00000000 00000010    00000000 00000001
 2:  00000000 00000100    00000000 00000011
 .....
15:  10000000 00000000    01111111 11111111
 .....
```

After you have done this, write down a similar table by hand that contains n, 10^b, and $10^n - 1$ for $n = 0, 1, 2, \ldots, 7$. Write the numbers in base 10 in your table. Do you see the similarity between the two tables? *Hint:* Use the following code:

```
int    i, power = 1;

for (i = 0; i < 32; ++i) {
   printf("%2d: ", i);
   bit_print(power);
   printf("   ");
   bit_print(power = 1);
   putchar('\n');
   power *= 2;
}
```

8 Write a function that takes as its input a string of decimal integers. Each character
   in the string can be thought of as a decimal digit. The digits should be converted to
   4-bit binary strings and packed into an int. If an int has 32 bits, then as many as 8
   digits can be packed into it. When you test your function, here is what you might
   see on the screen:

```
Input a string of decimal digits:  12345678

12345678 = 0001 0010 0011 0100 0101 0110 0111 1000
```

Also, write an inverse function. It should unpack an int and return the original
string. *Hint:* Here is one way to begin a conversion function:

```
int convert(char *s)
{
   char   *p;
   int    a = 0;       /* turn all bits off */

   for (p = s; *p != '\0'; ++p) {
      a <<= 4;
      switch (*p) {
      case '1':
         a |= 1;
         break;
      case '2':
         . . . . .
```

9 Some of the binary representations of the numbers in this chapter are easy to check
   for correctness, and some are not. Use bit_print() to check some of the more diffi-

cult representations. Try, for example, 70707 and its bitwise complement. Did we really get it right in the text?

10   Suppose that integers have a 16-bit two's complement representation. Write down the binary representation for -1, -5, -101, -1023. *Hint:* Recall that the two's complement representation of negative integers is obtained by taking the bit representation of the corresponding positive integer, complementing it, and adding 1.

11   Carole, Barbara, and Debra all vote on sixteen separate referendums. Assume that each individual's vote is stored bitwise in a 16-bit integer. Write a function definition that begins

```
short majority(short a, short b, short c)
{
    .....
```

This function should take as input the votes of Carole, Barbara, and Debra stored in a, b, and c, respectively. It should return the bitwise majority of a, b, and c.

12   Write a function definition that begins

```
int circular_shift(int a, int n)
{
    .....
```

This function should left-shift a by n positions, where the high-order bits are reintroduced as the low-order bits. Here are two examples of a circular shift operation defined for a char instead of an int:

| 10000001 | circular shift 1 yields | 00000011 |
| 01101011 | circular shift 3 yields | 01011011 |

Write a program that uses bit_print() to test your function.

13   Write a function that will reverse the bit representation of an int. Here are two examples of a reversing operation defined for a char instead of an int:

| 01110101 | reversed yields | 10101110 |
| 10101111 | reversed yields | 11110101 |

14   Write a function that will extract every other bit position from a 32-bit expression. The result should be returned as a 16-bit expression. Your function should work on machines having either 2- or 4-byte words.

15 Does your machine shift in sign bits? Here is some code that will help you to determine this:

```
int       i = -1;       /* turn all bits on */
unsigned  u = -1;

if (i >> 1 == u >> 1)
    printf("Zeros are shifted in.\n");
else
    printf("Sign bits are shifted in.\n");
```

Explain why this code works.

16 A twentieth-century date can be written with integers in the form *day/month/year*. An example is 1/7/33, which represents 1 July 1933. Write a function that stores the day, month, and year compactly. Since we need 31 different values for the day, 12 different values for the month, and 100 different values for the year, we can use 5 bits to represent the day, 4 bits to represent the month, and 7 bits to represent the year. Your function should take as input the day, month, and year as integers, and it should return the date packed into a 16-bit integer. Write another function that does the unpacking. Write a program to test your functions.

17 Write a function that acts directly on a packed date (see exercise 16) and produces the next calendar day in packed form. Contrast this to the program you wrote in exercise 2.

18 Rewrite the program given in Section 3.12, "Problem Solving: Boolean Variables," in Chapter 3. Use the 5 low-order bits in the char variable b to represent the five boolean variables b1, ..., b5.

19 Rewrite the program from exercise 18 to take advantage of machine arithmetic. Show by hand-simulation that the effect of adding 1 to the bit representation for b is equivalent to the effect of the nested for statements. In this exercise, your program should generate the table using a single unnested for statement.

20 Write an interactive program that asks the user to input an integer n. Use bit_print() to write out the binary representation of n, $2 \times n$, $4 \times n$, and $8 \times n$. Can you explain what happens? *Hint:* In base 10, what happens to a number when you multiply it by 10^k for $k = 1, 2, 3$?

21 Suppose you are on a two's complement machine that does not provide bitwise complementation. Implement the operation by writing a function bit_complement()

that only uses arithmetic operations. *Hint:* If a is a variable of type int, and binary complementation is available, then the expressions

```
-a          and          ~a + 1
```

have the same value.

22 Consider the function pack() given in Section 7.7, "Packing and Unpacking." The body of the function consists of four statements. Rewrite the function so that these four statements are collapsed into a single return statement.

23 Rewrite the function pack() so that only arithmetic operations are used.

24 Most machines implement a plain char as either a signed char or as an unsigned char. How is a plain char implemented on your machine? Try the following code:

```
char           c  = 128;      /* turn the high bit on */
signed char    sc = 128;
unsigned char  uc = 128;

printf("c = %d  sc = %d  uc = %d\n", c, sc, uc);
```

Although a variable of type char is stored in memory in a single byte, as an expression, it gets promoted to an int. Change the %d formats to %u. Do you see the effects of the promotion?

25 Suppose that a system implements a plain char as an unsigned char. Explain the effect of the following code:

```
char   c = EOF;

if (c == EOF)
    printf("Truth!\n");
else
    printf("This needs to be explained!\n");
```

We are assuming that *stdio.h* has been included. If your system implements a plain char as a signed char, then to see how this code would run on a different system, just change the declaration to

```
unsigned char   c = EOF;
```

Hint: Look in *stdio.h* to find the value of EOF. Then read Section 7.10, "System Considerations," carefully. If you are still mystified, use bit_print() to see what is happening.

26 How multicharacter character constants such as 'abc' get stored is system-dependent. Since programmers sometimes write 'abc' instead of "abc", some compilers provide a warning when multicharacter character constants get used, even if the use is proper. What happens on your system? Try the following code:

```
int   c = 'abc';

printf("'abc' = ");
bit_print(c);
printf("\n");
```

Here is the output on a Sun workstation:

```
'abc' = 00000000 01100011 01100010 01100001
```

Explain why this output makes sense. *Hint:* Consult the ASCII character codes in Appendix C. *Caution:* If you are working on a machine with 2-byte words, use 'ab' instead of 'abc'.

8

FUNCTIONS, POINTERS, AND STORAGE CLASSES

8.1   POINTER DECLARATION AND ASSIGNMENT

8.2   ADDRESSING AND DEREFERENCING

8.3   POINTERS TO void

8.4   CALL-BY-REFERENCE

8.5   SCOPE RULES

8.6   STORAGE CLASSES
      THE STORAGE CLASS auto
      THE STORAGE CLASS extern
      THE STORAGE CLASS register
      THE STORAGE CLASS static

8.7   STATIC EXTERNAL VARIABLES

8.8   DEFAULT INITIALIZATION

8.9   AN EXAMPLE: PROCESSING CHARACTERS

8.10 FUNCTION DECLARATIONS AND DEFINITIONS

8.11 THE TYPE QUALIFIERS const AND volatile

8.12 STYLE

8.13 COMMON PROGRAMMING ERRORS

8.14 SYSTEM CONSIDERATIONS

8.15 SUMMARY

8.16 EXERCISES

When an expression is passed as an argument to a function, a copy of the value of the expression is made, and it is the copy, not the original, that is passed to the function. This mechanism is known as *call-by-value*, and it is strictly adhered to in C. Suppose that v is a variable and f() is a function. If we write v = f(v), then a value returned by the function can change v in the calling environment. Apart from this, the function call f(v) by itself cannot change v. This is because only a copy of the value of v is passed to f(). In other programming languages, however, a function call by itself *can* change the value of v in the calling environment. The mechanism that accomplishes this is known as call-by-reference.

It is often convenient to have functions modify the values of the variables referred to in the argument list. To get the effect of call-by-reference in C, we must use pointers in the parameter list in the function definition, and pass addresses of variables as arguments in the function call. Before we explain this in detail, however, we need to understand how pointers work.

In C pointers have many uses. In this chapter we explain how they are used as arguments to functions. In the two chapters that follow, we will explain their use with arrays and strings. In Chapter 13 we will show how pointers are used with structures, and in Chapter 14 we will see how pointers are used when dealing with files.

In this chapter we also discuss scope rules and storage classes. Global variables are known throughout the program, unless they are masked by a redeclaration in a function or a block.

8.1   POINTER DECLARATION AND ASSIGNMENT

Pointers are used in programs to access memory and manipulate addresses. We have already seen the use of addresses as arguments to scanf(). A function call such as scanf("%d", &v) causes an appropriate value to be stored at a particular address in memory.

If v is a variable, then &v is the address, or location, in memory of its stored value. The address operator & is unary and has the same precedence and right-to-left associativity as the other unary operators. Pointer variables can be declared in programs and then used to take addresses as values. The declaration

```
int   i, *p;
```

declares i to be of type int and p to be of type "pointer to int." The legal range of values for any pointer always includes the special address 0 and a set of positive integers that are interpreted as machine addresses on a particular C system. Typically, the symbolic constant NULL is defined as 0 in *stdio.h*. Some examples of assignment to the pointer p are

```
p = &i;
p = 0;
p = NULL;            /* equivalent to p = 0; */
p = (int *) 1307;    /* an absolute address in memory */
```

In the first example we think of p as "referring to i," or "pointing to i," or "containing the address of i." The compiler decides what address to use to store the value of the variable i. This will vary from machine to machine and may even be different for different executions on the same machine. The second and third examples show assignments of the special value zero to the pointer p. In the last example the cast (int *) is necessary to avoid a compiler error. The type in the cast is "pointer to int." The last example is unusual because programmers ordinarily do not assign absolute addresses to pointers, except for the special value zero. This special value does not need to be cast.

8.2   ADDRESSING AND DEREFERENCING

We want to examine some elementary code and show some diagrams to illustrate what is happening in memory. Let us start with the declaration

```
int   a, b, *p;
```

This causes the compiler to allocate space in memory for two int's and a pointer to int. At this point the contents of the variables are garbage, because no values have been assigned.

We used question marks in the diagram because we do not know what values are stored in the three variables. After the assignment statements

```
a = b = 7;
p = &a;
```

have been executed, we have

Now we can use the pointer p to access the value stored in a. This is done through the *dereference*, or *indirection*, operator *. This operator is unary, and it has the same precedence and right-to-left associativity as the other unary operators. Since p is a pointer, the expression *p has the value of the variable that p points to. The name *indirection* is taken from machine-language programming. The direct value of p is a memory location, whereas *p is the indirect value of p, namely the value at the memory location stored in p. Consider the statement

```
printf("*p = %d\n", *p);        /* 7 gets printed */
```

Since p points to a, and a has value 7, the dereferenced value of p is 7, and that is what gets printed. Now consider

```
*p = 3;
printf("a = %d\n", a);        /* 3 gets printed */
```

The first statement is read, "The object pointed to by p is assigned the value 3." Since p points to a, the stored value of a in memory is overwritten with the value 3. Thus when we print out the value of a, 3 gets printed. At this point, this is what we have in memory:

Our next statement causes p to point at b.

```
p = &b;
```

This time, we draw our diagram differently to show what is happening in memory.

We do not really care about the place in memory where p is stored; our only concern is the object that p is pointing to. Now consider the code

```
*p = 2 * *p - a;
printf("b = %d\n", b);     /* 11 gets printed */
```

We read the first statement as follows: "The object pointed to by p is assigned the value 2 times what p is pointing to minus a." Note that the expression *p on the right side of the assignment is evaluated first. This is because the dereference operator * has higher precedence than the binary arithmetic operators.

Now let us suppose that we want to read in a value for a from the keyboard. Although there is no advantage in doing so, we can use the pointer p to accomplish this.

```
p = &a;
printf("Input an integer: ");
scanf("%d", p);                    /* put it at the address of a */
```

When scanf() is invoked, the characters typed at the keyboard are converted to a decimal integer value, and that value is placed at the address p. We can think of a pointer as an address, and conversely, we can think of an address as a pointer. If we type 77 when prompted, this is what we have in memory:

In a certain sense, the dereference operator * is the inverse of the address operator &. Consider the following code:

```
float   x, y, *p;

p = &x;
y = *p;
```

First p is assigned the address of x. Then y is assigned the value of the object pointed to by p. The two statements are equivalent to

```
y = *&x;
```

which in turn is equivalent to

```
y = x;
```

A pointer variable can be initialized in a declaration, but the notation is confusing to the beginning programmer. Here is an example:

```
int   a, *p = &a;
```

This declaration tells the compiler that p is a pointer to int and that the initial value of p is &a. *Caution:* Do *not* read this as "The object pointed to by p is initialized to the address of a." Also note that

```
int   *p = &a, a;      /* wrong */
```

will not work. The compiler must allocate space in memory for a before p can be initialized with its address. The compiler does not have the ability to look ahead.

In the following function definition, the parameter p is a pointer to int. We can use it to initialize variables in a declaration:

```
void f(int *p)
{
   int   a = *p, *q = p;


   . . . . .
}
```

This declares a to be an int and initializes it to the object p is pointing to, and it declares q to be a pointer to int and initializes it to p.

The following table illustrates how some pointer expressions are evaluated. Be careful to read the pointer initializations correctly.

Declarations and initializations		
int i = 3, j = 5, *p = &i, *q = &j, *r; double x;		
Expression	*Equivalent expression*	*Value*
p == & i	p == (& i)	1
p = i + 7	p = (i + 7)	/* illegal */
* * & p	* (* (& p))	3
r = & x	r = (& x)	/* illegal */
7 * * p / * q + 7	(((7 * (* p))) / (* q)) + 7	11
* (r = & j) *= * p	(* (r = (& j))) *= (* p)	15

In ANSI C, the only integer value that can be assigned to a pointer is the special value zero. To assign any other value, a cast must be used. In contrast to this, pointers and integers can be freely mixed in traditional C.

In the above table we attempted to assign `r` the value `&x`. Since `r` is a pointer to `int`, and the expression `&x` is of type pointer to `double`, this is illegal. Also note that in the above table we used the expression

```
7 * * p / * q + 7
```

If instead we had written

```
7 * * p /* q + 7            /* trouble? */
```

we would find that the compiler treats `/*` as the start of a comment. This can result in a difficult bug.

Let us write a short program that illustrates the distinction between a pointer value and its dereferenced value. Also, we will illustrate how the `%p` format can be used to print pointer values, or addresses.

```
#include <stdio.h>

main()
{
   int   i = 777, *p = &i;

   printf(" Value of i: %d\n", *p);
   printf("Address of i: %u or %p\n", p, p);
}
```

Here is the output of this program on our system:

```
Value of i: 777
Address of i: 234880252 or dfffcfc
```

The actual location of a variable in memory is system-dependent. The operator `*` takes the value of `p` to be a memory location and returns the value stored at this location appropriately interpreted according to the type declaration of `p`. We used the `%u` format to print the address of `i` as an unsigned decimal integer, and we used the `%p` format to print the address of `i` in whatever way is natural for the system. On our system this is a hexadecimal integer. The `%p` format is not available in some traditional C systems. In MS-DOS, the `%u` format does not always work (see exercise 13).

8.3   POINTERS TO void

In traditional C, pointers of different types are considered to be assignment compatible. In ANSI C, however, one pointer can be assigned to another only when they both have the same type, or when one of them is of type pointer to void. Thus we can think of void * as a generic pointer type. The following table shows examples of both legal and illegal pointer assignments.

Declarations	

`int    *p;`
`float  *q;`
`void   *v;`	

Legal assignments	*Illegal assignments*

`p = 0;`
`p = (int *) 1;`
`p = v = q;`
`p = (int *) q;`
	`p = 1;`
	`v = 1;`
	`p = q;`

In later chapters we will discuss `calloc()` and `malloc()`, which provide dynamic storage allocation for arrays and structures. These functions are in the standard library. Since they return a pointer to void, we can write

```
int   *a;

a = calloc(...);
```

In traditional C, we would need to use a cast:

```
a = (int *) calloc(...);      /* traditional C */
```

In traditional C, the type char * is used as a (sort of) generic pointer type, but this requires the use of casts. The type void * does not exist in traditional C.

8.4   CALL-BY-REFERENCE

Whenever variables are passed as arguments to a function, their values are copied to the corresponding function parameters, and the variables themselves are not changed in the calling environment. This call-by-value mechanism is strictly adhered to in C. In this section we describe how *addresses* of variables can be used as arguments to functions so as to achieve the effect of call-by-reference.

For a function to effect call-by-reference, pointers must be used in the parameter list in the function definition. Then, when the function is called, addresses of variables must be passed as arguments. The function swap() in the following program illustrates these ideas.

```
#include <stdio.h>

void swap(int *, int *);

main()
{
    int   a = 3, b = 7;

    printf("%d %d\n", a, b);      /* 3  7 is printed */
    swap(&a, &b);
    printf("%d %d\n", a, b);      /* 7  3 is printed */
}
```

Since the addresses of a and b are passed as arguments to swap(), the function is able to interchange the values of a and b in the calling environment.

```
void swap(int *p, int *q)
{
    int   tmp;

    tmp = *p;
    *p = *q;
    *q = tmp;
}
```

DISSECTION OF THE swap() FUNCTION

■ ```
void swap(int *p, int *q)
{
    int   tmp;
```

The type of the function is void, which means that no value is returned. The two parameters p and q are of type pointer to int. The variable tmp is local to this function. We think of it as temporary storage. When we call this function in main() with &a and &b as arguments, this is what we have in memory at this point.

■ ```
tmp = *p;
*p = *q;
*q = tmp;
```

We read this as follows:

> The variable tmp is assigned the value of the object pointed to by p.
>
> The object pointed to by p is assigned the value of the object pointed to by q.
>
> The object pointed to by q is assigned the value tmp.

After these three statements have been executed, here is what we have in memory:

If pointers are new to you, you should draw a diagram of what is in memory after each statement has been executed (see exercise 2).

The effect of call-by-reference is accomplished by

1   Declaring a function parameter to be a pointer

2   Using the dereferenced pointer in the function body

3   Passing an address as an argument when the function is called

8.5   SCOPE RULES

The *scope* of an identifier is that part of the program text where the identifier is known or accessible. This idea depends on the notion of a *block*, which is a compound statement with declarations.

The basic rule of scoping is that identifiers are accessible only within the block in which they are declared. They are unknown outside the boundaries of that block. This would be an easy rule to follow, except that programmers, for a variety of reasons, choose to use the same identifier in different declarations. We then have the question of which object the identifier refers to. Let us give a simple example of this state of affairs.

```
{
    int a = 2;              /* outer block a */
    printf("%d\n", a);      /* 2 is printed */
    {
        int a = 7;          /* inner block a */
        printf("%d\n", a);  /* 7 is printed */
    }                       /* back to the outer block */
    printf("%d\n", ++a);    /* 3 is printed */
}
```

An equivalent piece of code would be

```
{
    int a_outer = 2;
    printf("%d\n", a_outer);
    {
        int a_inner = 7;
        printf("%d\n", a_inner);
    }
    printf("%d\n", ++a_outer);
}
```

Each block introduces its own nomenclature. An outer block name is valid unless an inner block redefines it. If redefined, the outer block name is hidden, or masked, from the inner block. Inner blocks may be nested to arbitrary depths that are determined by system limitations.

8.6   STORAGE CLASSES

Every variable and function in C has two attributes: *type* and *storage class*. The four storage classes are automatic, external, register, and static, with corresponding keywords

```
auto      extern      register      static
```

By far the most common storage class for variables is automatic. However, the programmer needs to know about all the storage classes. They all have important uses.

THE STORAGE CLASS **auto**

Variables declared within function bodies are automatic by default. Thus automatic is the most common of the four storage classes. If a compound statement starts with variable declarations, then these variables can be acted on within the scope of the enclosing compound statement. A compound statement with declarations is called a *block* to distinguish it from one that does not begin with declarations.

Declarations of variables within blocks are implicitly of storage class automatic. The keyword auto can be used to explicitly specify the storage class. An example is

```
auto int     a, b, c;
auto float   f;
```

Because the storage class is automatic by default, the keyword auto is seldom used.

When a block is entered, the system allocates memory for the automatic variables. Within that block, these variables are defined and are considered "local" to the block. When the block is exited, the system releases the memory that was set aside for the automatic variables. Thus the values of these variables are lost. If the block is reentered, the system once again allocates memory, but previous values are unknown. The body of a function definition constitutes a block if it contains declarations. If it does, then each invocation of the function sets up a new environment.

THE STORAGE CLASS extern

One method of transmitting information across blocks and functions is to use external variables. When a variable is declared outside a function, storage is permanently assigned to it, and its storage class is extern. A declaration for an external variable can look just the same as a declaration for a variable that occurs inside a function or block. Such a variable is considered to be global to all functions declared after it, and upon exit from the block or function, the external variable remains in existence. The following program illustrates these ideas:

```
# include <stdio.h>

int   a = 1, b = 2, c = 3;          /* global variables */
int   f(void);                      /* function prototype */

main()
{
   printf("%3d\n", f());            /* 12 is printed */
   printf("%3d%3d%3d\n", a, b, c);  /*  4  2  3 is printed */
}

int f(void)
{
   int   b, c;                      /* b and c are local */
                                    /* global b, c are masked */

   a = b = c = 4;
   return (a + b + c);
}
```

Note that we could have written

```
   extern int   a = 1, b = 2, c = 3;   /* global variables */
```

This use of extern will cause some traditional C compilers to complain. Although this is allowable in ANSI C, it is not required. Variables defined outside of a function have external storage class, even if the keyword extern is not used. Such variables cannot have automatic or register storage class. The keyword static can be used, but its use is special, as explained in Section 8.7, "Static External Variables."

The keyword extern is used to tell the compiler to "look for it elsewhere, either in this file or in some other file." Let us rewrite the last program to illustrate a typical use of the keyword extern.

In file file1.c:

```c
#include <stdio.h>

int   a = 1, b = 2, c = 3;      /* external variables */
int   f(void);

main()
{
   printf("%3d\n", f());
   printf("%3d%3d%3d\n", a, b, c);
}
```

In file file2.c:

```c
int f(void)
{
   extern int    a;              /* look for it elsewhere */
   int           b, c;

   a = b = c = 4;
   return (a + b + c);
}
```

The two files can be compiled separately. The use of extern in the second file tells the compiler that the variable a will be defined elsewhere, either in this file or in some other. The ability to compile files separately is important when writing large programs.

External variables never disappear. Since they exist throughout the execution life of the program, they can be used to transmit values across functions. They may, however, be hidden if the identifier is redefined. Another way of conceiving of external variables is to think of them as being declared in a block that encompasses the whole program.

Information can be passed into a function two ways: by use of external variables and by use of the parameter mechanism. Although there are exceptions, the use of the parameter mechanism is the preferred method. This tends to improve the modularity of the code, and it reduces the possibility of undesirable side effects.

One form of side effect occurs when a function changes a global variable from within its body rather than through its parameter list. Such a construction is error prone. Correct practice is to effect changes to global variables through the parameter and return mechanisms. Adhering to this practice improves modularity and readability, and since changes are localized, programs are typically easier to write and maintain.

All functions have external storage class. This means that we can use the keyword extern in function definitions and in function prototypes, if we wish to do so. For example,

```
extern double   sin(double);
```

is a valid function prototype for the sin() function, and for its function definition we can write

```
extern double sin(double x)
{
    . . . . .
```

THE STORAGE CLASS register

The storage class register tells the compiler that the associated variables should be stored in high-speed memory registers, provided it is physically and semantically possible to do so. Since resource limitations and semantic constraints sometimes make this impossible, this storage class defaults to automatic whenever the compiler cannot allocate an appropriate physical register. Typically, the compiler has only a few such registers available. Many of these are required for system use and cannot be allocated otherwise.

Basically, the use of storage class register is an attempt to improve execution speed. When speed is a concern, the programmer may choose a few variables that are most frequently accessed and declare them to be of storage class register. Common candidates for such treatment include loop variables and function parameters. Here is an example:

```
{
    register int   i;

    for (i = 0; i < LIMIT; ++i) {
        . . . . .
    }
}       /* block exit will free the register */
```

The declaration

```
    register i;         is equivalent to         register int i;
```

If a storage class is specified in a declaration and the type is absent, then the type is int by default.

Note that in our example the register variable i was declared as close to its place of use as possible. This is to allow maximum availability of the physical registers, using them only when needed. Always remember that a register declaration is taken only as *advice* to the compiler.

THE STORAGE CLASS static

Static declarations have two important and distinct uses. The more elementary use is to allow a local variable to retain its previous value when the block is reentered. This is in contrast to ordinary automatic variables, which lose their value upon block exit and must be reinitialized. The second and more subtle use is in connection with external declarations. This will be discussed in the next section.

As an example of the value-retention use of static, we will write the outline of a function that behaves differently depending on how many times it has been called.

```
void f(void)
{
   static int   cnt = 0;

   ++cnt;
   if (cnt % 2 == 0)
       . . . . .            /* do something */
   else
       . . . . .            /* do something different */
}
```

The first time the function is invoked, the variable cnt is initialized to zero. On function exit, the value of cnt is preserved in memory. Whenever the function is invoked again, cnt is not reinitialized. Instead, it retains its previous value from the last time the function was called. The declaration of cnt as a static int inside of f() keeps it private to f(). If it were declared outside of the function, then other functions could access it, too.

8.7   STATIC EXTERNAL VARIABLES

The second and more subtle use of `static` is in connection with external declarations. With external constructs it provides a "privacy" mechanism that is very important for program modularity. By privacy, we mean visibility or scope restrictions on otherwise accessible variables or functions.

At first glance, static external variables seem unnecessary. External variables already retain their values across block and function exit. The difference is that static external variables are scope-restricted external variables. The scope is the remainder of the source file in which they are declared. Thus they are unavailable to functions defined earlier in the file or to functions defined in other files, even if these functions attempt to use the `extern` storage class keyword.

```
void f(void)
{
    .....           /* v is not available here */
}

static int   v;     /* static external variable */

void g(void)
{
    .....           /* v can be used here */
}
```

Let us use this facility to provide a variable that is global to a family of functions, but at the same time is private to the file. We will write two pseudo random number generators, both of which use the same seed. (The algorithm is based on linear congruential methods; see *The Art of Computer Programming*, 2nd ed., vol. 2, *Seminumerical Algorithms*, by Donald Ervin Knuth [Reading, Mass.; Addison-Wesley, 1981]).

```
/* A family of pseudo random number generators. */

#define   INITIAL_SEED      17
#define   MULTIPLIER        25173
#define   INCREMENT         13849
#define   MODULUS           65536
#define   FLOATING_MODULUS  65536.0


static unsigned   seed = INITIAL_SEED;   /* external, but
                                              private to this file */
unsigned random(void)
{
   seed = (MULTIPLIER * seed + INCREMENT) % MODULUS;
   return seed;
}

double probability(void)
{
   seed = (MULTIPLIER * seed + INCREMENT) % MODULUS;
   return (seed / FLOATING_MODULUS);
}
```

The function random() produces an apparently random sequence of integer values between 0 and MODULUS. The function probability() produces an apparently random sequence of floating values between 0 and 1.

Notice that a call to random() or probability() produces a new value of the variable seed that depends on its old value. Since seed is a static external variable, it is private to this file and its value is preserved between function calls. We can now create functions in other files that invoke these random number generators without worrying about side effects.

A last use of static is as a storage class specifier for function definitions and prototypes. This causes the scope of the function to be restricted. Static functions are visible only within the file in which they are defined. Unlike ordinary functions, which can be accessed from other files, a static function is available throughout its own file, but no other. Again, this facility is useful in developing private modules of function definitions.

```
void f(int a)
{
    .....    /* g() is available here, but not in other files */
}

static int g(void)
{
    .....
}
```

8.8   DEFAULT INITIALIZATION

In C, both external variables and static variables that are not explicitly initialized by the programmer are initialized to zero by the system. This includes arrays, strings, pointers, structures, and unions. For arrays and strings, this means that each element is initialized to zero; for structures and unions, this means that each member is initialized to zero. In contrast to this, automatic and register variables usually are not initialized by the system. This means they start with garbage values. Although some C systems do initialize automatic variables to zero, this feature should not be relied on; to do so makes the code nonportable.

8.9   AN EXAMPLE: PROCESSING CHARACTERS

A function that uses a `return` statement can pass back to the calling environment a single value. If more than one value is needed in the calling environment, then addresses must be passed as arguments to the function. To illustrate this idea, let us write a program that processes characters in a particular way. Here is what we want to accomplish:

> Read characters from the input stream until `EOF` is encountered.
>
> Change any lowercase letter to an uppercase letter.
>
> Print three words to a line with a single space between each word.
>
> Count the number of characters and the number of letters printed.

In this program we will consider a word to be a sequence of nonwhite space characters of maximal length. Here is main():

```
#include <stdio.h>
#include <ctype.h>

#define   NWORDS   3                    /* number of words per line */

int    process(int *, int *, int *);

main()
{
    int    c, nchars = 0, nletters = 0;

    while ((c = getchar()) != EOF)
        if (process(&c, &nchars, &nletters) == 1)
            putchar(c);
    printf("\n%s%5d\n%s%5d\n\n",
        "Number of characters:", nchars,
        "Number of letters:   ", nletters);
}
```

The processing of each character takes place in the function process(). Since the values of the variables c, nchars, and nletters are to be changed in the calling environment, addresses of these variables are passed as arguments to process(). Notice that c is an int rather than a char. This is because c must eventually take on the special value EOF, which is not a character. Notice also that a character gets written to the screen only if process() returns the value 1. In this context we think of 1 as signaling that the character has been appropriately processed and that it is ready to print. We will use the value 0 to signal that the character is not to be printed. This case will occur when contiguous white space characters occur. Let us now see how process() does its work.

```
int process(int *p, int *nchars_ptr, int *nletters_ptr)
{
   static int   cnt = 0, last_char = ' ';

   if (isspace(last_char) && isspace(*p))
      return 0;
   if (isalpha(*p)) {
      ++*nletters_ptr;
      if (islower(*p))
         *p = toupper(*p);
   }
   else if (isspace(*p))
      if (++cnt % NWORDS == 0)
         *p = '\n';
      else
         *p = ' ';
   ++*nchars_ptr;
   last_char = *p;
   return 1;
}
```

Before we dissect this function, we want to show some output from the program. First we compile the program and put the executable code in the file *process*. Then we create a file called *data* with the following lines in it:

```
    she sells sea shells
by      the      seashore
```

Notice that we have deliberately put contiguous blanks into the file. Now, if we give the command

process < data

here is what appears on the screen:

```
SHE SELLS SEA
SHELLS BY THE
SEASHORE
Number of characters:   37
Number of letters:      30
```

DISSECTION OF THE *process()* FUNCTION

- ```
  int process(int *p, int *nchars_ptr, int *nletters_ptr)
  {
      static int   cnt = 0, last_char = ' ';
  ```

The type of the function is `int`, which means that it returns an `int` value. The parameters of the function are three pointers to `int`. Although we think of p as a pointer to a character, its declaration here should be consistent with its use in `main()`. The local variables `cnt` and `last_char` are of storage class `static`. Thus they will be initialized only once, and their values will be retained between function calls. If these variables were of storage class `auto`, they would be reinitialized every time the function is called.

- ```
  isspace(last_char)
  ```

The macro `isspace()` is defined in *ctype.h*. It returns a nonzero value (*true*) if its argument is a blank, tab, or newline.

- ```
  if (isspace(last_char) && isspace(*p))
      return 0;
  ```

If the last character seen was a white space character, and the character pointed to by p is also a white space character, the value 0 is returned to the calling environment. Back in the calling environment, that is, back in `main()`, when this value is received, the current character is not printed.

- ```
  if (isalpha(*p)) {
      ++*nletters_ptr;
      if (islower(*p))
          *p = toupper(*p);
  }
  ```

If the character pointed to by p is a letter, then we increment the value of the object pointed to by `nletters_ptr`. If, moreover, the value of the object pointed to by p is a lowercase letter, then the object pointed to by p is assigned the corresponding uppercase letter.

■ `+++*nletters_ptr;`

Let us consider this statement in some detail. The increment operator ++ and the indirection operator * are both unary and associate from right to left. Thus

```
++(*nletters_ptr);
```

is an equivalent statement. What is being incremented is the dereferenced value in the calling environment. Note carefully that the expression

`+++*nletters_ptr`   is not equivalent to   `*nletters_ptr++`

The latter expression is equivalent to

```
*(nletters_ptr++)
```

which causes the current pointer value to be dereferenced and then the pointer itself to be incremented. This is an instance of pointer arithmetic; see Chapter 9 for further discussion.

■
```
else if (isspace(*p))
    if (++cnt % NWORDS == 0)
        *p = '\n';
    else
        *p = ' ';
```

If the character pointed to by p is a white space character, then `last_char` cannot also be a white space character; we have already handled that case. No matter what this character is, we want to print a newline or a blank, depending on the incremented value of `cnt`. Since the symbolic constant NWORDS has the value 3, we print a newline every third time, and the other two times we print a blank. The effect of this is to print at most three words to a line, with a single blank between them.

■
```
+++*nchars_ptr;
last_char = *p;
return 1;
```

First we increment the value of the object pointed to by `nchars_ptr`. Then we assign to `last_char` the value of the object pointed to by p. Finally, we return the value 1 to the calling environment to indicate that a character is to be printed.

8.10 FUNCTION DECLARATIONS AND DEFINITIONS

To the compiler, function declarations are generated in various ways: by function invocation, by function definition, and by explicit declarations and prototypes. If a function call such as f(x) is encountered before any declaration, definition, or prototype for the function occurs, then the compiler assumes a default declaration of the form

```
int f();
```

Nothing is assumed about the parameter list for the function. Now suppose that the following function definition occurs first:

```
int f(x)         /* traditional C style */
double x;
{
    . . . . .
```

This provides both declaration and definition to the compiler. Again, nothing is assumed about the parameter list. It is the programmer's responsibility to pass only a single argument of type double. A function call such as f(1) can be expected to fail. Now suppose that, instead, we use the following new style definition:

```
int f(double x)     /* ANSI C style */
{
    . . . . .
```

The compiler now knows about the parameter list as well. In this case, if an int is passed as an argument, then it will be converted appropriately to a double.

A function prototype is a special case of a function declaration. A good programming style is to give either the function definition (new style), or the function prototype, or both before a function is used. A major reason for including standard header files is because they contain function prototypes.

There are certain limitations for function definitions and prototypes. The function storage class specifier, if present, can be either extern or static, but not both; auto and register cannot be used. The types "array of . . ." and "function returning . . ." cannot be returned by a function. However, a pointer representing an array or a function can be returned. The only storage class specifier that can occur in the parameter type list is register. Parameters cannot be initialized.

8.11   THE TYPE QUALIFIERS const AND volatile

The ANSI committee has added the keywords const and volatile to the C language. They are not available in traditional C. Since const and volatile are used in declarations to tell the compiler how identifiers can be used, they are called *type qualifiers*.

Let us first discuss how const gets used. Typically, in a declaration const comes after the storage class, if any, but before the type. Consider the declaration

```
static const int   k = 3;
```

We read this as "k is a constant int with static storage class." Since the type for k has been qualified by const, we can initialize k, but thereafter k cannot be assigned to, incremented, or decremented. Even though a variable has been qualified with const, it still cannot be used to specify an array size in another declaration.

```
const int   n = 3;
int         v[n];        /* the compiler will complain */
```

Thus a const-qualified variable is not equivalent to a symbolic constant.

An unqualified pointer should not be assigned the address of a const-qualified variable. The following code will cause the compiler to complain:

```
const int   a = 7;
int         *p = &a;     /* the compiler will complain */
```

The reason for this is that since p is an ordinary pointer to int, we could use it later in an expression such as ++*p. However, that would change the stored value of a, violating the concept that a is constant. If, on the other hand, we write

```
const int   a = 7;
const int   *p = &a;
```

then the compiler will be happy. The last declaration is read "p is a pointer to a constant int, and its initial value is the address of a." Note that p itself is not constant. We can assign it to some other address. We may not, however, assign a value to *p. The object pointed to by p should not be modified.

Suppose we want p itself to be constant, but not a. This is achieved with the declarations

```
int         a;
int * const   p = &a;
```

We read the last declaration as "p is a constant pointer to int, and its initial value is the address of a." Thereafter, we may not assign a value to p, but we may assign a value to *p. Now consider

```
const int        a = 7;
const int * const    p = &a;
```

The last declaration tells the compiler that p is a constant pointer to a constant int. Neither p nor *p can be assigned to, incremented, or decremented.

In contrast to const, the type qualifier volatile is seldom used. A volatile object is one that can be modified in some unspecified way by the hardware. Consider the declaration

```
extern const volatile int    real_time_clock;
```

The extern means "look for it elsewhere, either in this file or in some other file." The qualifier volatile indicates that the object may be acted on by the hardware. Since const is also a qualifier, the object may not be assigned to, incremented, or decremented within the program.

8.12   STYLE

One often finds p, q, and r used as identifiers for pointer variables in a program. This is a natural convention, with p standing for "pointer," and q and r being the next letters in the alphabet. In a similar fashion p1, p2, . . . are also used as identifiers for pointer variables. Other common ways to designate that an identifier is a pointer is to prepend p _ to a name, as in p_hi and p_lo, or to append _ptr, as in nchars_ptr.

An alternative declaration style for a pointer is

```
char* p;
```
                    which is equivalent to   `char *p;`

Some programmers prefer this style because the * is now more closely associated with the type being pointed to. One must be careful, however, because

```
char*    p, q, r;
```
                    is not equivalent to   `char    *p, *q, *r;`

Instead, it is equivalent to

```
char    *p, q, r;
```

Our next concern deals with functions that have a *side effect*. This occurs when a function call changes the stored value in memory of a variable in the calling environment. A good programming style is to effect such changes by using the `return` mechanism or the parameter mechanism. To illustrate these ideas, let us rewrite our *swap* program.

```
#include <stdio.h>

int     a = 3, b = 7;            /* global variables */
void    swap(void);             /* function prototype */

main()
{
    printf("%d %d\n", a, b);    /* 3 7 is printed */
    swap();
    printf("%d %d\n", a, b);    /* 7 3 is printed */
}
```

We have moved the declaration of a and b outside of `main()`, making these variables global. Now we rewrite the `swap()` function.

```
void swap(void)         /* very bad programming style */
{
    extern int    a, b;
    int           tmp;

    tmp = a;
    a = b;
    b = tmp;
}
```

The modification of the global variables a and b is a side effect of the function call `swap()`. With this programming style large programs can be very difficult to read and maintain. Ideally, one writes code that is locally intelligible.

8.13 COMMON PROGRAMMING ERRORS

Beginning programmers often make conceptual mistakes when learning to use pointers. A typical example of this is

```
int   *p = 3;
```

Here an attempt is being made to initialize the value of the object pointed to by p. But this is an initialization of p itself, and most likely not what was intended. Suppose that we try to fix this by writing

```
int   *p = &i, i = 3;
```

Now there is a more subtle error. C does not provide look-ahead capability. At the point where p is initialized to the address of i, space for the variable i has not yet been allocated. To correct this we can write

```
int   i = 3, *p = &i;
```

First space for i is allocated, and i is initialized to 3; then space for p is allocated, and p is initialized to the address of i.

When dealing with pointers, the programmer must learn to distinguish carefully between a pointer p and its dereferenced value *p. To minimize any chance for confusion, one should use names for pointer variables that indicate pointer usage. Here is an example of what *not* to do. Suppose that v1 and v2 are floating variables and that we want to interchange their values in the calling environment by the function call swap(&v1, &v2). To code swap() one could write

```
void swap(float *v1, float *v2)          /* poor style */
{
    . . . . .
```

But now there is confusion. In main(), the identifiers v1 and v2 are used as names of variables of type float, but in swap() the same identifiers are used as names of variables of type pointer to float. It would be much better to use p_v1 and p_v2. Using names that clearly indicate pointer usage helps the programmer minimize mistakes, and helps others who read the code to understand its intent.

Of course, not every value is stored in an accessible memory location. It is useful to keep in mind the following prohibitions:

Constructs *not* to be pointed at

Do not point at constants.

```
&3                              /* illegal */
```

Do not point at ordinary expressions.

```
&(k + 99)                       /* illegal */
```

Do not point at register variables.

```
register  v;
&v                              /* illegal */
```

The address operator can be applied to variables and array elements. If a is an array, then expressions such as &a[0] and &a[i+j+7] make sense (see Chapter 9).

One common use for a block is for debugging purposes. Imagine we are in a section of code where a variable, say v, is misbehaving. By inserting a block temporarily into the code, we can use local variables that do not interfere with the rest of the program.

```
{                               /* debugging starts here */
    static int   cnt = 0;

    printf("*** debug: cnt = %d   v = %d\n", ++cnt, v);
}
```

The variable cnt is local to the block. It will not interfere with another variable of the same name in an outer block. Since its storage class is static, it retains its old value when the block is reentered. Here, it is being used to count the number of times the block is executed. (Perhaps we are inside a for loop.) We are assuming that the variable v has been declared in an outer block, and is therefore known in this block. We are printing its value for debugging purposes. Later, after we have fixed our code, this block becomes extraneous, and we remove it.

8.14   SYSTEM CONSIDERATIONS

In traditional C, integer values can be assigned to a pointer, but in ANSI C, only the special value zero can be assigned to a pointer. This is true regardless of the pointer type. Some compilers issue an error message; others only issue a warning. They are all supposed to issue an error message, but many ANSI C compilers are used in an environment where both old and new C code must be compiled.

Programs that make explicit use of absolute addresses are frequently nonportable.

Different systems have different address spaces, and they may use their address spaces in noncompatible ways. If you must write programs with absolute addresses, it is best to use the `#define` facility to localize any possible system-dependent code.

Pointer expressions should not be of mixed type. As an example, suppose that `p` is of type pointer to `char` and `q` is of type pointer to `int`. Then the assignment expression `p = q` has mixed pointer type. Although such expressions are considered illegal in ANSI C, many compilers will only issue a warning. In Turbo C, for example, we get

```
Suspicious pointer conversion in . . .
```

The proper style is to use casts. For example, we could write

```
p = (char *) q;
```

When writing portable code, the programmer must heed all compiler warnings. What is a warning on one system may be prohibited on another.

In ANSI C, the `%p` format can be used in a `printf()` statement to print pointer values. Typically, these are hexadecimal numbers. This format is not available in some traditional C compilers.

The preferred placement of function prototypes is either in a header file that gets included or at the top of the file but after the `#include`'s, `#define`'s, and `typedef`'s. This gives the function prototypes file visibility. In ANSI C, function prototypes placed in a block (in the body of a function, for example) are supposed to have just the scope of that block. In traditional C, function declarations were often given file visibility no matter where they were placed in the file. Some ANSI C compilers continue to do this with respect to both function prototypes and function declarations, even though it is technically wrong to do so. In some instances this can cause porting difficulties.

8.15   SUMMARY

1   A pointer variable usually takes as values either NULL or addresses of other variables.

2   The address operator `&` and the indirection, or dereferencing, operator `*` are unary operators with the same precedence and right-to-left associativity as the other unary operators. If `v` is a variable, then the expression

```
*&v            is equivalent to            v
```

Remember, however, that if `v` has storage class `register`, then the operation `&v` is not allowed.

3 In C, the call-by-value mechanism is strictly adhered to. This means that when an expression occurs as an argument to a function, a copy of the value of the expression is made, and it is this copy that is passed to the function. Thus a function call such as f(v) by itself cannot change the stored value of v in the calling environment.

4 The effect of call-by-reference can be achieved by using pointers, the address operator &, and the dereferencing operator *.

5 To achieve the effect of call-by-reference, the programmer must use a pointer as a formal parameter in the header of the function definition. Then the assignment of a value to the deferenced pointer in the body of the function can change the value of a variable in the calling environment. When such a function is called, an address is passed as an actual argument.

6 The four storage classes are auto, extern, register, and static. The storage class auto is the most common. Automatic variables appear and disappear with block entry and exit. They can be hidden when an inner block redeclares an outer block identifier.

7 The keyword extern means "look for it elsewhere, either in this file or in some other."

8 All variables declared outside of functions have external storage class; the keyword extern does not have to occur. These variables may be used throughout the program. They can be hidden by redeclaration, but their values cannot be destroyed.

9 All functions have external storage class. The type specifier of a function is int unless explicitly declared otherwise. The type of the expression in the return statement must be compatible with the type of the function.

10 The storage class register can be used to try to improve execution speed. It is semantically equivalent to automatic.

11 The storage class static is used to preserve exit values of variables. It is also used to restrict the scope of external identifiers.

12 Scope rules are the visibility constraints associated with identifiers. The keyword static used with external identifiers provides a form of privacy that is very important for program modularity. Consider the following code:

```
static void f(int k)
{
    . . . . .
}

static int   a, b, c;
. . . . .
```

The function f() is known throughout this file but in no other. The variables a, b, and c are known only in this file, and only below the place where they are declared.

13 External and static variables that are not explicitly initialized by the programmer are initialized to zero by the system.

8.16   EXERCISES

1 What gets printed by the following code?

```
int    i = 5, *p = &i;

printf("%p %d %d %d %d\n", p, *p + 2, **&p, 3**p, **& p+4);
```

Note that we used the %p format to print a pointer value. All ANSI C compilers understand this format. What happens if you change the %p to %d? In UNIX, it probably will work, but in MS-DOS, it probably will fail. If MS-DOS is available to you, try the %u format as well.

2 Consider the following code:

```
char    c1 = 'A', c2 = 'B', tmp;
char    *p = &c1, *q = &c2;

tmp = *p;
*p = *q;
*q = tmp;
```

Draw a diagram of what is in memory after each of the declarations and statements has been executed.

3 Consider the code

```
double    *p, *q;

p = 3;
q = 7 - 5 - 2;
```

Your compiler should complain about one of these lines but not the other. Explain why. If you use pointers to int rather than pointers to double, will your compiler be any happier?

4 If i and j are int's, and p and q are pointers to int, which of the following assignment expressions are illegal?

```
p = &i          p = &*&i         i = (int) p      q = &p
*q = &j         i = (*&)j        i = *&*&j        i = (*p)++ + *q
```

5 Write a program with the declaration

```
char    a, b, c, *p, *q, *r;
```

that prints out the locations assigned to all these variables by your compiler. From the values that are printed out, can you tell how many bytes are allocated for each of the variables?

6 Write a function that shifts the stored value of five character variables in a circular fashion. Your function should work in the following way. Suppose that c1, c2, . . . , c5 are variables of type char, and suppose that the values of these variables are 'A', 'B', . . . , 'E', respectively. The function call shift(&c1, &c2, &c3, &c4, &c5) should cause the variables c1, c2, . . . , c5 to have the values 'B', 'C', 'D', 'E', 'A', respectively. Your function definition should start as follows:

```
void shift(char *p1, char *p2, char *p3, char *p4, char *p5)
{
    . . . . .
```

Test your function by calling it five times and printing out in turn BCDEA, CDEAB, DEABC, EABCD, and ABCDE.

7 Write a function that orders the stored values of three characters. Suppose, for example, that c1, c2, and c3 are character variables having the values 'C', 'B', and 'D', respectively. Then the function call order_chars(&c1, &c2, &c3) should cause the stored values of c1, c2, and c3 to be 'B', 'C', and 'D', respectively. Write a program that tests your function.

8 The program that we wrote to process characters in Section 8.9 is short enough so that one could do away with the function process() and write all the code in main(). Of course, we did the work in process() to illustrate how pointers can be used. Rewrite the program, making no use of pointers.

9 In Section 7.7, "Packing and Unpacking," we wrote the function unpack(). It can unpack 1 byte at a time from an int. Rewrite the function so that it unpacks all the bytes at once. On a machine with 4-byte words, begin your function as follows:

```
/* Unpack the packed int p into 4 characters. */

void unpack(int p, char *pa, char *pb, char *pc, char *pd)
{
    unsigned   mask = 255;      /* turn on the low-order byte */
    .....
```

Write a program to check your function. Your program should use the bit_print() function presented in Chapter 7.

10 How many bytes are used by your C system to store pointer variables? Does it take less space to store a pointer to char than to store a pointer to long double? Use the sizeof operator to find out. Write a program that prints a table of values that shows the number of bytes needed to store a pointer to each of the fundamental types.

11 Since the symbol * represents both the indirection operator and the multiplication operator, it is not always immediately clear what is intended. Consider the following code:

```
int    i = 2, j = 4, k = 6;
int    *p = &i, *q = &j, *r = &k;

printf("%d\n", * p * * q * * r);
printf("%d\n", ++ * p * -- * q * ++ * r);
```

What gets printed? Write down your answers, and then execute the code to check them. Rewrite the expressions in the printf() statements in two ways. First, remove all the blanks in the two expressions. Does your compiler get confused when you do this? Second, leave a blank around each binary operator, but remove the blanks between any unary operator and whatever it is operating on. Does your compiler produce the same answers as before? If you think formatting is for sissies, change all the multiplication operators to division and redo this exercise. It may give you a surprise!

12 The following program has a conceptual mistake; see if you can spot it.

```
#include <stdio.h>

#define    LUCKY_NUMBER 777

main()
{
    int    *p = LUCKY_NUMBER;

    printf("Is this my lucky number?  %d\n", *p);
}
```

On our system the program produces the following output:

```
Is this my lucky number?   24864
```

Can you explain this output?

13 Just as there are pointers to int, there are pointers to pointers to int. Write a test program with the declaration

```
int   v = 7, *p = &v, **q = &p;
```

The identifier q is a pointer to pointer to int, and its initial value is the address of p. To test this concept, use the statement

```
printf("%d\n%d\n%d\n", q, *q, **q);
```

to print some values. Does an expression such as q == &p make sense? Include this expression in your test program. *Caution:* If you are using the MS-DOS operating system, then you must be careful when printing pointer values. The %p format can be expected to work, and of course it will work in UNIX as well. The %u format will work in the small memory model, but not in the larger memory models. Try the following code:

```
printf("%p\n%p\n%d\n", q, *q, **q);
printf("---\n");
printf("%u\n%u\n%u\n", q, *q, **q);
```

When you examine your output, you will be able to tell if something is wrong.

14 In this exercise we continue with the ideas discussed in exercise 13. Consider the code

```
int   v = 7, *p = &v, **q = &p;

printf("%d\n%d\n%d\n%d\n%d\n%d\n%d\n%d\n",
     &v, *&v, &p, *&p, **&p, &q, *&q, **&q, ***&q);
```

The output has an interesting pattern. Can you explain why some of the numbers repeat? Notice that we have used the combination *&, but not &*. Are there situations where &* is semantically correct? *Caution:* In MS-DOS, try replacing all the %d formats with %u. If that does not seem right, replace all the %d formats with %p except for the second, the fifth, and the last.

15 Extend the ideas presented in exercise 14 by writing a test program where r is declared to be a pointer to pointer to pointer to int.

16 In ANSI C, at most one storage class can be specified in a declaration. What happens when you try the following code on your system?

```
#include <stdio.h>

static extern int   a = 1;

main()
{
    printf("a = %d\n", a);
}
```

The point of this exercise is that you want to use a static external variable, but the compiler will not let you declare one. What should you do?

17 If you use const in a declaration and then try to perform an inappropriate initialization or assignment, your compiler will complain. Whether it is an error or a warning is system-dependent. Try the following code on your system:

```
const float   x = 7.7;
float          *p = &x;    /* compiler error or warning? */

printf("x = %g\n", *p);
```

Rewrite the code, keeping the const but at the same time making the compiler happy.

9

ARRAYS AND POINTERS

9.1   ONE-DIMENSIONAL ARRAYS
         INITIALIZATION
         SUBSCRIPTING
9.2   AN EXAMPLE: COUNTING EACH LETTER SEPARATELY
9.3   THE RELATIONSHIP BETWEEN ARRAYS AND POINTERS
9.4   POINTER ARITHMETIC AND ELEMENT SIZE
9.5   PASSING ARRAYS TO FUNCTIONS
9.6   A SORTING ALGORITHM: BUBBLE SORT
9.7   MULTIDIMENSIONAL ARRAYS
         TWO-DIMENSIONAL ARRAYS
         TWO-DIMENSIONAL ARRAYS AND FUNCTIONS
         THREE-DIMENSIONAL ARRAYS
         INITIALIZATION
9.8   DYNAMIC MEMORY ALLOCATION
9.9   STYLE
9.10   COMMON PROGRAMMING ERRORS
9.11   SYSTEM CONSIDERATIONS
9.12   SUMMARY
9.13   EXERCISES

An array is a sequence of data items that are of the same type, indexable, and stored contiguously. Typically, arrays are a data type that is used to represent a large number of homogeneous values. The elements of an array are accessed by the use of subscripts. Arrays of all types are possible, including arrays of arrays. Strings are just arrays of characters, but they are sufficiently important to be treated separately in the next chapter.

A typical array declaration allocates memory starting from a base address. The array name is in effect a pointer constant to this base address. This chapter carefully explains this relationship of array to address. Another key point is how to pass arrays as parameters to functions. A number of carefully worked examples illustrate these points.

9.1 ONE-DIMENSIONAL ARRAYS

Programs often use homogeneous data. For example, if we want to manipulate some grades, we might declare

```
int    grade0, grade1, grade2;
```

However, if the number of grades is large, it is cumbersome to represent and manipulate the data by means of unique identifiers. Instead, we can use an array, which is a derived type. Individual elements of the array are accessed using a subscript, also called an *index*. The brackets [ ] are used to contain the subscripts of an array. To use grade[0], grade[1], and grade[2] in a program, we would declare

```
int   grade[3];
```

where the integer 3 in the declaration represents the size of the array, or the number of elements in the array. The indexing of array elements always starts at 0. This is one of the characteristic features of the C language.

A one-dimensional array declaration is a type followed by an identifier with a bracketed constant integral expression. The value of the constant expression, which must be positive, is the size of the array; it specifies the number of elements in the array. To store the elements of the array, the compiler assigns an appropriate amount of memory, starting from a base address.

To illustrate some of these ideas, let us write a small program that fills an array, prints out values, and sums the elements of the array.

```
#include <stdio.h>

#define   N   5

main()
{
    int   a[N];               /* allocate space for a[0], ..., a[4] */
    int   i, sum = 0;

    for (i = 0; i < N; ++i)                    /* fill the array */
        a[i] = 7 + i * i;
    for (i = 0; i < N; ++i)                    /* print the array */
        printf("a[%d] = %d    ", i, a[i]);
    for (i = 0; i < N; ++i)                    /* sum the elements */
        sum += a[i];
    printf("\nsum = %d\n", sum);               /* print the sum */
}
```

The output of this program is

```
a[0] = 7    a[1] = 8    a[2] = 11    a[3] = 16    a[4] = 23
sum = 65
```

The array a requires space in memory to store four integer values. Let us suppose that our machine stores an int in 4 bytes. If a[0] is stored at location 1000, then the remaining array elements are stored successively at locations 1004, 1008, 1012, and 1016.

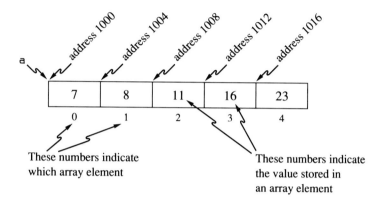

It is considered good programming practice to define the size of an array as a symbolic constant. Since much of the code may depend on this value, it is convenient to be able to change a single #define line to process arrays of different sizes. Notice how the various parts of the for statement are neatly tailored to provide a terse notation for dealing with array computations.

INITIALIZATION

Arrays may be of storage class automatic, external, static, or constant, but not register. As with simple variables, arrays can be initialized within a declaration. An *array initializer* is a sequence of initializing values written as a brace-enclosed, comma-separated list. An example is

```
float   x[7] = {-1.1, 0.2, 33.0, 4.4, 5.05, 0.0, 7.7};
```

This initializes x[0] to -1.1, x[1] to 0.2, and so forth. When a list of initializers is shorter than the number of array elements to be initialized, the remaining elements are initialized to zero. If an external or static array is not initialized, then the system initializes all elements to zero automatically. Uninitialized automatic and constant arrays start with garbage values—that is, with arbitrary values that happen to be in memory when the array is allocated. In traditional C only external and static arrays could be initialized using an array initializer. ANSI C allows automatic and constant arrays to be initialized as well.

If an array is declared without a size and is initialized to a series of values, it is implicitly given the size of the number of initializers. Thus

```
int a[] = {3, 4, 5, 6};          and          int a[4] = {3, 4, 5, 6};
```

are equivalent declarations.

SUBSCRIPTING

Assume that a declaration of the form

```
int   i, a[size];
```

has been made. Then we can write a[i] to access an element of the array. More generally, we may write a[*expr*], where *expr* is an integral expression, to access an element of the array. We call *expr* a *subscript*, or *index*, of a. The value of a subscript must lie in the range 0 to *size* − 1. An array subscript value outside this range will cause a run-time error. When this happens, the condition is called "overrunning the bounds of the array" or "subscript out of bounds." It is a common programming error. The effect of the error is system-dependent and can be quite confusing. One frequent result is that the value of some unrelated variable will be returned or modified. Thus the programmer must ensure that all subscripts stay within bounds.

9.2   AN EXAMPLE: COUNTING EACH LETTER SEPARATELY

In previous chapters we showed how to count digits, letters, and so on. By using an array, we can easily count the occurrence of each uppercase letter separately. Here is a program that does this.

```
/* Count each uppercase letter separately. */

#include <stdio.h>
#include <ctype.h>

main()
{
    int   c, i, letter[26];

    for (i = 0; i < 26; ++i)          /* initialize array to zero */
        letter[i] = 0;
    while ((c = getchar()) != EOF)    /* count the letters */
        if (isupper(c))
            ++letter[c - 'A'];
    for (i = 0; i < 26; ++i) {        /* print the results */
        if (i % 6 == 0)
            printf("\n");
        printf("%5c:%4d", 'A' + i, letter[i]);
    }
    printf("\n\n");
}
```

Among our files is one that contains the current version of this chapter. If we compile the program into *cnt_abc* and then give the command

  cnt_abc < chapter9

the following appears on the screen:

```
A:  75   B:  52   C: 219   D:  14   E: 121   F:  13
G:   9   H:  13   I: 121   J:   1   K:   1   L:  39
M:  25   N:  44   O:  38   P: 243   Q:   1   R:  37
S:  73   T:  96   U:   7   V:   3   W:  17   X:   9
Y:  11   Z:  27
```

DISSECTION OF THE *cnt_abc* PROGRAM

■ `int   c, i, letter[26];`

The count for each of the 26 capital letters will be stored in the array `letter`. It is important to remember that the elements of the array are `letter[0]`, `letter[1]`, . . . , `letter[25]`. Forgetting that array subscripting starts at 0 causes many errors. The variable `i` will be used as a subscript.

■ `for (i = 0; i < 26; ++i)          /* initialize array to zero */`
   `letter[i] = 0;`

Automatic arrays must be explicitly initialized. This `for` loop follows a standard pattern for processing all the elements of an array. It is a C programming cliché. The subscripting variable is initialized to 0. The termination test is to see if the upper bound is exceeded.

■ `while ((c = getchar()) != EOF)   /* count the letters */`
   `if (isupper(c))`
      `++letter[c - 'A'];`

The library function `getchar()` is used repeatedly to read a character in the input stream and assign its value to `c`. The `while` loop is exited when the end-of-file sentinel is detected. The macro `isupper()` from `<ctype.h>` is used to test whether `c` is an uppercase letter. If it is, then an appropriate element of the array `letter` is incremented.

■ `++letter[c - 'A'];`

This line of code is system-dependent. On ASCII machines the expression `c - 'A'` has the value 0 if `c` has the value `'A'`, the value 1 if `c` has the value `'B'`, and so forth. Thus the uppercase letter value of `c` is mapped into the range of values 0 to 25. Because brackets have higher precedence than `++`, an equivalent statement is

   `++(letter[c - 'A']);`

Thus we see that `letter[0]` is incremented if `c` has the value `'A'`, `letter[1]` is incremented if `c` has the value `'B'`, and so forth.

```
■ for (i = 0; i < 26; ++i) {          /* print the results */
      if (i % 6 == 0)
         printf("\n");
      printf("%5c:%4d", 'A' + i, letter[i]);
   }
```

Once again the same for loop cliché is used to process the array letter. Every sixth time through the loop, a newline is printed. As i runs from 0 to 25, the expression 'A' + i is used to print A through Z, with each letter followed by a colon and the appropriate count.

9.3   THE RELATIONSHIP BETWEEN ARRAYS AND POINTERS

An array name by itself is an address, or pointer value, and pointers and arrays are almost identical in terms of how they are used to access memory. However, there are differences, and these differences are subtle and important. A pointer is a variable that takes addresses as values. An array name is a particular fixed address that can be thought of as a constant pointer. When an array is declared, the compiler must allocate a base address and a sufficient amount of storage to contain all the elements of the array. The base address of the array is the initial location in memory where the array is stored; it is the address of the first element (index 0) of the array. Suppose that we write the declaration

```
#define   N   100

int   a[N], *p;
```

and that the system causes memory bytes numbered 300, 304, 308, . . . , 696 to be the addresses of a[0], a[1], a[2], ... , a[99], respectively, with location 300 being the base address of a. The two statements

```
    p = a;          and          p = &a[0];
```

are equivalent and would assign 300 to p. Pointer arithmetic provides an alternative to array indexing. The two statements

```
    p = a + 1;          and          p = &a[1];
```

are equivalent and would assign 304 to p. Assuming that the elements of a have been assigned values, we can use the following code to sum the array.

```
sum = 0;
for (p = a; p < &a[N]; ++p)
    sum += *p;
```

In this loop the pointer variable p is initialized to the base address of the array a. Then the successive values of p are equivalent to &a[0], &a[1], . . . , &a[N-1]. In general, if i is a variable of type int, then p + i is the *i*th offset from the address p. In a similar manner a + i is the *i*th offset from the base address of the array a. Here is another way of summing the array.

```
sum = 0;
for (i = 0; i < N; ++i)
    sum += *(a + i);
```

Just as the expression *(a + i) is equivalent to a[i], so is the expression *(p + i) equivalent to p[i]. Here is yet another way of summing the array.

```
p = a;
sum = 0;
for (i = 0; i < N; ++i)
    sum += p[i];
```

Although in many ways arrays and pointers can be treated alike, there is one essential difference. Because the array a is a constant pointer and not a variable, expressions such as

```
a = p          ++a          a += 2
```

are illegal. We cannot change the address of a.

9.4 POINTER ARITHMETIC AND ELEMENT SIZE

Pointer arithmetic is one of the powerful features of C. If the variable p is a pointer to a particular type, then the expression p + 1 yields the correct machine address for storing or accessing the next variable of that type. In a similar fashion pointer expressions such as p + i and ++p and p += i all make sense. If p and q are both pointing to elements of an array, then p - q yields the int value representing the number of array elements between p and q. Even though pointer expressions and arithmetic expressions have a similar appearance, there is a critical difference in interpretation between the two types of expressions. The following code illustrates the difference.

```
main()
{
    double   a[2], *p, *q;

    p = &a[0];                    /* points at base of array */
    q = p + 1;                    /* equivalent to q = &a[1]; */
    printf("%d\n", q - p);              /* 1 is printed */
    printf("%d\n", (int) q - (int) p);    /* 8 is printed */
}
```

What is printed by the last statement is system-dependent. On many systems a double is stored in 8 bytes. Hence the difference of the two machine addresses interpreted as integers is 8.

9.5   PASSING ARRAYS TO FUNCTIONS

In a function definition a formal parameter that is declared as an array is actually a pointer. When an array is being passed, its base address is passed call-by-value. The array elements themselves are not copied. As a notational convenience, the compiler allows array bracket notation to be used in declaring pointers as parameters. To illustrate this, we write a function that sums the elements of an array of type int.

```
int sum(int a[], int n)   /* n is the size of the array */
{
    int   i, s = 0;

    for (i = 0; i < n; ++i)
        s += a[i];
    return s;
}
```

As part of the header of a function definition, the declaration

    `int a[];`   is equivalent to   `int *a;`

On the other hand, as declarations within the body of a function, they are *not* equivalent. The first will create a constant pointer (and no storage), whereas the second will create a pointer variable.

Suppose that v has been declared to be an array with 100 elements of type `int`. After the elements have been assigned values, we can use the above function `sum()` to add various of the elements of v. The following table illustrates some of the possibilities:

Various ways that sum() might be called

Invocation	What gets computed and returned
sum(v, 100)	v[0] + v[1] + ··· + v[99]
sum(v, 88)	v[0] + v[1] + ··· + v[87]
sum(&v[7], k - 7)	v[7] + v[8] + ··· + v[k - 1]
sum(v + 7, 2 * k)	v[7] + v[8] + ··· + v[2 * k + 6]

The last function call illustrates again the use of pointer arithmetic. The base address of v is offset by 7, and `sum()` initializes the local pointer variable a to this address. This causes all address calculations inside the function call to be similarly offset.

9.6   A SORTING ALGORITHM: BUBBLE SORT

Algorithms that order information are critical to searching large databases. Think of the dictionary or the telephone book. In both cases it is relatively easy and convenient to look up information, because the information is sorted in alphabetic, or lexicographic, order. Sorting is a very useful problem solving technique. Moreover, the question of how to sort efficiently is an important area of study in its own right.

Efficient sorting algorithms typically require on the order of $n \log n$ comparisons to sort an array with n elements. A bubble sort is inefficient because it requires n^2 comparisons. Nonetheless, for small arrays its performance is usually acceptable. After we present the code for `bubble()`, we will illustrate in detail how the function works on a particular array of integers. We will use the function `swap()`, written in Chapter 8.

```
void  swap(int *, int *);

void bubble(int a[], int n)       /* n is the size of a[] */
{
    int   i, j;

    for (i = 0; i < n - 1; ++i)
        for (j = n - 1; i < j; --j)
            if (a[j-1] > a[j])
                swap(&a[j-1], &a[j]);
}
```

Suppose we declare

```
int    a[] = {7, 3, 66, 3, -5, 22, -77, 2};
```

and then invoke bubble(a, 8). The following table shows the elements of the array a[] after each pass of the outer loop:

Unordered data:	7	3	66	3	−5	22	−77	2
First pass:	−77	7	3	66	3	−5	22	2
Second pass:	−77	−5	7	3	66	3	2	22
Third pass:	−77	−5	2	7	3	66	3	22
Fourth pass:	−77	−5	2	3	7	3	66	22
Fifth pass:	−77	−5	2	3	3	7	22	66
Sixth pass:	−77	−5	2	3	3	7	22	66
Seventh pass:	−77	−5	2	3	3	7	22	66

At the start of the first pass, a[6] is compared with a[7]. Since the values are in order, they are not exchanged. Then a[5] is compared with a[6], and since these values are out of order, they are exchanged. Then a[4] is compared with a[5], and so forth. Adjacent out-of-order values are exchanged. The effect of the first pass is to "bubble" the smallest value in the array into the element a[0]. In the second pass a[0] is not examined and therefore left unchanged, while a[6] is compared first with a[7], and so forth. After the second pass, the next to the smallest value is in a[1]. Since each pass bubbles the next smallest element to its appropriate array position, the algorithm after n - 1 passes will have put all the elements in order. Notice that in this example all the elements have been ordered after the fifth pass. It is possible to modify the algorithm to terminate earlier by adding a variable that detects if no exchanges are made in a given pass (see exercise 7).

9.7   MULTIDIMENSIONAL ARRAYS

The C language allows arrays of any type, including arrays of arrays. With two bracket pairs, we obtain a two-dimensional array. This idea can be iterated to obtain arrays of higher dimension. With each bracket pair, we add another array dimension.

Examples of declarations of arrays	*Remarks*
int a[100];	a one-dimensional array
int b[2][7];	a two-dimensional array
int c[5][3][2];	a three-dimensional array

A k-dimensional array has a size for each of its k dimensions. If we let s_i represent the size of its ith dimension, then the declaration of the array will allocate space for $s_1 \times s_2 \times \cdots \times s_k$ elements. In the above table, b has 2×7 elements, and c has $5 \times 3 \times 2$ elements. Starting at the base address of the array, all the array elements are stored contiguously in memory.

TWO-DIMENSIONAL ARRAYS

Even though array elements are stored contiguously one after the other, it is often convenient to think of a two-dimensional array as a rectangular collection of elements with rows and columns. For example, if we declare

```
int   a[3][5];
```

then we can think of the array elements arranged as follows:

	col 1	*col 2*	*col 3*	*col 4*	*col 5*
row 1	a[0][0]	a[0][1]	a[0][2]	a[0][3]	a[0][4]
row 2	a[1][0]	a[1][1]	a[1][2]	a[1][3]	a[1][4]
row 3	a[2][0]	a[2][1]	a[2][2]	a[2][3]	a[2][4]

To illustrate these ideas, let us write a program that fills a two-dimensional array, prints out values, and sums the elements of the array.

```
#include <stdio.h>

#define   M   3      /* number of rows */
#define   N   4      /* number of columns */

main()
{
    int   a[M][N], i, j, sum = 0;

    for (i = 0; i < M; ++i)         /* fill the array */
        for (j = 0; j < N; ++j)
            a[i][j] = i + j;
    for (i = 0; i < M; ++i) {       /* print array values */
        for (j = 0; j < N; ++j)
            printf("a[%d][%d] = %d    ", i, j, a[i][j]);
        printf("\n");
    }
    for (i = 0; i < M; ++i)         /* sum the array */
        for (j = 0; j < N; ++j)
            sum += a[i][j];
    printf("\nsum = %d\n\n", sum);
}
```

The output of this program is

```
a[0][0] = 0    a[0][1] = 1    a[0][2] = 2    a[0][3] = 3
a[1][0] = 1    a[1][1] = 2    a[1][2] = 3    a[1][3] = 4
a[2][0] = 2    a[2][1] = 3    a[2][2] = 4    a[2][3] = 5

sum = 30
```

In processing every element of a multidimensional array, each dimension requires a single for loop.

Because of the relationship between arrays and pointers, there are numerous ways to access elements of a two-dimensional array.

Expressions equivalent to a[i][j]

```
*(a[i] + j)
(*(a + i))[j]
*((*(a + i)) + j)
*(&a[0][0] + 5*i + j)
```

The parentheses are necessary because the brackets [ ] have higher precedence than the indirection operator *. We can think of a[i] as the *i*th row of a (counting from 0), and we can think of a[i][j] as the element in the *i*th row, *j*th column of the array (counting from 0). The array name a by itself is equivalent to &a[0]; it is a pointer to an array of 5 int's. The base address of the array is &a[0][0], not a. Starting at the base address of the array, the compiler allocates contiguous space for 15 int's. For any array, the mapping between pointer values and array indices is called the *storage mapping function*. For the array a, the storage mapping function is specified by noting that

a[i][j]   is equivalent to   *(&a[0][0] + 5*i + j)

TWO-DIMENSIONAL ARRAYS AND FUNCTIONS

When a multidimensional array is a formal parameter in a function definition, all sizes except the first must be specified, so that the compiler can determine the correct storage mapping function. After the elements of the array a given above have been assigned values, the following function can be used to sum the elements of the array. Note carefully that the column size must be specified.

```
int sum(int a[][5])
{
    int   i, j, sum = 0;

    for (i = 0; i < 3; ++i)
       for (j = 0; j < 5; ++j)
          sum += a[i][j];
    return sum;
}
```

In the header of the function definition, the following parameter declarations are equivalent:

int a[][5]   int (*a)[5]   int a[3][5]

Because of operator precedence, the parentheses are necessary. The constant 3 acts as a reminder to human readers of the code, but the compiler disregards it.

THREE-DIMENSIONAL ARRAYS

Arrays of dimension higher than two work in a similar fashion. Let us describe how three-dimensional arrays work. If we declare

```
int   a[7][9][2];
```

then the compiler will allocate space for $7 \times 9 \times 2$ contiguous int 's. The base address of the array is &a[0][0][0], and the storage mapping function is specified by noting that

a[i][j][k]   is equivalent to   *(&a[0][0][0] + 9*2*i + 2*j + k)

If an expression such as a[i][j][k] is used in a program, the compiler uses the storage mapping function to generate object code to access the correct array element in memory. Although normally it is not necessary to do so, the programmer can make direct use of the storage mapping function. Here is a function that will sum the elements of the array a:

```
int sum(int a[][9][2])
{
    int   i, j, k, sum = 0;

    for (i = 0; i < 7; ++i)
        for (j = 0; j < 9; ++j)
            for (k = 0; k < 2; ++k)
                sum += a[i][j][k];
    return sum;
}
```

In the header of the function definition, the following parameter declarations are equivalent:

```
int a[][9][2]       int a[7][9][2]       int (*a)[9][2]
```

The constant 7 acts as a reminder to human readers of the code, but the compiler disregards it. The other two constants are needed by the compiler to generate the correct storage mapping function.

INITIALIZATION

There are a number of ways to initialize a multidimensional array. Let us begin our discussion by considering the following three initializations, which are equivalent:

```
int   a[2][3] = {1, 2, 3, 4, 5, 6};
int   a[2][3] = {{1, 2, 3}, {4, 5, 6}};
int   a[ ][3] = {{1, 2, 3}, {4, 5, 6}};
```

If there are no inner braces, then each of the array elements a[0][0], a[0][1], . . . , a[1][2] is initialized in turn. Note that the indexing is by rows. If there are fewer initializers than elements in the array, then the remaining elements are initialized to zero. If the first bracket pair is empty, then the compiler takes the size from the number of inner brace pairs. All sizes except the first must be given explicitly.

Now consider the initialization

```
int   a[2][2][3] = {
         {{1, 1, 0}, {2, 0, 0}},
         {{3, 0, 0}, {4, 4, 0}}
      };
```

An equivalent initialization is given by

```
int   a[][2][3] = {{{1, 1}, {2}}, {{3}, {4, 4}}};
```

If the initializers are fully and consistently braced, then wherever there are not enough initializers listed, the remaining elements are initialized to zero.

In general, if an array of storage class automatic is not explicitly initialized, then array elements start with garbage values. Static and external arrays, however, are initialized to zero by default. Here is a simple way to initialize all array elements to zero:

```
int   a[2][2][3] = {0};
```

9.8   DYNAMIC MEMORY ALLOCATION

C provides calloc() and malloc() in the standard library for dynamic memory allocation. The function prototypes are in *stdlib.h*. Rather than having an array size given by a specific constant in a program, it may be desirable to allow the user to input the array size, or to obtain the array size in a computation. A function call of the form calloc(*n*, *object_size*)

returns a pointer to enough space in memory to store *n* objects, each of *object_size* bytes. Both *n* and *object_size* should be positive. If the system is unable to allocate the requested memory, the pointer value NULL is returned.

In ANSI C, the type size_t is given by a typedef in *stdlib.h*. Typically, the type is *unsigned*, but it can vary from one system to another. This type definition is used in the function prototypes for calloc() and malloc():

```
void    *calloc(size_t, size_t);
void    *malloc(size_t);
```

Since the pointer returned by the functions has type void *, it can be assigned to other pointers without casting. The storage set aside by calloc() is automatically initialized to zero, whereas the storage set aside by malloc() is not initialized, and therefore starts with garbage values. The name calloc comes from "contiguous allocation." The name malloc comes from "memory allocation."

To illustrate the use of calloc(), let us write a small program that prompts the user to input an array size interactively.

```
#include <stdio.h>
#include <stdlib.h>

main()
{
    int    *a, i, n, sum = 0;

    printf("\n%s",
        "An array will be created dynamically.\n\n"
        "Input an array size n followed by n integers:  ");
    scanf("%d", &n);
    a = calloc(n, sizeof(int));      /* allocate space for n int's */
    for (i = 0; i < n; ++i)
        scanf("%d", &a[i]);
    for (i = 0; i < n; ++i)
        sum += a[i];
    free(a);                         /* free the space */
    printf("\n%s%7d\n%s%7d\n\n",
        " Number of elements:", n,
        "Sum of the elements:", sum);
}
```

Notice that we invoked free(a) to release the space allocated by calloc() back to the system. In this small program, this is not necessary; the space will be released when the program exits. The function prototype for free() is given in *stdlib.h* as

```
void    free(void *ptr);
```

Space allocated by calloc() and malloc() remains in use for the duration of the program unless it is explicitly released by the programmer. Space is *not* released on function exit.

In the above program, we allocated space dynamically for the array a by using calloc(). Here is the line that we typed:

```
a = calloc(n, sizeof(int));    /* allocate space for n int's */
```

Instead of using calloc(), we could have used malloc(). To do so we would write

```
a = malloc(n * sizeof(int));    /* allocate space for n int's */
```

The only difference is that malloc() does not initialize the allocated space to zero. Since our program did not require the array to be initialized to zero, we could just as well have used malloc(). For arrays, however, we tend to use calloc().

9.9   STYLE

As the examples of this chapter have shown, it is often desirable to use a symbolic constant to define the size of an array. This constant allows the programmer to make a single modification if code is needed to process an array of a different size.

A for loop that is to be used to do ten things repetitively can be written

```
for (i = 1; i <= 10; ++i)
    . . . . .
```

or it can be written

```
for (i = 0; i < 10; ++i)
    . . . . .
```

Which form is used depends on just what is in the body of the loop. However, in cases where either form can be used, C programmers generally favor the second form. The reason for this is clear: When dealing with arrays, the second form is the correct programming idiom. Because arrays are used extensively in programming tasks, most experienced C programmers begin counting from 0 rather than 1.

A generally important style consideration is to structure a program so that each elementary task is accomplished by its own function. This approach is at the heart of structured programming. However, this can lead to inefficient code when processing arrays. Let us look at a specific example.

```c
/* Compute various statistics. */

#include <stdio.h>

#define   N   10                    /* size of the array */

double   average(double *, int);
double   maximum(double *, int);
double   sum(double *, int);

main()
{
   int       i;
   double    a[N];

   printf("Input %d numbers:  ", N);
   for (i = 0; i < N; ++i)
      scanf("%lf", &a[i]);
   printf("\n%s%5d\n%s%7.1f\n%s%7.1f\n%s%7.1f\n\n",
      "      Array size:", N,
      "Maximum element:", maximum(a, N),
      "         Average:", average(a, N),
      "             Sum:", sum(a, N));
```

We have written main() so that it calls three other functions, each one computing a desired value. Let us write these functions next.

```
double maximum(double a[], int n)
{
    int      i;
    double   max = a[0];

    for (i = 0; i < n; ++i)
        if (max < a[i])
            max = a[i];
    return max;
}


double average(double a[], int n)
{
    return (sum(a, n) / (double) n);
}


double sum(double a[], int n)
{
    int      i;
    double   s = 0.0;

    for (i = 0; i < n; ++i)
        s += a[i];
    return s;
}
```

Two of these three functions use a for loop to process the elements of an array, and average() calls sum() to do its work. For the sake of efficiency, we could restructure our program as follows. First we rewrite main().

```
/* Compute various statistics more efficiently. */

#include <stdio.h>

#define    N    10

void    stats(double *, int, double *, double *, double *);

main()
{
    int     i;
    double  a[N], average, max, sum;

    printf("Input %d numbers:  ", N);
    for (i = 0; i < N; ++i)
        scanf("%lf", &a[i]);
    stats(a, N, &average, &max, &sum);
    printf("\n%s%5d\n%s%7.1f\n%s%7.1f\n%s%7.1f\n\n",
    "    Array size:", N,
    "Maximum element:", max,
    "        Average:", average,
    "            Sum:", sum);
}
```

Now we write the function stats(), using a single for loop to compute all the desired values.

```
void stats(double a[], int n,
          double *p_average,
          double *p_max,
          double *p_sum)
{
    int    i;

    *p_max = *p_sum = a[0];
    for (i = 1; i < n; ++i) {
        *p_sum += a[i];
        if (*p_max < a[i])
            *p_max = a[i];
    }
    *p_average = *p_sum / (double) n;
}
```

The second version avoids repeated function-call overhead. It calls stats() once in place of the 3×N function calls of the first version. This example is so small that efficiency is not really an issue. However, when code is to be used in a serious working environment, the ideas that we have presented are often relevant. In general, along with clarity and correctness, efficiency is an important consideration in programming.

9.10 COMMON PROGRAMMING ERRORS

The most common programming error with arrays is using a subscript value that is out of bounds. Suppose that 10 is the size of an array a[] of integers. If we were to write

```
sum = 0;
for (i = 1; i <= 10; ++i)
   sum += a[i];
```

we would get an error. The value at the address corresponding to a[10] would be used, but the value in memory at this address would be unpredictable.

In many programming languages, when an array of size n is declared, the corresponding subscript range is from 1 to n. It is very important to remember that C uses 0 as a lower bound and $n - 1$ as an upper bound. Bounds-checking is an important programming skill to cultivate. It is often useful to hand-simulate programs on small arrays before processing very large arrays.

When the programmer uses dynamic memory allocation, a common programming error is to forget to release space. In small programs this usually is not a problem. If, however, we are in a loop and we repeatedly allocate space, use it, and then forget to release it, the program can fail unexpectedly because no more space is available.

9.11 SYSTEM CONSIDERATIONS

If efficiency is an issue, then programmers prefer

malloc(n * sizeof(*something*))   instead of   calloc(n, sizeof(*something*))

unless the allocated space must be initialized to zero. For most programs, the difference in execution time is not noticeable.

Space in memory is a limited resource. When calloc() or malloc() is invoked to allocate space dynamically, the programmer should check to see that the call succeeded. The following code shows how this can be done with `calloc()`:

```
int    *a, n;

.....                                   /* get n from somewhere */
if ((a = calloc(n, sizeof(int)) == NULL) {
   printf("\nERROR: calloc() failed - bye!\n\n");
   exit(1);
}
```

If we are writing a lot of code, and we need to call `calloc()` and `malloc()` repeatedly, then we write graceful versions of these functions. Here is a graceful version of `calloc()`:

```
void *gcalloc(size_t n, size_t sizeof_something)     /* graceful function */
{
   void    *p;

   if ((p = calloc(n, sizeof_something)) == NULL) {
      printf("\nERROR: calloc() failed - bye!\n\n");
      exit(1);
   }
   return p;
}
```

In any serious coding effort, graceful functions are essential. We will see this idea again in Section 14.7 in Chapter 14.

9.12 SUMMARY

1 An array is a sequence of data items that are of the same type, indexable, and stored contiguously. Arrays can be used to deal with a large number of homogeneous values. A declaration such as

```
int    a[100];
```

makes a an array of `int`'s. The compiler allocates contiguous space in memory for 100 `int`'s and numbers the elements of a from 0 to 99.

2　Elements of the array are accessed by expressions such as a[i]. More generally, we can use a[*expr*], where the subscript, or index, *expr* is an integral expression having a nonnegative value that does not overrun the upper bound of a. It is the programmer's responsibility to make sure that an array index stays within bounds.

3　When an array name is passed as an argument to a function, only a copy of the base address of the array is actually passed. In the header to a function definition, the declaration

```
int   a[];           is equivalent to           int   *a;
```

In the header to a function definition, the declaration of a multidimensional array must have all sizes specified except the first (see exercise 9).

4　An array can be initialized by assigning an appropriate-length list of values within braces. If an external or static array is declared but not initialized, then all the elements of the array are automatically initialized to zero. Automatic arrays that are not initialized start with garbage values.

5　Arrays of any type can be created, including arrays of arrays. For example,

```
double   a[30][50];
```

declares a to be an array of "array of 50 double's." The elements of a are accessed by expressions such as a[i][j].

9.13　EXERCISES

1　Explain the following terms:
   (a) lower bound
   (b) subscript
   (c) out of bounds

2　The following array declarations have several errors. Identify each of them.

```
#define   SIZE   4

main()
{
    int   a[SIZE] = {0, 2, 2, 3, 4};
    int   b[SIZE - 5];
    int   c[3.0];
    . . . . .
```

3   Write a function that sums the even-indexed elements and odd-indexed elements of an array of double's separately. Each element of the array contributes to one of the two sums, depending on whether the index of the element is even or odd. Your function definition should look something like

```
void sum(double a[],
        int   n,                        /* n is the size of a[] */
        double *even_index_sum_ptr,
        double *odd_index_sum_ptr)
{
    . . . . .
```

4   Write a function that computes two sums from the elements of an array of integers. Each element of the array contributes to one of the two sums, depending on whether the element itself is even or odd. Your function definition should look something like

```
void sum(int a[],
        int n,
        int *even_element_sum_ptr,
        int *odd_element_sum_ptr)
{
    . . . . .
```

5   Modify the *cnt_abc* program to also count each lowercase letter separately.

6   This exercise is designed to test your understanding of pointer arithmetic. Suppose that SIZE is a symbolic constant with value 100. If we make the declaration

```
char    a[SIZE], *p = a;
int     i;
```

then the compiler allocates 100 bytes of contiguous storage in memory, with the array name a pointing to the base address of this storage. We are deliberately using an array of char's, because each char is stored in 1 byte. The pointer p is initialized to have the same value as a. Now we want to fill the array in a very simple way.

```
for (i = 0; i < SIZE; ++i)
   a[i] = i;
```

The elements of the array have been assigned the consecutive values 0, 1, 2, ..., 99. Now consider

```
printf("%d\n", *(p + 3));
printf("%d\n", *(char *)((int *) p + 3));
printf("%d\n", *(char *)((double *) p + 3));
```

What gets printed? The answer to this question is system-dependent. Explain why this is so, and explain what would get printed on a machine different from your own. *Hint:* Consider the expression

```
(int *) p + 3
```

Of the two operators that are acting, which has the higher precedence? Use this information to help you determine which element of the array this pointer expression is pointing to. Now consider

```
(char *) pointer_expression
```

This casts the pointer expression to be a pointer to char. Now consider

```
*(char *) pointer_expression
```

How do the two unary operators that are acting associate?

7   Write a program that uses the bubble() function to sort an array of integers. Write another version of your program, modifying bubble() so that it terminates after the first pass in which no two elements are interchanged. Time the two versions of your program. Which version is faster?

8   Write a program that finds the maximum and minimum elements of a two-dimensional array. Do all of this within main(). See the next exercise.

9   Rewrite the program that you wrote for exercise 8, using a function that has a two-dimensional array in its parameter list. *Hint:* When a multidimensional array occurs as a parameter in a header to a function definition, the size for each dimension, except the first dimension, must be specified. The effect of this is to hard-wire the function so that it can be used only for certain arrays. Consider

```
double sum(double a[][5], int m)      /* m is the number of rows */
{
    .....
```

In this example we specified 5 as the column size of a. This information is needed by the compiler to handle expressions of the form a[i][j] within the function. We can invoke this function by writing sum(a, 3) if a is a 3-by-5 array in the calling environment, or we can write sum(a, 7) if a is a 7-by-5 array in the calling environment. In general, we can pass to sum() any *n*-by-5 array. From all of this you may gather that C does not handle multidimensional arrays gracefully, but that is not true. There is more to the story. However, since it involves a more sophisticated use of pointers, we cannot tell the rest of the story here.

10 Write a program that keeps sales data for 10 years by month. The array should have a month index of size 12. Given this data, compute by sorted order the months of the year for which sales are best.

11 There are many known sorting methods. Here is the heart of a simple transposition sort.

```
for (i = 0; i < SIZE; ++i)
    for (j = i + 1; j < SIZE; ++j)
        if (a[i] > a[j])
            swap(&a[i], &a[j]);
```

Write a program that implements this sort. After your program is working, modify it so that all the elements of the array are printed after each pass of the outer loop. Suppose, for example, that the size of your array is 8, and that its starting values are

   7   3   66   3   −5   22   −77   2

Your program should print the following on the screen:

```
Unordered data:     7     3    66     3    -5    22   -77     2
   After pass 1:   -77     7    66     3     3    22    -5     2
   After pass 2:   -77    -5    66     7     3    22     3     2
   . . . . .
```

12 The output of the program that you wrote for exercise 11 illustrated the effects of a particular sorting method acting on a particular array. In this exercise we want to dig a little deeper. Modify the program that you wrote for exercise 11 so that every time two elements are interchanged, the array is written out with the interchanges underlined. With the array of size 8 previously suggested, your program should print the following on the screen:

```
 3     7    66    3    -5    22   -77    2
--    --

-5     7    66    3     3    22   -77    2
--                --
```

. . . . .

13 Write a program that reads *n* integers into an array, and then prints on a separate
line the value of each distinct element along with the number of times that it occurs.
The values should be printed in descending order. Suppose, for example, that you
input the values

```
-7  3  3  -7  5  5  3
```

as the elements of your array. Then your program should print

```
5 occurs 2 times
3 occurs 3 times
-7 occurs 2 times
```

Use your program to investigate the output of rand(). First use rand() to create a
file, say *rand_out*, containing 100 random integers in the range 1 to 10. Recall that
this can be done with a for loop of the form

```
for (i = 1; i <= 100; ++i) {
    printf("%7d", rand() % 10 + 1);
    if (i % 10 == 0)
        printf("\n");
}
```

Since we have not yet explained how one writes to a file (see Chapter 14), you will
have to write a small program, call it *cr_rand* (for "create random"), and then give
the command

cr_rand > rand_out

to redirect the output of the program.

14 Rewrite the previous program to make use of calloc(). Suppose that the file
rand_out has as its first entry the number of random numbers contained in that file.

Write your program to read that first entry into a variable named size. Suppose that the variable rand_array has been declared as a pointer to int. You can dynamically allocate storage by making use of calloc() as follows:

```
rand_array = calloc(size, sizeof(int));
```

The pointer rand_array can be treated as an array after space has been allocated. For example, to fill the array, you can write

```
for (i = 0; i < size; ++i)
   scanf("%d", &rand_array[i]);
```

15 Recall that the semantics of the assignment operator += is specified by the rule that

variable op= expression

is equivalent to

variable = variable op (expression)

with the exception that if *variable* is itself an expression, it is evaluated only once. This means, for example, that

a[*expr*] += 2   as compared to   a[*expr*] = a[*expr*] + 2

need not have the same effects. This is an important technical point. Try the following code:

```
int   a[] = {3, 3, 3}, i = 0;
int   b[] = {3, 3, 3}, j = 0;

a[++i] += 2;                /* perfectly acceptable */
b[++j] = b[++j] + 2;        /* legal, but unacceptable */
for (i = 0; i < 3; ++i)
   printf("a[%d] = %d    b[%d] = %d\n", i, a[i], i, b[i]);
```

On most systems, the arrays a[] and b[] end up with different values. What gets printed on your system?

10

STRINGS AND POINTERS

10.1 THE END-OF-STRING SENTINEL \0

10.2 INITIALIZATION OF STRINGS

10.3 AN EXAMPLE: HAVE A NICE DAY

10.4 USING POINTERS TO PROCESS A STRING

10.5 PROBLEM SOLVING: COUNTING WORDS

10.6 PASSING ARGUMENTS TO main()

10.7 STRING HANDLING FUNCTIONS IN THE STANDARD LIBRARY

10.8 STYLE

10.9 COMMON PROGRAMMING ERRORS

10.10 SYSTEM CONSIDERATIONS

10.11 SUMMARY

10.12 EXERCISES

In C, a *string* is a one-dimensional array of type char. A character in a string can be accessed either as an element in an array or by making use of a pointer to char. The flexibility this provides makes C especially useful in writing string processing programs. The standard library provides many useful string handling functions.

While string processing can be viewed as a special case of array processing, it has characteristics that give it a unique flavor. Important to this is the use of the character value \0 to terminate a string. This chapter includes a number of example programs that illustrate string processing ideas. Again, as in the previous chapter, we will see that arrays and pointers are closely related. The type pointer to char is conceptually a string. Our examples will illustrate the pointer arithmetic and dereferencing needed to properly process string data.

10.1   THE END-OF-STRING SENTINEL \0

By convention a string is terminated by the *end-of-string* sentinel \0, or null character. A constant string such as "abc" is stored in memory as 4 characters, the last one being \0. Thus the length of the string "abc" is 3, but the size of the string is 4. To allocate storage in memory for a string, we could write

```
#define   MAXWORD   100

main()
{
    char   w[MAXWORD];
    . . . . .
```

After storage has been allocated, there are a number of ways of getting character values into the string w. First, we can do it character by character as follows:

```
w[0] = 'A';
w[1] = 'B';
w[2] = 'C';
w[3] = '\0';
```

Notice that we ended the string with the null character.

Another way to get character values into w is to make use of scanf(). The format %s is used to read in a string. The process can be thought of as having three distinct steps. The statement

```
scanf("%s", w);
```

first positions the input stream to an initial nonwhite space character. Second, nonwhite space characters are read in and placed in memory beginning at the base address of w. Finally, the process stops when a white space character or EOF is encountered. At that point a null character is placed in memory to end the string. Since an array name is a pointer to the base address of the array, the expression w is equivalent to &w[0]. Because the size of w is 100, we can enter up to 99 characters on the keyboard and still have the string sentinel \0 stored. If more are entered, we will overrun the bounds of w.

There are other ways of getting values into the string w. Later in this chapter we discuss the use of functions in the standard library.

The sentinel \0 is also called a *delimiter*. It allows a simple test to detect the end of a string. It is useful to think of strings as having a variable length delimited by the null character, but with a maximum length determined by the size of the string. The size of a string must include the storage needed for the null character. As with all arrays, the programmer must make sure that string bounds are not overrun.

Note carefully that 'a' and "a" are different. The first is a character constant, and the second is a string constant. The string "a" is an array of characters with two elements, the first with value 'a' and the second with value '\0'.

10.2 INITIALIZATION OF STRINGS

Recall that arrays can be initialized. This feature works with character arrays as well. However, the compiler allows for an initialization of the form

```
char   s[] = "abc";
```

which is taken to be equivalent to

```
char   s[] = {'a', 'b', 'c', '\0'};
```

By default, the size of the array is one more than the string length. Thus in this example the size is 4.

A pointer to `char` can also be initialized with a constant string, but the interpretation is different. Here is an example:

```
char   *p = "abc";
```

Recall that an array name by itself is treated as a pointer to the base of the array in memory. A string constant, like all other constants, is stored in memory by the compiler. (The programmer does not provide space for constants.) Thus "abc" gets stored in memory by the compiler. At the same time it is an "array name by itself," and as such, it is treated by the compiler as a pointer to the base of the array in memory. The variable p is being initialized with this pointer value.

Thus the difference between initializing an array with a constant string and initializing a pointer with a constant string is that the array contains the individual characters followed by the null character, while the pointer is assigned the address of the constant string in memory.

10.3   AN EXAMPLE: HAVE A NICE DAY

Since a string is an array of characters, one way to process a string is to use array notation with subscripts. We want to write an interactive program to illustrate this. Our program will read a line of characters typed by the user into a string, print the string in reverse order, and then sum the letters in the string.

```c
/* Have a nice day! */

#include    <stdio.h>
#include    <ctype.h>

#define   MAXSTRING   100

main()
{
   char    c, name[MAXSTRING];
   int     i, sum = 0;

   printf("\nHi!  What is your name?  ");
   for (i = 0; (c = getchar()) != '\n'; ++i) {
      name[i] = c;
      if (isalpha(c))                           /* sum the letters */
         sum += c;
   }
   name[i] = '\0';
   printf("\n%s%s%s\n%s",
      "Nice to meet you ", name, ".",
      "Your name spelled backwards is ");
   for (--i; i >= 0; --i)
      putchar(name[i]);
   printf("\n%s%d%s\n\n%s\n",
      "and the letters in your name sum to ", sum, ".",
      "Have a nice day!");
}
```

Suppose that we execute this program and enter "C. B. Diligent" when prompted. Here is what appears on the screen:

```
Hi!  What is your name?  C. B. Diligent

Nice to meet you C. B. Diligent.
Your name spelled backwards is tnegiliD .B .C
and the letters in your name sum to 949.

Have a nice day!
```

DISSECTION OF THE *nice_day* PROGRAM

■ ```
#include   <stdio.h>
#include   <ctype.h>
```

The standard header file *stdio.h* contains the function prototype for printf(). It also contains the macro definitions for getchar() and putchar(). The standard header file *ctype.h* contains the macro definition for isalpha().

■ ```
#define   MAXSTRING   100
```

The symbolic constant MAXSTRING will be used to set the size of the character array name. We are making the assumption that the user of this program will not type in more than 100 characters.

■ ```
char   c, name[MAXSTRING];
int   i, sum = 0;
```

The variable c is of type char. The identifier name is of type "array of char," and its size is MAXSTRING. In C, all array subscripts start at 0. Thus name[0], name[1], . . . , name[MAXSTRING - 1] are the elements of the array. The variables i and sum are of type int; sum is initialized to 0.

■ ```
printf("\nHi!  What is your name?  ");
```

This is a prompt to the user. The program now expects a name to be typed in followed by a carriage return.

■ `(c = getchar()) != '\n'`

This expression consists of two parts. On the left we have

    `(c = getchar())`

Unlike other languages, assignment in C is an operator (see Chapter 2). Here, `getchar()` is being used to read a character from the keyboard and to assign it to c. The value of the expression as a whole is the value of whatever is assigned to c. Parentheses are necessary because the order of precedence of the `=` operator is less than that of the `!=` operator. Thus

    `c = getchar() != '\n'`   is equivalent to   `c = (getchar() != '\n')`

which is syntactically correct, but not what we want.

■
```
for (i = 0; (c = getchar()) != '\n'; ++i) {
    name[i] = c;
    if (isalpha(c))
        sum += c;
}
```

The variable i is initially assigned the value 0. Then `getchar()` gets a character from the keyboard, assigns it to c, and tests to see if it is a newline character. If it is not, the body of the for loop is executed. First, the value of c is assigned to the array element `name[i]`. Next, the macro `isalpha()` is used to determine whether c is a lower- or uppercase letter. If it is, sum is incremented by the value of c. As we saw in Chapter 5, a character in C has the integer value corresponding to its ASCII encoding. For example, `'a'` has value 97, `'b'` has value 98, and so forth. Finally, the variable i is incremented at the end of the for loop. The for loop is executed repeatedly until a newline character is received.

■ `name[i] = '\0';`

After the for loop is finished, the null character `\0` is assigned to the element `name[i]`. By convention all strings end with a null character. Functions that process strings, such as `printf()`, use the null character `\0` as an end-of-string sentinel. We now can think of the array name in memory as

C	.		B	.		D	i	l	i	g	e	n	t	\0	*	...	*
0	1	2	3	4	5	6	7	8	9	10	11	12	13	14	15		99

Notice that * has been used to indicate that the contents of all the characters beyond \0 in the array are not known.

- ```
  printf("\n%s%s%s\n%s",
      "Nice to meet you ", name, ".",
      "Your name spelled backwards is ");
  ```

The format %s is used to print a string. Here, the array name is one of four string arguments being printed. The elements of the array are printed one after another until the end-of-string sentinel \0 is encountered. The effect of this statement is to print on the screen

```
Nice to meet you C. B. Diligent.
Your name spelled backwards is
```

- ```
  for (--i; i >= 0; --i)
      putchar(name[i]);
  ```

If we assume that "C. B. Diligent" followed by a carriage return was typed in, then i has value 14 at the beginning of this for loop. (Do not forget to count from 0, not 1.) After i has been decremented, the subscript corresponds to the last character of the name that was typed in. Thus the effect of this for loop is to print the name on the screen backwards.

- ```
  printf("\n%s%d%s\n\n%s\n",
      "and the letters in your name sum to ", sum, ".",
      "Have a nice day!");
  ```

We print the sum of the letters in the name typed in by the user, and then we print a final message.

10.4 USING POINTERS TO PROCESS A STRING

In the last section we illustrated string processing with the use of subscripts. In this section we want to use pointers to process a string. Also, we want to show how strings can be used as arguments to functions.

Let us write a small interactive program that reads into a string a line of characters input by the user. Then the program will use this to create a new string and print it.
  ```

```
/* Character processing: change a line. */

#include <stdio.h>

#define   MAXLINE   100

main()
{
    char    line[MAXLINE], *change(char *);
    void    read_in(char *);

    printf("\nWhat is your favorite line?  ");
    read_in(line);
    printf("\n%s\n\n%s\n\n",
        "Here it is after being changed:", change(line));
}
```

After prompting the user, this program uses read_in() to put characters into line. Then line is passed as an argument to change(), which returns a pointer to char. The returned pointer value is printed by printf() in the format of a string. Here is the function read_in():

```
void read_in(char s[])
{
    int    c, i = 0;

    while ((c = getchar()) != EOF && c != '\n')
        s[i++] = c;
    s[i] = '\0';
}
```

The parameter s is of type pointer to char. We could just as well have written

```
void read_in(char *s)
{
    . . . . .
```

In the while loop, successive characters are taken from the input stream and placed one after another into the array with base address s. When a newline character is received, the loop is exited, and a null character is put into the array to act as the end-of-string sentinel. Notice that this function allocates no space. In main() space is allocated with the declaration of line. We are making the assumption that the user will type in less than MAXLINE characters. When line is passed as an argument to read_in(), a copy of the base address of the array is made, and this value is taken on by the parameter s. The array elements themselves are not copied, but they are accessible in read_in() via this base address.

```
char *change(char *s)
{
    static char    new_string[MAXLINE];
    char           *p = new_string;

    *p++ = '\t';
    for ( ; *s != '\0'; ++s)
        if (*s == 'e')
            *p++ = 'E';
        else if (*s == ' ') {
            *p++ = '\n';
            *p++ = '\t';
        }
        else
            *p++ = *s;
    *p = '\0';
    return new_string;
}
```

This function takes a string and copies it, changing every e to E and replacing every blank by a newline and a tab. Suppose we run the program and type in the line

```
she sells sea shells
```

after receiving the prompt. Here is what appears on the screen:

```
What is your favorite line? she sells sea shells

Here it is after being changed:

    shE
    sElls
    sEa
    shElls
```

We want to explain in some detail how the function change() works.

DISSECTION OF THE change( ) FUNCTION

■ `char *change(char *s)`
```
{
    static char    new_string[MAXLINE];
    char           *p = new_string;
```

The first `char *` tells the compiler that this function returns a value of type pointer to `char`. The parameter `s` and the local variable `p` are both declared to be of type pointer to `char`. Since `s` is a parameter in a function header, we could just as well have written

```
char *change(char s[])
{
    . . . . .
```

However, since `p` is a local variable and not a parameter, a similar declaration for `p` would be wrong. The array `new_string` is declared to have static storage class, and space is allocated for `MAXLINE` characters. The reason for static rather than automatic is explained below. The pointer `p` is initialized to the base address of `new_string`.

■ `*p++ = '\t';`

This one line of code is equivalent to

```
*p = '\t';
++p;
```

The situation is analyzed as follows. Since the operators `*` and `++` are both unary and associate from right to left, the expression `*p++` is equivalent to `*(p++)`. Thus the `++` operator is causing `p` to be incremented. In contrast, the expression `(*p)++` would cause the value of what is pointed to by `p` to be incremented, which is something quite different. Since the `++` operator occurs on the right side of `p` rather than the left, the incrementing of `p` occurs after the total expression `*p++ = '\t'` has been evaluated. Assignment is part of the evaluation process, and this causes a tab character to be assigned to what is pointed to by `p`. Since `p` points to the base address of `new_string`, a tab character is assigned to `new_string[0]`. After the incrementing of `p` occurs, `p` points to `new_string[1]`.

■ `for ( ; *s != '\0'; ++s)`

Each time through the `for` loop, a test is made to see if the value of what is pointed to by `s` is the end-of-string sentinel. If not, then the body of the `for` loop is executed, and `s` is incremented. The effect of incrementing a pointer to `char` is to cause it to point at the next character in the string.

■ `if (*s == 'e')`
    `*p++ = 'E';`

In the body of the `for` loop, a test is made to see if `s` is pointing to the character `e`. If it is, then the character `E` is assigned to the object `p` is pointing to, and then `p` is incremented.

■ `else if (*s == ' ') {`
    `*p++ = '\n';`
    `*p++ = '\t';`
  `}`

Otherwise, a test is made to see if `s` is pointing to a blank character. If it is, then a newline character is assigned to the object `p` is pointing to, followed by the incrementing of `p`, followed by the assignment of a tab character to the object `p` is pointing to, followed by the incrementing of `p`.

■ `else`
    `*p++ = *s;`

Finally, if the character to which `s` is pointing is neither an `e` nor a blank, then the object `p` is pointing to is assigned the value of the object `s` is pointing to, followed by the incrementing of `p`. The effect of this `for` loop is to copy the string passed as an argument to `change()` into the string with base address `&new_string[1]`, except that each `e` is replaced by an `E`, and each blank is replaced by a newline and a tab.

■ `*p = '\0';`

When the `for` loop is exited, the object pointed to by `p` is assigned an end-of-string sentinel.

■ `return new_string;`

The array name `new_string` is returned. An array name by itself is treated as a pointer to the base of the array in memory. Since `new_string` is of storage class static, it is preserved in memory on function exit. If `new_string` were automatic instead, then the memory allocated to `new_string` would not be preserved on function exit. If the memory gets overwritten, then the final `printf()` statement in `main()` will not work properly.

10.5   PROBLEM SOLVING: COUNTING WORDS

The example in the last section illustrated the use of pointers and pointer arithmetic to process a string. In this section we want to give another illustration of this. We will write a function that counts the number of words in a string. For the purposes of this function, a sequence of nonwhite space characters will constitute a word.

```
/* Count the number of words in a string. */

#include <ctype.h>

int word_cnt(char *s)
{
   int    cnt = 0;

   while (*s != '\0') {
      while (isspace(*s))                    /* skip white space */
         ++s;
      if (*s != '\0') {                      /* found a word */
         ++cnt;
         while (!isspace(*s) && *s != '\0')   /* skip the word */
            ++s;
      }
   }
   return cnt;
}
```

This is a typical string processing function. Pointer arithmetic and dereferencing are used to search for various patterns or characters.

10.6   PASSING ARGUMENTS TO main()

C provides for arrays of any type, including arrays of pointers. Although this is an advanced topic that we do not wish to treat in detail, we need to use arrays of pointers to char to write programs that use command line arguments. Two arguments, conventionally called argc and argv, can be used with main() to communicate with the operating system. Here is a program that prints its command line arguments.

```
/* Echo the command line arguments. */

#include <stdio.h>

main(int argc, char *argv[])
{
    int    i;

    printf("argc = %d\n", argc);
    for (i = 0; i < argc; ++i)
        printf("argv[%d] = %s\n", i, argv[i]);
}
```

The variable argc provides a count of the command line arguments. The array argv is an array of pointers to char, and can be thought of as an array of strings. Since the element argv[0] always contains the name of the command itself, the value of argc is always 1 or more. Suppose we compile the above program and put the executable code in the file *my_echo*. If we give the command

> *my_echo*

the following gets printed on the screen:

```
argc = 1
argv[0] = my_echo
```

Now suppose that we give the command

> *my_echo try this*

Here is what appears on the screen:

```
argc = 3
argv[0] = my_echo
argv[1] = try
argv[2] = this
```

The parameter argv could just as well have been declared as follows:

```
char    **argv;
```

It is a pointer to pointer to char that can be thought of as an array of pointers to char, which in turn can be thought of as an array of strings. Notice that we have not allocated any space for the strings on the command line. The system does this for us and passes information to main() via the two arguments argc and argv.

10.7 STRING HANDLING FUNCTIONS IN THE STANDARD LIBRARY

The standard library contains many useful string handling functions. They all require that strings passed as arguments be null terminated, and they all return either an integer value or a pointer to char. The following list describes some of the available functions. (All the string handling functions are described in Appendix A.) The function prototypes are given in the header file *string.h*. This file should be included when using these string handling functions.

Some string handling functions in the standard library

■ char *strcat(char *s1, const char *s2);

This function takes two strings as arguments, concatenates them, and puts the result in s1. The programmer must ensure that s1 points to enough space to hold the result. The string s1 is returned.

■ int strcmp(const char *s1, const char *s2);

Two strings are passed as arguments. An integer is returned that is less than, equal to, or greater than zero, depending on whether s1 is lexicographically less than, equal to, or greater than s2.

■ char *strcpy(char *s1, const char *s2);

The string s2 is copied into s1 until \0 is moved. Whatever exists in s1 is overwritten. It is assumed that s1 has enough space to hold the result. The value s1 is returned.

■ unsigned strlen(const char *s);

A count of the number of characters before \0 is returned.

There is nothing special about these functions. They are written in C and are all quite short. Variables in them are often declared to have storage class register to make them execute more quickly. Here is one way the function strlen() could be written:

```
unsigned strlen(const char *s)
{
    register int   n = 0;

    for ( ; *s != '\0'; ++s)
        ++n;
    return n;
}
```

String handling functions are illustrated in the next table. Note carefully that it is the programmer's responsibility to allocate sufficient space for strings that are passed as arguments to functions. Overrunning the bounds of a string is a common programming error.

Declarations and initializations	
`char   s1[] = "beautiful big sky country",` `       s2[] = "how now brown cow";`	
Expression	*Value*
`strlen(s1)`	25
`strlen(s2 + 8)`	9
`strcmp(s1, s2)`	*negative integer*
Statements	*What gets printed*
`printf("%s", s1 + 10);`	big sky country

`strcpy(s1 + 10, s2 + 8);`
`strcat(s1, "s!");`
`printf("%s", s1);`
	beautiful brown cows!

Before using any string functions in the standard library, the programmer must provide the function prototypes. Typically, the programmer writes the line

```
#include <string.h>
```

to include the header file *string.h*. This header file contains all the prototypes of the string handling functions in the standard library.

10.8 STYLE

There are two styles of programming that can be used to process strings: array notation with subscripts, or pointers and pointer arithmetic. Although both styles are common, there is a tendency for experienced programmers to favor the use of pointers. In some C systems the pointer versions may execute faster.

Since the null character is always used to delimit a string, it is a common programming style to explicitly test for \0 when processing a string. However, it is not necessary to do so. The alternative is to use the length of the string. As an example of this we could write

```
n = strlen(s);
for (i = 0; i <= n; ++i)
   if (islower(s[i]))
      s[i] = toupper(s[i]);
```

to capitalize all the letters in the string s. This style of string processing is certainly acceptable. Notice, however, that a for loop of the form

```
for (i = 0; i <= strlen(s); ++i)
   . . . . .
```

is inefficient. This code causes the length of s to be recomputed every time through the loop.

It is sometimes convenient to use a pointer to char to point at a constant string. As an example of this, consider

```
char    *p;

p = "RICH";
printf("C. B. DeMogul is %s %s %s!\n", p, p, p);
```

which is an alternative to

```
printf("C. B. DeMogul is %s %s %s!\n", "RICH", "RICH", "RICH");
```

In this example the repetitive use of p saves a little space. Compilers allocate separate storage for each constant string, even if one is the same as another.

Where possible, the programmer should use a function in the standard library rather than code an equivalent routine, even when the specially coded routine would have a marginal gain in efficiency. The functions in the standard library are designed to be portable across systems.

Although it is considered poor programming practice to do so, a pointer to a constant string can change the contents of the string on most systems. For an explicit example, see exercise 8.

10.9   COMMON PROGRAMMING ERRORS

A common programming error is overrunning the bounds of a string. As with other arrays, it is the programmer's responsibility to make sure that enough space is allocated for a string. Consider

```
char    s[17], *strcpy();

strcpy(s, "Have a nice day!\n");
```

Here the programmer made a careful count of the characters in the string to be copied into s, but forgot to allocate space for the null character, too. Overrunning the bounds of a string can easily occur with a function call such as strcat(s1, s2). The concatenation of the two strings must fit within the space allocated for s1.

Another common programming error is to forget to terminate a string with the null character. On most systems this type of error cannot be caught by the compiler. The effect of the error can be sporadic; sometimes the program may run correctly and other times not. This kind of error can be very difficult to find.

Other common errors include writing 'a' for "a", or vice versa. Usually the compiler will find this kind of mistake. Also, using a function call such as scanf("%s", &w) to read a string into the character array w is an error. Since w is itself a pointer, the correct function call is scanf("%s", w).

10.10   SYSTEM CONSIDERATIONS

In ANSI C, string constants that are separated by zero or more white space characters are concatenated by the compiler into one long string. Traditional C compilers do not support this feature. Here is an example:

```
char    *long_string;

long_string = "A list of words:\n"
              "\n"
              "   1   abacus\n"
              "   2   bracelet\n"
              "   3   cafeteria\n";
```

In this particular example the advantage is that the string embodies the look it will have when it gets printed. Traditional C compilers do not support this feature.

The standard library contains 17 string handling functions (see Appendix A). It is considered good programming practice to use these functions rather than write your own. They enhance portability to other systems. Note, however, that not all the string handling functions are supported by older compilers. The new ANSI C standard has added many functions.

10.11   SUMMARY

1   Strings are one-dimensional arrays of type char. The null character \0 is used to delimit a string. Systems functions such as printf() will work properly only on null terminated strings.

2   A function call such as scanf("%s", w) can be used to read a sequence of nonwhite space characters into the string w. After all the characters have been read in, scanf() automatically ends the string with the null character.

3   Strings may be initialized. An initialization of the form

```
char    *s[] = "cbd";
```

is taken by the compiler to be equivalent to

```
char    *s[] = {'c', 'b', 'd', '\0'};
```

4   String processing can be done by making use of array notation with subscripts and by making use of pointers and pointer arithmetic. Because of this flexibility, C is used extensively for string processing.

5   C provides access to the command line arguments. This is done by making use of the two parameters argc and argv in the function definition of main(). The parameter argc is an int; its value is the number of command line arguments. The

rameter `argv` is an array of pointers to `char`; it can be thought of as an array of strings. The system places the command line arguments in memory as strings and causes the elements of the array `argv` to point to them. The value of `argc` is always 1 or more, and the string pointed to by `argv[0]` is always the name of the command.

6   The standard library contains many useful string handling functions. For example, a function call such as `strcmp(s1, s2)` can be used to lexicographically compare the strings `s1` and `s2`.

10.12   EXERCISES

1   Rewrite the *nice_day* program using pointers and pointer arithmetic throughout.

2   Rewrite the function `word_cnt()` using array notation with subscripts. Write an interactive program that reads in lines typed by the user, and then reports to the user the number of words in the line. Your program should allow for very long lines. Experiment to see what happens when you type in a line that is so long it runs off the screen.

3   Write a function `search()` that searches the alphabetic characters in a string. From among the letters that occur in the string, the function is to find the letter that occurs least, but at least once, and the letter that occurs most. Report this information back to the calling environment along with the count of the occurrences of the two letters. Your function definition should start as follows:

```
void search(char s[], char *p_least, char *p_most,
            int *p_least_cnt, int *p_most_cnt)
{
    . . . . .
```

Treat lower- and uppercase letters separately. Make sure that you handle gracefully the case when there are no letters in the string. Write a program to test your function.

4   Write a function that when invoked as `bubble_string(s)` causes the characters in the string `s` to be bubble sorted. If `s` contains the string `"xylophone"`, then the statement

```
printf("%s\n", bubble_string(s));
```

should cause `ehlnoopxy` to be printed.

5 Modify the *my_echo* program so that it has the following effect. If the command line

   my_echo pacific sea

is typed, then the following should be printed:

```
pacific
sea
```

Make a further modification so that if the option −*c* is present, the arguments are printed with capital letters. Do not print out the argument that contains the option.

6 Write your own version of the library function strncmp(). The function prototype and a description of how the function behaves are given in Appendix A.

7 In this exercise we use a multidimensional array of pointers to char. Complete the following table.

Declarations and initializations		

char   *p[2][3] = {
    "abc", "defg", "hi", "jklmno",
    "pqrstuvw", "xyz"
};		

Expression	*Equivalent expression*	*Value*
***p	p[0][0][0]	'a'
**p[1]		
**(p[1] + 2)		
((p + 1) + 1)[7]		/* error */
(*(*(p + 1) + 1))[7]		
*(p[1][2] + 2)		

8 Constant strings on many systems can have their value altered. This is a very bad coding practice. Here is an example of what *not* to do. Explain what gets printed and why.

```
#include <stdio.h>

main()
{
    char    *p, *q;

    p = q = " RICH";
    printf("C. B. DeMogul is%s%s%s!\n", p, p, p);
    *++q = 'p';
    *++q = 'o';
    *++q = 'o';
    *++q = 'r';
    printf("C. B. DeMogul is%s%s%s!\n", p, p, p);
}
```

Note. On some systems this form of constant string alteration is detected and prohibited.

9 Write an interactive program that makes use of scanf() to read in seven strings input by the user. The program should print the seven strings as a list, and then sort them alphabetically and print a new list. Use the function strcmp() to assist in the sorting of the strings. Also, use the preprocessing directive

```
#define    N_STRINGS    7
```

to write your program in such a way that it can sort a different number of strings by changing only this line.

10 (Advanced) Write a program similar to the one you wrote in exercise 9 that sorts and prints command line arguments.

11

THE PREPROCESSOR
AND SOFTWARE
METHODOLOGY

11.1   THE USE OF #include

11.2   THE USE OF #define
       SYNTACTIC SUGAR

11.3   MACROS WITH
       ARGUMENTS

11.4   THE TYPE DEFINITIONS
       AND MACROS IN *stddef.h*

11.5   PROBLEM SOLVING:
       SORTING WITH qsort()

11.6   AN EXAMPLE: MACROS
       WITH ARGUMENTS

11.7   CONDITIONAL
       COMPILATION

11.8   PREDEFINED MACROS

11.9   THE OPERATORS # AND ##

11.10 THE assert() MACRO

11.11 THE USE OF #error
       AND #pragma

11.12 LINE NUMBERS

11.13 CORRESPONDING
       FUNCTIONS

11.14 SOFTWARE METHODOLOGY

11.15 DEVELOPING A LARGE
       PROGRAM

11.16 AN EXAMPLE: PRINTING
       IN COLUMNS

11.17 STYLE

11.18 COMMON PROGRAMMING
       ERRORS

11.19 SYSTEM CONSIDERATIONS

11.20 SUMMARY

11.21 EXERCISES

The C language uses the preprocessor to extend its power and notation. In this chapter we present a detailed discussion of the preprocessor, including new features added by the ANSI C committee. We begin by explaining the use of `#include`. Then we thoroughly discuss the use of the `#define` macro facility. Macros can be used to generate in-line code that takes the place of a function call. Their use can reduce program execution time.

Lines that begin with a `#` are called *preprocessing directives*. These lines communicate with the preprocessor. In ANSI C, the `#` can be preceded on the line by white space, whereas in traditional C, it must occur in column 1. The syntax for preprocessing directives is independent of the rest of the C language. The effect of a preprocessing directive starts at its place in a file and continues until the end of that file, or until its effect is negated by another directive. It is always helpful to keep in mind that the preprocessor does not "know C."

11.1   THE USE OF #include

We have already used preprocessing directives such as

```
#include <stdio.h>
#include <stdlib.h>
```

Another form of the #include facility is given by

```
#include "filename"
```

This causes the preprocessor to replace the line with a copy of the contents of the named file. A search for the file is made first in the current directory and then in other system-dependent places. With a preprocessing directive of the form

```
#include <filename>
```

the preprocessor looks for the file only in the other places and not in the current directory. In UNIX systems, the standard header files such as *stdio.h* and *stdlib.h* are typically found in */usr/include*. In general, where the standard header files are stored is system-dependent.

There is no restriction on what a #include file can contain. In particular, it can contain other preprocessing directives that will be expanded by the preprocessor in turn.

11.2   THE USE OF #define

Preprocessing directives with #define occur in two forms:

```
#define    identifier    token_string opt
```

```
#define    identifier(identifier, . . . , identifier)    token_string opt
```

The *token_string* is optional. A long definition of either form can be continued to the next line by placing a backslash \ at the end of the current line. If a simple #define of the first form occurs in a file, the preprocessor replaces every occurrence of *identifier* by *token_string* in the remainder of the file, except in quoted strings. Consider the example

```
#define    SECONDS_PER_DAY    (60 * 60 * 24)
```

In this example the token string is (60 * 60 * 24), and the preprocessor will replace every occurrence of the symbolic constant SECONDS_PER_DAY by that string in the remainder of the file.

The use of simple #define's can improve program clarity and portability. For example, if special constants such as π or the speed of light c are used in a program, they should be defined.

```
#define   PI    3.14159
#define   C     299792.458    /* speed of light in km/sec */
```

Other special constants that are used in programs are also best coded as symbolic constants.

```
#define   EOF      (-1)        /* typical end-of-file value */
#define   MAXINT   2147483647  /* largest 4-byte integer */
```

Program limits that are programmer decisions can also be specified symbolically.

```
#define   ITERS   50      /* number of iterations */
#define   SIZE    250     /* array size */
#define   EPS     1.0e-9  /* a numerical limit */
```

In general, symbolic constants aid documentation by replacing what might otherwise be a mysterious constant with a mnemonic identifier. They aid portability by allowing constants that may be system-dependent to be altered once. They aid reliability by restricting to one place the check on the actual representation of the constant.

SYNTACTIC SUGAR

It is possible to alter the syntax of C toward some user preference. A frequent programming error is to use the token = in place of the token == in logical expressions. A programmer could use

```
#define   EQ    ==
```

to defend against such a mistake. This superficial alteration of the programming syntax is called *syntactic sugar*. Another example of this is to change the form of the while statement by introducing "do," which is an ALGOL style construction.

```
#define   do   /* blank */
```

With these two #define lines at the top of the file, the code

```
while (i EQ 1) do {
    . . . . .
```

will become, after the preprocessor pass,

```
while (i == 1) {
    . . . . .
```

One must keep in mind that since do will disappear from anywhere in the file, the
do-while statement cannot be used.

11.3   MACROS WITH ARGUMENTS

So far, we have considered only simple #define preprocessing directives. We now want
to discuss how one can use the #define facility to write macro definitions with parameters. The general form is given by

> #define   *identifier*(*identifier*, . . . , *identifier*)   *token_string*_{opt}

There can be no space between the first identifier and the left parenthesis. Zero or more
identifiers can occur in the parameter list. An example of a macro definition with a
parameter is

```
#define   SQ(x)   ((x) * (x))
```

The identifier x in the #define is a parameter that is substituted for in later text. The
substitution is one of string replacement without consideration of syntactic correctness.
For example, with the argument 7 + w the macro call

> SQ(7 + w)   expands to   ((7 + w) * (7 + w))

In a similar fashion

> SQ(SQ(*p))   expands to   ((((*p) * (*p))) * (((*p) * (*p))))

This seemingly extravagant use of parentheses is to protect against the macro expand-
ing an expression that would then lead to an unanticipated order of evaluation. It is

important to understand why all the parentheses are necessary. This will be discussed
in detail in Section 11.18, "Common Programming Errors," along with the very common error

```
#define   SQ(x)   ((x) * (x));   /* error */
```

Here, the unwanted semicolon can cause problems (see Section 11.18). Even though
forewarned, the programmer will still make this mistake, because it becomes almost
second nature to end each line with a semicolon.

Macros are frequently used to replace function calls by in-line code, which is more
efficient. For example, instead of writing a function to find the minimum of two values,
a programmer could write

```
#define   min(x, y)   (((x) < (y)) ? (x) : (y))
```

After this definition, an expression such as

```
m = min(u, v)
```

gets expanded by the preprocessor to

```
m = (((u) < (v)) ? (u) : (v))
```

The arguments of min() can be arbitrary expressions of compatible type. Also, we can
use min() to build another macro. For example, if we need to find the minimum of four
values, we can write

```
#define   min4(a, b, c, d)   min(min(a, b), min(c, d))
```

A macro definition can use both functions and macros in its body. Here are some
examples:

```
#define   SQ(x)      ((x) * (x))
#define   CUBE(x)    (SQ(x) * (x))
#define   F_POW(x)   sqrt(sqrt(CUBE(x)))   /* fractional power: 3/4 */
```

A preprocessing directive of the form

```
#undef identifier
```

will undefine a macro. It causes the previous definition of a macro to be forgotten.

11.4   THE TYPE DEFINITIONS AND MACROS IN *stddef.h*

C provides the typedef facility so that an identifier can be associated with a specific type. A simple example is

```
typedef   char   uppercase;
```

This makes uppercase a type that is synonymous with char, and it can be used in declarations just as other types are used. An example is

```
uppercase   c, u[100];
```

The typedef facility allows the programmer to use type names that are appropriate for a specific application (see Chapters 7 and 13).

In this section we are concerned with the implementation-specific type definitions and macros that are given in the header file *stddef.h*. They can occur in other standard header files as well. Here is how the type definitions might appear:

```
typedef   int        ptrdiff_t;    /* pointer difference type */
typedef   short      wchar_t;      /* wide character type */
typedef   unsigned   size_t;       /* the sizeof type */
```

The type ptrdiff_t tells what type is obtained with an expression involving the difference of two pointers. In MS-DOS, this depends on the memory model being used. In UNIX, the type is usually int.

The type wchar_t is provided to support languages with character sets that will not fit into a char. Some C compilers are not interested in providing such support. If that is the case, the type definition would probably be

```
typedef   char   wchar_t;    /* same as a plain char */
```

Recall that the sizeof operator is used to find the size of a type or of an expression. For example, sizeof(double) on most systems is 8. The type size_t is the type of the result of the sizeof operator. This is implementation-dependent, but it must be an unsigned integral type. We will see the use of size_t in our discussion of qsort() in Section 11.5.

The macro NULL is also given in *stddef.h*. It is an implementation-defined null pointer constant. It usually is given by

```
#define   NULL   0
```

11.5   PROBLEM SOLVING: SORTING WITH qsort()

Programmers, for a variety of reasons, need to be able to sort data. If the amount of data is small, or the program does not have to run fast, we can use a bubble sort or a transposition sort to accomplish the task. If, however, there is a lot of data and speed of execution is a concern, then we can use the function qsort() provided by the standard library. (The name *qsort* stands for "quick sort.")

The function qsort() is useful because it is a lot faster than a bubble sort or a simple transposition sort, and it is quite easy to implement. The function prototype for qsort() is in *stdlib.h*. It is equivalent to

```
void qsort(void *array, size_t n_els, size_t el_size,
           int compare(const void *, const void *));
```

Notice that the type size_t is used. Many other functions in the standard library also use this type. When qsort() is called, its first argument is the array to be sorted, its second argument is the number of elements in the array, its third argument is the number of bytes in an element, and its fourth argument is a function, called the *comparison function*, which is used to compare elements in the array. In the function prototype for qsort() given above, the declaration of the fourth parameter is

```
int compare(const void *, const void *)
```

This is itself a function prototype, the prototype for the comparison function. The comparison function takes as arguments two pointers to void. When qsort() gets invoked, these two pointers will point to elements of the array. The comparison function returns an int that is less than, equal to, or greater than zero, depending on whether its first argument is considered to be less than, equal to, or greater than its second argument. The two pointers are of type void *, because they are meant to be generic. As we will see, qsort() can be used to sort arrays of any type. The type qualifier const tells the compiler that the objects pointed to by the two pointers may not be modified (see Section 8.11 in Chapter 8).

Let us write a test program that illustrates the use of qsort(). In our program we fill an array, print it, sort it with qsort(), and then print it again.

```
#include <stdio.h>
#include <stdlib.h>
#include <time.h>

#define   N   11                              /* size of the array */

int    cmp(const void *vp, const void *vq);     /* comparison fct */
void   fill_array(double *a, int n);
void   prn_array(double *a, int n);

main()
{
   double   a[N];

   fill_array(a, N);
   prn_array(a, N);
   qsort(a, N, sizeof(double), cmp);
   prn_array(a, N);
}

int cmp(const void *vp, const void *vq)
{
   const double   *p = vp;
   const double   *q = vq;
   double         diff = *p - *q;

   return ((diff >= 0.0) ? ((diff > 0.0) ? -1 : 0) : +1);
}

void fill_array(double *a, int n)
{
   int   i;

   srand(time(NULL));                          /* seed rand() */
   for (i = 0; i < n; ++i)
     a[i] = (rand() % 1001) / 10.0;
}
```

```
void prn_array(double *a, int n)
{
   int    i;

   for (i = 0; i < n; ++i) {
      if (i % 6 == 0)
         putchar('\n');
      printf("%12.1f", a[i]);
   }
   putchar('\n');
}
```

We want to discuss a number of points about this test program, but before we do so, let us look at some typical output:

```
      67.1        88.0        10.7        10.2        87.0        28.4
       3.1        32.5        69.3        16.8        76.5

      88.0        87.0        76.5        69.3        67.1        32.5
      28.4        16.8        10.7        10.2         3.1
```

DISSECTION OF THE *try_qsort* PROGRAM

■ `#define   N   11                          /* size of the array */`

To test the function qsort(), we will create an array of size N. After we get the code to work for a small array, we can test it on a larger array.

■ `int    cmp(const void *vp, const void *vq);    /* comparison fct */`
  `void   fill_array(double *a, int n);`
  `void   prn_array(double *a, int n);`

These are function prototypes. We can name our comparison function whatever we want, but the type of the function and the number and type of its arguments must agree with the last parameter in the function prototype for qsort().

```
■ main()
  {
     double   a[N];

     fill_array(a, N);
     prn_array(a, N);
     qsort(a, N, sizeof(double), cmp);
     prn_array(a, N);
  }
```

In main(), we declare a to be an array of double's. Since the purpose of our program is to test qsort(), we do not do anything exciting. All we do is fill the array, print it, use *qsort()* to sort it, and then print the array again.

```
■ qsort(a, N, sizeof(double), cmp);
```

When qsort() is invoked, we must pass it the base address of the array to be sorted, the number of elements in the array, the number of bytes required to store an element, and the name of our comparison function.

```
■ int cmp(const void *vp, const void *vq)
  {
     . . . . .
```

This is the start of the function definition for our comparison function. The letter v in vp and vq is mnemonic for "void." In the body of main() we pass the name of our comparison function as the last argument to qsort(). This occurs in the statement

```
     qsort(a, N, sizeof(double), cmp);
```

In the body of qsort(), which the programmer does not have access to, pointers to elements of the array a will be passed to cmp(). The programmer is not concerned with the internal details of qsort(). The programmer only has to write the comparison function with the understanding that the parameters vp and vq are pointers to elements of the array.

```
■ int cmp(const void *vp, const void *vq)
  {
     const double   *p = vp;
     const double   *q = vq;
     double         diff = *p - *q;
     . . . . .
```

In the body of our comparison function, we initialize vp to p and vq to q. If we do not qualify p and q with const, the compiler will complain (see Section 8.11 in Chapter 8). The variables p and q are of type pointer to double because the elements of the array a are of type double. We initialize diff to the difference of the objects pointed to by p and q.

■ `return ((diff >= 0.0) ? ((diff > 0.0) ? -1 : 0) : +1);`

If diff is positive, we return −1; if diff is zero, we return 0; and if diff is negative, we return 1. This causes the array to be sorted in descending order. Suppose we replace this line with

```
if (diff < 0.0)
   return -1;
if (diff == 0.0)
   return 0;
return 1;
```

This will cause the array to be sorted in ascending order.

■ ```
void fill_array(double *a, int n)
{
   int   i;
   srand(time(NULL));   /* seed rand() */
   . . . . .
```

Typically, the function call time(NULL) returns the number of seconds that have elapsed since 1 January 1970. ANSI C does not guarantee this, but this convention is widely followed. Passing time(NULL) to srand() causes the array a to be filled with different values every time the program is invoked.

■ ```
for (i = 0; i < n; ++i)
   a[i] = (rand() % 1001) / 10.0;
```

The expression rand() % 1001 has an int value in the interval 0 to 1000. Since we are dividing this by the double value 10.0, the value of what is assigned to a[i] is in the interval 0 to 100.

11.6   AN EXAMPLE: MACROS WITH ARGUMENTS

In this section we again fill arrays and sort them with qsort(), but this time we use macros with arguments. We will call our program *sort*.

Let us write our program in two files, a header file *sort.h* and a *.c* file. In the header file we put our #include's, our #define's, and all our function prototypes.

In file sort.h:

```
#include <stdio.h>
#include <stdlib.h>
#include <string.h>
#include <time.h>

#define   M   32                              /* size of a[] */
#define   N   11                              /* size of b[] */

#define   fractional_part(x)   (x - (int) x)
#define   random_char()        (rand() % 26 + 'a')
#define   random_float()       (rand() % 100 / 10.0)

#define   FILL(array, sz, type)      \
   if (strcmp(type, "char") == 0)    \
      for (i = 0; i < sz; ++i)       \
         array[i] = random_char();   \
   else                              \
      for (i = 0; i < sz; ++i)       \
         array[i] = random_float()

#define   PRINT(array, sz, cntrl_string)  \
   for (i = 0; i < sz; ++i)               \
      printf(cntrl_string, array[i]);     \
   putchar('\n')

int   compare_fractional_part(const void *, const void *);
int   lexico(const void *, const void *);
```

DISSECTION OF THE *sort.h* HEADER FILE

■ `#include <stdio.h>`
  `#include <stdlib.h>`
  `#include <string.h>`
  `#include <time.h>`

The header file *stdio.h* contains the macro definition for NULL and the function proto-type for printf(). The header file *stdlib.h* contains the function prototypes for rand(), srand(), and qsort(). The header file *time.h* contains the function prototype for time(). The function call time(NULL) will be used to seed the random number generator.

■ `#define   fractional_part(x)   (x - (int) x)`

If x is a positive float, then the expression x - (int) x yields the fractional part of x.

■ `#define   random_char()        (rand() % 26 + 'a')`

When rand() is invoked, it returns an integer value randomly distributed between 0 and MAX_RAND, a symbolic constant defined in stdlib.h. Since MAX_RAND is typically more than 32 thousand, the expression rand() % 26 yields an integer value randomly distributed between 0 and 25. Since 'a' + 25 has the value 'z', the expression

    rand() % 26 + 'a'

produces a character value randomly distributed between 'a' and 'z'.

■ `#define   random_float()       (rand() % 100 / 10.0)`

The value of the expression rand() % 100 is an integer randomly distributed between 0 and 99. Since the expression 10.0 is of type double, the value produced by rand() % 100 is promoted to a double, and the expression

    rand() % 100 / 10.0

as a whole is also of type double. Its value is between 0 and 9.9.

```
■ #define   FILL(array, sz, type)          \
    if (strcmp(type, "char") == 0)   \
      for (i = 0; i < sz; ++i)            \
          array[i] = random_char();   \
      else                           \
        for (i = 0; i < sz; ++i)         \
          array[i] = random_float()
```

In this macro definition, array, sz, and type are parameters. Unlike function definitions, no type checking gets done. It is the programmer's responsibility to call the macro with arguments of the appropriate type. Note that the variable i is used in the body of the macro. Since it is not declared here, it has to be declared in main() where the macro gets called. Consider the macro call

```
FILL(a, n, "char");
```

When the macro gets expanded, we obtain

```
if (strcmp("char", "char") == 0)
    for (i = 0; i < n; ++i)
        a[i] = random_char();
else
    for (i = 0; i < n; ++i)
        a[i] = random_float();
```

The identifiers array, sz, and type have been replaced by a, n, and "char", respectively. Note carefully that all but the last semicolon came from the preprocessor expansion mechanism.

```
■ #define   PRINT(array, sz, cntrl_string)  \
    for (i = 0; i < sz; ++i)                 \
      printf(cntrl_string, array[i]);        \
    putchar('\n')
```

This macro can be used to print the values of elements of an array. Note that the control string for printf() is a parameter in the macro definition.

```
■ int   compare_fractional_part(const void *, const void *);
  int   lexico(const void *, const void *);
```

These are prototypes of comparison functions that will be passed to qsort(). Notice that with respect to type, they match the function prototype of the comparison function in the function prototype for qsort().

Now let us consider the rest of the code for our program. At the top of the file *sort.c* we have

```
#include "sort.h"

main()
{
    char    a[M];
    float   b[N];
    int     i;

    srand(time(NULL));
    FILL(a, M , "char");
    PRINT(a, M, "%-2c");
    qsort(a, M, sizeof(char), lexico);
    PRINT(a, M, "%-2c");
    printf("---\n");
    FILL(b, N, "float");
    PRINT(b, N, "%-6.1f");
    qsort(b, N, sizeof(float), compare_fractional_part);
    PRINT(b, N, "%-6.1f");
}
```

In main(), we fill an array, print it, sort it, and print it again. Then we repeat the process, but this time with an array of a different type. Notice that each time we invoke qsort(), we use a different comparison function. Here is the output of our program:

```
q m z r h l a j o e t b k w l t z t v i e m h p f y b p s w a j
a a b b e e f h h i j j k l l m m o p p q r s t t t v w w y z z
---
9.4   0.2   5.1   6.7   5.4   5.3   6.1   9.6   2.8   8.8   8.5
6.1   5.1   0.2   5.3   5.4   9.4   8.5   9.6   6.7   8.8   2.8
```

Finally, we want to look at the two comparison functions. Pointers to void are used because this is required by the function prototype of qsort() in *stdlib.h*. We will carefully explain how these pointers get used in the comparison functions.

```
int compare_fractional_part(const void *vp, const void *vq)
{
    const float   *p = vp, *q = vq;
    float         x;

    x = fractional_part(*p) - fractional_part(*q);
    return ((x < 0.0) ? -1 : (x == 0.0) ? 0 : +1);
}

int lexico(const void *vp, const void *vq)
{
    const char    *p = vp, *q = vq;

    return (*p - *q);
}
```

DISSECTION OF THE **compare_fractional_part**() FUNCTION

■ `int compare_fractional_part(const void *vp, const void *vq)`
  `{`
  `. . . . .`

This function takes two const qualified pointers to void as arguments and returns an int. Because of this, the function can be passed as an argument to qsort().

■ `int compare_fractional_part(const void *vp, const void *vq)`
  `{`
  `    const float   *p = vp, *q = vq;`
  `    float         x;`
  `. . . . .`

The letter v in vp and vq is mnemonic for "void." Since pointers to void cannot be dereferenced, we declare p and q to be pointers to float and initialize them with vp and vq, respectively. Since an ANSI C compiler will complain if a const qualified pointer is assigned to one that is not const qualified, we declare p and q to be const qualified. Notice that we did not declare x to be const qualified. If we had done so, we would be able to give x a value only by initializing it.

■ x = fractional_part(*p) - fractional_part(*q);
  return ((x < 0.0) ? -1 : (x == 0.0) ? 0 : +1);

The difference of the fractional parts of the objects pointed to by p and q is assigned to x. Then -1, 0, or $+1$ is returned, depending on whether x is negative, zero, or positive. Thus when we call qsort() with compare_decimal_part() passed as an argument, the elements in the array get sorted according to their fractional parts.

Observe that in the function lexico() we defined p and q to be pointers to const char and initialized them with vp and vq, respectively. Then we returned the difference of what is pointed to by p and q. Thus when we call qsort() with lexico passed as an argument, the elements in the array get sorted lexicographically.

11.7   CONDITIONAL COMPILATION

The preprocessor has directives for conditional compilation. They can be used for program development and for writing code that is more easily portable from one machine to another. Each preprocessing directive of the form

    #if   *constant_integral_expression*
    #ifdef   *identifier*
    #ifndef   *identifier*

provides for conditional compilation of the code that follows until the preprocessing directive

    #endif

is reached. For the intervening code to be compiled, after #if the constant expression must be nonzero (*true*), and after #ifdef or after #if defined, the named identifier must have been defined previously in a #define line, without an intervening

    #undef *identifier*

having been used to undefine the macro. After #ifndef the named identifier must be currently undefined.

The integral constant expression used in a preprocessing directive cannot contain the sizeof operator or a cast. It may, however, use the defined preprocessing operator. This operator is available in ANSI C, but not necessarily in traditional C. The expression defined *identifier*   is equivalent to   defined(*identifier*)

It evaluates to 1 if the identifier is currently defined, and evaluates to 0 otherwise. Here is an example of how it can be used:

```
#if defined(HP9000) || defined(SUN4) && !defined(VAX)
   .....         /* machine-dependent code */
#endif
```

Sometimes `printf()` statements are useful for debugging purposes. Suppose that at the top of a file we write

```
#define   DEBUG   1
```

and then throughout the rest of the file we write lines such as

```
#if DEBUG
   printf("debug:   a = %d\n", a);
#endif
```

Since the symbolic constant `DEBUG` has nonzero value, the `printf()` statements will be compiled. Later, these lines can be omitted from compilation by changing the value of the symbolic constant `DEBUG` to 0.

An alternate scheme is to define a symbolic constant having no value. Suppose that at the top of a file we write

```
#define   DEBUG
```

Then we can use the `#ifdef` or `#if defined` forms of conditional compilation. For example, if we write

```
#ifdef DEBUG
   .....
#endif
```

then the intervening lines of code will be compiled. When we remove the `#define` line that defines `DEBUG` from the top of the file, the intervening lines of code will not be compiled.

Suppose that we are writing code in a large software project. We may be expected to include at the top of all our code certain header files supplied by others. Our code may depend on some of the function prototypes and on some of the macros in these header files, but since the header files are for the project as a whole, our code might not use everything. Moreover, we may not even know all the things that eventually will be in the header files. To prevent the clash of macro names, we can use the #undef facility:

```
#include "everything.h"

#undef    PIE
#define   PIE  "I like apple."
. . . . .
```

If PIE happens to be defined in *everything.h*, then we have undefined it. If it is not defined in *everything.h*, then the #undef directive has no effect.

Here is a common use of conditional compilation. Imagine that you are in the testing phase of program development and that your code has the form

statements
more statements
and still more statements

For debugging or testing purposes, you may wish to temporarily disregard, or block out, some of your code. To do this, you can try to put the code into a comment.

statements
/
more statements
/
and still more statements

However, if the code to be blocked out contains comments within it, this method will result in a syntax error. The use of conditional compilation solves this problem.

statements
#if 0
more statements
#endif
and still more statements

The preprocessor has control structures that are similar to the if-else statement in C. Each of the #if forms can be followed by any number of lines, possibly containing preprocessing directives of the form

#elif *constant_integral_expression*

possibly followed by the preprocessing directive

#else

and, finally, followed by the preprocessing directive

#endif

Note that #elif is a contraction for "else-if." The flow of control for conditional compilation is analogous to that provided by if-else statements.

11.8   PREDEFINED MACROS

In ANSI C there are five predefined macros. They are always available, and they cannot be undefined by the programmer. Each of these macro names includes two leading and two trailing underscore characters.

Predefined Macro	*Value*
__DATE__	A string containing the current date.
__FILE__	A string containing the file name.
__LINE__	An integer representing the current line number.
__STDC__	If the implementation follows ANSI Standard C, then the value is a nonzero integer.
__TIME__	A string containing the current time.

In exercise 6 we show how to test what the effects of these macros are on your system.

11.9   THE OPERATORS # AND

The preprocessing operators # and ## are available in ANSI C but not in traditional C. The unary operator # causes "stringization" of a formal parameter in a macro definition. Here is an example of its use:

```
#define   message_for(a, b) \
          printf(#a " and " #b ": We love you!\n")

main()
{
   message_for(Carole, Debra);
}
```

When the macro is invoked, each parameter in the macro definition is replaced by its corresponding argument, with the # causing the argument to be surrounded by double quotes. Thus, after the preprocessor pass, we obtain

```
main()
{
   printf("Carole" " and " "Debra" ": We love you!\n");
}
```

Because string constants separated by white space are concatenated, this printf() statement is equivalent to

```
printf("Carole and Debra: We love you!\n");
```

In the next section we will see how the "stringization" operator # is used in assertions.

The binary operator ## is used to merge tokens. Here is an example of how the operator is used:

```
#define   X(i)   x ## i

X(1) = X(2) = X(3);
```

After the preprocessor pass, we are left with the line

```
x1 = x2 = x3;
```

11.10   THE assert() MACRO

ANSI C provides the assert() macro in the standard header file *assert.h*. This macro can be used to ensure that the value of an expression is what you expect it to be. Suppose that you are writing a critical function, and you want to be sure that the arguments satisfy certain conditions. Here is an example of how assert() can be used to do this:

```
#include <assert.h>

void f(char *p, int n)
{
    .....
    assert(p != NULL);
    assert(n > 0 && n < 5);
    .....
```

If an assertion fails, then the system will print out a message and abort the program. Although the assert() macro is implemented differently on each system, its general behavior is always the same. Here is one way that the macro might be written:

```
#if defined(NDEBUG)
    #define   assert(ignore)   ((void) 0)   /* ignore it */
#else
    #define   assert(expr)                      \
        if (!(expr)) {                          \
           printf("\n%s%s\n%s%s\n%s%d\n\n",     \
              "Assertion failed: ", #expr,      \
              "in file ", __FILE__,             \
              "at line ", __LINE__);            \
           abort();                             \
        }
#endif
```

Note that if the macro NDEBUG is defined, then all assertions are ignored. This allows the programmer to use assertions freely during program development, and then to effectively discard them later by defining the macro NDEBUG. The function abort() is in the standard library (see Appendix A).

11.11   THE USE OF **#error** AND **#pragma**

ANSI C has added the `#error` and `#pragma` preprocessing directives. The following code demonstrates how `#error` can be used:

```
#if A_SIZE < B_SIZE
    #error "Incompatible sizes"
#endif
```

If during compilation the preprocessor reaches the `#error` directive, then a compile-time error will occur, and the string following the directive will be printed on the screen. In our example, we used the `#error` macro to enforce the consistency of two symbolic constants. In an analogous fashion, the directive can be used to enforce other conditions.

The `#pragma` directive is provided for implementation-specific uses. Its general form is

```
#pragma    tokens
```

It causes a behavior that depends on the particular C compiler. Any `#pragma` that is not recognized by the compiler is ignored.

11.12   LINE NUMBERS

A preprocessing directive of the form

```
#line    integral_constant    "filename"
```

causes the compiler to renumber the source text so that the next line has the specified constant and to believe that the current source file name is *filename*. If no file name is present, then only the renumbering of lines takes place. Normally, line numbers are hidden from the programmer and occur only in reference to warnings and syntax errors.

11.13   CORRESPONDING FUNCTIONS

In ANSI C, many of the macros with parameters that are given in the standard header files are supposed to have corresponding functions in the standard library. As an example, suppose we want to access the function isalpha() instead of the macro. One way to do this is to write

```
#undef isalpha
```

somewhere in the file before isalpha() is invoked. This has the effect of discarding the macro definition, forcing the compiler to use the function instead. We would still include the header file *ctype.h* at the top of the file, because in addition to macros, the file contains function prototypes.

Another way to obtain the function instead of the macro is to write

```
(isalpha)(c)
```

The preprocessor does not recognize this construct as a macro. The compiler, however, recognizes it as a function call.

11.14   SOFTWARE METHODOLOGY

Some of the concerns of software methodology for writing code are correctness, readability, portability, maintainability, and ease of code development. These issues become more important as program size grows. For all of these issues, modularity is a key idea. C provides the function facility to write modular code. This facility allows the programmer to break the code into manageable pieces.

Modularity is a fundamental concept of software methodology. It is the grouping together of logically related units of code and data in such a way that the details of implementation are hidden from other sections of the program. Each of these groups is called a *module*. Ideally, a module should present only the simplest interface to the rest of the program. This is important because critical errors can occur in the interactions between sections of a program. Another important effect of this isolation is to greatly enhance reusability, the ability to reuse a module in the same or subsequent programs. In C, a module corresponds to a file.

11.15   DEVELOPING A LARGE PROGRAM

Typically, a large program is written in a separate directory as a collection of *.h* and *.c* files, with each *.c* file containing one or more function definitions. Each *.c* file can be recompiled as needed, saving time for both the programmer and the machine. We discuss this further in Chapter 15, where we explain about libraries and the use of *make*.

Let us suppose that we are developing a large program called *pgm*. At the top of each of our *.c* files we put the line

```
#include "pgm.h"
```

Our header file *pgm.h* contains prototypes of all our functions, our macro definitions, templates of our enumeration types, and templates of our structure and union types. At the top of *pgm.h* we put directives such as

```
#include <stdio.h>
#include <stdlib.h>
 . . . . .
```

Thus *pgm.h* contains program elements that are appropriate for our program as a whole. Since each of our *.c* files includes *pgm.h*, it acts as the "glue" that binds our program together.

When a program consists of multiple files, each of the files can be compiled separately, as necessary. Separate compilation can facilitate the edit-compile-test cycle of code development. That is, when a new function is added to the program, or an old function is corrected or redesigned, all the other functions do not have to be recompiled. In developing a large program, this can save a lot of time. In Section 11.19, "System Considerations," we will discuss the mechanics of separate compilation. In Chapter 15 we will discuss the *make* utility, which automatically keeps track of the files that need to be recompiled.

11.16   AN EXAMPLE: PRINTING IN COLUMNS

In this section we will write a program composed of functions written in separate files that does some text processing. The program will read from the standard input file and write to the standard output file. Words in the input file will be written in columns, and possibly capitalized, too. Let us use *mk_cols* as the name of the program. If we want the words in *infile* printed in seven columns and at the same time printed in uppercase letters, then an appropriate command would be

> *mk_cols −7 −u < infile > outfile*

We are using the UNIX convention that command line options are flagged with a minus sign (see exercise 20 for further discussion). The −7 option indicates that seven columns are desired. We will print in three columns by default. The −u option indicates that uppercase letters are desired.

Since this is a serious program, we write it in a separate directory. By convention, the name of the directory is the name of the program. Here is the command that we use to create our directory:

> *mkdir mk_cols*

In the directory *mk_cols* we begin our program development by creating a READ_ME file. This is a place where we keep notes to ourselves concerning the development of the program, improvements planned for the future, and the like. We continually modify and add to this file as we proceed.

In file READ_ME:

```
29 Oct 92

Carole, Barbara, and Debra suggested the -u option.
Uppercase words printed in columns is just what they needed.

Next month, after I learn about dynamic memory allocation,
I need to add a -s option to sort the words. I want to print
alphabetically down the columns rather than across.
```

Next, we start writing our header file. This file also gets modified and added to as we proceed. Here is the final result:

In file mk_cols.h:

```
#ifndef MK_COLS_H
#define MK_COLS_H

#include <ctype.h>
#include <stdio.h>
#include <stdlib.h>
#include <string.h>

#define    MAXWORD        100
#define    N_COLS         3                    /* default value */
#define    SCREEN_WIDTH   80

typedef   enum no_yes {no, yes}   no_yes;

void   get_options(int argc, char **argv,
                   int *n_cols_ptr, no_yes *u_case_ptr);
void   mk_cols(int n_cols, no_yes u_case);
void   prn_info(char *pgm_name);

#endif
```

Although the first, second, and last lines in the header file are not essential, the construct embodied in them is useful in certain situations (see exercise 24).

Next we write main(). This is where we invoke other functions as needed. Notice that it is conceptually easy to add another function call to do other work if we want to modify the program.

In file main.c:

```
#include "mk_cols.h"

main(int argc, char **argv)
{
   int     n_cols;
   no_yes  u_case;

   get_options(argc, argv, &n_cols, &u_case);
   mk_cols(n_cols, u_case);
}
```

The next function is `get_options()`. This is where we process the command line arguments to see what options, if any, are present. We also do some checking for errors, but we do not try to catch all of them. If, for example, we type -7X as an option, the program does not catch the error.

In file get_options.c:

```
#include "mk_cols.h"

void get_options(int argc, char **argv,
                 int *n_cols_ptr, no_yes *u_case_ptr)
{
    char    *pgm_name = argv[0];
    int     i, n_cols = N_COLS;              /* default value */
    no_yes  u_case = no;                     /* default value */

    for (i = 1; i < argc; ++i) {
        if (*argv[i] != '-') {
            printf("ERROR: Inappropriate argument.\n");
            prn_info(pgm_name);
            exit(1);
        }
        if (strcmp(argv[i], "-h") == 0) {
            prn_info(pgm_name);
            exit(1);
        }
        if (isdigit(argv[i][1]))
            sscanf(argv[i] + 1, "%d", &n_cols);
        else if (strcmp(argv[i], "-u") == 0)
            u_case = yes;
        else {
            printf("ERROR: Unknown option.\n");
            prn_info(pgm_name);
            exit(1);
        }
    }
    *n_cols_ptr = n_cols;
    *u_case_ptr = u_case;
}
```

We want to discuss the following code in detail:

```
if (isdigit(argv[i][1]))
    sscanf(argv[i] + 1, "%d", &n_cols);
```

Recall that `argv` is an array of pointers to `char`. The element `argv[i]` points to the first character of the *i*th word (counting from zero) on the command line. Thus `argv[i][j]` is the *j*th character (counting from zero) of the *i*th word (counting from zero) on the command line. Suppose that we have given the command

   mk_cols −*12* . . .

If i has the value 1, then `argv[i]` points to the first character in the string "-12", and `argv[i][1]` is the second character in the string. Since that character is a digit, we want to read in a value for `n_cols`, which indicates the number of columns to be used for printing the words in the input stream. To read in the value, we use `sscanf()`, the string version of `scanf()`. This function is in the standard library, and its function prototype is in *stdio.h*. Instead of reading characters from the standard input file, the function `sscanf()` reads them from its first argument, which must be of type pointer to `char` (a string). The remaining arguments are the same as the arguments to `scanf()`, namely a control string followed by a list of addresses that match the formats in the control string. Here, the first argument to `sscanf()` is

```
argv[i] + 1
```

Since `argv[i]` is a pointer to `char`, adding 1 to it causes the expression to point to the next character. This is an example of pointer arithmetic. Again, let us assume that we have typed the command

   mk_cols −*12* . . .

When i has value 1, this is what we have in memory:

Thus we see that `sscanf()` reads two characters, converts them to a decimal integer, and stores the value at the address of `n_cols`.

In get_options(), we call prn_info() and then exit() if the −h option is typed, or if the user makes an error.

In file prn_info.c:

```
#include "mk_cols.h"

void prn_info(char *pgm_name)
{
   printf("\n%s%s%s\n\n%s%s%s\n\n%s\n\n",
      "Usage:   ", pgm_name, " [-h] [-N] [-u]",
      "Example: ", pgm_name, " -7 < input > output",
      "Words from the standard input file are printed in N columns.");
   printf("%s\n%s\n%s%d\n%s\n\n",
      "Options:",
      "   -h   help option, print this message",
      "   -N   number of columns, by default ", N_COLS,
      "   -u   uppercase option, change lowercase letters to uppercase");
}
```

When this function is invoked, here is what gets printed on the screen:

```
Usage:   mk_cols [-h] [-N] [-u]

Example: mk_cols -7 < input > output

Words from the standard input file are printed in N columns.

Options:
   -h   help option, print this message
   -N   number of columns, by default 3
   -u   uppercase option, change lowercase letters to uppercase
```

We are using the convention that optional items on the command line (the options themselves in our case) are printed in brackets. This convention is widely used in both MS-DOS and UNIX.

In main(), after we have obtained the command line options, we invoke mk_cols(). This is where most of the work gets done.

In file mk_cols.c:

```c
#include "mk_cols.h"

static void    capitalize(char *w);
static char *  get_word(char *w);

void mk_cols(int n_cols, no_yes u_case)
{
   char   w[MAXWORD];
   int    col_cnt, col_width, i, n_blanks;

   col_cnt = n_blanks = 0;
   col_width = SCREEN_WIDTH / n_cols;
   while (get_word(w) != NULL) {
      if (u_case == yes)
         capitalize(w);
      for (i = 0; i < n_blanks; ++i)         /* pad with blanks */
         putchar(' ');
      printf("%s", w);                       /* print the word */
      if (++col_cnt >= n_cols) {
         putchar('\n');
         col_cnt = n_blanks = 0;
      }
      else
         n_blanks = col_width - strlen(w);
   }
   if (col_cnt != 0)
      putchar('\n');
}

static void capitalize(char *w)
{
   for ( ; *w != '\0'; ++w)
      if (islower(*w))
         *w = toupper(*w);
}
```

```
static char *get_word(char *w)
{
   char    *p = w;
   int     c;

   while (isspace(c = getchar()))      /* skip white space */
      ;
   if (c == EOF)
      return NULL;
   *p++ = c;
   while (!isspace(c = getchar()) && c != EOF)
      *p++ = c;
   *p = '\0';
   return w;
}
```

DISSECTION OF THE *mk_cols.c* MODULE

■ #include "mk_cols.h"

```
static void    capitalize(char *w);
static char *  get_word(char *w);
```

At the top of the file we include the header file *mk_cols.h* and then list the prototypes of the functions that are private to this file. Since the functions are static external, they are known only within this module, or file. In another file we could have other private functions with the same name.

■ void mk_cols(int n_cols, no_yes u_case)
```
   {
      char    w[MAXWORD];
```

The parameters n_cols and u_case indicate the number of columns and whether words should be capitalized, respectively. The array w will provide work space to store words read from the standard input file.

■ `col_width = SCREEN_WIDTH / n_cols;`

The algorithm for computing the column width is straightforward. Suppose, for example, we want to print our words in three columns. We divide the screen width, which is 80, by the number of columns, which is 3. Since integer division is performed, any fractional part is discarded. The resulting value is assigned to `col_width`. Suppose the file *input* contains the line

```
She sells sea shells by the seashore.
```

Then the command

mk_cols −3 < input

causes the following to be printed on the screen:

```
She                       sells                     sea
shells                    by                        the
seashore.
```

Each column is 26 characters wide.

■
```
while (get_word(w) != NULL) {
   if (u_case == yes)
      capitalize(w);
   .....
```

As long as `get_word()` is able to get another word and store it in `w`, the body of the `while` loop is repeatedly executed. If the value of `u_case` is `yes`, then we capitalize `w`. After this, we print blanks as necessary to achieve the correct spacing and then print the word `w`.

■
```
static void capitalize(char *w)
{
   .....
```

The storage type `static` used in this context means that this function is private to this file (see Section 8.7 in Chapter 8).

■
```c
static char *get_word(char *w)
{
    char  *p = w;
    int    c;
```

Even though c will be assigned character values, eventually it will hold the value EOF, which is not a character. Thus c is declared to be an int rather than a char.

■
```c
while (isspace(c = getchar()))      /* skip white space */
    ;
if (c == EOF)
    return NULL;
```

First we read from the input stream, discarding any white space characters. After that, if there are no more characters, we return NULL to indicate that we were not able to read a word.

■
```c
*p++ = c;
```

If we do not return NULL, then c is a nonwhite space character. The variable c is assigned to what is pointed to by p. Then p is incremented so that it points to the next character in the string w.

■
```c
while (!isspace(c = getchar()) && c != EOF)
    *p++ = c;
```

As long as we are able to read a nonwhite space character into c, we assign c to what is pointed to by p and then increment p to point to the next character in the string w.

■
```c
*p = '\0';
return w;
```

When we exit the while loop, we assign the null character to what is pointed to by p. The null character \0 serves as the end-of-string sentinel. Finally, w is returned to indicate that we found a word.

11.17 STYLE

A common programming style is to use names ending in *.h* for header files. Of course, the #include facility can be used to include any file, not just those ending in *.h*. There are no restrictions on what can be put into a header file, but it is not considered good programming style to put function definitions there. If functions exist in separate files, they should be in *.c* files that can be compiled separately. It is considered bad programming style to use the #include facility to include a *.c* file.

The use of "syntactic sugar" (see Section 11.2) is not considered good programming style. One can argue that its use is acceptable in personal code, but most serious code must be read and maintained by many people. The beginning programmer may prefer EQ for ==, but the experienced programmer will certainly prefer ==.

By convention, capital letters are used for the names of symbolic constants defined in a macro. Although any identifier can be used, the use of capitals allows the reader of a program to readily identify text that will be expanded by the preprocessor. In contrast to this, macros with arguments often have lowercase names. An example is

```
#define   max(x, y)   (((x) > (y)) ? (x) : (y))
```

Since the programmer intends to use this in place of a function, the lowercase name seems appropriate. Note that macros such as assert() and isspace() that are supplied by the system also have lowercase names.

Function prototypes are written at the bottom of a header file, because they typically need the programming constructs that come earlier in the file. In a module (a *.c* file), however, they usually are written near the top of the file, just before the first function definition. We used this style in the module *mk_cols.c* in Section 11.16. Instead, we could have written

```
#include "mk_cols.h"

void mk_cols(int n_cols, no_yes u_case)
{
    static void    capitalize(char *w);
    static char    *get_word(char *w);
    . . . . .
```

Some compilers will make function prototypes that are placed within the body of a function visible throughout the file, even though in ANSI C they should be visible only within the function. Other compilers will issue a warning. The preferred style is to give function prototypes file visibility by placing them before any function definitions.

11.18   COMMON PROGRAMMING ERRORS

Recall that in Section 11.3 we gave a fully parenthesized macro definition of SQ(). In this section we want to explain fully why all the parentheses are necessary. First, suppose that we had defined the macro as

```
#define   SQ(x)   x * x
```

With this definition

```
SQ(a + b)          expands to          a + b * a + b
```

which, because of operator precedence, is not the same as

```
((a + b) * (a + b))
```

Now suppose that we had defined the macro as

```
#define   SQ(x)   (x) * (x)
```

With this definition

```
4 / SQ(2)          expands to          4 / (2) * (2)
```

which, because of operator precedence, is not the same as

```
4 / ((2) * (2))
```

Finally, let us suppose that we had defined the macro as

```
#define   SQ (x)   ((x) * (x))
```

With this definition

```
SQ(7)          expands to          (x)   ((x) * (x)) (7)
```

which is not even close to what was intended. If in the macro definition there is a space between the macro name and the left parenthesis that follows, then the rest of the line is taken as replacement text.

Even when a macro is written in a robust fashion as in the example

```
#define   SQ(x)    ((x) * (x))
```

things can go wrong. If, for example, we were to write SQ(++k), the macro call would get expanded to

```
((++k) * (++k))
```

which is certainly not what we intended. If SQ(++k) were a function call instead of a macro call, there would be no problem. The expression ++k would be evaluated, and a copy of that value would be passed to the function.

Another common programming error is to end a #define line with a semicolon, making it part of the replacement string when it is not wanted. As an example of this, consider

```
#define   SQ(x)    ((x) * (x));
```

The semicolon here was typed by mistake—a mistake that is easily made since programmers often end a line of code with a semicolon. When used in the body of a function, the line

```
x = SQ(y);           gets expanded to           x = ((y) * (y));;
```

The last semicolon creates an unwanted null statement. If we were to write

```
if (x == 2)
   x = SQ(y);
else
   ++x;
```

we would get a syntax error caused by the unwanted null statement. The extra semicolon does not allow the else to be attached to the if statement.

Although macros with arguments in many cases act like functions, they are different because the preprocessor expands them into in-line code. Because of this, the programmer can make mistakes. Consider the following macro:

```
#define   PRN(array, size)   printf("\n");                    \
                             for (i = 0; i < size; ++i)   \
                                 printf("%5d", array[i])
```

Suppose that we want to use this macro to print an array five times. To accomplish this, we might write

```
for (j = 0; j < 5; ++j)
   PRN(a, n);
```

This, however, will not produce the desired results. The preprocessor will expand these two lines of code into new code that is equivalent to

```
for (j = 0; j < 5; ++j)
   printf("\n");
for (i = 0; i < n; ++i)
   printf("%5d", a[i]);
```

We will get five newlines and a single printout of the array. If an error such as this occurs, it can be quite mystifying. To guard against this type of error, one can use braces in the macro definition.

11.19   SYSTEM CONSIDERATIONS

Most C systems are able to provide the programmer with the result of the (conceptual) preprocessor pass, prior to compilation. On some systems the preprocessing is done as a separate step; on other systems it is done along with compilation. Either method is acceptable in ANSI C.

Using macros with arguments is intrinsically error prone. This is true for experienced programmers, as well as for beginners. To debug code with macros, the programmer needs access to the output of the preprocessor.

Suppose that we are having trouble with a macro that we are using in, say, *pgm.c*. In UNIX, we can give the command

cc −E pgm.c

This causes the preprocessor to write its results on the screen. No compilation will occur. Similar facilities exist in the MS-DOS world. In Turbo C, for example, we would give the command

cpp pgm.c

This causes the preprocessor to write its results in the file *pgm.i.* (The name *cpp* is mnemonic for "C preprocessor.") Many compilers write the output of the (conceptual) preprocessor pass into a *.i* file. (The *.i* suffix is mnemonic for "intermediate" code.)

In ANSI C, the compiler changes a comment into a single blank character. In traditional C, how comments are treated is system-dependent. In many traditional systems, comments are completely removed. Thus A/* comment */B becomes AB, which we can think of as pasting A and B. In ANSI C, the preprocessing operator ## is provided to paste tokens. This operator is not available in traditional C.

ANSI C provides for the separate compilation of modules. To compile the *.c* files that comprise the *mk_cols* program, we can give the command

> *cc main.c get_options.c mk_cols.c prn_info.c*

In UNIX, this command causes the compiler to produce *.o* files corresponding to each of the *.c* files, and it causes the loader to write the executable code into *a.out*, overwriting anything that may be there already. The *.o* files are called *object files*. The loader uses them to make the executable file. In MS-DOS, the object files have a *.obj* extension, and the executable file is written into a file having the same name as the first file on the command line, except it has the extension *.exe.* See Section 15, "The C Compiler," in Chapter 15 for further discussion.

11.20 SUMMARY

1   The preprocessor provides facilities for file inclusion and for defining macros. Files may be included by using preprocessing directives of the form

> #include <*filename*>
> #include "*filename*"

2   A #define preprocessing directive can be used to give a symbolic name to a token string. The preprocessor substitutes the string for the symbolic name in the source text before compilation.

3   The use of the #define facility to define symbolic constants enhances readability and portability of programs.

4   The preprocessor provides a general macro facility with argument substitution. A macro with parameters is defined by a preprocessing directive of the form

> #define   *identifier(identifier, . . . , identifier)*   *token_string*$_{opt}$

An example is given by

```
#define   swap(x, y)   {int t; t = x; x = y; y = t;}
```

This macro provides in-line code to perform the swap of two values. It is not a function call.

5 The preprocessor provides for conditional compilation to aid in program testing, to facilitate porting, and so on. Lines beginning with `#if`, `#ifdef`, `#ifndef`, `#elif`, `#else`, and `#endif` are used for this.

6 The `defined` operator can be used with preprocessing directives. An example is

```
#if (defined(HP3000) || defined(SUN3)) && !defined(SUN4)
    .....        /* machine-dependent code */
#endif
```

7 An effective way to block out sections of code for debugging purposes is to use

```
#if 0
.....
#endif
```

8 The function `qsort()` is provided by the standard library. Its function prototype is in *stdlib.h*. When sorting a lot of data, the use of `qsort()` is much faster than a bubble sort or a simple transposition sort.

9 The preprocessing operators `#` and `##` are available in ANSI C, but not in traditional C. The `#` operator is unary. It can be applied to a formal parameter in the body of the macro. It causes replacement text to be surrounded by double quotes. This effect is called *stringization*. The `##` operator is binary. It causes the pasting together of two tokens.

10 The macro `assert()` is defined in the system header file *assert.h*. Assertions are used to ensure that expressions have appropriate values. They are available in both ANSI C and traditional C.

11 A common programming methodology for creating a large program is to write functions in separate modules (files). An essential part of this methodology is to create appropriate header files that can be included at the top of the modules. In these header files we put `#include`'s, `#define`'s, `typedef`'s, templates of `enum`'s, other templates, and function prototypes. These header files provide the "glue" between the modules that constitute the program.

11.21   EXERCISES

1   Experiment with your system. The following preprocessing directive gives π correct to 41 significant digits.

```
#define    PI    3.14159265358979323846264338327950288841972
```

Write a test program containing this #define line and the statements

```
printf("pi = %.40f\n", PI);
printf("pi = %.50f\n", PI);
```

What gets printed? (Don't believe everything you read.)

2   Write a macro definition for XOR(), called *exclusive or*. A macro call such as XOR(a, b) should be true if a is true and b is false, or if a is false and b is true. In all other cases the macro call should be false. For example, XOR(0, 1) should be true, and XOR(1, 1) should be false. In contrast to this, the expression 1 || 1 is true. Write a program that tests your XOR() macro.

3   Write macro definitions for XOR_3() and XOR_4() that can be considered extended versions of the "exclusive or" operator. In general, the macro XOR_*n*() would have *n* parameters in its macro definition. The macro call XOR_3(a, b, c) should be true if and only if one of the three arguments a, b, and c is true, and all the others are false. Similarly, the macro call XOR_4(a, b, c, d) should be true if and only if one of the four arguments a, b, c, and d is true, and all the others are false. Write a program that tests your macros. *Hint:* Use nested for loops in your test program.

4   Can XOR be defined as a macro so that one could write a XOR b instead of XOR(a, b)? That is, can XOR be defined to be a binary operator in the same sense as && and ||?

5   Write a macro definition PRN_STRING(x) that prints the string x followed by an integer representing the length of the string and a newline character. There should be three spaces between the end of the string and the number. Write a program to test your macro.

6   What are the effects of the predefined macros available on your system? Try the following code:

```
printf("%s%s\n%s%s\n%s%d\n%s%d\n%s%s\n",
    "__DATE__ = ", __DATE__,
    "__FILE__ = ", __FILE__,
    "__LINE__ = ", __LINE__,
    "__STDC__ = ", __STDC__,
    "__TIME__ = ", __TIME__);
```

7 In traditional C, some compilers allow the preprocessor to change a string constant. In ANSI C, this is not allowed. What happens with your compiler? To find out, put the following lines in a file, say *try_me.c*:

```
#include <stdio.h>

#define   test(s)   printf("%s\n", s)   /* what happens to %s? */

main()
{
    test("abc");
}
```

Create another file that contains the results of the preprocessor pass on your system. On a UNIX system, for example, you can do this with the command

   cc −E try_me.c > tmp

In Turbo C, we invoke the preprocessor directly with the command

   cpp try_me.c

The output of the preprocessor is written to a *.i* file, in this case *try_me.i*. Now read the file to see what the effects of the preprocessor were. The file *try_me.c* has two lines that contain the word test. Delete all the other lines in the file. What is left is certainly not a C program. Does it make sense to run it through the preprocessor? Will the preprocessor complain? Try it.

8 Write a macro definition for PRN3() so that it behaves in the following way. If x, y, and z have the values 1.1, 2.2, and 3.3, respectively, then the statement

   PRN3(x, y, z);

should cause the following line to be printed:

```
x has value 1.1
y has value 2.2
z has value 3.3
```

Write a program that tests your macro. *Hint:* Use stringization to get the arguments printed as strings.

9   Macro definitions are not always as safe as function definitions, even when all the arguments are enclosed in parentheses. Write the macro definition for max(x, y, z) so that it produces a value corresponding to the largest of its three arguments. Construct some expressions to use in max() that produce unanticipated results.

10 What is the largest floating point constant available on your system? Is this constant in *math.h*? *Hint:* Try the following program:

```c
#include <math.h>

main()
{
    printf("HUGE_VAL = %.16e\n", HUGE_VAL);
}
```

11 The following program uses the stringization operator. What gets printed?

```c
#include <stdio.h>

#define   PRN(x)   \
          printf("%s%s%s%d\n", "value of ", #x, ": ", x)

#define   PRN2(x, y)   \
          PRN(x); PRN(y)

#define   PRN4(x1, x2, x3, x4)   \
          PRN2(x1, x2); PRN2(x3, x4)

main()
{
    int   a[] = {2, 3, 5, 7, 11, 13, 17, 19};   /* prime numbers */

    PRN4(a[0], a[1], a[2], a[3]);
    PRN4(a[4], a[5], a[6], a[7]);
}
```

Suppose that we rewrite the printf() expression as

```
printf("%s%2d\n", "value of " #x ": ", x)
```

Does this make sense? Try it.

12 Modify the program in exercise 11 by declaring the array a to be of type char instead of int. The program should still produce the same output. Does it? Make a further change to the program by replacing the macro PRN() with the function

```
void PRN(int x)
{
    printf("%s%2d\n", "value of " #x ": ", x);
}
```

What happens now? Does the program behave the same?

13 Write a program that uses the following macro to fill an array.

```
#define   FILL(array, size)               \
              for (i = 0; i < size; ++i)   \
                  array[i] = rand() % 100
```

One difficulty with using a backslash to continue a line is that blanks and tabs are not allowed after the backslash. If the programmer makes this kind of mistake, it is not visible. Deliberately put some blanks after the first backslash character to see how your compiler handles this error. On most systems the compiler will produce weird error messages that do not pinpoint the trouble. Capture the output of the preprocessor pass in a file and examine it. You will see that something is wrong, but again it will be difficult to see just what is causing the error.

14 The use of a macro such as the one given in exercise 13 is error prone. This is because i is not a parameter. Let us rewrite the macro as follows:

```
#define   FILL(array, size) {              \
              int   i;                      \
              for (i = 0; i < size; ++i)    \
                  array[i] = rand() % 100;  \
          }
```

Now i is a variable that is local to the block enclosing it. Use this macro in a program that contains the following lines:

```
int    a[3], b[7];

if (rand() % 2 == 0)
    FILL(a, 3);
else
    FILL(b, 7);
```

Your program will not compile. Do you know why? *Hint:* Examine the output of the preprocessor.

15 In ANSI C, the nesting of comments is not allowed. However, some compilers, such as Turbo C, provide an option for this. Write a program to see how your compiler treats the following line:

```
/* is this /* really */ a comment? */
```

Also, check to see that the construct

```
#if 0
    .....
#endif
```

can be used on your system to block out code, including code that is commented. *Warning:* Even if a compiler provides an option for the nesting of comments, you should not use this feature if you want your code to be portable to other systems.

16 Experiment with the *mk_cols* program. Execute it with the −*h* command line options, causing prn_info() to be called. Rename the program and do it again. Do you see why it is better not to hardwire the name of a program into the code? Suppose *text* is the name of a file with some text in it. Try the command

   mk_cols −4 −u < text

so that you understand the effects of the program. What happens if you interchange the two options on the command line?

17 Rewrite the *mk_cols* program, adding the −*l* option to indicate that the words are to be printed with lowercase letters. Write the program in such a way that either −*l* or −*u* can occur as a command line option, but not both.

18 In the *mk_cols* program we defined a word to be a string of nonwhite space characters of maximal length. Thus, for example, a hyphenated word such as *end-of-file*

is considered to be a single word. Rewrite the program so that a word is defined to be a string of alphabetic characters of maximal length. All other characters should be discarded. With this new definition *end-of-file* will be treated as three separate words, and the hyphens will be discarded.

19   Redesign the *mk_cols* program to use the function get_number() instead of get_word() if a −n option is typed on the command line. The function get_number() should select characters such as 1.23 and −77 from the input file, discarding all other characters.

20   In MS-DOS, the following command will list the files in a directory in multiple columns:

  dir /w

In UNIX, the comparable command is

  ls −C

By convention, command line options are flagged with a slash character in MS-DOS and with a minus sign in UNIX. In the *mk_cols* program we hardwired the UNIX minus sign flag into the code. In this exercise we want to redesign the program so that it can be ported easily to either an MS-DOS or UNIX environment. First, add the line

```
#define   FLAG   '-'      /* UNIX flag character */
```

to the header file. Then rewrite the code so that only this line has to be modified to port the code to an MS-DOS machine.

21   Execute the following program so that you understand its effects.

```
#include <stdio.h>

#define   greetings(a, b, c)  \
          printf(#a ", " #b ", and " #c ":   Hello!\n")

main()
{
    greetings(Alice, Bob, Carole);
}
```

Experiment to find out if there can be white space following the unary stringization operator. Explain why Alice, Bob, and Carole do not have to be declared. *Hint:* Examine the output of the preprocessor.

22 In Section 11.6 we discussed the *sort* program and showed the output from the program on our system. If you examine the output, you will see that 8.8 gets printed before 2.8. Modify the compare_fractional_part() function so that if the fractional parts of two numbers are equal, then the numbers are printed in their natural order.

23 Implement the *sort* program, making sure that it compiles without warnings. Then rewrite the lexico() function as follows:

```
int lexico(const void *p, const void *q)
{
    return (*((char *) p) - *((char *) q));
}
```

Your compiler should be happy with this function. Is it? Explain why this function is equivalent to the previous one.

24 Consider the header file *mk_cols.h* that we used in Section 11.16 to build the *mk_cols* program:

```
#ifndef MK_COLS_H
#define MK_COLS_H

. . . . .
#endif
```

In this exercise we want to explain why the construct embodied in the first, second, and last lines can be useful. First try the following experiment. Concatenate the *.h* file and all the *.c* files into a single *.c* file. In UNIX, we can do this with the command

    cat mk_cols.h main.c get_options.c mk_cols.c prn_info.c > tmp.c

Now compile *tmp.c* and execute the resulting program so that you understand that its effects are the same as those of the *mk_cols* program. After you have done this, remove the first, second, and last lines in *mk_cols.h*, and then repeat the experiment. You will see that your compiler is unhappy. Explain why. Suppose you want to share your program with a friend. With the original header file, you can do this by concatenating all the files into a single *.c* file and then sending it via e-mail. Of course, you can send each file separately, and then send instructions to your friend on what to do with them, but it is simpler to deal with just one file. Just for the record, there are ways of assembling together a lot of files, sending the result via e-mail, and then disassembling it at the other end. We could, for example, use the *shar* utility. But even if you know how to use *shar* (it is not difficult), you may not find it easy to explain its use via e-mail to your friend.

12

RECURSION

12.1 RECURSIVE PROBLEM SOLVING

12.2 AN EXAMPLE: DRAWING PATTERNS ON THE SCREEN

12.3 STRING HANDLING USING RECURSION

12.4 THE DIVIDE-AND-CONQUER METHODOLOGY

12.5 STYLE

12.6 COMMON PROGRAMMING ERRORS

12.7 SYSTEM CONSIDERATIONS

12.8 SUMMARY

12.9 EXERCISES

Recursion is a function invoking itself, either directly or indirectly. Some programming tasks are naturally solved with the use of recursion, which can be considered an advanced form of flow of control. Recursion is an alternative to iteration.

Recursion will be explained using some simple example programs. One particularly nice example is a function that draws different patterns on the screen. Another example is the recursive calculation of string length. Recursion is a programming technique that naturally implements the divide-and-conquer problem solving methodology, a powerful strategy that will be explained along with an example taken from sorting algorithms.

12.1   RECURSIVE PROBLEM SOLVING

A function is said to be *recursive* if it calls itself, either directly or indirectly. In C all functions can be used recursively. In its simplest form the idea of recursion is straightforward.

```
#include <stdio.h>

void   count_down(int n);

main()
{
   count_down(10);
}

void count_down(int n)
{
   if (n) {
      printf("%d !  ", n);
      count_down(n - 1);
   }
   else
      printf("\nBLAST OFF\n");
}
```

This program prints

```
10 !  9 !  8 !  7 !  6 !  5 !  4 !  3 !  2 !  1 !
BLAST OFF
```

This could have been accomplished by using an iterative statement enclosing the printf(). What is new here is that count_down() invokes itself.

Another simple example of a recursive function is the following, which computes the sum of the first *n* positive integers.

```
int sum(int n)
{
   if (n <= 1)
      return n;
   else
      return (n + sum(n - 1));
}
```

The recursive function sum() is analyzed as illustrated in the following table. First the base case is considered; then working out from the base case, the other cases are considered.

Function call	Value returned
sum(1)	1
sum(2)	2 + sum(1) or 2 + 1
sum(3)	3 + sum(2) or 3 + 2 + 1
sum(4)	4 + sum(3) or 4 + 3 + 2 + 1

Simple recursive routines follow a standard pattern. Typically there is a base case that is tested for on entry to the function. Then there is a general recursive case in which one of the variables, often an integer, is passed as an argument in such a way as to ultimately lead to the base case. In sum() the variable n was reduced by 1 each time until the base case with n equal to 1 was reached.

Recursion is a very powerful problem solving technique. The key is to identify a general case. A pitfall is to forget to reach the base case that terminates the recursion.

When an integer *n* is passed to sum(), the recursion activates *n* nested copies of the function before returning level by level to the original call. This means that *n* function calls are used in the computation. Most simple recursive functions can be rewritten in an equivalent iterative form. Since function calls usually require more computation than iteration, why use recursion at all? If the code is easier to write and maintain using recursion, and run-time efficiency is not critical, then the use of recursion is justified.

In the remainder of this chapter we present examples that illustrate the ideas and power of recursion. The following program first prompts the user to type in a line, and then by means of a recursive function reprints the line backwards.

```
/* Write a line backwards. */

#include <stdio.h>

void  prn_it(void);

main()
{
   printf("Input a line:  ");
   prn_it();
   printf("\n\n");
}

void prn_it(void)
{
   char   c;

   if ((c = getchar()) != '\n')
      prn_it();
   putchar(c);
}
```

If the user types in the line sing a song of sixpence when prompted, then the following appears on the screen:

```
Input a line:  sing a song of sixpence

ecnepxis fo gnos a gnis
```

DISSECTION OF THE *wr_bkwds* PROGRAM

■ printf("Input a line: ");
  prn_it();

The invocation of the recursive function prn_it() occurs after a prompt to the user. The user writes a line and terminates it by hitting a carriage return, which is the character \n.

■ if ((c = getchar()) != '\n')
    prn_it();

As each character is read in, it initiates a new call to prn_it(). Each call has its own local storage for the variable c in which the individual characters of the input line get stored. Each call is stacked until the newline character is read.

■ putchar(c);

Only after the newline character is read does anything get written. Each invocation of prn_it() now prints the value stored in its local variable c. First the newline character is outputted, then the character just before it, and so on, until the first character is outputted. Thus the input line is reversed.

An interesting variation on this theme is to read in a line of words and print the line back out with the order of the words reversed. Here is a program that does this.

```
#include <ctype.h>
#include <stdio.h>

#define    MAXWORD    100

void    prn_it_by_word(void);
void    get_word(char *);

main()
{
    printf("Input a line:  ");
    prn_it_by_word();
    printf("\n\n");
}

void prn_it_by_word(void)
{
    char    w[MAXWORD];

    get_word(w);
    if (w[0] != '\n')
        prn_it_by_word();
    printf("%s ", w);
}
```

```
void get_word(char *s)
{
    static char   c = '\0';

    if (c == '\n')
        *s++ = c;
    else
        while (!isspace(c = getchar()))
            *s++ = c;
    *s = '\0';
}
```

If the user types in the line deep in the heart of texas when prompted, then the following appears on the screen:

```
Input a line:  deep in the heart of texas

texas of heart the in deep
```

Notice that the variable c has storage class static, so that when a newline character is read in and assigned to c, that sentinel value will not be lost on exit from the function. The initialization of c occurs only when the function get_word() is invoked for the first time. This is because the storage class of c is static. On subsequent function calls, the value of c is whatever was there when the previous call exited. Since static storage is guaranteed to be initialized to zero, the explicit initialization of c is not really necessary. Nonetheless, it reminds the reader that the initial value of the variable c is the null character.

    The next example illustrates a recursive function that manipulates characters in a string. It can easily be rewritten as an equivalent iterative function.

```
/* Reverse the characters between s[j] and s[k] recursively. */

#include <stdio.h>

void    reverse(char *s, int j, int k);
void    swap(char *, char *);

main()
{
   char    phrase[] = "by the sea, by the beautiful sea";

   reverse(phrase, 3, 17);
   printf("%s\n", phrase);
}

void reverse(char *s, int j, int k)
{
   if (j < k) {
      swap(&s[j], &s[k]);
      reverse(s, ++j, --k);
   }
}

void swap(char *p, char *q)
{
   char    tmp;

   tmp = *p;
   *p = *q;
   *q = tmp;
}
```

Here is the output from our program:

```
by eht yb ,aes eht beautiful sea
```

Notice that the characters from position 3 to position 17 have been reversed, counting from zero.

12.2   AN EXAMPLE: DRAWING PATTERNS ON THE SCREEN

Elaborate patterns can be drawn on the screen with the use of recursive functions. We will illustrate this with a simple example.

```
#include <stdio.h>

#define   SYMBOL   '*'
#define   OFFSET   0
#define   LENGTH   19

void  display(char, int, int);
void  draw(char, int);

main()
{
   display(SYMBOL, OFFSET, LENGTH);
}

void display(char c, int m, int n)
{
   if (n > 0) {
      draw(' ', m);
      draw(c, n);
      putchar('\n');
      display(c, m + 2, n - 4);
   }
}

void draw(char c, int k)
{
   if (k > 0) {
      putchar(c);
      draw(c, k - 1);
   }
}
```

The function main() calls display(), which in turn calls draw() and display(). Thus display() is recursive. The function draw() prints k copies of a character c. We have written this function to be recursive as well. Here is what appears on the screen when we execute this program:

```
* * * * * * * * * * * * * * * * * * *
  * * * * * * * * * * * * * * *
    * * * * * * * * * *
      * * * * * * *
        * * *
```

12.3 STRING HANDLING USING RECURSION

A string consists of contiguous characters in memory, ending with the null character \0. Conceptually, we can think of a string as either the null string, consisting of just the null character, or as a character followed by a string. This definition of a string describes it as a recursive data structure. We can use this to code some basic string handling functions recursively.

In Chapter 10 we showed how the standard library function strlen() could be coded as an iteration. Here we show how it can be coded recursively.

```
/* Recursive string length. */

int r_strlen(char *s)
{
    if (*s == '\0')
        return 0;
    else
        return (1 + r_strlen(s + 1));
}
```

The base case tests for the empty string. The recursion is invoked as r_strlen(s + 1), where s + 1 is a pointer expression. The expression points one character further down the string.

The elegance of this recursive formulation is paid for in a loss of run-time efficiency. If a string is length k, computing it will require $k + 1$ function calls of r_strlen(). An optimizing compiler could avoid this penalty.

String comparison is somewhat more complicated. We will write a recursive version of the standard library function strncmp(). It lexicographically compares at most the first *n* characters of two strings.

```
/* Recursive string n compare. */

int r_strncmp(char *s1, char *s2, int n)
{
    if (*s1 != *s2 || *s1 == '\0' || n == 1)
        return (*s1 - *s2);
    else
        return (r_strncmp(++s1, ++s2, --n));
}
```

This function looks at the first character of the two strings pointed at by s1 and s2. If the two characters are different, or both of them are the null character, or the value of n is 1, then the value returned is the difference of the two characters. Otherwise the function recurs, incrementing both string pointers and decrementing n. The recursion will terminate at the first position where the two strings differ, or at the position where both of the characters are null, or after at most n – 1 recursions.

12.4   THE DIVIDE-AND-CONQUER METHODOLOGY

A typical place where recursion is used is in coding a divide-and-conquer algorithm. Such an algorithm divides the problem into smaller pieces, solves each piece either directly or by recursion, and recombines the solution of the parts into the solution of the whole.

Let us use the divide-and-conquer method to find both the maximum and minimum elements in an array of integers. In 1972 in the article "A Sorting Problem and Its Complexity" (*Communications of the ACM*, 15, no. 6), one of the authors, Ira Pohl, published the best possible algorithm for this problem. The criterion for "best" is the least number of comparisons needed. For simplicity, we will treat here only the case where the number of elements in the array is a power of 2. In the exercises at the end of the chapter we continue our discussion of the algorithm and modify it to remove the power of 2 restriction.

```
/* The best possible minmax algorithm - Pohl, 1972 */

/* The size of the array a is n; it must be a power of 2. */
/* The code can be rewritten to remove this restriction.  */

void minmax(int a[], int n, int *min_ptr, int *max_ptr)
{
    int   min1, max1, min2, max2;

    if (n == 2)
        if (a[0] < a[1]) {
            *min_ptr = a[0];
            *max_ptr = a[1];
        }
        else {
            *min_ptr = a[1];
            *max_ptr = a[0];
        }
    else {
        minmax(a, n/2, &min1, &max1);
        minmax(a + n/2, n/2, &min2, &max2);
        if (min1 < min2)
            *min_ptr = min1;
        else
            *min_ptr = min2;
        if (max1 < max2)
            *max_ptr = max2;
        else
            *max_ptr = max1;
    }
}
```

DISSECTION OF THE minmax() FUNCTION

■
```
if (n == 2)
    if (a[0] < a[1]) {
        *min_ptr = a[0];
        *max_ptr = a[1];
    }
    else {
        *min_ptr = a[1];
        *max_ptr = a[0];
    }
```

This is the base case. The smaller of the two elements a[0] and a[1] will be assigned to the value pointed to by min_ptr, and the larger of the two elements will be assigned to the value pointed to by max_ptr.

■
```
else {
    minmax(a, n/2, &min1, &max1);
    minmax(a + n/2, n/2, &min2, &max2);
```

This is the divide-and-conquer step. The array a is divided into two halves. The first invocation finds the minimum and maximum among the elements a[0], . . . , a[n/2 -1]. The second invocation looks for the minimum and maximum among the second half of the elements a[n/2], . . . , a[n-1]. Note that a is a pointer expression having the value &a[0], and that a + n/2 is a pointer expression having the value &a[n/2].

■
```
if (min1 < min2)
    *min_ptr = min1;
else
    *min_ptr = min2;
```

The minimum values from the two halves are compared, and the smaller of the two values is assigned to the object pointed to by min_ptr, the overall minimum.

■
```
if (max1 < max2)
    *max_ptr = max2;
else
    *max_ptr = max1;
```

Similarly the overall maximum value is assigned to the object pointed to by max_ptr.

This algorithm has theoretical, as well as practical, implications. Further ideas are discussed in exercises 11 and 12 at the end of this chapter. In particular, exercise 12 concerns the removal of the power of 2 restriction on the size of the array a[].

Many algorithms for sorting use the divide-and-conquer technique. An especially important one is the sorting algorithm "quicksort"; see *A Book on C* by Al Kelley and Ira Pohl (Menlo Park, Calif.: Benjamin/Cummings, 1990).

12.5 STYLE

In most common uses of recursion there is a simple, equivalent iterative program. Recursion simplifies the coding by suppressing the need for local variables that keep track of different indices. Iteration is often a more efficient method of solution. Which method to code is frequently a matter of taste.

Let us write a simple recursive program that computes the average value of an array.

```
double average(double a[], int n)      /* n is the size of a[] */
{
   if (n == 1)
      return a[0];
   else
      return ((a[n - 1] + (n - 1) * average(a, n - 1)) / n);
}
```

In such cases, where the recursion is elementary, there is a simple transformation to an iterative form using a while or for loop. Here is the iterative form of the function average().

```
double average(double a[], int n)      /* n is the size of a[] */
{
   double   sum = 0.0;
   int      i;

   for (i = 0; i < n; ++i)
      sum += a[i];
   return (sum / n);
}
```

In this case the iterative form of the function is simpler. It also avoids $n - 1$ function calls, where n is the size of the array being averaged. A common programming style is to choose the iterative version over the recursive version of a function if both versions are simple. Nonetheless, many algorithms are commonly coded using recursion. One such algorithm is "quicksort." Another is the greatest common divisor algorithm given in exercise 9 at the end of this chapter.

12.6 COMMON PROGRAMMING ERRORS

The most common errors in recursive functions lead to infinite loops. We shall use the recursive definition of factorial to illustrate several common pitfalls.

For a nonnegative integer n, the factorial of n, written $n!$, is defined by

$$0! = 1, \qquad n! = n(n - 1) \cdots 3 \cdot 2 \cdot 1 \qquad \text{for } n > 0$$

or equivalently,

$$0! = 1, \qquad n! = n((n - 1)!) \qquad \text{for } n > 0$$

Thus, for example, $5! = 5 \cdot 4 \cdot 3 \cdot 2 \cdot 1 = 120$. Using the recursive definition of factorial, it is easy to write a recursive version of the factorial function.

```
int factorial(int n)     /* recursive version */
{
   if (n <= 1)
      return 1;
   else
      return (n * factorial(n - 1));
}
```

This code is correct and will work properly within the limits of integer precision available on a given system. However, since the numbers $n!$ grow large very fast, the function call factorial(n) yields a valid result only for a few values of n. On our system the function call factorial(12) returns a correct value, but if the argument to the function is greater than 12, an incorrect value is returned. This type of programming error is common. Functions that are logically correct can return incorrect values if the logical operations in the body of the function are beyond the integer precision available to the system.

Now let us suppose that the programmer has incorrectly coded the factorial function, omitting the base case. This leads to an infinite loop.

```
long factorial_forever(long n)
{
   return (n * factorial_forever(n - 1));
}
```

Suppose that the base case is coded, but only for n having the value 1. Now the function will work properly with argument values in the range 1 to 12, but if the function is called with an argument that is zero or negative, an infinite loop will occur.

```
long factorial_positive(long n)
{
   if (n == 1)
      return 1;
   else
      return (n * factorial_positive(n - 1));
}
```

Another common error, not specifically tied to the use of recursion, is the incorrect use of the decrement operator. In many recursions there is a variable, say n, that is used to pass an argument of lower value to the function in the recursion step. For some algorithms --n is a correct argument; for others it is not. Consider

```
long factorial_decrement(long n)
{
   if (n <= 1)
      return 1;
   else
      return (n * factorial_decrement(--n));
}
```

In the second return statement we used the expression

```
n * factorial_decrement(--n)
```

which uses the variable n twice. Because the decrement operator has a side effect, when it is applied to the second n, it may also affect the value of the first n. This type of programming error is common, especially when recursive functions are coded.

12.7   SYSTEM CONSIDERATIONS

Recursive function calls require memory for each invocation. Since many invocations are active at the same time, the operating system may run out of available memory. Obviously, this is more of a problem on small systems than on large ones. Of course, if you are writing code meant to run on many systems, you must know and respect all the system limitations.

Let us write a program that will show us the depth of recursion that can occur on our Turbo C system. The depth varies from one system to another, and depends on the recursive function that is being used. Nonetheless, our experiment will give us some indication of our machine limits. We will use the recursive function sum() presented at the beginning of this chapter, but modify it to use long integers. This modification avoids overflow problems for large values of n. The function call sum(n) activates n nested copies of the function. Thus n indicates the depth of recursion.

```
/* Test the depth of recursion for sum() */

#include <stdio.h>

long    sum(long);

main()
{
   long    n = 0;

   for ( ; ; n += 100)
      printf("recursion test:  n = %ld sum = %ld\n", n, sum(n));
}

long sum(long n)
{
   if (n <= 1)
      return n;
   else
      return (n + sum(n - 1));
}
```

Warning: This program may fail catastrophically and require you to reboot the system. Here are the last few lines printed by this program on our system:

```
.....
recursion test:  n = 7900  sum = 31208950
recursion test:  n = 8000  sum = 32004000
recursion test:  n = %ld  sum = %ld
```

The program fails at this point without returning control to the operating system. This shows that failure occurs after the depth of the recursion exceeds 8000 calls to sum(). The system is allowing very deep recursions to occur before some system limit is reached. Note carefully that it is not the number of recursive calls per se that causes the failure; it is the depth of the recursion, more than 8000, that causes the problem.

12.8 SUMMARY

1   A function is said to be *recursive* if it calls itself, either directly or indirectly. Recursion is an advanced form of flow of control.

2   Recursion typically consists of a base case or cases and a general case. It is important to make sure that the function will terminate.

3   Any recursive function can be written in an equivalent iterative form. Due to system overhead in calling functions, a recursive function may be less efficient than an equivalent iterative one. However, the difference is often very slight. When a recursive function is easier to code and maintain than an equivalent iterative one, and the penalty for using it is slight, the recursive form is preferable.

12.9   EXERCISES

1   The following program writes BLAST OFF first. Explain its behavior.

```
#include <stdio.h>

void count_down(int n)
{
    if (n) {
        count_down(n - 1);
        printf("%d !  ", n);
    }
    else
        printf("\nBLAST OFF\n");
}

main()
{
    count_down(10);
}
```

2   Write a recursive function that tests whether a string is a palindrome, which is a string, such as "abcba" or "otto", that reads the same in both directions. Write a program that tests your function. For comparison write an iterative version of your program as well.

3   Consider the following recursive function. On some systems the function will return correct values, whereas on other systems it will return incorrect values. Explain why. Write a test program to see what happens on your system.

```
int sum(int n)
{
    if (n <= 1)
        return n;
    else
        return (n + sum(--n));
}
```

4   Examine the base case of the recursive function r_strncmp() carefully. Will the following base case also work? Which is more efficient? Explain.

```
if (*s1 != *s2 || *s1 == '\0' || *s2 == '\0' || n == 1)
    return (*s1 - *s2);
```

5 Write a recursive version of the standard library function strcmp(). If s1 and s2 are strings, then the function call r_strcmp(s1, s2) should return an integer value that is negative, zero, or positive, depending on whether s1 is lexicographically less than, equal to, or greater than s2. Use main() given below to test your function. Compile your program and put the executable code in the file *test*. If *infile* is a file containing many words, then the command

   test < *infile*

can be used to test your program.

```
#include <string.h>
#include <stdio.h>

#define   MAXWORD   30      /* max number of characters in a word */
#define   N         50      /* number of words in the array */

int   r_strcmp(char *, char *);

main()
{
    int    i, j;
    char   word[N][MAXWORD],    /* an array of N words */
           temp[MAXWORD];

    for (i = 0; i < N; ++i)
       scanf("%s", word[i]);
    for (i = 0; i < N - 1; ++i)
       for (j = i + 1; j < N; ++j)
          if (r_strcmp(word[i], word[j]) > 0) {
             strcpy(temp, word[i]);
             strcpy(word[i], word[j]);
             strcpy(word[j], temp);
          }
    for (i = 0; i < N; ++i)
       printf("%s\n", word[i]);
}
```

6   Write a recursive version of the standard library function strcpy(). If s1 and s2 are strings, then the function call r_strcpy(s1, s2) should overwrite whatever is in s1 with the contents of s2, and the pointer value of the first argument, namely s1, should be returned. See Appendix A for a description of strcpy().

7   Although it is considered bad programming style to overwrite a constant string, we do so in this exercise in order to emphasize an important point. Consider the two statements

```
printf("%s\n", strcpy("try this", "and this"));
printf("%s\n", strcpy("and", "also this"));
```

One of these statements works correctly, whereas the other can be expected to cause difficulty. Why? Rewrite the function r_strcpy() that you wrote for exercise 6 so that if the type of error exhibited here occurs, an error message is printed, and the program stops. Even though the function is recursive, make sure that you check for the error only once. *Hint:* Make use of a static variable.

8   A function that calls another function, which in turn calls the original function, is said to be *corecursive*. Note that corecursive functions occur in pairs. Write a program that counts the number of alphabetic characters in a string and sums the digits in the string. For example, the string "A0is444apple7" has 8 alphabetic characters, and the digits in the string sum to 19. Write a pair of corecursive functions to help carry out the tasks. Use count_alph() to count the alphabetic characters, and use sum_digit() for summing the digits. These two functions should call each other. For comparison, write a noncorecursive function that performs the two tasks in a direct, more natural fashion. *Hint:* If necessary, use static variables.

9   The greatest common divisor of two positive integers is the largest integer that is a divisor of both of them. For example, 6 and 15 have 3 as their greatest common divisor, and 15 and 22 have 1 as their greatest common divisor. The following recursive function computes the greatest common divisor of two positive integers. First write a program to test the function, and then write and test an equivalent iterative function.

```
int gcd(int a, int b)
{
    int    r;

    if ((r = a % b) == 0)
        return b;
    else
        return gcd(b, r);
}
```

10 Write a recursive lookup function to search an array in sorted order. Write a program to test your function. Use random() to fill an array a[] of size n, and use bubble _sort() to sort the array. The function call look_up(v, a, n) should be used to look for the value v in the array a[]. If just one of the elements of the array, say a[i], has the value v, then i should be returned. If two or more of the elements of the array have the value v, then the index of any one of them is an acceptable answer. If none of the elements of the array have the value v, then −1 should be returned. The base case is to look at the "middle" element a[n/2]. If this element has the value v, then n/2 is returned; otherwise recursion is used to look for v in

a[0], . . . , a[n/2 - 1]   or   a[n/2 + 1], . . . , a[n - 1]

whichever is appropriate. For example, if the value of v is less than a[n/2], then v should be looked for in the first part of the array and the appropriate recursion would be

```
return (look_up(v, a, n/2));
```

11 The following code can be used to test the recursive function minmax() given in Section 12.4. The value of n is entered interactively; the function calloc() is used to create an array a[] of size n dynamically; the array is filled with randomly distributed integer values; and finally the minimum and maximum values of the array are computed in two ways: recursively, by calling minmax(), and iteratively. Since all of this occurs repeatedly inside a loop, we use the standard library function free() to give the storage pointed to by a back to the system at the end of the for loop.

```
#include <stdio.h>
#include <stdlib.h>

void   minmax(int *, int, int *, int *);

main()
{
   int   *a, i,
          n,                 /* n is the size of a[] */
          r_min, r_max,      /* recursive min and max */
          i_min, i_max;      /* iterative min and max */

   printf("Input a power of 2: ");
   while (scanf("%d", &n) == 1 && n > 0) {
      a = calloc(n, sizeof(int));
      for (i = 0; i < n; ++i)
         a[i] = rand();
      minmax(a, n, &r_min, &r_max);
      printf("\n%s%d%9s%d\n",
         "recursion: min = ", r_min, "max = ", r_max);
      i_min = i_max = a[0];
      for (i = 1; i < n; ++i) {
         i_min = (i_min < a[i]) ? i_min : a[i];
         i_max = (i_max > a[i]) ? i_max : a[i];
      }
      printf("%s%d%9s%d\n\n",
         "iteration: min = ", i_min, "max = ", i_max);
      free(a);
      printf("Input a power of 2: ");
   }
}
```

The value of n is the size of the array a[]. For each value of n that is a power of 2, the minimum and maximum values of the array are computed in two ways: recursively and iteratively. How many comparisons are used in each of these computations? *Hint:* Use hand simulation to find the answer when n takes on values that are powers of 2 of low order.

12 It is not at all obvious that the recursive algorithm minmax() is "best" in the sense of requiring the least number of comparisons. That there cannot exist a better

algorithm is proved in the paper by Ira Pohl cited in Section 12.4. In this exercise we want to show how to modify the algorithm so that arrays of any size can be handled. The modified function may not have the property that it is the "best" possible, but nonetheless it is still a very efficient algorithm. The interested reader can compare the minmax() function given in this exercise with the version given on page 51 of the first edition of *A Book on C* by Ira Pohl and Al Kelley (Menlo Park, Calif.: Benjamin/Cummings, 1984).

```
void minmax(int a[], int n,                    /* n is a the size of a[] */
            int *min_ptr, int *max_ptr)
{
   int   min1, max1, min2, max2;

   if (n == 1)
      *min_ptr = *max_ptr = a[0];
   else {
      minmax(a, n/2, &min1, &max1);
      minmax(a + n/2, n - n/2, &min2, &max2);
      if (min1 < min2)
         *min_ptr = min1;
      else
         *min_ptr = min2;
      if (max1 < max2)
         *max_ptr = max2;
      else
         *max_ptr = max1;
   }
}
```

Write a program to test this function. Notice that it is still a divide-and-conquer algorithm and that it handles arrays of all sizes correctly. The base case now occurs when n has value 1. In the best possible algorithm, given in Section 12.4, the base case occurs when n has the value 2. The value 2 is, of course, a power of 2. But 1 is also a power of 2. Can the original minmax() be modified so that n with value 1 is the base case and the algorithm still remains "best"? Perhaps the base case with n having value 2 was used to emphasize the "2-ness" of the algorithm. After all, when n has value 1, the algorithm is not too complicated.

There is one more minor detail that needs to be considered. The algorithm in this exercise uses the argument n - n/2, whereas the comparable argument in the original algorithm is the expression n/2. Explain why.

13 (Advanced) A knight is a chess piece that moves in the pattern of an "ell" (L). The chessboard has 64 squares, and the knight can make 2 legal moves if placed at a corner square of the chessboard and can make 8 legal moves if placed in the middle square of the board. Write a function that computes the number of legal moves that a knight can make when starting at a specific square on the board. Associate that number with the square. This is called the *connectivity* of the square as viewed by the knight. Write a program that finds and prints the number of legal moves associated with each square on the board. The numbers should be printed as an 8×8 array corresponding to the 64 squares on a chessboard, with each number representing the connectivity of its square. This array is the connectivity of the chessboard as viewed by the knight.

14 (Advanced—see the 1967 article "A Method for Finding Hamiltonian Paths and Knight's Tours" by Ira Pohl, in *Communications of the ACM*, 10, no. 7). A knight's tour is a path the knight takes that covers all 64 squares without revisiting any square. Warnsdorf's rule states that to find a knight's tour, one starts from a corner square and goes to a square that has not yet been reached and has smallest connectivity. An *adjacent* square is one the knight can immediately move to. When a square is visited, all of the connectivity numbers of adjacent squares are decremented. Employ Warnsdorf's rule to find a knight's tour. Print out an 8×8 array corresponding to the chessboard, and in each position print the number of moves it took the knight to reach that square.

15 (Advanced) Pohl's improvement to Warnsdorf's rule was to suggest that ties be broken recursively (see exercise 14). Warnsdorf's rule is called a *heuristic*. It is not guaranteed to work. Still, it is very efficient for a combinatorially difficult problem. Sometimes two squares have the same smallest connectivity. To break the tie, compute recursively which square leads to a further smallest connectivity and choose that square. On the ordinary 8×8 chessboard, from any starting square, the Warnsdorf-Pohl rule was always found to work. Implement this heuristic algorithm and run it for five different starting squares, printing each tour.

13

STRUCTURES
AND LINKED LISTS

13.1   DECLARING STRUCTURES
13.2   ACCESSING A MEMBER
13.3   OPERATOR PRECEDENCE AND ASSOCIATIVITY: A FINAL LOOK
13.4   STRUCTURES, FUNCTIONS, AND ASSIGNMENT
13.5   PROBLEM SOLVING: STUDENT RECORDS
13.6   INITIALIZATION OF STRUCTURES
13.7   THE USE OF typedef
13.8   SELF-REFERENTIAL STRUCTURES
13.9   LINEAR LINKED LISTS
            DYNAMIC STORAGE ALLOCATION
13.10   LIST OPERATIONS
13.11   COUNTING AND LOOKUP
13.12   INSERTION AND DELETION
13.13   STYLE
13.14   COMMON PROGRAMMING ERRORS
13.15   SYSTEM CONSIDERATIONS
13.16   SUMMARY
13.17   EXERCISES

The structure type allows the programmer to aggregate components into a single, named variable. A structure has components that are individually named. These components are called *members*. Since the members of a structure can be of various types, the programmer can create aggregates of data that are suitable for a problem. Like arrays and pointers, structures are considered a derived type.

In this chapter we show how to declare structures and how to use them to represent a variety of familiar examples, such as a playing card or a student record. Critical to processing structures is the accessing of their members. This is done with either the member operator "." or the structure pointer operator ->. These operators, along with () and [], have the highest precedence. After these operators have been introduced, a complete table of precedence and associativity for all the operators of C is given.

Many examples are given in the chapter to show how structures are processed. An example that implements a student record system is given to show the use of structures and the accessing of its members. The use of self-referential structures to create linked lists is explained, and code necessary for the processing of linked lists is presented.

13.1   DECLARING STRUCTURES

Structures are a means of aggregating a collection of data items of possibly different types. As a simple example, let us define a structure that will describe a playing card. The spots on a card that represent its numeric value are called *pips*. A playing card, such as the three of spades, has a pip value, 3, and a suit value, "spades." Structures allow us to group variables together. We can declare the structure type

```
struct card {
    int     pips;
    char    suit;
};
```

to capture the information needed to represent a playing card. In this declaration struct is a keyword, card is the structure tag name, and the variables pips and suit are members of the structure. The variable pips will take values from 1 to 13 representing ace to king, and the variable suit will take values from 'c', 'd', 'h', and 's', representing the suits clubs, diamonds, hearts, and spades.

This declaration creates the derived data type struct card. The declaration can be thought of as a template; it creates the type struct card, but no storage is allocated. The tag name can now be used to declare variables of this type. The declaration

```
struct card   c1, c2;
```

allocates storage for the identifiers c1 and c2, which are of type struct card. To access the members of c1 and c2, we use the structure member operator ".". Suppose that we want to assign to c1 the values representing the five of diamonds and to c2 the values representing the queen of spades. To do this we can write

```
c1.pips = 5;
c1.suit = 'd';
c2.pips = 12;
c2.suit = 's';
```

A construct of the form

structure_variable . member_name

is used as a variable in the same way a simple variable or an element of an array is used. The member name must be unique within the specified structure. Since the member must always be prefaced or accessed through a unique structure variable identifier, there is no confusion between two members having the same name in different structures. An example is

```
struct fruit {
    char    name[15];
    int     calories;
};

struct vegetable {
    char    name[15];
    int     calories;
};

struct fruit      a;
struct vegetable  b;
```

Having made these declarations, we can access a.calories and b.calories without ambiguity.

Within a single declaration, it is possible to create a structure type (make the template) and declare variables of that type at the same time. An example of this is

```
struct card {
    int     pips;
    char    suit;
} c, deck[52];
```

The identifier card is the structure tag name. The identifier c is declared to be a variable of type struct card, and the identifier deck is declared to be an array of type struct card. Another example of this is

```
struct {
    char    *last_name;
    int     student_id;
    char    grade;
} s1, s2, s3;
```

which declares s1, s2, and s3 to represent three student records, but does not include a tag name for use in later declarations. Suppose, instead, that we had written

```
struct student {
   char    *last_name;
   int     student_id;
   char    grade;
};
```

This declaration, unlike the previous one, has student as a structure tag name, but no variables are declared of this type. It can be thought of as a template. Now we can write

```
struct student    temp, class[100];
```

This declares temp and class to be of type struct student. Only at this point will storage be allocated for these variables. The template of a structure type by itself does not cause storage to be allocated.

13.2   ACCESSING A MEMBER

We have already seen the use of the member operator ".". In this section we give further examples of its use and introduce the structure pointer operator ->.

Suppose that we are writing a program called *class_info*, which generates information about a class of 100 students. We can begin by creating a header file. Note that we use the name "cl_info.h" to conform to MS-DOS length restrictions on file names. On systems without this limitation, "class_info.h" would be more mnemonic.

In file cl_info.h:

```
#define   CLASS_SIZE    100

struct student {
   char    *last_name;
   int     student_id;
   char    grade;
};
```

This header file can now be used to share information with the modules making up the program. Suppose in another file we write

```
#include "cl_info.h"

main()
{
    struct student   temp, class[CLASS_SIZE];
    . . . . .
```

We can assign values to the members of the structure variable temp by using statements such as

```
temp.grade = 'A';
temp.last_name = "Bushker";
temp.student_id = 590017;
```

Now suppose that we want to count the number of failing students in a given class. To do this, we can write a function that accesses the grade member. Here is a function fail() that counts the number of F grades in the array class[].

```
/* Count the failing grades. */

#include "cl_info.h"

int fail(struct student class[])
{
    int   i, cnt = 0;

    for (i = 0; i < CLASS_SIZE; ++i)
        cnt += class[i].grade == 'F';
    return cnt;
}
```

DISSECTION OF THE fail() FUNCTION

■ `int fail(struct student class[])`
  ```
  {
      int   i, cnt = 0;
  ```

The parameter `class` is of type "pointer to `struct student`." We can think of it as a one-dimensional array of structures. Parameters of any type, including structure types, can be used in headers to function definitions.

■ `for (i = 0; i < CLASS_SIZE; ++i)`

We are assuming that when this function is called, an array of type `struct student` and of size `CLASS_SIZE` will be passed as an argument.

■ `cnt += class[i].grade == 'F';`

An expression such as this demonstrates how C can be concise. C is operator rich. To be fluent in its use, the programmer must be careful about precedence and associativity. This statement is equivalent to

```
cnt += (((class[i]).grade) == 'F');
```

The member `grade` of the *i*th element (counting from zero) of the array of structures `class` is selected. A test is made to see if it is equal to `'F'`. If equality holds, then the value of the expression

```
class[i].grade == 'F'
```

is 1, and the value of `cnt` is incremented. If equality does not hold, then the value of the expression is 0, and the value of `cnt` remains unchanged. A clearer but more verbose equivalent is

```
if (class[i].grade == 'F')
   ++cnt;
```

■ `return cnt;`

The number of failing grades is returned to the calling environment.

C provides the structure pointer operator `->` to access the members of a structure via a pointer. This operator is typed on the keyboard as a minus sign followed by a "greater than" sign. If a pointer variable is assigned the address of a structure, then a member of the structure can be accessed by a construct of the form

pointer_to_structure   -\>   *member_name*

An equivalent construct is given by

(*\ *pointer_to_structure*). *member_name*

The parentheses are necessary here. The operators `->` and ".", along with () and [], have the highest precedence, and they associate from left to right. Because of this, the above construct without parentheses would be equivalent to

* *(pointer_to_structure. member_name)*

In complicated situations the two accessing modes can be combined in complicated ways. The following table illustrates their use in a straightforward manner.

Declarations and assignments		

`struct student    temp, *p = &temp;`
 	
`temp.grade = 'A';`
`temp.last_name = "Bushker";`
`temp.student_id = 590017;`		

Expression	*Equivalent expression*	*Conceptual value*
`temp.grade`	`p -> grade`	A
`temp.last_name`	`p -> last_name`	Bushker
`temp.student_id`	`p -> student_id`	590017
`(*p).student_id`	`p -> student_id`	590017

13.3 OPERATOR PRECEDENCE AND ASSOCIATIVITY: A FINAL LOOK

We now want to display the entire precedence and associativity table for all the C operators. The operators "." and -> have been introduced in this chapter. These operators, together with () and [], have the highest precedence.

Operators	Associativity
() [] . -> ++ (*postfix*) -- (*postfix*)	left to right
++ (*prefix*) -- (*prefix*) ! ~ sizeof (*type*) + (*unary*) - (*unary*) & (*address*) * (*dereference*)	right to left
* / %	left to right
+ -	left to right
<< >>	left to right
< <= > >=	left to right
== !=	left to right
&	left to right
^	left to right
|	left to right
&&	left to right
||	left to right
?:	right to left
= += -= *= /= %= >>= <<= &= ^= |=	right to left
, (*comma operator*)	left to right

The comma operator has the lowest precedence of all the operators of C (see exercise 19). The commas used in declarations and in argument lists to functions are not comma operators.

As we saw in Chapter 6, the unary operator sizeof can be used to find the number of bytes needed to store an object in memory. For example, the value of the expression sizeof(struct card) is the number of bytes needed by the system to store a variable of type struct card. On most systems the type of the expression is unsigned. Later in this chapter we will see that the `sizeof` operator is used extensively when creating linked lists.

While the complete table of operators is extensive, some simple rules apply. The primary operators are function parentheses, subscripting, and the two addressing primitives for accessing a member of a structure. These four operators are of highest precedence. Unary operators come next, followed by the arithmetic operators. Arithmetic operators follow the usual convention; namely, multiplicative operators have higher precedence than additive operators. Assignments of all kinds are of lowest precedence, with the exception of the still lowlier comma operator. A programmer who does not know the rules of precedence and associativity in a particular situation should either look the rules up or use parentheses.

13.4 STRUCTURES, FUNCTIONS, AND ASSIGNMENT

Traditional C systems allow a pointer to a structure type to be passed as an argument to a function and returned as a value. ANSI C allows structures themselves to be passed as arguments to functions and returned as values. In this environment, if `a` and `b` are two variables of the same structure type, the assignment expression `a = b` is allowed. It causes each member of `a` to be assigned the value of the corresponding member of `b`. See Section 13.15, "System Considerations," for further remarks.

To illustrate the use of structures with functions, we will use the structure type `struct card`. For the remainder of this chapter, assume the header file *card.h* contains the declaration for this structure.

In file card.h:

```
struct card {
    int     pips;
    char    suit;
};
```

Let us write functions that will assign values to a card, extract the member values of a card, and print the values of a card. We will assume that the header file *card.h* has been included wherever needed.

```
void assign_values(struct card *c_ptr, int p, char s)
{
   c_ptr -> pips = p;
   c_ptr -> suit = s;
}

void extract_values(struct card *c_ptr, int *p_ptr, char *s_ptr)
{
   *p_ptr = c_ptr -> pips;
   *s_ptr = c_ptr -> suit;
}
```

These functions access a card by using a pointer to a variable of type struct card.
The structure pointer operator -> is used throughout to access the required member.
Next, let us write a card printing routine that takes a pointer to struct card and prints its
values using extract_values().

```
void prn_values(struct card *c_ptr)
{
   int    p;              /* pips value */
   char   s;              /* suit value */
   char   *suit_name;
   void   extract_values(struct card *, int *, char *);

   extract_values(c_ptr, &p, &s);
   switch (s) {
   case 'c' :
      suit_name = "clubs";
      break;
   case 'd' :
      suit_name = "diamonds";
      break;
   case 'h' :
      suit_name = "hearts";
      break;
   case 's' :
      suit_name = "spades";
      break;
   default:
      suit_name = "error";
   }
   printf("card:  %d of %s\n", p, suit_name);
}
```

Finally, we want to illustrate how these functions can be used. First, we assign values to a deck of cards, and then as a test we print out the heart suit.

```
main()
{
    int           i;
    struct card   deck[52];
    void          assign_values(struct card *, int, char );
    void          prn_values(struct card *);

    for (i = 0; i < 13; ++i) {
        assign_values(deck + i, i + 1, 'c');
        assign_values(deck + i + 13, i + 1, 'd');
        assign_values(deck + i + 26, i + 1, 'h');
        assign_values(deck + i + 39, i + 1, 's');
    }
    for (i = 0; i < 13; ++i)        /* print out the hearts */
        prn_values(deck + i + 26);
}
```

Notice how this code uses address arithmetic to assign and print values for the different suits. Thus the cards in the heart suit are printed by the statement

```
prn_values(deck + i + 26);
```

which is equivalent to

```
prn_values(&deck[i + 26]);
```

Functions can be designed to work with structures as parameters, rather than with pointers to structures. To illustrate this, let us rewrite the function extract_values().

```
void extract_values(struct card  c, int *p_ptr, char *s_ptr)
{
    *s_ptr = c.suit;
    *p_ptr = c.pips;
}
```

In C the value of an argument that is passed to a function is copied when the function is invoked. This call-by-value mechanism was discussed in Chapter 4 and Chapter 8. Because of this, when a structure is passed as an argument to a function, the structure is copied when the function is invoked. For this reason, passing the address of the structure is more efficient than passing the structure itself.

13.5   PROBLEM SOLVING: STUDENT RECORDS

In C, structures, pointers, and arrays may be combined to create complicated data structures. Problem solving is greatly aided by matching a data structure to the information that is manipulated. Usually a real-world object, such as student, is best described as a set of characteristics. In C, struct is an encapsulation mechanism for such a data aggregate. Once aggregated, the object is treated conceptually as a student, instead of a collection of specific characteristics.

We will start with our previous example of struct student and develop it into a more comprehensive data structure for a student record. We begin by defining the various types needed, as follows:

In file student.h:

```
#define   CLASS_SIZE   50
#define   NCOURSES     10      /* number of courses */

struct student {
    char    *last_name;
    int     student_id;
    char    grade;
};

struct date {
    short   day;
    char    month[10];
    short   year;
};

struct personal {
    char            name [20];
    struct date     birthday;
};

struct student_data {
    struct personal    p;
    int                student_id;
    char               grade[NCOURSES];
};
```

Notice that struct student_data is constructed with nested structures. One of its members is the structure p, which has as one of its members the structure birthday. After the declaration

```
struct student_data   temp;
```

has been made, the expression

```
temp.p.birthday.month[0]
```

has as its value the first letter of the month of the birthday of the student whose data is in temp. Structures such as date and personal are used in database applications.

Let us write the function read_date() to enter data into a variable of type struct date. When the function is called, the address of the variable must be passed as an argument to the function.

```
#include "student.h"

void read_date(struct date *d)
{
    printf("Enter   day(int)   month(string)   year(int):  ");
    scanf("%hd%s%hd", &d -> day, d -> month, &d -> year);
}
```

DISSECTION OF THE *read_date()* FUNCTION

■ void read_date(struct date *d)
```
{
    printf("Enter   day(int)   month(string)   year(int):  ");
```

The parameter d has type "pointer to struct date." The printf() statement prompts the user for information.

■ &d -> day

This is an address. Because & is of lower precedence than -> , this expression is equivalent to

```
&(d -> day)
```

First the pointer d is used to access the member day. Then the address operator & is applied to this member to obtain its address.

■ d -> month

This is an address. The pointer d is being used to access a member that is an array. An array name by itself is a pointer, or address. It points to the base address of the array.

■ scanf("%hd%s%hd", &d -> day, d -> month, &d -> year);

The function scanf() is used to read in three values and to store them at appropriate addresses. Recall that in the header file *student.h*, the two members day and year of struct date were declared to be of type short. The format %hd is used to convert characters in the standard input stream (keyboard) to a value of type short. (The h used to modify the conversion character d in the format comes from the second letter in the word *short*.)

The function read_date() can be used to read information into a variable of type struct student_data. For example, the code

```
struct student_data    temp;

read_date(&temp.p.birthday);
```

can be used to place information into the appropriate member of temp.

Here is a function to enter grades:

```
void read_grades(char g[])
{
   int    i;

   printf("Enter %d grades:  ", NCOURSES);
   for (i = 0; i < NCOURSES; ++i)
      scanf(" %c", &g[i]);
}
```

The control string " %c" is being used to read in a single nonwhite space character. The blank just before the % matches optional white space in the input stream. This function could be called to read a list of grades into temp as follows:

```
read_grades(temp.grade);
```

The argument `temp.grade` is an address (pointer) because it refers to a member of a structure that is an array, and an array name by itself is the base address of the array. Thus when the function is invoked, it causes the values of `temp.grade` in the calling environment to be changed.

Basically, understanding structures comes down to understanding how to access their members. As a further example let us now write a function that takes data stored in the long form in `struct student_data` and converts it to the short form stored in `struct student`.

```
#include "student.h"

void extract( struct student_data   *s_data,
              int                    n,
              struct student         *undergrad)
{
    undergrad -> student_id = s_data -> student_id;
    undergrad -> last_name = s_data -> p.name;
    undergrad -> grade = s_data -> grade[n];
}
```

13.6 INITIALIZATION OF STRUCTURES

All external and static variables, including structure variables, that are not explicitly initialized are automatically initialized by the system to zero. In traditional C, external and static structures can be initialized by the programmer. In ANSI C, we can also initialize automatic structures. The syntax is similar to that used with arrays. A structure variable can be followed by an equal sign = and a list of constants contained within braces. If not enough values are used to assign all the members of the structure, the remaining members are assigned the value zero by default. Some examples are

```
struct card    c = {12, 's'};    /* the queen of spades */

struct fruit    frt = {"plum", 150};

struct complex {
   double    real;
   double    imaginary;
}   m[3][3] = {
   {{1.0, -0.5}, {2.5, 1.0}, { 0.7, 0.7}},
   {{7.0, -6.5}, {-0.5, 1.0}, {45.7, 8.0}},
};    /* m[2][] is assigned zeroes */
```

13.7　THE USE OF typedef

Before we continue with a discussion of structures and linked lists, we want to describe the typedef facility. In practice, the typedef facility is often used to rename a structure type. We will see this in Section 13.9.

　C provides a number of fundamental types such as char and int, and a number of derived types such as arrays and pointers. The language also provides the typedef mechanism, which allows a type to be explicitly associated with an identifier. Some examples are

```
typedef    char *    string;
typedef    int       INCHES, FEET, YARDS;
typedef    float     vector[10];
typedef    double    (*PFD)(double);    /* ptr to fct returning double */
```

In each of these type definitions, the named identifiers can be used later to declare variables or functions in the same way ordinary types can be used. Thus

```
INCHES    length, width;
string    s1 = "abc", s2 = "xyz";
vector    x;
```

declares the variables length and width to be of type INCHES, which is synonymous with the type int, and declares the variables s1 and s2 to be of type string, which is synonymous with char *. The declaration of x is more interesting. One way to think of the declaration for x is to mentally replace the word `vector` in the `typedef` with x. An equivalent declaration for x would be

```
float    x[10];
```

In a similar fashion, the declaration

```
PFD   f;              is equivalent to          double   (*f)(double);
```

What is gained by allowing the programmer to create a new nomenclature for an existing type? One gain is in abbreviating long declarations. Another is having type names that reflect the intended use. Furthermore, if there are system-sensitive declarations, such as an `int` that is 4 bytes on one system and 2 bytes on another, and these differences are critical to the program, then the use of `typedef` may make the porting of the software easier.

Let us illustrate the use of `typedef` by defining a small number of functions that operate on vectors and matrices.

```
#define   N   3      /* the size of all vectors and matrices */

typedef   double   scalar;
typedef   scalar   vector[N];
typedef   scalar   matrix[N][N];
```

We have used the `typedef` mechanism to create the types `scalar`, `vector`, and `matrix`, which is both self-documenting and conceptually appropriate. Our programming language has been extended in a natural way to incorporate these new types as a domain. Notice how `typedef` can be used to build hierarchies of types. For example, we could have written

```
typedef   vector   matrix[N];
```

in place of

```
typedef   scalar   matrix[N][N];
```

The use of `typedef` to create type names such as `scalar`, `vector`, and `matrix` allows the programmer to think in terms of the application. Now we are ready to create functions that provide operations over our domain.

```
void add(vector x, vector y, vector z)     /* x = y + z */
{
    int i;

    for (i = 0; i < N; ++i)
        x[i] = y[i] + z[i];
}


scalar dot_product(vector x, vector y)
{
    int      i;
    scalar   sum = 0.0;

    for (i = 0; i < N; ++i)
        sum += x[i] * y[i];
    return sum;
}


void multiply(matrix a, matrix b, matrix c)    /* a = b * c */
{
    int    i, j, k;

    for (i = 0; i < N; ++i)
        for (j = 0; j < N; ++j) {
            a[i][j] = 0.0;
            for (k = 0; k < N; ++k)
                a[i][j] += b[i][k] * c[k][j];
        }
}
```

13.8   SELF-REFERENTIAL STRUCTURES

In this section we define structures with pointer members that refer to the structure type containing them. These are called *self-referential* structures. Self-referential structures often require storage management routines to explicitly obtain and release memory.

Let us define a structure with a member field that points at the same structure type. We wish to do this in order to have an unspecified number of such structures linked together.

```
struct list {
    int         data;
    struct list *next;
};
```

Each variable of type struct list has two members, data and next. The pointer variable next is called a *link*. Each structure is linked to a succeeding structure by way of the member next. These structures are conveniently displayed pictorially, with links shown as arrows.

data   next

The pointer variable next contains an address of either the location in memory of the successor struct list element or the special value NULL, which is usually defined in *stdio.h* as a symbolic constant with value 0. The value NULL is used to denote the end of the list. To see how all this works, let us begin with the declaration

```
struct list    a, b, c;
```

We want to manipulate the structure variables a, b, and c to create a linked list. We begin by performing some assignments on these structures.

```
a.data = 1;
b.data = 2;
c.data = 3;
a.next = b.next = c.next = NULL;
```

The result of this code is described pictorially as follows:

a

| 1 | NULL |

b

| 2 | NULL |

c

| 3 | NULL |

Next, let us chain the three structures together.

```
a.next = &b;
b.next = &c;
```

These pointer assignments result in linking a to b to c.

Now the links allow us to retrieve data from successive elements. For example,

```
a.next -> data                 has value 2
a.next -> next -> data         has value 3
```

13.9   LINEAR LINKED LISTS

A *linear linked list* is like a clothesline on which the data structures hang sequentially. There is a head pointer addressing the first element of the list, and each element points at a successor element, with the last element having a link value NULL. Typically, a linked list is created dynamically. In this section we will show how this is done.

   Let us begin by creating a header file that will be included with the list processing functions that we will write in the sections that follow. This header file includes the file *stdio.h* because that is where NULL is defined.

   In file list.h:

```
#include <stdio.h>

typedef   char   DATA;      /* we will use char in examples */

struct linked_list {
   DATA                 d;
   struct linked_list   *next;
};

typedef   struct linked_list   ELEMENT;
typedef   ELEMENT *            LINK;
```

   In the header file *list.h* we used typedef to create names of types that are more suggestive of their use. Notice that although DATA is simply the type char, conceptually it could be a more complicated type, such as an array or a structure (see exercise 11).

DYNAMIC STORAGE ALLOCATION

The declaration of `struct linked_list` in *list.h* does not allocate storage. It acts as a template for the storage that the system will allocate later when variables and arrays of this type are declared. We used the `typedef` facility to rename the type as `ELEMENT`, because we wish to think of it as an element in our list. What makes self-referential structure types such as `ELEMENT` especially useful is that utility functions exist to allocate storage dynamically. The function `malloc()` is provided in the standard library. A function call of the form

    malloc(*size*)

returns a pointer to enough storage for an object of *size* bytes. The function `malloc()` takes a single argument of type `size_t` and returns a pointer to `void` that points to the base of the storage allocated by the function. The type `size_t` is an unsigned integer type that is suitable for holding the sizes of objects in bytes. Since the value returned is of type pointer to `void`, it can be assigned to any other pointer regardless of its type. If `head` is a variable of type `LINK`, then

    head = malloc(sizeof(ELEMENT));

obtains a piece of memory from the system adequate to store an `ELEMENT` and assigns its base address to the pointer `head`. As in the above example, a function call to `malloc()` often uses the `sizeof` operator. The `sizeof` operator calculates the number of bytes required to store a particular object.

Suppose that we want to dynamically create a linear linked list to store the three characters *n, e,* and *w*. The following code will do this:

    head = malloc(sizeof(ELEMENT));
    head -> d = 'n';
    head -> next = NULL;

This creates a single-element list.

head ——→ | n | NULL |

A second element is added by the assignments

```
head -> next = malloc(sizeof(ELEMENT));
head -> next -> d = 'e';
head -> next -> next = NULL;
```

Now there is a two-element list.

Finally we add the last element.

```
head -> next -> next = malloc(sizeof(ELEMENT));
head -> next -> next -> d = 'w';
head -> next -> next -> next = NULL;
```

Now we have a three-element list pointed at by head and ending with the sentinel value NULL.

13.10 LIST OPERATIONS

The basic operations on linear linked lists include the following:

1. Creating a list
2. Counting the elements
3. Looking up an element
4. Inserting an element
5. Deleting an element

We will demonstrate the techniques for programming such operations on lists. The use of recursive functions is natural, since lists are a recursively defined construct.

Each routine will require the specifications in the header file *list.h*. Observe that d in these examples could be redefined as a more complicated data structure.

As a first example we will write a function that will produce a list from a string. The function will return a pointer to the head of the resulting list. The heart of the function creates a list element by allocating storage and assigning member values.

```
/* List creation by recursion. */

#include "list.h"

LINK string_to_list(char s[])
{
   LINK   head;

   if (s[0] == '\0')      /* base case */
      return NULL;
   else {
      head = malloc(sizeof(ELEMENT));
      head -> d = s[0];
      head -> next = string_to_list(s + 1);
      return head;
   }
}
```

Notice once more how recursion has a base case, the creation of the empty list, and a general case, the creation of the remainder of the list.

DISSECTION OF THE string_to_list() FUNCTION

■ `LINK string_to_list(char s[])`
```
{
   LINK   head;
```

When a string is passed as an argument, a linked list of the characters in the string is created. Since a pointer to the head of the list will be returned, the type specifier in the header to this function definition is LINK.

■ `if (s[0] == '\0')     /* base case */`
    `return NULL;`

When the end-of-string sentinel is detected, NULL is returned, and as we will see, the recursion terminates. The value NULL is also used to mark the end of the linked list.

■ `else {`
    `head = malloc(sizeof(ELEMENT));`

If the string s[] is not the null string, then malloc() is used to retrieve enough bytes to store an object of type ELEMENT. The pointer variable head now points at the block of storage provided by malloc().

■ `head -> d = s[0];`

The member d of the allocated ELEMENT is assigned the first character in the string s[].

■ `head -> next = string_to_list(s + 1);`

The pointer expression s + 1 points to the remainder of the string. The function is called recursively with s + 1 as an argument. The pointer member next is assigned the pointer value that is returned by string_to_list(s + 1). This recursive call returns as its value a LINK or, equivalently, a pointer to ELEMENT, which points to the remaining sublist.

■ `return head;`

The function exits with the address of the head of the list.

13.11   COUNTING AND LOOKUP

In this section we will write two more recursive functions that perform list operations. The first function is count(). It can be used to count the elements in a list. It involves recurring down the list and terminating when the NULL pointer is found. If the list is empty, the value 0 is returned; otherwise, the number of elements in the list is returned.

```
/* Count a list recursively. */

#include "list.h"

int count(LINK head)
{
    if (head == NULL)
        return 0;
    else
        return (1 + count(head -> next));
}
```

The next function searches a list for a particular element. If the element is found, a pointer to that element is returned; otherwise the NULL pointer is returned.

```
/* Lookup c in the list pointed to by head. */

#include "list.h"

LINK lookup(DATA c, LINK head)
{
    if (head == NULL)
        return NULL;
    else if (c == head -> d)
        return head;
    else
        return (lookup(c, head -> next));
}
```

13.12 INSERTION AND DELETION

One of the most useful properties of lists is that insertion takes a fixed amount of time once the position in the list is found. In contrast, if one wished to place a value in a large array, retaining all other array values in the same sequential order, the insertion would take, on average, time proportional to the length of the array. The values of all elements of the array that came after the newly inserted value would have to be moved over one element.

Let us illustrate insertion into a list by having two adjacent elements pointed at by p1 and p2, and inserting between them an element pointed at by q.

Before insertion:

After insertion:

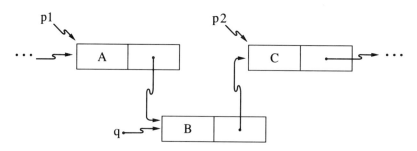

Here is a function that accomplishes the task:

```
/* Inserting an element in a linked list. */

#include "list.h"

void insert(LINK p1, LINK p2, LINK q)
{
   p1 -> next = q;    /* insertion */
   q -> next = p2;
}
```

Deleting an element is very simple in a linear linked list. The predecessor of the element to be deleted has its link member assigned the address of the successor to the deleted element. Let us first illustrate graphically the situation before deletion:

The next line of code

```
q = p -> next;
```

causes q to point at the element that we want to delete.

Now consider the statement

```
p -> next = q -> next;
```

After this statement is executed, we have

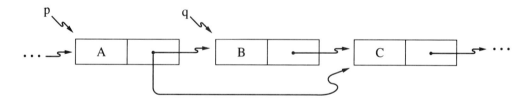

As the diagram shows, the element containing B is no longer accessible and is of no use. Such an inaccessible element is called *garbage*. Since memory is frequently a critical resource, it is desirable that this storage be returned to the system for later use. This may be done with the standard library function free(). The function call

```
free(q)
```

makes again available to the system the storage pointed at by q that was previously allocated dynamically by malloc() or calloc(). Since free() takes an argument of type pointer to void, the pointer q can be of any type.

Using `free()`, we will write a deletion routine that returns dynamically allocated list storage to the system.

```
/* Recursive deletion of a list. */

#include "list.h"

void delete_list(LINK head)
{
    if (head != NULL) {
        delete_list(head -> next);
        free(head);                     /* release storage */
    }
}
```

13.13   STYLE

It is good programming style to aggregate related data into a structure. By declaring a structure, the programmer can create a data type suitable for a problem. The declaration should list each member on its own line, properly indented.

```
struct automobile {
    char    name[15];      /* example: buick */
    int     year;          /* example: 1983 */
    double  cost;          /* example: 2390.95 */
};
```

It is usually good programming practice to associate a tag name with a structure type. It is both convenient for further declarations and for documentation.

If extensive use is going to be made of a structure declaration, it is appropriate to use the `typedef` facility to create a new name for the type. In the case of `struct automobile` we could use

```
typedef   struct automobile CAR;
```

The new type name does not have to be in capital letters; we could just as well have used `Car` or `car`. In some styles, fully capitalized identifiers are reserved for preprocessor identifiers. The choice depends on personal taste.

A common programming style is to write structure declarations in header files that can then be included where needed. If the declaration of a structure type needs to be altered later, this is accomplished by changing its declaration in the header file. Perhaps later we will discover that we want CAR to have a member describing the horsepower of an automobile. This is easily done by adding a line such as

```
int    horsepower;    /* example: 225 */
```

to the structure declaration in the header file.

13.14 COMMON PROGRAMMING ERRORS

When working with self-referential structures, a common programming error is to access the wrong place in memory. For example, if a linear linked list is not properly terminated by a NULL pointer, some form of unexpected run-time error will occur.

Another common programming error is to mix up the order in the use of typedef. For example,

```
typedef   ELEMENT   struct linked_list;    /* wrong */
```

is incorrect because the identifier ELEMENT has to follow the type struct linked_list, not precede it. Notice also that a typedef construction is followed by a semicolon.

Our last programming error involves the comparison of two variables of the same structure type, say a and b. Although the assignment expression

```
a = b
```

is legal, the use of the expression

```
a == b    /* wrong */
```

to test for equality of two structures is not allowed. Because the operators = and == are so visually similar, beginning programmers sometimes make this mistake.

13.15   SYSTEM CONSIDERATIONS

C has evolved with time. Traditional C systems allow pointers to structures to be passed as arguments to functions and returned as values. ANSI C compilers also allow structures themselves to be passed as arguments and returned as values. In addition, these compilers allow structure assignment. Programmers writing code that is meant to be backward-compatible must take into account restrictions that may be present in older compilers.

Traditional C does not allow initialization of structure variables of storage class automatic. Maintaining compatibility with older systems requires that only static and external structure variables be initialized.

In database applications, structures often have tens, even hundreds, of members. If a structure is passed as an argument to a function, then a copy of the structure is made when the function is invoked. If the structure is large, and a local copy is not really needed, then for the sake of efficiency it is better to pass a pointer to the structure rather than the structure itself.

Operating systems differ in their requirements for aligning storage on boundaries. For example, some systems may require that an int be aligned on a word boundary; others may not. Because of this, when space for a structure is allocated, it can happen that the space required for the structure as a whole is more than the sum of the space required for each of its members. Moreover, the space requirement for the structure as a whole may depend on the order of the members within the structure (see exercise 18). This seldom concerns the programmer, except when memory is a scarce resource. Turbo C has the *tcc* option *-a*, which forces word-boundary alignment. This option is also available in the integrated environment; see the manual. The default in Turbo C is byte alignment.

13.16   SUMMARY

1   A structure is an aggregation of subparts treated as a single variable. The subparts of the structure are called members.

2   Structure members are accessed by the member operator "." and the structure pointer operator ->. If s is a structure variable with a member named m, then s.m refers to the value of the member m within s. If p is a pointer that points at s, then p -> m and s.m are equivalent expressions. Both "." and -> have highest precedence among C operators.

3   Structures can be members of other structures. Considerable complexity is possible when nesting structures, pointers, and arrays within each other. Care should be taken that the proper variables are being accessed.

4   A self-referential structure uses a pointer member to address a structure of the same type. Self-referential structures can be used to create a linear linked list. Each element points to the next element, except the last element, which has the value NULL for its pointer member.

5   The function malloc() is used to dynamically allocate storage. It takes an argument of type size_t and returns a pointer to void that is the base address of the allocated storage. The type size_t is an unsigned integer type. It is defined in *stdlib.h*.

6   Standard algorithms for list processing are naturally implemented recursively. Frequently, the base case is the detection of the NULL link. The general case recurs by moving one element over in the linked list.

13.17   EXERCISES

1   Suppose that the following structure is used to write a dieting program:

```
structure food {
    char    name[15];
    int     portion_weight;
    int     calories;
};
```

What is the tag name of this structure? How would one declare an array meal[10] of this type? Let us say that a 4-ounce apple contains 200 calories. How would you assign values to the three members of meal[0] to represent such an apple?

2   Write a program that counts the number of calories in a given meal. The meal would be stored in the array meal[]. The program should write each course of the meal.

3   The following function is supposed to assign values to a card, but does not work as expected. Describe what goes wrong.

```
#include "card.h"

struct card *assign_values(
        int    p,      /* pips value assigned */
        char   s       /* suit value assigned */
)
{
    card   *c_ptr;

    c_ptr -> pips = p;
    c_ptr -> suit = s;
    return c_ptr;
}
```

4   Create a structure that can describe a restaurant. It should have members that include the name, address, average cost, and type of food. Suppose that an array of structures representing restaurants has been created. Write a function that prints out all restaurants of a given food type in order of cost, least costly first.

5   When playing poker or other card games, it is usual to arrange a hand to reflect its values. Write a program that arranges and prints out a hand of five cards in sorted order by pips value. Assume that an ace is highest in value, a king is next highest in value, and so forth.

6   Using the student record example in Section 13.5, write a function that prints the average for each student in a class. Let an A grade have value 4, a B grade have value 3, and so forth.

7   Write a function that prints out students in order of their date of birth, oldest first. The original set of student records need not be in any order.

8   Write a function prn_student_data() that prints in a nice format all the information in a variable of type struct student_data.

9   Define a structure that contains the name of a food, its calories per serving, its food type (such as meat or fruit), and its costs. Write a program that is able to produce a balanced meal. The foods should be stored as an array of structures. The program should construct a meal so as to come from four different food types and to meet calorie and cost constraints. It should be capable of producing a large number of different menus.

10   The following declarations do not compile correctly. Explain what is wrong with the declarations and rewrite them.

```
struct husband {
    char         name[10];
    int          age;
    struct wife  spouse;
} a;

struct wife {
    char            name[10];
    int             age;
    struct husband  spouse;
} b;
```

11 Modify the header file *list.h* by replacing the typedef line with

```
struct s_data {
    char  name[10];
    int   age;
    int   weight;
};

typedef  struct s_data  DATA;
```

Write a function create_list() that transforms an array of type DATA into a linear linked list. Write another function that counts the number of people above both a given age and a given weight.

12 Given a linear linked list of the type found in exercise 11, write a function sort_by_age() that sorts the list by age. Write another function sort_by_name() that sorts the list lexicographically by name.

13 Write an iterative version of the function count() that was presented in Section 13.10.

14 Write an insertion function that inserts an element at the first position in the list following an element storing a particular DATA item. You should use lookup() to find the element. If the element is not present, the insertion should occur at the end of the list.

15 Explain why the parentheses are necessary in the construct

   (*pointer_to_structure).member_name

Write a test program that uses the construct. Will your program compile if the parentheses are removed?

16 In simple situations a typedef can be replaced by a #define. Sometimes, however, this can lead to unexpected errors. Rewrite the header file *list.h* as follows:

```
#include <stdio.h>

#define   DATA   char     /* we will use char in examples */

struct linked_list {
    DATA                d;
    struct linked_list  *next;
};

#define   ELEMENT   struct linked_list
#define   LINK      ELEMENT *
```

After you have done this, check to see that the functions string_to_list(), count(), and lookup() can all be compiled just as before. The function insert(), however, does not compile. Explain why. Modify the function so that it does compile.

17 The function insert(), which we wrote in Section 13.12, assumed that p1 and p2 were pointing to adjacent elements in a linked list. What happens if p1 and p2 are pointing to elements in the list that are not adjacent?

18 On some systems, the following two structures are not stored in the same number of bytes.

```
struct s1 {
    char   c1;
    char   c2;
    int    i;
};

struct s2 {
    char   c1;
    int    i;
    char   c2;
};
```

The statement

```
printf("%d\n%d\n", sizeof(struct s1), sizeof(struct s2));
```

causes system-dependent values to be printed. What are the space requirements for these structures on the C systems available to you? On some systems, such as Borland's Turbo C, byte and word alignment options exist. On such systems, try this with both settings.

19 In a comma expression of the form

expr1 , *expr2*

expr1 is evaluated first, then *expr2*, and the comma expression as a whole has the value and type of its right operand. An example of a comma expression is

```
a = 1, b = 2
```

If b has been declared to be an int, then the value of this comma expression is 2 and its type is int. Here is a for loop that prints a column of even integers and a column of odd integers. Which commas are comma operators and which are not? Rewrite the code so that no comma operators are used.

```
int    i, j;

for (i = 0, j = 1; i < LIMIT; i += 2, j += 2)
    printf("%12d%12d\n", i, j);
```

14

INPUT/OUTPUT
AND FILES

14.1 THE OUTPUT FUNCTION
printf()

14.2 THE INPUT FUNCTION
scanf()
DIRECTIVES IN THE
CONTROL STRING
ORDINARY CHARACTERS
WHITE SPACE
CHARACTERS
CONVERSION
SPECIFICATIONS
FLOATING NUMBERS IN
THE INPUT STREAM
USING THE SCAN SET
THE RETURN VALUE
A scanf() EXAMPLE

14.3 THE FUNCTIONS sprintf()
AND sscanf()

14.4 THE FUNCTIONS fprintf()
AND fscanf()

14.5 ACCESSING FILES

14.6 AN EXAMPLE: DOUBLE-
SPACING A FILE

14.7 USING TEMPORARY FILES
AND GRACEFUL FUNCTIONS

14.8 ACCESSING A FILE
RANDOMLY

14.9 STYLE

14.10 COMMON PROGRAMMING
ERRORS
THE FUNCTION sscanf() IS
DIFFERENT

14.11 SYSTEM CONSIDERATIONS

14.12 SUMMARY

14.13 EXERCISES

In this chapter we explain how to use some of the input/output functions in the standard library, including the functions printf() and scanf(). Although we have used these functions throughout this text, many details still need to be explained. We present extensive tables showing the effects of various formats. The standard library provides functions related to printf() and scanf() that can be used for dealing with files and strings; their use is explained here.

General file input/output is important in applications where data reside in files on disks and tapes. We will show how to open files for processing and how to use a pointer to a file. Some applications need temporary files. Examples are given to illustrate their use.

14.1 THE OUTPUT FUNCTION printf()

The printf() function has two nice properties that allow flexible use at a high level. First, a list of arguments of arbitrary length can be printed, and second, the printing is controlled by simple conversion specifications, or formats. The function printf() delivers its character stream to the standard output file stdout, which is normally connected to the screen. The argument list to printf() has two parts:

control_string   and   *other_arguments*

In the example

```
printf("she sells %d %s for $%f", 99, "sea shells", 3.77);
```

we have

control_string: `"she sells %d %s for $%f"`
other_arguments: `99, "sea shells", 3.77`

The expressions in *other_arguments* are evaluated and converted according to the formats in the control string and then placed in the output stream. Characters in the control string that are not part of a format are placed directly in the output stream. The % symbol introduces a conversion specification, or format. A single conversion specification is a string that begins with % and ends with a conversion character.

`printf()`	
Conversion character	**How the corresponding argument is printed**
c	as a character
d, i	as a decimal integer
u	as an unsigned decimal integer
o	as an unsigned octal integer
x, X	as an unsigned hexadecimal integer
e	as a floating point number; example: 7.123000e+00
E	as a floating point number; example: 7.123000E+00
f	as a floating point number; example: 7.123000
g	in the e-format or f-format, whichever is shorter
G	in the E-format or f-format, whichever is shorter
s	as a string
p	the corresponding argument is a pointer to void; its value gets printed as a hexadecimal number
n	the corresponding argument is a pointer to an integer into which gets printed the number of characters written so far; the argument is not converted
%	with the format %% a single % is written to the output stream; there is no corresponding argument to be converted

The function printf() returns as an int the number of characters printed. In the example

```
printf("she sells %d %s for $%f", 99, "sea shells", 3.77);
```

we can match the formats in the control string with their corresponding arguments in the argument list.

Format	Corresponding argument
%d	99
%s	"sea shells"
%f	3.77

Explicit formatting information may be included in a conversion specification. If it is not included, then defaults are used. For example, the format %f with corresponding argument 3.77 will result in 3.770000 being printed. The number is printed with six digits to the right of the decimal point by default.

Between the % that starts a conversion specification and the conversion character that ends it, there may appear in order

- zero or more flag characters that modify the meaning of the conversion specification. These flag characters are discussed below.

- an optional positive integer that specifies the minimum *field width* of the converted argument. The place where an argument is printed is called its *field*, and the number of spaces used to print an argument is called its *field width*. If the converted argument has fewer characters than the specified field width, then it will be padded with spaces on the left or right, depending on whether the converted argument is right- or left-adjusted. If the converted argument has more characters than the specified field width, then the field width will be extended to whatever is required. If the integer defining the field width begins with a zero and the argument being printed is right-adjusted in its field, then zeros rather than spaces will be used for padding.

- an optional *precision*, which is specified by a period followed by a nonnegative integer. For d, i, o, u, x, and X conversions it specifies the minimum number of digits to be printed. For e, E, and f conversions it specifies the number of digits to the right of the decimal point. For g and G conversions it specifies the maximum number of significant digits. For an s conversion it specifies the maximum number of characters to be printed from a string.

- an optional h or l, which is a "short" or "long" modifier, respectively. If an h is followed by a d, i, o, u, x, or X conversion character, the conversion specification applies to a short int or unsigned short int argument. If an h is followed by an n conversion character, the corresponding argument is a pointer to a short int or unsigned short int. If an l is followed by a d, i, o, u, x, or X conversion character, the conversion specification applies to a long int or unsigned long int argument. If an l is followed by an n conversion character, the corresponding argument is a pointer to a long int or unsigned long int.

■ an optional L, which is a "long" modifier. If an L is followed by an e, E, f, g, or G conversion character, the conversion specification applies to a long double argument.

The flag characters are

■ a minus sign, which means that the converted argument is to be left-adjusted in its field. If there is no minus sign, then the converted argument is to be right-adjusted in its field.

■ a plus sign, which means that a nonnegative number that comes from a signed conversion is to have a + prepended. This works with the conversion characters d, i, e, E, f, g, and G. All negative numbers start with a minus sign.

■ a space, which means that a nonnegative number that comes from a signed conversion is to have a space prepended. This works with the conversion characters d, i, e, E, f, g, and G. If both a space and a + flag are present, the space flag is ignored.

■ a #, which means that the result is to be converted to an "alternate form" that depends on the conversion character. With conversion character o, the # causes a zero to be prepended to the octal number being printed. In an x or X conversion, the # causes 0x or 0X to be prepended to the hexadecimal number being printed. In a g or G conversion, it causes trailing zeros to be printed. In an e, E, f, g, or G conversion, it causes a decimal point to be printed, even with precision 0. The behavior is undefined for other conversions.

■ a zero, which means that zeros instead of spaces are used to pad the field. With d, i, o, u, x, X, e, E, f, g, and G conversion characters, this can result in numbers with leading zeros. Any sign and any 0x or 0X that gets printed with a number will precede the leading zeros.

In a format, the field width or precision or both may be specified by a * instead of an integer, which indicates that a value is to be obtained from the argument list. Here is an example of how the facility can be used:

```
int     m, n;
double  x = 333.7777777;

.....                           /* get m and n from somewhere */
printf("x = %*.*f\n", m, n, x);
```

If the argument corresponding to the field width has a negative value, then it is taken as a - flag followed by a positive field width. If the argument corresponding to the precision has a negative value, then it is taken as if it were missing.

The conversion specification %% can be used to print a single percent symbol in the output stream. It is a special case because there is no corresponding argument to be converted. For all the other formats there should be a corresponding argument. If there are not enough arguments, the behavior is undefined. If there are too many arguments, the extra ones are evaluated but otherwise ignored.

The field width is the number of spaces used to print the argument. The default is whatever is required to properly display the value of the argument. Thus the integer value 255 (decimal) requires three spaces for decimal conversion d or octal conversion o, but only two spaces for hexadecimal conversion x.

When an argument is printed, characters appropriate to the conversion specification are placed in a field. The characters appear right-adjusted unless a minus sign is present as a flag. If the specified field width is too short to properly display the value of the corresponding argument, the field width will be increased to the default. If the entire field is not needed to display the converted argument, then the remaining part of the field is padded with blanks on the left or right, depending on whether the converted argument is right- or left-adjusted. The padding character on the left can be made a zero by specifying the field width with a leading zero.

The precision is specified by a nonnegative number that occurs to the right of the period. For string conversions this is the maximum number of characters to be printed from the string. For e, E, and f conversions it specifies the number of digits to appear to the right of the decimal point.

Examples of character and string formats are given in the next table. We use double quote characters to visually delimit the field. They do not get printed.

Declarations and initializations
`char c = 'A', s[] = "Blue moon!";`

Format	Corresponding argument	How it is printed in its field	Remarks
`%c`	`c`	`"A"`	field width 1 by default
`%2c`	`c`	`" A"`	field width 2, right-adjusted
`%-3c`	`c`	`"A  "`	field width 3, left-adjusted
`%s`	`s`	`"Blue moon!"`	field width 10 by default
`%3s`	`s`	`"Blue moon!"`	more space needed
`%.6s`	`s`	`"Blue m"`	precision 6
`%-11.8s`	`s`	`"Blue moo   "`	precision 8, left-adjusted

Examples of formats used to print numbers are given in the next table. Again we use double quote characters to visually delimit the field. They do not get printed.

Declarations and initializations
`int    i = 123;` `double x = 0.123456789;`

Format	Corresponding argument	How it is printed in its field	Remarks
`%d`	`i`	`"123"`	field width 3 by default
`%05d`	`i`	`"00123"`	padded with zeros
`%7o`	`i`	`"    173"`	right-adjusted, octal
`%-9x`	`i`	`"7b       "`	left-adjusted, hexadecimal
`%-#9x`	`i`	`"0x7b     "`	left-adjusted, hexadecimal
`%10.5f`	`x`	`"   0.12346"`	field width 10, precision 5
`%-12.5e`	`x`	`"1.23457e-01 "`	left-adjusted, e-format

14.2 THE INPUT FUNCTION scanf()

The function scanf() has two nice properties that allow flexible use at a high level. The first is that a list of arguments of arbitrary length can be scanned, and the second is that the input is controlled by simple conversion specifications, or formats. The function scanf() reads characters from the standard input file stdin. The argument list to scanf() has two parts:

control_string   and   *other_arguments*

In the example

```
char     a, b, c, s[100];
int      n;
double   x;

scanf("%c%c%c%d%s%lf", &a, &b, &c, &n, s, &x);
```

we have

control_string: "%c%c%c%d%s%lf"
other_arguments: &a, &b, &c, &n, s, &x

The other arguments following the control string consist of a comma-separated list of pointer expressions, or addresses. Note that in the above example, writing &s would be wrong; the expression s by itself is an address.

DIRECTIVES IN THE CONTROL STRING

The control string for scanf() is composed of three kinds of *directives*: ordinary characters, white space, and conversion specifications. We want to discuss each of these in detail.

ORDINARY CHARACTERS

Characters in the control string other than white space characters and characters in a conversion specification are called *ordinary characters*. Ordinary characters must be matched in the input stream. Here is an example:

```
float    amount;

scanf("$%f", &amount);
```

The character $ is an ordinary character. An attempt will be made to match a $ in the input stream. If the match succeeds, then white space, if any, will be skipped, and characters that can be converted to a floating value will be matched. The converted value will be placed in memory at the address of amount.

In our next example, each of the three characters a, b, and c constitute an ordinary character directive.

```
scanf("abc");
```

First the character a will be matched, then the character b, and finally the character c. If at some point scanf() fails to make a match, the offending character is left in the input stream and scanf() returns. If the call to scanf() succeeds, then the characters immediately following a, b, and c in the input stream will be ready for processing.

WHITE SPACE CHARACTERS

White space characters in the control string that are not in a conversion specification are matched with optional white space in the input stream. Consider the example

```
char    c1, c2, c3;

scanf(" %c %c %c", &c1, &c2, &c3);
```

If the input stream contains the letters *a*, *b*, and *c*, with or without leading white space and with or without intervening white space, then *a*, *b*, and *c*, will be read into c1, c2, and c3, respectively. A white space directive causes white space, if any, in the input stream to be skipped. Because of this, the following two statements are equivalent:

```
scanf(" %c %c %c", &c1, &c2, &c3);
scanf("\t%c \t  %c\n%c", &c1, &c2, &c3);
```

CONVERSION SPECIFICATIONS

In a control string for scanf(), a conversion specification directive begins with a % and ends with a conversion character. It determines how characters in the input stream are matched and converted.

scanf()		
Unmodified conversion character	*Characters in the input stream that are matched*	*Type of the corresponding argument*
c	any character, including white space	char *
d	an optionally signed decimal integer	int *
i	an optionally signed decimal, octal, or hexadecimal integer such as 77 or 077 or 0x77	int *
u	an optionally signed decimal integer	unsigned *
o	an optionally signed octal integer, leading 0 not needed	unsigned *
x, X	an optionally signed hexadecimal integer, leading 0x or 0X not allowed	unsigned *
e, E, f, g, G	an optionally signed floating point number	float *
s	a sequence of nonwhite space characters	char *
p	what is produced by %p in printf(), usually an unsigned hexadecimal integer	void **
n, %, [. . .]	(See the next table.)	

Three conversion characters are of a special nature, and one of these, [. . .], is not even a character, although the construct is treated as such. We discuss these in the next table.

scanf()	
Unmodified conversion character	**Remarks**
n	No characters in the input stream are matched. The corresponding argument is a pointer to int, into which gets printed the number of characters read so far.
%	The conversion specification %% causes a single % character in the input stream to be matched. There is no corresponding argument.
[. . .]	The set of characters inside the brackets [ ] is called the *scan set*. It determines what gets matched and read in. (See the explanation given below.) The corresponding argument is a pointer to the base of an array of characters that is large enough to hold the characters that are matched, along with a terminating null character \0 that gets appended automatically.

Between the % and the conversion character there may be

■ an optional * that indicates assignment suppression, followed by an optional integer that defines a maximum scan width, followed by an optional h, l, or L that modifies the conversion character.

■ the modifier h, which can precede a d, i, o, u, x, or X conversion character. It indicates that the converted value is to be stored in a short int or in an unsigned short int.

■ the modifier l, which can precede either a d, i, o, u, x, or X conversion character or an e, E, f, g, or G conversion character. In the first case it indicates that the converted value is to be stored in a long int or in an unsigned long int. In the second case it indicates that the converted value is to be stored in a double.

■ the modifier L, which can precede an e, E, f, g, or G conversion character. It indicates that the converted value is to be stored in a long double.

The characters in the input stream are converted to values according to the conversion specifications in the control string and placed at the address given by the corresponding pointer expression in the argument list. Except for character input, a scan field consists of contiguous nonwhite characters that are appropriate to the specified conversion. The scan field ends when an inappropriate character is reached, or the scan width, if specified, is exhausted, or the end-of-file mark is encountered, whichever comes first.

The scan width is the number of characters scanned to retrieve the argument value. The default is whatever is in the input stream. The specification `%s` skips white space and then reads in nonwhite space characters until a white space character is encountered, or the end-of-file mark is encountered, whichever comes first. In contrast to this, the specification `%5s` skips white space and then reads in nonwhite characters, stopping when a white space character is encountered, or five characters have been read in, or the end-of-file mark is encountered, whichever comes first. When a string is read in, it is presumed that enough space has been allocated in memory to hold the string and an end-of-string sentinel `\0`, which will be appended.

The format `%nc` can be used to read in the next *n* characters, including white space characters. It is presumed that enough space has been allocated in memory to hold them. The null character `\0` does not get appended.

FLOATING NUMBERS IN THE INPUT STREAM

Floating numbers in the input stream are formatted as an optional sign followed by a digit string with an optional decimal point, followed by an optional exponential part. The exponential part consists of e or E, followed by an optional sign, followed by a digit string. Some examples are

```
77              /* gets converted to a floating value */
+7.7e1          /* equivalent to 77 */
770.0E-1        /* equivalent to 77 */
+0.003
```

Remember: The input stream is not C code; different rules apply.

USING THE SCAN SET

A conversion specification of the form `%[` *string* `]` indicates that a special string is to be read in. The set of characters inside the brackets `[ ]` is called the *scan set*. If the first character in the scan set is not a circumflex character ^, then the string is to be made up only of the characters in the scan set. Thus the format `%[abc]` will input a string containing only the letters a, b, and c, and will stop if any other character appears in the input stream, including a blank. In contrast to this, if the first character in the scan set is a circumflex, then the string is to be made up of all characters other than those in scan set. Thus the format `%[^abc]` will input a string terminated by any of a, b, or c, but not by white space. Consider the code

```
char    store[30];

scanf("%29[AB \t\n]", store);
```

This will read into the character array store a string containing at most 29 characters. The string will consist of the letters A and B and the white space characters blank, tab, and newline. Whatever is read into store will be terminated with \0.

Programmers usually think of a line as a string of characters, including blanks and tabs, that ends with a newline character. One way to read a line into memory is to use an appropriate scan set. Consider the following code:

```
char    line[300];

while (scanf(" %[^\n]", line) == 1)
    printf("%s\n", line);
```

The effect of this code is to skip any blank lines and to remove leading white space from any other lines. Let us give an explicit example. We first create a program containing the above lines, compile it, and put the executable code in the file *pgm*. Then we put the following lines in *infile*:

```
A is for

    apple and
                alphabet pie.
```

When we give the command

pgm < infile > outfile

here is what we find in *outfile*:

```
A is for
apple and
alphabet pie.
```

In addition to the scanf() family of functions, C also provides the functions gets() and fgets() to read lines from a file (see exercise 9).

THE RETURN VALUE

When scanf() is invoked, an input failure can occur or a matching failure can occur. An input failure occurs when there are no characters in the input stream. When this happens, EOF (typically -1) is returned. When a matching failure occurs, the offending character is left in the input stream and the number of successful conversions up to that point is returned. This number is zero if no conversions have occurred. If scanf() succeeds, then the number of successful conversions is returned. Again, this number can be zero.

A scanf() EXAMPLE

We want to present an example that illustrates some of the capability of the scanf() function. We will describe in detail the matching process that occurs with a particular input stream. Here is our example:

```
char    c, *cntrl_string, save[7], store[15];
int     a, cnt;

cntrl_string = "%d , %*s %% %c %[abc] %*s %5s %s";
cnt = scanf(cntrl_string, &a, &c, save, store, &store[5]);
```

With the following characters in the input stream

```
23 , ignore_this  %  C  abacus  read_in_this**
```

the value 23 is placed in a, the comma is matched, the string "ignore_this" is ignored, the % is matched, the character C is placed in the variable c, the string "abac" is placed in save[0] through save[4] with the terminating \0 in save[4], the "us" in abacus is ignored, the string "read_" is placed in store[0] through store[5] with the terminating \0 in store[5], and finally the string "in_this**" is placed in store[5] through store[14] with the terminating \0 in store[14]. Since five successful conversions were made, the value 5 is returned by scanf().

scanf()			
Directive in control string	**Type of the corresponding argument**	**What is in the input stream**	**Remarks**
ab%2c	char *	abacus	ab gets matched, ac gets converted
%3hd	short *	-7733	-77 gets converted
%4li	long *	+0x66	+0x6 gets converted (hexadecimal)
-%2u	unsigned *	-123	- gets matched, 12 gets converted
+ %lu	unsigned long *	+-123	+ gets matched, -123 gets converted
+ %lu	unsigned long *	+ -123	+ gets matched, -123 gets converted
+ %lu	unsigned long *	+- 123	+ gets matched, *error*, - cannot be converted
%3e	float *	+7e-2	+7e gets converted
%4f	float *	7e+22	7e+2 gets converted
%5lf	double *	-1.2345	-1.23 gets converted
%4Lf	long double *	12345	1234 gets converted
%p	void **	*system-dependent*	can read in what printf() *with* %p writes on output

14.3   THE FUNCTIONS sprintf() AND sscanf()

The functions sprintf() and sscanf() are string versions of the functions printf() and scanf(), respectively. Their function prototypes, found in *stdio.h*, are

```
int    sprintf(char *s, const char *format, ...);
int    sscanf(const char *s, const char *format, ...);
```

The ellipsis ... indicates to the compiler that the function takes a variable number of arguments. A statement of the form

```
sprintf(string, control_string, other_arguments);
```

writes to the character array *string*. The conventions for *control_string* and *other_arguments* conform to those of printf(). In a similar fashion, a statement of the form

```
sscanf(string, control_string, other_arguments);
```

reads from the character array *string*.

Let us look at an example:

```
char    in_string[] = "1 2 3 go";
char    out_string[100], tmp[100];
int     a, b, c;

sscanf(in_string, "%d%d%d%s", &a, &b, &c, tmp);
sprintf(out_string, "%s %s %d%d%d\n", tmp, tmp, a, b, c);
printf("%s", out_string);
```

Here is what gets printed:

```
go go 123
```

First, the function sscanf() reads three integers and a string from in_string, putting them into a, b, c, and tmp, respectively. Then the function sprintf() writes to out_string. Finally, we use printf() to print out_string on the screen. *Caution:* It is the programmer's responsibility to provide adequate space in memory for the output of sprintf().

14.4   THE FUNCTIONS fprintf() AND fscanf()

The functions fprintf() and fscanf() are file versions of the functions printf() and scanf(), respectively. Before we discuss their use, we need to know how C deals with files.

The header file *stdio.h* contains a number of constructs that pertain to files. Among these is the identifier FILE, which is a structure type whose members describe the current state of a file. To use files, the programmer need not know any details concerning the FILE structure type.

Also defined in *stdio.h* are the three file pointers stdin, stdout, and stderr. We sometimes refer to them as files, even though they are actually pointers.

Written in C	Name	Remark
stdin	standard input file	connected to the keyboard
stdout	standard output file	connected to the screen
stderr	standard error file	connected to the screen

The header file *stdio.h* contains function prototypes for many file handling functions. Here are the prototypes for fprintf() and fscanf():

```
int    fprintf(FILE *ofp, const char *format, ...);
int    fscanf(FILE *ifp, const char *format, ...);
```

The ellipsis ... indicates to the compiler that the function takes a variable number of arguments. A statement of the form

fprintf(*file_ptr*, *control_string*, *other_arguments*);

writes to the file pointed to by *file_ptr*. The conventions for *control_string* and *other_arguments* conform to those of printf(). In particular,

fprintf(stdout, ...);   is equivalent to   printf(...);

In a similar fashion, a statement of the form

fscanf(*file_ptr*, *control_string*, *other_arguments*);

reads from the file pointed to by *file_ptr*. In particular,

fscanf(stdin, ...);   is equivalent to   scanf(...);

In the next section we will show how to use fopen() to open files, how to use fprintf() and fscanf() to access them, and how to use fclose() to close files.

14.5   ACCESSING FILES

Files have several important properties. They have a name. They must be opened and closed. They can be written to, or read from, or appended to. Conceptually, until a file is opened, nothing can be done to it. It is like a closed book. When it is opened, we can have access to it at its beginning or end. To prevent accidental misuse, we must tell the system which of the three activities—reading, writing, or appending—we will be performing on it. When we are finished using the file, we close it.

Abstractly, a file can be thought of as a stream of characters. After a file has been opened, the stream can be accessed with file handling functions in the standard library. Consider the following code:

```
#include <stdio.h>

main()
{
    int     sum = 0, val;
    FILE    *ifp, *ofp;

    ifp = fopen("my_file", "r");    /* open for reading */
    ofp = fopen("outfile", "w");    /* open for writing */
    .....
```

This opens two files in the current directory: *my_file* for reading and *outfile* for writing. (The identifier ifp is mnemonic for "infile pointer," and the identifier ofp is mnemonic for "outfile pointer.") After a file has been opened, the file pointer is used exclusively in all references to the file. Suppose that *my_file* contains integers. If we want to sum them and put the result in *outfile*, we can write

```
while (fscanf(ifp, "%d", &val) == 1)
    sum += val;
fprintf(ofp, "The sum is %d.\n", sum);
```

Note that fscanf(), like scanf(), returns the number of successful conversions. After we have finished using the files, we can close them by writing

```
fclose(ifp);
fclose(ofp);
```

A function call of the form fopen(*file_name, mode*) opens the named file in a particular mode and returns a file pointer. There are a number of possibilities for the mode.

Mode	Meaning
"r"	open text file for reading
"w"	open text file for writing
"a"	open text file for appending
"rb"	open binary file for reading
"wb"	open binary file for writing
"ab"	open binary file for appending

Each of these modes can end with a + character. This means that the file is to be opened for both reading and writing.

Mode	Meaning
"r+"	open text file for reading and writing
"w+"	open text file for writing and reading
. . . . .	

Opening for reading a file that cannot be read, or does not exist, will fail. In this case fopen() returns a NULL pointer. Opening a file for writing causes the file to be created if it does not exist and causes it to be overwritten if it does. Opening a file in append mode causes the file to be created if it does not exist and causes writing to occur at the end of the file if it does.

When a + occurs in the mode, the file is opened in update mode (for both reading and writing). Consider the code

```
FILE    *fp;

fp = fopen("my_file", "r+");      /* open for reading and writing */
```

This opens *my_file* for input first, but both input and output may be performed on the file. However, input may not be directly followed by output unless the end-of-file mark has been reached or an intervening call to fseek(), fsetpos(), or rewind() has occurred. Similarly, output may not be directly followed by input without an intervening call to fflush(), fseek(), fsetpos(), or rewind() occurring.

In the UNIX operating system there is no distinction between binary and text files, except in their contents. The file mechanism is the same for both types of files. In MS-DOS, and in some other operating systems too, there are different file mechanisms for each of the two types of files; see exercise 22 for further discussion.

A detailed description of the file handling functions, such as fopen() and fclose(), can be found in Appendix A, "The Standard Library." The reader should consult the appendix as necessary to understand how the various functions are used.

14.6   AN EXAMPLE: DOUBLE-SPACING A FILE

Let us illustrate the use of some file handling functions by writing a program to double-space a file. In main() we open files for reading and writing that are passed as command line arguments. After the files have been opened, we invoke double_space() to accomplish the task of double-spacing.

```c
#include <stdio.h>
#include <stdlib.h>

void   double_space(FILE *, FILE *);
void   prn_info(char *);

main(int argc, char **argv)
{
   FILE   *ifp, *ofp;

   if (argc != 3) {
      prn_info(argv[0]);
      exit(1);
   }
   ifp = fopen(argv[1], "r");     /* open for reading */
   ofp = fopen(argv[2], "w");     /* open for writing */
   double_space(ifp, ofp);
   fclose(ifp);
   fclose(ofp);
}

void double_space(FILE *ifp, FILE *ofp)
{
   int   c;

   while ((c = getc(ifp)) != EOF) {
      putc(c, ofp);
      if (c == '\n')
         putc('\n', ofp);   /* found a newline - duplicate it */
   }
}

void prn_info(char *pgm_name)
{
   printf("\n%s%s%s\n\n%s%s\n\n",
      "Usage: ", pgm_name, " infile  outfile",
      The contents of infile will be double-spaced ",
      "and written to outfile.");
}
```

Suppose that we have compiled this program and put the executable code in the file *dbl_space*. When we give the command

   dbl_space file1   file2

the program will read from *file1* and write to *file2*. The contents of *file2* will be the same as *file1*, except that every newline character will have been duplicated.

DISSECTION OF THE *dbl_space* PROGRAM

■ `#include <stdio.h>`
  `#include <stdlib.h>`

  `void   double_space(FILE *, FILE *);`
  `void   prn_info(char *);`

We have included *stdlib.h* because it contains the function prototype for `exit()`, which gets used in `prn_info()`. The identifier `FILE` is a structure defined in *stdio.h*. To make use of files, we do not need to know system implementation details of how the file mechanism works. The function prototype for `double_space()` shows that it takes two file pointers as arguments.

■ `main(int argc, char **argv)`
  `{`
  `   FILE   *ifp, *ofp;`

  `   if (argc != 3) {`
  `      prn_info(argv[0]);`
  `      exit(1);`
  `   }`

The identifiers `ifp` and `ofp` are file pointers. The names are mnemonic for "infile pointer" and "outfile pointer," respectively. The program is designed to access two files entered as command line arguments. If there are too few or too many command line arguments, `prn_info()` is invoked to print information about the program, and `exit()` is invoked to exit the program. By convention, `exit()` returns a nonzero value when something has gone wrong.

```
■ ifp = fopen(argv[1], "r");    /* open for reading */
  ofp = fopen(argv[2], "w");    /* open for writing */
```

We can think of `argv` as an array of strings. The function `fopen()` is used to open the file named in `argv[1]` for reading. The pointer value returned by the function is assigned to `ifp`. In a similar fashion, the file named in `argv[2]` is opened for writing.

```
■ double_space(ifp, ofp);
```

The two file pointers are passed as arguments to `double_space()`, which then does the work of double-spacing. One can see that other functions of this form could be written to perform whatever useful work on files was needed.

```
■ fclose(ifp);
  fclose(ofp);
```

The function `fclose()` from the standard library is used to close the files pointed to by `ifp` and `ofp`. It is good programming style to close files explicitly in the same function in which they were opened. Any files not explicitly closed by the programmer are closed automatically by the system on program exit.

```
■ void double_space(FILE *ifp, FILE *ofp)
  {
     int  c;
     .....
```

This is the start of the function definition for `double_space()`. The identifier `c` is an `int`. Although it will be used to store characters obtained from a file, eventually it will be assigned the value `EOF`, which is not a character.

```
■ while ((c = getc(ifp)) != EOF) {
     putc(c, ofp);
     if (c == '\n')
        putc('\n', ofp);   /* found a newline - duplicate it */
  }
```

The macro `getc()` reads a character from the file pointed to by `ifp` and assigns the value to `c`. If the value of `c` is not `EOF`, then `putc()` is used to write `c` into the file pointed to by `ofp`. If `c` is a newline character, another newline character is written into the file as well. This has the effect of double spacing the output file. This process continues repeatedly until an `EOF` is encountered. The macros `getc()` and `putc()` are defined in *stdio.h*.

14.7 USING TEMPORARY FILES AND GRACEFUL FUNCTIONS

In ANSI C, the programmer can invoke the library function tmpfile() to create a temporary binary file that will be removed when it is closed or on program exit. The file is opened for updating with the mode "wb+". In MS-DOS, a binary file can also be used as a text file. In UNIX, there is only one mechanism for a file. Except for their contents, binary and text files are the same.

In this section we want to write an elementary program that illustrates the use of tmpfile(). Our program will also present a graceful version of fopen(). Let us name our program *dbl_with_caps*. Here is what we want to accomplish:

> Open the file named on the command line in update mode for reading and writing.
>
> Open a temporary file in update mode for writing and reading.
>
> Copy the contents of the first file into the temporary file, capitalizing any lowercase letters as we do so.
>
> Write a marker line at the bottom of the first file, so that we can easily distinguish what was already in the file from what we are going to add.
>
> Copy the contents of the temporary file to the bottom of the first file, thereby doubling its contents.

```
#include <ctype.h>
#include <stdio.h>
#include <stdlib.h>

FILE   *gfopen(char *file_name, char *mode);

main(int argc, char **argv)
{
   int    c;
   FILE   *fp, *tmp_fp;

   if (argc != 2) {
      fprintf(stderr, "\n%s%s%s\n\n%s\n\n",
         "Usage:  ", argv[0], "  file_name",
         "The file will be doubled and some letters capitalized.");
      exit(1);
   }
   fp = gfopen(argv[1], "r+");         /* open for reading and writing */
   tmp_fp = tmpfile();                 /* open for writing and reading */
   while ((c = getc(fp)) != EOF)
      putc(toupper(c), tmp_fp);        /* capitalize lowercase letters */
   fprintf(fp, "---\n");               /* print marker line at bottom */
   rewind(tmp_fp);                     /* mv file pos indicator to top */
   while ((c = getc(tmp_fp)) != EOF)   /* copy tmp file at the bottom */
      putc(c, fp);
}

FILE *gfopen(char *fn, char *mode)     /* graceful version of fopen() */
{
   FILE   *fp;

   if ((fp = fopen(fn, mode)) == NULL) {
      fprintf(stderr, "Cannot open %s - bye!\n", fn);
      exit(1);
   }
   return fp;
}
```

Before we explain the program, let us see its effects. Suppose that in file *apple* we have the line

```
A is for apple and alphabet pie.
```

After we give the command

dbl_with_caps apple

the contents of the file *apple* will be

```
A is for apple and alphabet pie.
---
A IS FOR APPLE AND ALPHABET PIE.
```

DISSECTION OF THE *dbl_with_caps* PROGRAM

■ `fp = gfopen(argv[1], "r+");`

We are using a graceful version of fopen() to open a file for both reading and writing. If for some reason the file cannot be opened, a message will be printed and the program exited. In contrast to this, consider the statement

```
fp = fopen(argv[1], "r+");      /* dangerous! */
```

If for some reason argv[1] cannot be opened, fopen() returns the NULL pointer. No warning gets printed on the screen telling the user that something is wrong.

■ `tmp_fp = tmpfile();`

ANSI C provides the function tmpfile() to open a temporary file. The file mode is "wb+", meaning the file is a binary file that is opened for both writing and reading. A binary file can also be used as a text file. On program exit, the temporary file will be removed by the system. Consult Appendix A, "The Standard Library," for the function prototype and other details.

■ `while ((c = getc(fp)) != EOF)`
`    putc(toupper(c), tmp_fp);`

The macros getc() and putc() are defined in *stdio.h*. They are being used to read from one file and to write to another. The function prototype for toupper() is given in *ctype.h.* If c is a lowercase letter, toupper(c) returns the corresponding uppercase letter; otherwise, it returns c. *Caution:* Some ANSI C compilers do not get this right. (Hopefully, they will improve with time.) You may have to write

```
while ((c = getc(fp)) != EOF)
    if (islower(c))
        putc(toupper(c), tmp_fp);
    else
        putc(c, tmp_fp);
```

■ fprintf(fp, "---\n");

Since we encountered the end-of-file marker in the stream pointed to by fp, we can switch from reading to writing. Here, we are writing a marker line that will serve to delineate the two parts of the file.

■ rewind(tmp_fp);

This causes the file position indicator for the stream pointed to by tmp_fp to be set to the beginning of the file. This statement is equivalent to

```
fseek(tmp_fp, 0, 0);
```

See Appendix A, "The Standard Library," for the function prototypes and for an explanation of fseek().

■ while ((c = getc(tmp_fp)) != EOF)
    putc(c, fp);

Now we are reading from the stream pointed to by tmp_fp and writing to the stream pointed to by fp. Note that a call to rewind() occurred before we switched from writing to reading on the stream pointed to by tmp_fp.

■ FILE *gfopen(char *fn, char *mode)   /* graceful version of fopen() */
  {
  . . . . .

This is a graceful version of fopen(). If something goes wrong, a message is printed on the screen and the program is exited. Note that we wrote to stderr. In this program, we could just as well have written to stdout. However, in other programs that use this function, there is an advantage to writing to stderr (see exercise 13).

14.8 ACCESSING A FILE RANDOMLY

In addition to accessing one character after another in a file (sequential access), we can access characters in different places (random access). The library functions ftell() and ftell() are used to access a file randomly. An expression of the form

ftell(*file_ptr*)

returns the current value of the file position indicator. The value represents the number of bytes from the beginning of the file, counting from zero. Whenever a character is read from the file, the system increments the position indicator by 1. Technically, the file position indicator is a member of the structure pointed to by *file_ptr*. The file pointer itself does not point to individual characters in the stream. This is a conceptual mistake that many beginning programmers make.

The function fseek() takes three arguments: a file pointer, an integer offset, and an integer that indicates the place in the file from which the offset should be computed. A statement of the form

fseek(*file_ptr*, *offset*, *place*);

sets the file position indicator to a value that represents *offset* bytes from *place*. The value for *place* can be 0, 1, or 2, meaning the beginning of the file, the current position, or the end of the file, respectively. *Caution:* The functions fseek() and ftell() are guaranteed to work properly only on binary files. In MS-DOS, if we want to use these functions, the file should be opened with a binary mode. In UNIX, since there is only one file mechanism, any file mode will work.

A common exercise is to write a file backwards. Let us write a program that does this by accessing the file randomly.

```
#include <stdio.h>

#define    MAXSTRING    100

main()
{
    char    file_name[MAXSTRING];
    int     c;
    FILE    *ifp;

    fprintf(stderr, "\nInput a file name:  ");
    scanf("%s", file_name);
    ifp = fopen(file name, "rb");    /* binary mode for ms-dos */
    fseek(ifp, 0, 2);                /* move to the end of the file */
    fseek(ifp, -1, 1);               /* back up one character / 
    while (ftell(ifp) >= 0) {
        c = getc(ifp);               /* move ahead one character */
        putchar(c);
        fseek(ifp, -2, 1);           /* back up two characters */
    }
}
```

The prompt to the user is written to stderr so that the program will work properly with redirection (see exercise 13). We open the file with mode "rb" so that the program will work in both MS-DOS and UNIX.

14.9   STYLE

In ANSI C, different conversion characters can have the same effect. When possible, we use lowercase instead of uppercase conversion characters. Also, for portability reasons, when dealing with decimal integers, we prefer d to i. The latter is unavailable in many traditional C systems.

A good programming style is to check that fopen() does its work as expected. In any serious program such checks are essential. Suppose that we want to open *my_file* for reading. A common programming style used to do this is

```
if ((ifp = fopen("my_file", "r")) == NULL) {
    printf("\nCannot open my_file - bye!\n\n");
    exit(1);
}
```

If for some reason fopen() is unable to open the named file, the pointer value NULL is returned. We test for this value, and if we find it, we print a message and exit.

Another stylistic issue concerns the indiscriminate opening of files for writing. If fopen() is used to open a file for writing that already exists, then the contents of that file will be destroyed. Since files are potentially valuable, the user should be warned if a file already exists. One way to do this is to first check to see if the file can be opened for reading. If it can be, then the file exists. In this case, the user should be warned (see exercise 10).

Most operating systems allow only a limited number of files to be open at one time. When writing a large program, it is essential to keep track of which files are open. A good programming style is to close a file in the same function in which it was opened.

14.10 COMMON PROGRAMMING ERRORS

Beginning programmers sometimes forget that the file mode is a string, not a character. If you type

```
ifp = fopen("my_file", 'r');      /* wrong */
```

your compiler should at least give you a warning. The programmer is well advised to pay attention to all pointer warnings.

When using printf() and scanf(), or the file and string versions of these functions, it is easy to improperly match formats in the control string with the arguments that follow. Here is a specific example:

```
double   x;
FILE     *ifp, *ofp;

. . . . .
fscanf(ifp, "%f", &x);            /* wrong, use %lf instead */
fprintf(ofp, "x = %lf\n", x);     /* wrong, use %f instead */
```

For functions in the printf() family, the format "%lf" does not exist.

Many common errors are related to the use of files. An error that beginning programmers often make is to use the file name instead of the file pointer. After a file has been opened, the file pointer is to be used to access the file, not the file name. Constructs such as

```
fprintf(file_name, . . .);      /* wrong */
fclose(file_name);              /* wrong */
```

can cause unexpected run-time errors. Most compilers will issue a message warning of suspicious pointer conversion. All such warnings should be heeded.

Some other common errors are opening a file that is already open, closing a file that is already closed, writing to a file that is opened for reading, or reading from a file that is opened for writing. What happens in such cases is system-dependent. The compiler cannot catch mistakes of this kind. It is the programmer's responsibility to open, use, and close files properly.

When using the functions fprintf(), sprintf(), fscanf(), and sscanf(), a common programming error is to forget to use a pointer to FILE or a string, as the case may be, as the first argument.

```
fprintf("k = %d\n", k);     /* wrong, a file pointer missing */
```

This is a natural error to make, since the use of fprintf(), is very similar to the use of printf(). Your compiler will warn you, but you may have difficulty interpreting what the warning is about.

Here is a mistake that can be very hard to find. The difficulty is that the compiler cannot help you at all.

```
char    msg[100], wrk[100];
int     val;

.....                              /* get msg and val from somewhere */
sprintf("%s %d\n", msg, val);      /* wrong arguments */
```

Since the programmer has used two strings as the first two arguments to sprintf(), the compiler is happy, even though these are the wrong ones. The programmer's intent was to use sprintf() to write into wrk, which should be the first argument to sprintf().

When porting code to MS-DOS, there can be subtle problems. In UNIX, since all files are the same, it is common not to use the binary mode when opening a file. However, the functions fseek() and ftell() are guaranteed to work properly only on binary files.

The programmer often thinks of a file pointer as pointing to a stream of characters, which is certainly an acceptable mental image. The programmer should not, however, think of a file pointer as pointing to individual characters in the stream. This is not what happens. Technically, the file pointer points to a structure of type FILE, and the members of the structure keep track of what is happening in the file. (The programmer need not know the details concerning the structure itself.)

THE FUNCTION sscanf() IS DIFFERENT

We first discuss fscanf() and then show how sscanf() is different. Here is some code that we can use to read in nonwhite space characters one after another:

```
char    c;
FILE    *ifp;

. . . . .
while (fscanf(ifp, " %c", &c) == 1) {
    . . . . .                                /* do something */
```

The file mechanism uses the file position indicator to keep track of the current position in the file. Because of this, every time fscanf() is called, we get the next character in the file.

The function sscanf() is different. Suppose line is a string, and suppose that we want to access the nonwhite characters in line one after another. The following code fails!

```
while (sscanf(line, " %c", &c) == 1) {
    . . . . .                                /* do something */
```

Every time sscanf() is invoked, it accesses line from the beginning. There is no string position indicator mechanism that keeps track of where we are in the string (see exercise 5). The correct C idiom is to use a pointer, say p, as follows:

```
for (p = line; *p != '\0'; ++p) {
    if (!isspace(*p))
        . . . . .                            /* do something */
```

14.11   SYSTEM CONSIDERATIONS

On any machine, the use of calloc() or malloc() to dynamically allocate memory will fail if there is not enough memory. Because MS-DOS machines often have limited memory, the graceful versions of these functions are particularly useful in that environment.

Files are a limited resource. Only FOPEN_MAX files can be open at one time, including stdin, stdout, and stderr. The symbolic constant FOPEN_MAX is defined in *stdio.h*. A typical value for FOPEN_MAX is 20, although on some newer systems it is 64 or more.

In UNIX, there is only one file mechanism, whereas in MS-DOS there is a difference between binary files and text files. Both types of files can be used to store text. For further discussion see exercise 22.

When a file is opened in append mode, the file position indicator can be repositioned by invoking fseek() or rewind(). In MS-DOS, what was already in the file cannot be overwritten. In UNIX, it can be overwritten.

With time, there seems to be a need (or desire) to deal with larger files of all kinds. ANSI C added the standard library functions fgetpos() and fsetpos() to access files that are potentially very large. An implementation can design these functions to access files that are too large to be handled by the traditional functions ftell() and fseek(). See Appendix A for details.

14.12 SUMMARY

1 The functions printf() and scanf(), and the related file and string versions of these functions, all use conversion specifications in a control string to deal with a list of arguments of variable length.

2 The standard header file *stdio.h* must be included if files are to be used. It contains the definitions of the identifier FILE (a structure) and the file pointers stdin, stdout, and stderr. It also contains prototypes of many file handling functions and definitions for the macros getc() and putc().

3 A file can be thought of as a stream of characters. The stream can be accessed either sequentially or randomly. When a character is read from a file or written to a file, the file position indicator is incremented by 1.

4 The system opens the three standard files stdin, stdout, and stderr at the beginning of each program. The function printf() writes to stdout. The function scanf() reads from stdin. The files stdout and stderr are usually connected to the screen. The file stdin is usually connected to the keyboard. Redirection causes the operating system to make other connections.

5 The programmer can use fopen() and fclose() to open and close files, respectively. After a file has been opened, the file pointer is used to refer to the file.

6 The macro call getc(ifp) reads the next character from the file pointed to by ifp. Similarly, the macro call putc(c, ofp) writes the value of c in the file pointed to by ofp.

7 There are many kinds of file handling errors that the compiler cannot catch. An example is trying to write to a file that has been opened for reading. It is the programmer's responsibility to open, use, and close files properly.

8   Files are a scarce resource. The maximum number of files that can be open simultaneously is given by the symbolic constant FOPEN_MAX in *stdio.h*. For many systems this number is 20, although on some newer systems it is 64 or more. It is the programmer's responsibility to keep track of which files are open. On program exit, any open files are closed by the system automatically.

9   The standard library provides a collection of functions that access a file through its file pointer. For example, the function call

```
fgets(line, MAXLINE, ifp)
```

reads the next line of characters from the file pointed to by ifp.

10 In ANSI C, the function tmpfile() in the standard library can be used to open a temporary file. When a temporary file gets closed, the system removes it.

14.13   EXERCISES

1   Write a program that uses the directive %[\n] in a control string in a scanf() statement to read lines from a file named on the command line. Print every other line to stdout. *Hint:* Use a counter and test to see if it is even or odd.

2   The conversion specification %n is available in ANSI C, but not in traditional C. Can your compiler handle it correctly? Try the following code:

```
int   n1, n2;

printf("try %n me %n \n", &n1, &n2);
printf("n1 = %d  n2 = %d\n", n1, n2);
```

3   Can we give flag characters in a conversion specification in any order? The ANSI C document is not too specific about this point, but it seems that the intent is for any order to be acceptable. See what happens with your compiler when you try the following code:

```
printf("%0+17d\n", 1);
printf("%+017d\n", 1);
```

4 What is the effect of the following code?

```
char    s[300];

while (scanf("%*[^\n]%*[\n]%[^\n]%*[\n]", s) == 1)
    printf("%s\n", s);
```

Put these lines in a program, compile it, put the executable code in *pgm*, and then give the command

pgm < *my_file*

where the file *my_file* contains some lines of text. Do blank lines in *my_file* cause problems?

5 Accessing a string is not like accessing a file. When a file is opened, the file position indicator keeps track of where you are in the file. There is no comparable mechanism for a string. Write a program that contains the following lines:

```
char    c, s[] = "abc", *p = s;
int     i;
FILE    *ofp1, *ofp2;

ofp1 = fopen("tmp1", "w");
ofp2 = fopen("tmp2", "w");
for (i = 0; i < 3; ++i) {
    sscanf(s, "%c", &c);
    fprintf(ofp1, "%c", c);
}
for (i = 0; i < 3; ++i) {
    sscanf(p++, "%c", &c);
    fprintf(ofp2, "%c", c);
}
```

What gets written in tmp1 and tmp2? Explain.

6 Compile the following program and put the executable code into the file *try_me*:

```
#include <stdio.h>

main()
{
    fprintf(stdout, "A is for apple\n");
    fprintf(stderr, "and alphabet pie.\n");
}
```

Execute the program so you understand its effects. What happens when you redirect the output? Try the command

try_me > temp

Make sure you read the file *temp* after you do this. If UNIX is available to you, try the command

try_me > & temp

This causes the output that is written to stderr to be redirected, too. Make sure that you look at what is in *temp*. You may be surprised!

7 Write a program to number the lines in a file. The input file name should be passed to the program as a command line argument. The program should write to stdout. Each line in the input file should be written to the output file with the line number and a space prepended.

8 Modify the program you wrote in exercise 7 so that the line numbers are right-adjusted. The following output is *not* acceptable:

```
    . . . . .
9 This is line nine.
10 This is line ten.
```

If there are more than 10 lines but less than 100, then the line numbers should be printed using the "%2d" format; if there are more than 100 lines but less than 1000, then the line numbers should be printed using the "%3d" format; and so forth. If UNIX is available to you, try the command

nlines /usr/dict/words > outfile

where *nlines* is the name of your program. Examine the top and bottom of *outfile*, and a few places in between, to see if your program worked correctly. (The file is large—do not leave it lying around.)

9 Read about the functions fgets() and fputs() in Appendix A. Use fgets() to read lines from a file named on the command line. If the first nonwhite space characters on the line are //, then remove the // characters, along with any blanks and tabs that immediately precede and follow the // characters before writing the line to stdout. All other lines should be written to stdout without change. *Hint:* Use the following code:

```
char    line[MAXLINE], store[MAXLINE];
FILE    *ifp = stdin;


.....
while (fgets(line, MAXLINE, ifp) != NULL)
   if (sscanf(line, " // %[^\n]", store) == 1) {
      fputs(store, stdout);
      fputs("\n", stdout);      /* restore the newline */
   }
   else
      fputs(line, stdout);
}
```

10 Write a program called *wrt_rand* that creates a file of randomly distributed numbers. The file name is to be entered interactively. Your program should use three functions. Here is the first function:

```
void get_info(char *file_name, int *n_ptr)
{
   printf("\n%s\n\n%s",
      "This program creates a file of random numbers.",
      "How many random numbers would you like?  ");
   scanf("%d", n_ptr);
   printf("\nIn what file would you like them?  ");
   scanf("%s", file_name);
}
```

The second function to be used in your program is a "careful" version of fopen(). Its purpose is to warn the user if the output file already exists. (There are other ways of doing this.)

```
FILE *cfopen(char *file_name, char *mode)
{
    char    reply[2];
    FILE    *gfopen(char *, char *), *fp;

    if (strcmp(mode, "w") == 0
        && (fp = fopen(file_name, "r")) != NULL) {
            fclose(fp);
            printf("\nFile exists.  Overwrite it?  ");
            scanf("%1s", reply);
            if (*reply != 'y' && *reply != 'Y') {
                printf("\nBye!\n\n");
                exit(1);
            }
    }
    fp = gfopen(file_name, mode);
    return fp;
}
```

The third function is gfopen(), the graceful version of fopen(). We discussed this function in Section 14.7. *Hint:* To write your randomly distributed numbers neatly, use the following code:

```
for (i = 1; i <= n; ++i) {
    fprintf(ofp, "%12d", rand());
    if (i % 6 == 0 || i == n)
        fprintf(ofp, "\n");
}
```

11   In this exercise we examine a typical use of sscanf(). Suppose we are writing a serious interactive program that asks the user to input a positive integer. To guard against errors, we can pick up as a string the line typed by the user. Here is one way to process the string:

```
char    line[MAXLINE];
int     error, n;

do {
   printf("Input a positive integer:  ");
   fgets(line, MAXLINE, stdin);
   error = sscanf(line, "%d", &n) != 1 || n <= 0;
   if (error)
      printf("\nERROR: Do it again.\n");
} while (error);
```

This will catch some typing errors, but not all. If, for example, 23e is typed instead of 233, the error will not be caught. Modify the code so that if anything other than a digit string surrounded by optional white space is typed, the input is considered to be in error. Use these ideas to rewrite the *wrt_rand* program that you wrote in exercise 10.

12   Our program that double-spaces a file can be invoked with the command

   dbl_space infile outfile

If *outfile* exists, then it will be overwritten. This is potentially dangerous. Rewrite the program so it writes to stdout instead. Then the program can be invoked with the command

   dbl_space infile > outfile

This program design is much safer. Of all the system commands, only a few are designed to overwrite a file. After all, nobody likes to lose a file by accident.

13   Make a further modification to the program *dbl_space* that you wrote in exercise 12. Since the program is now intended to be used with redirection, it now makes sense to use

   fprintf(stderr, ...)   rather than   printf(...)

in the function definition for prn_info(). Since printf() writes to stdout, which in turn gets redirected, the user does not see the information on the screen. The symbol > is used to redirect what is written to stdout. It does not affect what is written to stderr. Try writing your program two ways: with the error message being written first to stderr and then to stdout. Experiment with the two versions of the program, with and without redirection, so you understand the different effects.

14 Make a further modification to the program *dbl_space* that you wrote in exercise 13. Implement a command line option of the form $-n$, where n can be 1, 2, or 3. If n is 1, then the output should be single-spaced. That is, two or more contiguous newline characters in the input file should be written as a single newline character in the output file. If n is 2, then the output file should be strictly double-spaced. That is, one or more contiguous newline characters in the input file should be re-written as a pair of newline characters in the output file. If n is 3, the output file should be strictly triple-spaced.

15 Write the function `getwords(ifp, k, words)` so that it reads k words from the file pointed to by `ifp` and places them in the string `words`, separated by newlines. The function should return the number of words successfully read and stored in `words`. Write a program to test your function.

16 Write the function `putstring(s, ofp)` so that it writes the string `s` into the file pointed to by `ofp`. Use the macro `putc()` to accomplish the task. Write a program to test your function.

17 Read about the `ungetc()` function in Appendix A. After three characters have been read from a file, can `ungetc()` be used to push three characters back onto the file? Write a program to test this.

18 Write a program that displays a file on the screen 20 lines at a time. The input file should be given as a command line argument. The program should display the next 20 lines after a carriage return has been typed. (This is an elementary version of the *more* utility in UNIX.)

19 Modify the program you wrote in exercise 18. Your program should display one or more files given as command line arguments. Also, allow for a command line option of the form -*n*, where *n* is a positive integer specifying the number of lines that are to be displayed at one time.

20 The library function `fgets()` can be used to read from a file a line at a time. Read about it in Appendix A. Write a program called *search* that searches for patterns. If the command

  search hello my_file

is given, then the string pattern *hello* is searched for in the file *my_file*. Any line that contains the pattern is printed. (This program is an elementary version of *grep*.) *Hint:* Use the following code:

```
char    line[MAXLINE], *pattern;
FILE    *ifp;

if (argc != 3) {
   .....
}
if ((ifp = fopen(argv[2], "r")) == NULL) {
   fprintf(stderr, "\nCannot open %s\n\n", argv[2]);
   exit(1);
}
pattern = argv[1];
while (fgets(line, MAXLINE, ifp) != NULL) {
   if (strstr(line, pattern) != NULL)
      .....
```

21 Modify the program that you wrote in exercise 20. If the command line option $-n$ is present, then the line number should be printed as well.

22 In the early days of MS-DOS, a control-z character embedded in a file was used as an end-of-file mark. Although this is not done now, if a file has a control-z in it, and it is opened as a text file for reading, characters beyond the control-z may be inaccessible. Write a program with the following lines in it:

```
char    cntrl_z = 26;     /* decimal value for control-z */
int     c;
FILE    *ifp, *ofp;

ofp = fopen("tmp", "w");
fprintf(ofp, "%s%c%s\n",
   "A is for apple", cntrl_z, " and alphabet pie.");
fclose(ofp);
ifp = fopen("tmp", "r");             /* open as a text file */
while ((c = getc(ifp)) != EOF)       /* print the file */
   putchar(c);
fclose(ifp);
printf("\n---\n");                   /* serves as a marker */
ifp = fopen("tmp", "rb");            /* open as a binary file */
while ((c = getc(ifp)) != EOF)       /* print the file */
   putchar(c);
```

What gets printed? (Does the program act differently on a UNIX system?) Try the MS-DOS command

type tmp

Only the characters before the control-z are printed. How do you know that there are more characters in the file? *Hint:* Try the *dir* command. Normally, control-z characters are not found in text files, but they certainly can occur in binary files. Subtle problems can occur if you open a binary file for processing with mode "r" instead of "rb".

23 Examine the following program carefully. What gets printed?

```
#include <stdio.h>

main()
{
    printf("Hello!\n");
    fclose(stdout);
    printf("Goodbye!\n");
}
```

15

SOFTWARE TOOLS

15.1   EXECUTING COMMANDS FROM WITHIN A C PROGRAM
15.2   ENVIRONMENT VARIABLES
15.3   THE C COMPILER
15.4   CREATING A LIBRARY
15.5   USING THE PROFILER
15.6   HOW TO TIME C CODE
15.7   THE USE OF *dbx*
15.8   THE USE OF *make*
15.9   THE USE OF *touch*
15.10 OTHER USEFUL TOOLS
15.11 STYLE
15.12 COMMON PROGRAMMING ERRORS
15.13 SYSTEM CONSIDERATIONS
15.14 SUMMARY
15.15 EXERCISES

There are two kinds of software tools: general utilities provided by the operating system for everyone, and specific utilities designed explicitly to help the programmer. Since operating system commands can be executed from within a C program, the programmer can use these commands as software tools to accomplish specific tasks.

Some tools are provided in one operating system, but not in another. For example, *make* is available in UNIX, but in MS-DOS it is an add-on feature. Nonetheless, *make* is available on many MS-DOS systems.

Software tools vary with time. Debuggers on newer systems tend to be much better than what was available before. The C compiler itself can be considered a software tool. Newer compilers usually conform to the ANSI C standard.

In this chapter we first discuss how to execute an operating system command from within a program. Then a number of the more important tools for programmers are discussed, including the compiler, *make, touch, grep*, beautifiers, and debuggers.

15.1 EXECUTING COMMANDS FROM WITHIN A C PROGRAM

The library function system() provides access to operating system commands. Thus whatever tools are provided by the operating system are also available to the C programmer. In both MS-DOS and UNIX, the command *date* causes the current date to be printed on the screen. If we want this information printed on the screen from within a program, we can write

```
system("date");
```

The string passed to system() is treated as an operating system command. When the statement is executed, control is passed to the operating system, the command is executed, and then control is passed back to the program.

In UNIX, *vi* is a commonly used text editor. Suppose that from inside a program we want to use *vi* to edit a file that has been given as a command line argument. We can write

```
char    command[MAXSTRING];

sprintf(command, "vi %s", argv[1]);
printf("vi on the file %s is coming up ...\n", argv[1]);
system(command);
```

A similar example works in MS-DOS, provided that we replace *vi* by an editor that is available on that system.

As a final example, let us suppose that we are tired of looking at all those capital letters produced by the *dir* command on our MS-DOS system. We can write a program that interfaces with this command and writes only lowercase letters on the screen.

```
#include <ctype.h>
#include <stdio.h>
#include <stdlib.h>

#define   MAXSTRING   100

main()
{
   char   command[MAXSTRING], *tmp_file_name;
   int    c;
   FILE   *ifp;

   temp_file_name = tmpnam(NULL);
   sprintf(command, "dir > %s", tmp_file_name);
   system(command);
   ifp = fopen(tmp_file_name, "r");
   while ((c = getc(ifp)) != EOF)
      putchar(tolower(c));
   remove(tmp_file_name);
}
```

First, we use the library function tmpnam() to create a temporary file name. Then we invoke system() to redirect the output of the *dir* command into the temporary file. Then we print on the screen the contents of the file, changing each uppercase letter to lowercase. Finally, when we are finished using the temporary file, we invoke the library function remove() to remove it. Consult Appendix A, "The Standard Library," for details about these functions.

15.2   ENVIRONMENT VARIABLES

Environment variables are available in both UNIX and MS-DOS. The following program will print them on the screen:

```
#include <stdio.h>

main(int argc, char *argv[], char *env[])
{
    int   i;

    for (i = 0; env[i] != NULL; ++i)
        printf("%s\n", env[i]);
}
```

Both of the parameters argv and env are of type pointer to pointer to char. We can think of them as arrays of pointers to char, or as arrays of strings. The system provides the strings, including the space for them. The last element in each of the arrays is a NULL pointer. In this program, we only make use of env. On our UNIX system, this program prints

```
BASE=/c/c/blufox
HOME=/c/c/blufox/center
SHELL=/bin/csh
TERM=vt102
USER=blufox
. . . . .
```

To the left of the equal sign is the environment variable; to the right of the equal sign is its value, which should be thought of as a string. On our MS-DOS system, this program prints

```
COMSPEC=C:\COMMAND.COM
BASE=d:\base
INCLUDE=d:\msc\include
. . . . .
```

Both MS-DOS and UNIX provide a command to display environment variables. In UNIX, the command is *env* or *printenv* (or both), and in MS-DOS, it is *set*. The output of the command is the same as the output of our program.

By convention, environment variables are usually capitalized. In a C program, we can access environment variables via the third parameter to main(), as we did in our last program, or we can use the function getenv() in the standard library. Its function prototype, which is in *stdlib.h*, is given by

```
char   *getenv(const char *name);
```

If the string passed as an argument is an environment variable, then the function returns the string (pointer to char) provided by the system that is the value of the variable. If the string passed as an argument is not an environment variable, then NULL is returned. Here is some code that illustrates the use of getenv():

```
printf("%s%s\n%s%s\n%s%s\n%s%s\n%s%s\n",
    "   User's name: ", getenv("NAME"),
    "   Login name: ", getenv("LOGNAME"),
    "         Shell: ", getenv("SHELL"),
    "          Base: ", getenv("BASE"),
    "Home directory: ", getenv("HOME"));
```

On our UNIX system, this prints the following:

```
   User's name: Al Kelley
   Login name: blufox
         Shell: /bin/csh
          Base: /c/c/blufox
Home directory: /c/c/blufox/center
```

In UNIX, certain environment variables, such as LOGNAME, SHELL, and HOME are provided by the system. To get others, we put lines such as

```
setenv  BASE  /c/c/blufox
setenv  NAME  "Al Kelley"
```

in our *.login* file.

15.3   THE C COMPILER

There are many C compilers, and an operating system may provide any number of them. Here are just a few of the possibilities:

Command	The C compiler that gets invoked
cc	C compiler from Bell Laboratories
cc	C compiler from Cray Research running under UNICOS
cc	C compiler from Hewlett-Packard running under HP-UX
cc	C compiler from Silicon Graphics running under IRIX
acc	C compiler from Sun Microsystems running under SunOS
gcc	GNU C compiler from the Free Software Foundation
hc	High C compiler from Metaware
occ	Oregon C compiler from Oregon Software
qc	Quick C compiler from Microsoft
tc	Turbo C compiler, integrated environment, from Borland
tcc	Turbo C compiler, command line version, from Borland

In this section we explain the use of the compiler and discuss some of the options that are generally available for compilers in UNIX. Many of these options are available for compilers in the MS-DOS world as well.

If a complete program is contained in a single file, say *pgm.c*, then the command

```
cc  pgm.c
```

translates the C code in *pgm.c* into executable object code and writes it in the file *a.out*. (In MS-DOS, the executable file is *pgm.exe*.) The command *a.out* executes the program. Now consider the command

```
cc  −o pgm  pgm.c
```

This causes the executable code to be written directly into the file *pgm*, overwriting the file if it already exists. Whatever is in *a.out* will not be disturbed. (In MS-DOS, the option is −*e*, and no space can follow it.)

The *cc* command actually does its work in three stages: first the preprocessor is invoked, then the compiler, and finally the loader. The loader, or linker, is what puts all the pieces together to make the final executable file. The −*c* option can be used to compile only—that is, to invoke the preprocessor and the compiler, but not the loader. This option is useful if we have a program written in more than one file. Consider the command

```
cc  −c  main.c  file1.c  file2.c
```

If there are no errors, corresponding object files ending in *.o* will be created. (In MS-DOS, object files end in *.obj*.) To create an executable file, we can compile a mixture of .*c* and .*o* files. Suppose, for example, that we have an error in *main.c*. After correcting the error, we can give the command

> *cc −o pgm main.c file1.o file2.o*

The use of .*o* files in place of .*c* files reduces compilation time. In addition to .*c* and .*o* files, we can also use .*s* files that have been created either by the assembler or by the compiler with the -S option, and we can use libraries created by the archiver (see Section 15.4). Library file names typically end in .*a*. (Library file names end in .*lib* in MS-DOS.)

Some useful options to the compiler

-c	Compile only, generate corresponding .*o* files.
-g	Generate code suitable for the debugger.
-o *name*	Put executable output code in *name*.
-p	Generate code suitable for the profiler.
-D *name=def*	Place at the top of each .*c* file the line #define *name def*
-E	Invoke the preprocessor but not the compiler.
-I *dir*	Look for #include files in the directory *dir*.
-M	Make a makefile.
-MM	Make a makefile, but do not include any dependencies on the standard header files.
-O	Attempt code optimization.
-S	Generate assembler code in corresponding .*s* files.

Your compiler may not support all of these options, and it may provide others. Or it may provide an equivalent option under a different name (flag character). Compilers in MS-DOS usually support different memory models. Consult the documentation for your compiler for a detailed list of options.

15.4 CREATING A LIBRARY

Many operating systems provide a utility to create and manage libraries. In UNIX, the utility is called the archiver, and it is invoked with the *ar* command. In the MS-DOS world, this utility is called the librarian, and it is an add-on feature. The Microsoft librarian, for example, is *lib*, whereas Borland's Turbo C librarian is *tlib*. By convention, library file names end in .*a* in UNIX, and end in .*lib* in MS-DOS. We will discuss the situation as it pertains to UNIX, but the general ideas apply to any librarian.

In UNIX, the archiver *ar* can be used to combine a group of files into a single file called a library. The standard C library is an example of such a file. On most UNIX systems, it is the file */lib/libc.a*, but it can exist wholly or in part in other files as well. If UNIX is available to you, try the command

> *ar   t   /lib/libc.a*

The key *t* is used to display titles, or names, of files in the library. There are more titles than you care to look at. To count them, you can give the command

> *ar   t   /lib/libc.a | wc*

This pipes the output of the *ar* command to the input of the *wc* command, causing lines, words, and characters to be counted. (The name *wc* stands for "word count.") It is not too surprising that the standard library grows with time. On our DEC VAX 11/780 the standard library contains 311 object files, whereas on a newer Sun machine it contains 529.

Let us illustrate how programmers can create and use libraries of their own. We will do this in the context of creating a "graceful library." In Section 14.7 in Chapter 14 we presented gfopen(), a graceful version of fopen(). In a directory named *g_lib* we have 11 such graceful functions, and we continue to add more from time to time. These are functions such as gfopen(), gfclose(), gcalloc(), gmalloc(), and so forth. Each is written in a separate file, but for the purpose of building a library, they could just as well be in one file. To reinforce the idea of these functions, here is the code for gcalloc():

```
#include <stdio.h>
#include <stdlib.h>

void *gcalloc(int n, unsigned sizeof_something)
{
   void   *p;

   if ((p = calloc(n, sizeof_something)) == NULL) {
      fprintf(stderr, "\nERROR: calloc() failed - bye.\n\n");
      exit(1);
   }
   return p;
}
```

To create our library, we must first compile the *.c* files to obtain corresponding *.o* files. After we have done this, we give the two commands

ar ruv g_lib.a gfopen.o gfclose.o gcalloc.o . . .
ranlib g_lib.a

The keys *ruv* in the first command stand for "replace, update, and verbose," respectively. This command causes the library *g_lib.a* to be created if it does not already exist. If it does exist, then the named *.o* files replace those of the same name already in the library. If any of the named *.o* files are not in the library, they are added to it. The *ranlib* command is used to randomize the library in a form that is useful for the loader.

Now suppose that we are writing a program that consists of *main.c* and two other *.c* files. If our program invokes gfopen(), we need to make our library available to the compiler (loader). The following command does this:

cc −o pgm main.c file1.c file2.c g_lib.a

Suppose that our program invokes a function but does not supply its function definition. The loader will search for this function first in *g_lib.a* and then in the standard library. The loader puts only those functions that are needed into the final executable file; it does not load the whole library.

If we write lots of programs, each consisting of many files, then each of the programs should be written in its own directory. Also, we should have a separate directory for our libraries such as *g_lib.a*, and another directory for associated header files such as *g_lib.h*. For each function in *g_lib.a*, we put its prototype in *g_lib.h*. This header file then gets included where needed. To manage all of this, we use the *make* utility (see Section 15.7).

15.5   USING THE PROFILER

In UNIX, if we use the *−p* option with the compiler, then extra code is generated, which gets placed in the object files and in the executable file (the program) produced by the compiler. When the program gets invoked, the extra code produces information that can be used to generate a profile of the execution. The information for the profile is written automatically to the file *mon.out*. This file is not readable by humans. To obtain the information in *mon.out*, the programmer must give the command

prof pgm

where *pgm* is the name of the program.

We want to provide an example of how this all works. To get started, we will write a program that uses two sorting routines to sort two identical arrays of integers. By using

the $-p$ option when we compile the program, we will be able to obtain an execution
profile that shows the relative efficiencies of two sorting routines.

We will use two sorting routines, a transposition sort that we write ourselves, and
qsort(), which is provided by the standard library.

In file compare_sorts.h:

```
#include <assert.h>
#include <stdio.h>
#include <stdlib.h>
#include "g_lib.h"

void    chk_arrays(int *a, int *b, int n);
int     compare(const void *p, const void *q)
void    prn_array(int *a, int n);
void    slow_sort(int *a, int n);
```

In file main.c:

```
#include "compare_sorts.h"

main()
{
    int    *a, *b, i, n;

    printf("\n%s\n\n%s",
        "Two identical arrays of integers will be sorted.",
        "Input the array size:  ");
    scanf("%d", &n);
    a = calloc(n, sizeof(int));
    b = calloc(n, sizeof(int));
    for (i = 0; i < n; ++i)
        a[i] = b[i] = rand() % 1000;
    qsort(a, n, sizeof(int), compare);
    slow_sort(b, n);
    chk_arrays(a, b, n);
    if (n < 100)
        prn_array(a, n);
}
```

We prompt the user to get the array size, and then use our graceful version of calloc()
to allocate space dynamically (see Section 15.4). After we fill the two arrays a and b
with randomly distributed integers in the range 0 to 999, we use slow_sort() and
qsort() to sort a and b, respectively. In chk_arrays(), we make certain that the arrays
have been sorted in ascending order and that the two arrays are still identical. If the
array size is less than 100, then we print the elements of a on the screen. During program development, this allows us to see that everything works as expected. When the
array size is large, we do not bother printing the results. We only want to get a profile of
the execution.

In file compare.c:

```
#include "compare_sorts.h"

int compare(const void *vp, const void *vq)
{
    const int   *p = vp, *q = vq;

    return (*p - *q);
}
```

Since compare gets passed as an argument to qsort(), the function definition for compare()
must be consistent with the function prototype of the corresponding parameter in the
function prototype for qsort(). In particular, we need the type qualifier const (see Section 8.11 in Chapter 8).

In file slow_sort.c:

```
#include "compare_sorts.h"

void slow_sort(int *a, int n)
{
    int   i, j, tmp;

    for (i = 0; i < n; ++i)
        for (j = i + 1; j < n; ++j)
            if (a[i] > a[j]) {
                tmp = a[i];
                a[i] = a[j];
                a[j] = tmp;
            }
}
```

In file chk_arrays.c:

```
#include "compare_sorts.h"

void chk_arrays(int *a, int *b, int n)
{
    int    i;

    for (i = 0; i < n - 1; ++i) {
        assert(a[i] == b[i]);
        assert(a[i] <= a[i+1]);
    }
    assert(a[i] == b[i]);
}
```

In file prn_array.c:

```
#include "compare_sorts.h"

void prn_array(int *a, int n)
{
    int    i;

    for (i = 0; i < n; ++i) {
        if (i % 12 == 0)
            putchar('\n');
        printf("%5d", a[i]);
    }
    putchar('\n');
}
```

Now we want to get a profile of the execution of our program. To do this, we first have to compile our code with the −p option:

*gcc   −p   −o compare_sorts   main.c   chk_arrays.c   compare.c   *
    prn_array.c   slow_sort.c   g_lib.a

The loader needs *g_lib.a*, because that library contains gcalloc(). Next, we give the command

compare_sorts

and enter 1000 when prompted. Program execution causes the file *mon.out* to be created. Finally, to get an execution profile, we give the command

prof compare_sorts

This causes a profile of the execution of the program to be printed on the screen. Here are some of the lines:

```
%time  cumsecs  #call  ms/call  name
 96.6     2.84      1  2839.90  _slow_sort
  1.4     2.88  11291     0.00  _compare
  1.4     2.92      1    40.00  _qsort
  0.7     2.94      1    20.00  _main
  0.0     2.94      1     0.00  __doprnt
  0.0     2.94      2     0.00  _calloc
  0.0     2.94      1     0.00  _chk_arrays
  0.0     2.94      1     0.00  _exit
```

Note that compare() was called more than 11000 times. This is because qsort() is recursive. If qsort() itself had been compiled with the −*p* option, then we would see how many times it called itself. Not all of the functions in the list are user-defined; some of them, such as _doprnt, are system routines. This profile shows that 96.6 percent of the time was spent executing slow_sort() and only 1.4 percent of the time was spent executing qsort(). An execution profile such as this can be very useful when working to improve execution time efficiency. If you know which of your functions are using the most time, you can work on them to reduce execution time. Also, if you know that a function uses only a small percentage of the running time, then you know very little will be gained by improving it.

15.6   HOW TO TIME C CODE

Most operating systems provide access to the underlying machine's internal clock. In this section we show how to use some timing functions. Because our functions are meant to be used in many programs, we put them into the library *u_lib.a*, our utility library.

Access to the machine's clock is made available in ANSI C through a number of functions whose prototypes are in *time.h*. This header file also contains a number of other constructs, including the type definitions for clock_t and time_t, which are useful for dealing with time. Typically, the two type definitions are given by

```
typedef    long    clock_t;
typedef    long    time_t;
```

and in turn, these types are used in the function prototypes. Here are the prototypes for the three functions that we will use in our timing routines:

```
clock_t    clock(void);
time_t     time(time_t *p);
double     difftime(time_t time1, time_t time0);
```

When a program is executed, the operating system keeps track of the processor time that is being used. When clock() is invoked, the value returned is the system's best approximation to the time used by the program up to that point. The clock units can vary from one machine to another. The macro

```
#define    CLOCKS_PER_SEC    60         /* machine-dependent */
```

is provided in *time.h*. It can be used to convert the value returned by clock() to seconds.

The function time() returns the number of seconds that have elapsed since 1 January 1970. Other units and other starting dates are possible, but these are the ones typically used. If the pointer argument passed to time() is not NULL, then the value returned gets assigned to what the argument is pointing to as well. One typical use of the function is

```
srand(time(NULL));
```

This seeds the random number generator. If two values produced by time() are passed to difftime(), the difference expressed in seconds is returned as a double.

We want to present a set of timing routines that can be used for many purposes, including the development of efficient code. We keep these functions in the file *time_keeper.c*.

```c
#include <stdio.h>
#include <stdlib.h>
#include <time.h>

#define   MAXSTRING   100

typedef struct {
   clock_t   begin_clock, save_clock;
   time_t    begin_time, save_time;
} time_keeper;

static time_keeper  tk;             /* known only to this file */

void start_time(void)
{
   tk.begin_clock = tk.save_clock = clock();
   tk.begin_time = tk.save_time = time(NULL);
}

double prn_time(void)
{
   char     s1[MAXSTRING], s2[MAXSTRING];
   int      field_width, n1, n2;
   double   clocks_per_sec = (double) CLOCKS_PER_SEC,
            user_time, real_time;

   user_time = (clock() - tk.save_clock) / clocks_per_sec;
   real_time = difftime(time(NULL), tk.save_time);
   tk.save_clock = clock();
   tk.save_time = time(NULL);

   /* print the values found, and do it neatly */

   n1 = sprintf(s1, "%.1f", user_time);
   n2 = sprintf(s2, "%.1f", real_time);
   field_width = (n1 > n2) ? n1 : n2;
   printf("%s%*.1f%s\n%s%*.1f%s\n\n",
      "User time: ", field_width, user_time, " seconds",
      "Real time: ", field_width, real_time, " seconds");
   return user_time;
}
```

Note that the structure tk is external to the functions and is known only in this file. It is used for communication between the functions in this file, and it cannot be accessed in some other file. Although we could have designed these functions so that tk gets passed as an argument, this would have been inappropriate. If this were done, the user would have to allocate space for tk and then write start_time(tk) and prn_time(tk) to invoke these functions. But the user is not interested in the internal workings of start_time() and prn_time(). Thus it is best to hide tk from the user.

When start_time() is invoked, the values returned from clock() and time() are stored in tk. When prn_time() is invoked, new values from clock() and time() are used to compute and print the elapsed user time and the elapsed real time, and new values are stored in tk. User time is whatever the system allocates to the running of the program; real time is wall-clock time. In a time-shared system they need not be the same.

The function prn_total_time() is also in the file, but we have not shown it. It is similar to prn_time(), except that the elapsed times are computed relative to the last invocation of start_time() rather than the last invocation of any of the three functions.

Since our timing routines are meant to be used in a variety of programs, we put them into *u_lib.a*, our utility library. The following commands do this:

cc −*c time_keeper.c;*   *ar ruv u_lib.a time_keeper.o;*   *ranlib u_lib.a*

In the header file *u_lib.h* we put the prototypes of the functions in *u_lib.a*. The header file then gets included elsewhere as needed.

Now we want to demonstrate how our timing routines can be used. In certain applications, fast floating point multiplication is desired. Should we use variables of type float or double? The following program can be used to test this:

```
/* Compare multiplication times. */

#include <stdio.h>
#include "u_lib.h"

#define   N   1000000

main()
{
    long    i;
    float   a, b = 3.333, c = 5.555;    /* arbitrary values */
    double  x, y = 3.333, z = 5.555;

    printf("\nNumber of multiples: %d\n\n", N);
    printf("Type float:\n");
    start_time();                       /* start timing */
    for (i = 0; i < N; ++i)
      a = b * c;
    prn_time();                         /* print time info */
    printf("Type double:\n");
    for (i = 0; i < N; ++i)
      x = y * z;
    prn_time();                         /* print time info */
}
```

On an older machine with a traditional C compiler, we find, much to our surprise, that single-precision multiplication is *slower* than double-precision multiplication! Perhaps this is explained by the fact that in traditional C, any float is automatically promoted to a double. On a newer machine with an ANSI C compiler, we find that single-precision multiplication is about 30% faster.

15.7 THE USE OF *dbx*

A debugger allows the programmer to step through the code a line at a time and to see the values of variables and expressions at each step. This can be extremely helpful in discovering why a program is not acting as the programmer expected. The programming world is full of debuggers, and *dbx* is not a particularly good one. It just happens to be one that is generally available on UNIX systems. In this section we want to describe the basics of using *dbx*.

Steps to follow to start using dbx

1   Go to a directory containing a C program.

2   Compile the program with the *-g* option (for debugging).

3   Give the command *dbx pgm*, where *pgm* is the name of the executable file. This invokes *dbx*. From now on, the commands we give are *dbx* commands.

4   Give a command such as *file main.c*. This sets the current file for *dbx*.

5   Give the command *list* to see the first 10 lines in the file. Give the command again to see the next 10 lines.

6   Give the command *stop at n*, where *n* is the line number of an executable line.

7   Give the command you would normally give to invoke *pgm*, except replace the word *pgm* with the word *run*. Example: *run 3*

8   At this point you can step through the program with the commands *step* and *next*. Use *step* to step into functions; use *next* to step over them. Use the command *print var* to print the current value of the variable *var*.

9   Give the command *quit* to quit.

This is just an outline of how to get started using *dbx*. Other useful commands are *alias* to see what aliases, if any, have been set, *continue* to continue program execution, and *help* to see a list of commands.

To cut down on the amount of typing needed to use *dbx*, the programmer can set aliases. Sometimes the system does this automatically. (There are slight variations in *dbx* from one system to another.) The programmer puts the aliases in the file *.dbxinit*, either in the current directory, or in the home directory, if the aliases are to be generally available. Here are the aliases we use:

In file .dbxinit:

```
alias a alias

a c cont;     a d delete;    a e edit;    a h help;    a l list;
a n next;     a p print;     a q quit;    a r run;     a j status;
a s step;     a w where;     a st stop;
```

In the MS-DOS world, debuggers are an add-on product. Both Microsoft and Borland, for example, provide excellent products. A UNIX workstation also may support add-on products. Although the programmer must expend some effort to learn to use a debugger, the effort can be well worth it.

15.8   THE USE OF *make*

For both the programmer and the machine, it is inefficient and costly to keep a moderate or large size program entirely in one file that has to be recompiled repeatedly. A much better strategy is to write the program in multiple *.c* files, compiling them separately as needed. The *make* utility can be used to keep track of source files and to provide convenient access to libraries and their associated header files. This utility is always available in UNIX and often available in MS-DOS, where it is an add-on feature. Its use greatly facilitates both the construction and the maintenance of programs.

Let us suppose that we are writing a program that consists of a number of *.h* and *.c* files. Typically, we would do this in a separate directory. The *make* command reads a file whose default name is *makefile*. This file contains the dependencies of the various modules, or files, making up the program, along with appropriate actions to be taken. In particular, it contains the instructions for compiling, or recompiling, the program. Such a file is called a *makefile*.

For simplicity, let us imagine that we have a program contained in two files, say *main.c* and *sum.c*, and that a header file, say *sum.h*, is included in each of the *.c* files. We want the executable code for this program to be in the file *sum*. Here is a simple makefile that can be used for program development and maintenance:

```
sum: main.o sum.o
        cc -o sum main.o sum.o

main.o: main.c sum.h
        cc -c main.c

sum.o: sum.c sum.h
        cc -c sum.c
```

The first line indicates that the file *sum* depends on the two object files *main.o* and *sum.o*. It is an example of a *dependency* line; it must start in column 1. The second line indicates how the program is to be compiled if one or more of the *.o* files have been changed. It is called an *action* line or a *command*. There can be more than one action following a dependency line. A dependency line and the action lines that follow it make up what is called a *rule. Caution:* Each action line must begin with a tab character. On the screen, a tab character looks like a sequence of blanks.

By default, the *make* command will make the first rule that it finds in the makefile. But dependent files in that rule may themselves be dependent on other files as specified in other rules, causing the other rules to be made first. These files, in turn, may cause yet other rules to be made.

The second rule in our makefile states that *main.o* depends on the two files *main.c* and *sum.h*. If either of these two files is changed, then the action line shows what must be done to update *main.o*. After this makefile has been created, the programmer can compile or recompile the program *sum* by giving the command

make

With this command, *make* reads the file *makefile*, creates for itself a dependency tree, and takes whatever action is necessary.

The dependency tree used
internally by *make*.

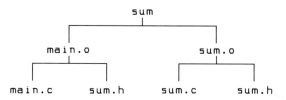

Certain rules are built into *make*, including the rule that a *.o* file depends on the corresponding *.c* file. Because of this, an equivalent makefile is given by

```
sum: main.o sum.o
        cc -o sum main.o sum.o

main.o: sum.h
        cc -c main.c

sum.o: sum.h
        cc -c sum.c
```

The *make* utility recognizes a number of built-in macros. Using one of them, we get yet another equivalent makefile:

```
sum: main.o sum.o
        cc -o sum main.o sum.o

main.o sum.o: sum.h
        cc -c $*.c
```

Here, the second rule states that the two *.o* files depend on *sum.h*. If we edit *sum.h*, then both *main.o* and *sum.o* must be remade. The macro `$*.c` expands to `main.c` when *main.o* is being made, and it expands to `sum.c` when *sum.o* is being made.

A makefile consists of a series of entries called *rules* that specify dependencies and actions. A rule begins in column 1 with a series of blank-separated target files, followed by a colon, followed by a blank-separated series of prerequisite files, also called *source* files. All the lines beginning with a tab that follow this are the actions, such as compilation, to be taken by the system to update the target files. The target files are dependent in some way on the prerequisite files and must be updated when the prerequisite files are modified.

In Section 15.5, "Using the Profiler," we wrote a program that used two routines to sort two identical arrays. Then we showed how to compile the program with the *-p* option so that we could get an execution profile. In reality, we used a makefile for program development. Here is the one that we used:

In file makefile:

```
# Makefile for compare_sorts.
# After execution, use prof to get a profile.

BASE    = /c/c/blufox
CC      = gcc
CFLAGS  = -p
EFILE   = $(BASE)/bin/compare_sorts
INCLS   = -I$(BASE)/include
LIBS    = $(BASE)/lib/g_lib.a

OBJS = main.o  chk_arrays.o  compare.o  \
       prn_array.o  slow_sort.o

$(EFILE): $(OBJS)
        @echo "linking ..."
        @$(CC)  $(CFLAGS)  -o $(EFILE)  $(OBJS)  $(LIBS)

$(OBJS): compare_sorts.h
        $(CC)  $(CFLAGS)  $(INCLS)  -c  $*.c
```

DISSECTION OF THE MAKEFILE FOR THE
compare_sorts PROGRAM

■ # Makefile for compare_sorts.
  # After execution, use prof to get a profile.

Comments can be put in a makefile. A comment begins with a *#* and extends to the end of the line.

■ BASE = /c/c/blufox

This is an example of a macro definition. The general form of a macro definition is

    macro_name = replacement_string

By convention, macro names are usually capitalized, but they do not have to be. The replacement string can contain white space. If a backslash \ occurs at the end of the line, then the replacement string continues to the next line. The macro BASE represents our base of operation on this particular machine. (It is not our home directory.)

■ CC   = gcc
  CFLAGS = -p

The first macro specifies the C compiler that we are using, in this case the GNU C compiler. The second macro specifies the options, if any, that will be used with the *gcc* command.

■ EFILE = $(BASE)/bin/compare_sorts
  INCLS = -I$(BASE)/include
  LIBS = $(BASE)/lib/g_lib.a

The first macro specifies the executable file, the second macro specifies a directory for include files proceeded by the *-I* option, and the third macro specifies our graceful library (see Section 15.4). We need this library, because it contains the object code for gcalloc(), the graceful version of *calloc()*. Since our programs often invoke functions that are in *g_lib.a*, we routinely make this library available to the compiler (loader). The prototypes of the functions in *g_lib.a* are kept in *g_lib.h*, and we will have to tell the compiler where to look for this header file.

■ OBJS = main.o   chk_arrays.o   compare.o   \
         prn_array.o   slow_sort.o

In this macro definition the replacement string is the list of object files that occurs on the right side of the equal sign. Note.that we used a backslash to continue the line. Although we put *main.o* first and then list the others alphabetically, order is unimportant.

■ `$(EFILE): $(OBJS)`
```
        @echo "linking ..."
        @$(CC)  $(CFLAGS)  -o $(EFILE)  $(OBJS)  $(LIBS)
```

The first line is a dependency line, and the other two lines specify the actions to be taken. Note carefully that they begin with a tab. (It looks like eight blank spaces on the screen.) The @ symbol means that the action line itself is not to be echoed on the screen. Macro invocation has the form

`$(`*macro_name*`)`

Thus the construct `$(EFILE)` is replaced by

`$(BASE)/bin/compare_sorts`

which in turn is replaced by

`/c/c/blufox/bin/compare_sorts`

Similarly, `$(OBJS)` is replaced by the list of object files, and so forth. Thus the dependency line states that the executable file depends on the object files. If one or more of the object files has been updated, then the specified actions occur. The second action line gets expanded to

```
@gcc  -p  -o /c/c/blufox/bin/compare_sorts  main.o    \
    chk_arrays.o compare.o prn_array.o slow_sort.o \
    /c/c/blufox/lib/g_lib.a
```

Although we have written it on three lines because of space limitations on the printed page, this is actually generated as a single line. The -p option causes the compiler to generate extra code suitable for the profiler. *Suggestion:* If make is new to you, build your makefiles without the @ symbol first. After you understand its effects, then you can use it to prevent echoing.

■ `$(OBJS): compare_sorts.h`
         `$(CC)  $(CFLAGS)  $(INCLS)  -c  $*.c`

The dependency line says that all the object files depend on the header file *compare_sorts.h*. If the header file has been updated, then all the object files have to be updated, too. This gets done through the action line. The construct $* that occurs at the end of the action line is a predefined macro called the *base file name macro*. It expands to the file name being built, excluding any extension. For example, if main.o is being built, then $*.c expands to main.c, and the action line becomes

```
gcc  -p  -I/c/c/blufox/include  -c  main.c
```

Certain dependencies are built into the *make* utility. For example, each .o file depends on the corresponding .c file. This means that if a .c file gets updated, then the actions specified for the corresponding .o file will be taken. For the makefile we are discussing here, this means that the .c file will be recompiled to produce a new .o file, and this in turn will cause all the object files to be relinked.

■ `-I/c/c/blufox/include`

An option of the form -I*dir* means "look in the directory *dir* for #include files." This option complements our use of libraries. At the top of each .c file making up this program we have the line

```
#include "compare_sorts.h"
```

and near the top of *compare_sorts.h* we have the line

```
#include "g_lib.h"
```

This header file contains the function prototypes for the functions in our library *g_lib.a*. The -I option tells the compiler where to find the header file if it is not in the current directory.

The *make* utility is not specific to C. It can be used to maintain programs in any language. More generally, it can be used in any kind of project that consists of files with dependencies and associated actions.

15.9   THE USE OF *touch*

The *touch* utility is always available in UNIX, and it is sometimes available in MS-DOS. Typically, it is available anywhere *make* is. The *touch* utility is used to put a new time on a file. This is often necessary when using *make*, which compares file times to determine what has to be done.

To illustrate the use of *touch*, let us assume that we have the makefile discussed in the previous section, along with the relevant *.h*, *.c*, and *.o* files. To put the current date on the file *compare_sorts.h*, we can give the command

   touch compare_sorts.h

This causes *compare_sorts.h* to have a more recent time than all the object files that depend on it. Now, if we give the command

   make

all the *.c* files will be recompiled and the object files linked to create a new executable file.

15.10   OTHER USEFUL TOOLS

Operating systems provide many useful tools for the programmer. Here we list a few of the tools found on UNIX systems, along with some remarks. Comparable utilities are sometimes available in MS-DOS.

Command	*Remarks*
cb	The C beautifier. It can be used to "pretty print" C code.
diff	Prints the lines that differ in two files.
grep	Searches for a pattern in one or more files.
indent	A C code "pretty printer" with lots of options.
wc	Counts lines, words, and characters in one or more files.

The *cb* utility reads from stdin and writes to stdout. It is not very powerful. To see what it can do, try the command

   cb < pgm.c

where *pgm.c* is poorly formatted. The utility *indent* is more powerful. It can be found on Berkeley and Sun versions of UNIX. To make serious use of it, you will need to read the online manual.

Tools such as *diff*, *grep*, and *wc* are of a general nature. They get used by everyone, not just programmers. Although these are UNIX tools, they are often available in MS-DOS as well, especially *grep*, which is very useful to programmers.

Finally, let us mention that C can be used in conjunction with other high-level tools, some of which are languages in their own right.

Utility	*Remarks*
awk	A pattern scanning and processing language.
csh	This shell, like *sh* and *ksh*, is programmable.
lex	Generates C code for lexical analysis.
sed	A stream editor that takes its commands from a file.
yacc	"Yet another compiler-compiler," used to generate C code.

Of particular importance are *lex* and *yacc*. More recent versions, called *flex* and *bison*, respectively, are available from the Free Software Foundation, Inc. They work in both MS-DOS and UNIX.

15.11   STYLE

A good programming style is to use system commands rather than writing the comparable utility yourself. Suppose, for example, that you need to find all the lines in a file named *data* that contain the word *beautiful*. You can accomplish this with the statement

```
system("grep beautiful data > tmp");
```

Inside your program, the file *tmp* can then be opened for further processing.

The beginning programmer often has difficulty understanding error and warning messages generated by the compiler. For this reason, there is a tendency to disregard the warnings. A good programming style is to rewrite code until it compiles with no warnings.

An efficient programming style is to use the sophisticated tools that are available to the programmer. Tools such as debuggers, profilers, *make*, and *touch* are nearly universal. For the development of all but the smallest programs, these tools are extremely useful. Of course, some effort is involved in learning to use these utilities, but the payback is large.

15.12   COMMON PROGRAMMING ERRORS

For the programmer, the compiler itself is the major software tool. A common error is to fail to set the warning level for the compiler at the highest level. All warnings should be heeded.

Beginning programmers often make the mistake of trying to write a large program in a single file. A better strategy is to break the program into modules and use *make* to keep track of dependencies.

A common error in the use of *make* is to forget that each action line must be preceded by a single tab. This is an easy mistake to make, because tabs are not visible.

When the programmer writes a makefile, it may have to be debugged. The command

```
make  −n
```

can be used to invoke *make* with the "no action" option. This option causes *make* to print on the screen what its actions would have been, without actually doing them.

When the flow of control in a program is not working as the programmer thinks it should, a "pretty printer" can be used as a debugging tool. The idea of using a "pretty printer" for debugging is not widely appreciated, but in some situations it can help a lot. For an example, see exercise 9.

15.13   SYSTEM CONSIDERATIONS

In today's world, the programmer often works across a network rather than on a single machine. In our environment, we routinely use a number of machines on campus, a machine at home, and various other machines around the country. One way to manage the complexity of this is to write code that depends on environment variables. Consider the following line from one of our *.login* files:

```
setenv BASE /c/c/blufox
```

This causes the environment variable BASE to have a string value that represents a certain directory on a particular machine. On another machine, the directory that we think of as "base" will be different, but since we write our software so that it accesses the environment variable BASE, this does not matter.

Many compilers support a "verbose" $-v$ option. It causes the compiler to print more information on the screen. The programmer should try this option to see if it has an effect.

In UNIX, the *make* utility reads instructions from either the file named *makefile* or *Makefile*. Some programmers prefer the name *Makefile* because it gets listed earlier when the *ls* command is used. Since the MS-DOS operating system is not case-sensitive, this distinction does not apply.

In UNIX, each action line in a makefile must begin with a tab character. In MS-DOS, this can be one or more blanks or tabs.

In many operating systems the output of a command or program that writes to stdout can be "piped" to another command or program that reads from stdin. The output of the first command becomes the input of the second command. Let us give an example of this. In MS-DOS, the command *dir* writes the current directory to stdout, and the command *sort* with no other command line arguments reads from stdin and writes to stdout. The output of *dir* can be piped to the input of *sort* by giving the command

   dir | sort

The symbol | represents a "pipe." In UNIX, a similar command will work, if we replace *dir* by *ls*. The concept of piping the output of one command to the input of another can be considered a way of getting software tools to work together.

Throughout this text we have used *tc* and *tcc* as the commands that invoke the Turbo C compiler from Borland. However, in 1991 Borland renamed these commands *bc* and *bcc*, respectively.

15.14 SUMMARY

1 An operating system command can be executed from within a program by invoking system(). In MS-DOS, the statement

```
system("dir");
```

will cause a list of directories and files to be listed on the screen. In UNIX, we replace "dir" by "ls".

2 The programmer can use getenv() to access environment variables on the system.

3 Most C compilers have a myriad of options. If you are doing serious work, it may pay to learn about all the options available on your compiler. Set the highest warning level. Heed all warnings.

4 Many operating systems provide a utility to create and manage libraries. In UNIX, the utility is called the *archiver*, and it is invoked with the *ar* command. In the MS-DOS world, this utility is called the *librarian*, and it is an add-on feature.

5 Using a library can save the programmer time and energy. The compilation process, however, then becomes more complex. The *make* utility can be used to help manage the complexity.

6 UNIX systems provide the *prof* utility to profile the execution of a program. Often, other profilers are available as well. For example, the *gprof* utility from Berkeley can be found on many UNIX systems. A profiler is often available on an MS-DOS system, although it is an add-on feature.

7 Debuggers are available on many systems. The newer ones provide a graphical interface for the user. The debugger *dbx* is old technology, but it is generally available on UNIX systems. This utility, even though it is not spiffy, can be very useful to the programmer.

8 The *make* utility can be used to keep track of source files and to provide convenient access to libraries and their associated header files.

9 The *touch* utility puts a new time on a file.

10 Some software tools, such as *diff* and *grep* are of a general nature. Everyone uses them, not just programmers. The *grep* utility is available on all UNIX systems and on many MS-DOS systems. Programmers routinely use it for a variety of tasks.

15.15 EXERCISES

1 First, write a program that lists all the environment variables on your system. If you are working on a UNIX system, give the command

   setenv ABC "Try me!"

This sets the environment variable *ABC*. In MS-DOS, the appropriate command is

   set ABC="Try me!"

Now run your program again. Is your new environment variable listed among the others alphabetically, or is it at the end? How do you get double quotes in the string assigned as a value to an environment variable?

2 If UNIX is available to you, give the command

   man sort

to read about the *sort* utility. Then experiment to see what the following program does:

```
#include <stdio.h>
#include <stdlib.h>

#define   MAXSTRING   100

main(int argc, char **argv)
{
    char   command[MAXSTRING];

    sprintf(command, "sort -r %s", argv[1]);
    system(command);
}
```

Actually, the program needs improvement. Rewrite it so that it prints a prompt to the user.

3   Is the Turbo C compiler available to you? If so, try the command

   tcc

This command by itself causes a list of all the options to be printed on the screen. This is a very nice feature. How many of the options do you know?

4   You already know how to write a bubble sort. Learn how to write quicksort; see, for example, *A Book on C* by Al Kelley and Ira Pohl (Menlo Park, Calif.: Benjamin/ Cummings, 1990). Investigate the efficiency of each of these sorting routines by using the profiler. You will find the information provided by *prof* more interesting. With respect to efficiency, there is no contest between qsort() and a transposition sort. Between qsort() and quicksort() there is.

5   In MS-DOS the command to clear the screen is *cls*; in UNIX it is *clear*. Try the command so that you understand its effect. Modify the *mk_cols* program that we presented in Section 11.15 in Chapter 11 so that the screen gets cleared at the beginning of the program. Use the function call system("cls") or system("clear") to accomplish this. What happens when the output is redirected? Does the screen still get cleared?

6   The last makefile that we presented in this chapter is a real one. Even though we dissected it, anyone who has not had experience with *make* will find the concepts difficult to grasp. If this utility is new to you, try the *make* command after you have created the following file:

In file makefile:

```
# Experiment with the make command!

go: hello date list
        @echo Goodbye!
hello:
        @echo Hello!
date:
        @date; date; date
list:
        @pwd; ls
```

What happens if you remove the @ characters? What happens if a file named *hello* or *date* exists?

7   Create the file listed below, and then give the command *make*. What gets printed? Write your answer first; then experiment to check it.

In file makefile:

```
# Experiment with the make command!

Start: A1 A2
        @echo Start
A1: A3
        @echo A1
A2: A3
        @echo A2
A3:
        @echo A3
```

8   (Advanced) Along with many utilities, the UNIX operating system is distributed with a few games. Many installations remove the games, because disk space is a scarce resource. It is, however, a common practice to leave one of the games on the system, the one that provides a random fortune. Sometimes the system administrator arranges for all users to get a fortune just prior to logout. (You can arrange for this yourself if you put the *fortune* command in your *.logout* file.) If UNIX is available to you, try the following command a number of times:

fortune

If this command has not been removed from the system, it will print a different fortune on the screen each time the command is invoked. If you give the command and see a fortune that you like, how can you capture it? (Perhaps you want to show it to your mother, or to send it via e-mail to a friend in Paris.) If you give the *fortune* command again, you will get a new fortune, not the one you had before. In this exercise you are to write a program that can capture a particular fortune. Begin by reading about the fortune command in the online manual. You can do this with the command

man fortune

Toward the end of the write-up, you will see the name of the file where all the fortunes are stored. On most systems, this file is unreadable to the public. We know from experience, however, that one fortune begins with the line

```
There are three possible parts to a date, of which
```

and ends with the line

```
-- Miss Manners' Guide to Excruciatingly Correct Behaviour
```

Your program should interactively ask the user to input a phrase to be searched for. Suppose the user types in "three possible parts to a date" when prompted. In your program you should do the following repeatedly:

1   Use the function call system("fortune > tmp") to capture a fortune in a file.
2   Search the file to see if it contains the desired phrase.
3   If it does, save the file, exit the loop, and send e-mail to notify the user.

The program may take a while, so it should be run in background. That is why notification by e-mail is appropriate. The following code can be used to send a message by e-mail to the user:

```
char    command[MAXSTRING], file_name[MAXSTRING],
        message[MAXLINE], *user = getenv("USER");

sprintf(message, "%s\n%s%s\n\n",
    "Found a fortune!",
    "It was saved in the file ", file_name);
sprintf(command, "echo \"%s\" | mail %s", message, user);
system(command);
```

9   The fact that a "pretty printer" can be used as a debugging tool is not widely appreciated. Put the following lines in the file *try_me.c*:

```c
#include <stdio.h>

main()
{
    int   a = 1, b = 2;

    if (a == 1)
        if (b == 2)
            printf("***\n");
    else
        printf("###\n");
}
```

Then give the command

   cb < try_me.c

You will see that the "pretty printer" *cb* aligns the code differently. Explain why.

16

FROM C TO C++

16.1 OUTPUT

16.2 INPUT

16.3 CLASSES AND ABSTRACT DATA TYPES

16.4 OVERLOADING

16.5 CONSTRUCTORS AND DESTRUCTORS

16.6 OBJECT-ORIENTED PROGRAMMING AND INHERITANCE

16.7 STYLE

16.8 COMMON PROGRAMMING ERRORS

16.9 SYSTEM CONSIDERATIONS

16.10 SUMMARY

16.11 EXERCISES

C++ is a modern extension of C to allow its use for object-oriented programming (OOP). Increasingly, C++ and C are being bundled together and made available for separate or joint use on the same system. In this chapter we give an overview of the C++ programming language. We also provide an introduction to the use of C++ as an object-oriented programming language. In the chapter a series of programs is presented, and the elements of each program are carefully explained. The programs increase in complexity, and the examples in the later sections illustrate some of the concepts of object-oriented programming. The approach is based on the three books *C++ for C Programmers, Turbo C++,* and *C++ for Pascal Programmers* by Ira Pohl (Menlo Park, Calif.: Benjamin/Cummings, 1990).

Each feature of C++ is explained briefly. The examples in this chapter give simple, immediate, hands-on experience with key features of the C++ language. The chapter introduces the reader to stream I/O, operator and function overloading, reference parameters, classes, constructors, destructors, and inheritance. The code is compatible with AT&T C++ and Borland Turbo C++.

Object-oriented programming is implemented in the class construct. The `class` construct in C++ is an extension of `struct` in C. The later examples in this chapter illustrate how C++ implements OOP (object-oriented programming) concepts, such as data hiding, ADTs (abstract data types), inheritance, and type hierarchies.

Several reasons exist for the C programmer to learn about C++:

C++ and C are increasingly being used together.

C is a starting point to learning C++.

With little additional effort, the C programmer can take advantage of several features that make C++ a "better C."

C++ is increasingly being used in colleges and industry, especially in advanced applications, where it is beginning to displace C.

This chapter cannot give more than a taste of OOP concepts. A good introduction to these concepts is given in *Object-Oriented Programming* by Timothy Budd (Menlo Park, Calif.: Addison-Wesley, 1991).

16.1   OUTPUT

Our first example is a program that prints on the screen the phrase "C++ is an improved C." The complete program is

```
// A first C++ program illustrating output.

#include <iostream.h>

main()
{
    cout << "C++ is an improved C.\n";
}
```

The program prints on the screen

```
C++ is an improved C.
```

DISSECTION OF THE *advert* PROGRAM

■ // A first C++ program illustrating output.

The double slash // is a new comment symbol. The comment runs to the end of the line. The old C bracketing comment symbols /* */ are still available for multiline comments.

■ `#include <iostream.h>`

The *iostream.h* header introduces I/O facilities for C++.

■ `cout << "C++ is an improved C.\n";`

This statement prints to the screen. The identifier `cout` is the name of the standard output stream. The operator `<<` passes the string `"C++ is an improved C.\n"` to standard out. Used in this way, the *output operator* `<<` is referred to as the *put to* or *insertion* operator.

The one-line comment symbol is the preferred C++ comment style. In general it is less error prone than the traditional C comment style, where leaving off the terminating symbol `*/` can create obscure errors.

We can rewrite our first program as follows.

```
// A first C++ program illustrating output.

#include <iostream.h>

main()
{
    cout << "C++ is an improved C." << "\n";
}
```

Although it is different from the first version, it produces the same output. Each time the `<<` is used with `cout`, printing continues from the position where it previously left off. In this case the newline character is output after a second use of the "put to" operator.

16.2 INPUT

We will write a program to convert to kilometers the distance in miles from the Earth to the moon. In miles this distance is, on average, 238,857 miles. This number is an integer. To convert miles to kilometers, we multiply by the conversion factor 1.609, a real number.

Our conversion program will use variables capable of storing integer values and real values. In C++ all variables must be declared before their use, but in contrast to their use in C, they need not be at the head of a block. Declarations may be mixed in with executable statements. Their scope, however, is still the block within which they are declared. Identifiers should be chosen to reflect their use in the program. In this way, they serve as documentation, making the program more readable.

```
// The distance to the moon converted to kilometers.

#include <iostream.h>

main()
{
    const long int moon = 238857;
    cout << "The moon's distance from Earth is " << moon;
    cout << " miles.\n";

    long int moon_kilo;
    moon_kilo = moon * 1.609;
    cout << "In kilometers this is " << moon_kilo;
    cout << " km.\n";
}
```

The output of the program is

```
The moon's distance from Earth is 238857 miles.
In kilometers this is 384320 km.
```

Since some machines have a 2-byte int, we have used variables of type long.

DISSECTION OF THE *moon* PROGRAM

■ `const long int moon = 238857;`

The keyword const is new in C++. It replaces some uses of the preprocessor command define to create named constants. Using this type modifier informs the compiler that the initialized value of moon cannot be changed.

■ `cout << "The moon's distance from Earth is " << moon;`

The stream I/O in C++ can discriminate among a variety of simple values without needing additional formatting information. Here the value of `moon` will be printed as an integer.

■ `long int moon_kilo;`
  `moon_kilo = moon * 1.609;`

Declarations can occur after executable statements. This allows declarations of variables to be nearer to their use.

Let us write a program that will convert a series of values from miles to kilometers. The program will be interactive. The user will type in a value in miles, and the program will convert this value to kilometers and print it out.

```
// Miles are converted to kilometers.

#include <iostream.h>

const double m_to_k = 1.609;
inline double convert(double mi) { return (mi * m_to_k); }

main()
{

    double   miles;

    do {
       cout << "Input distance in miles: ";
       cin >> miles;
       cout << "\nDistance is " << convert(miles) << " km.\n";
    } while (miles > 0);
}
```

This program uses the input stream variable `cin`, which is normally standard input. The *input operator* `>>` is called the *get from* or *extraction* operator, which assigns values from the input stream to a variable. This program illustrates both input and output.

DISSECTION OF THE *mi_km* PROGRAM

■ `const double m_to_k = 1.609;`
  `inline double convert(double mi) { return  (mi * m_to_k); }`

C++ reduces C's traditional reliance on the preprocessor. For example, instead of having to use `define`, special constants, such as the conversion factor 1.609, are simply assigned to variables specified as constants. The new keyword `inline` specifies that a function is to be compiled, if possible, as a macro. As a rule, `inline` should be done sparingly and only on short functions. Also note how the parameter `mi` is declared within the function parentheses. C++ uses function prototypes to define and declare functions.

■ `do {`
    `cout << "Input distance in miles: ";`
    `cin >> miles;`
    `cout << "\nDistance is " << convert(miles) << " km.\n";`
  `} while (miles > 0);`

The program repeatedly prompts the user for a distance in miles; it is terminated by a zero or negative value. The value placed in the standard input stream is automatically converted to a `double` value assigned to `miles`.

Many C++ programmers continue to use `printf()` and `scanf()` for their output and input. The advantage of using *iostream.h* is that it is type-safe. It is the system's responsibility to make sure the values being printed and read conform to their declarations. In using *stdio.h*-based I/O, the user is responsible for having the correct format string.

16.3   CLASSES AND ABSTRACT DATA TYPES

What is truly novel about C++ is its aggregate type `class`, which the language introduces. A `class` is an extension of the idea of `struct` in traditional C. A `class` provides the means for implementing a user-defined data type and associated functions and operators. Therefore a `class` is an implementation of an *abstract data type* (ADT). Let us write a `class` called `string` that will implement a restricted form of string.

```
// An elementary implementation of type string.

#include <string.h>
#include <iostream.h>

const int max_len = 255;

class string {
    char s[max_len];
    int  len;
public:
    void assign(const char* st) { strcpy(s, st); len = strlen(st); }
    int  length() { return (len); }
    void print() { cout << s << "\nLength: " << len << "\n"; }
};
```

Two important additions to the structure concept of traditional C are found in this example: (1) it has members that are functions, such as assign; and (2) it has both public and private members. The keyword public indicates the visibility or accessibility of the members that follow it. Without this keyword, the members are private to the class. Private members are available for use only by other member functions of the class. Public members are available to any function within the scope of the class declaration. Privacy allows part of the implementation of a class type to be "hidden." This restriction prevents unanticipated modifications to the data structure. Restricted access, or *data hiding*, is a feature of object-oriented programming.

The declaration of member functions allows the ADT to have particular functions act on its private representation. For example, the member function length returns the length of the string defined to be the number of characters up to but excluding the null character. The member function print() outputs both the string and its length. The member function assign() stores a character string into the hidden variable s and computes and stores its length in the hidden variable len.

We can now use this data type string as if it were a basic type of the language. It obeys the standard block structure scope rules of C. Other code that uses this type is called a *client*. The client can use the public members only to act on objects of type string.

```
// Test of the class string.

main()
{
    string    one, two;
    char      three[40] = {"My name is Charles Babbage."};

    one.assign("My name is Alan Turing.");
    two.assign(three);
    cout << three;
    cout << "\nLength: " << strlen(three) << "\n";
    if (one.length() <= two.length())              // print the shorter
        one.print();
    else
        two.print();
}
```

The variables one and two are of type string. The variable three is of type pointer to char and is not compatible with string. The member functions are called using the dot operator or "structure member selection operator." As is seen from their definitions, these member functions act on the hidden, private member fields of the named variables. One cannot write inside main the expression one.len expecting to access this member. The output of this example program is

```
My name is Charles Babbage.
Length: 27
My name is Alan Turing.
Length: 23
```

Conventional C practice uses the *string.h* header file in conjunction with the data type char * as a string type. However it requires that programmer's discipline themselves by not directly manipulating the underlying representation. In a C++ implementation the user has no choice but to operate on the public definition of string. The hidden representation can be altered by the class provider without requiring a change in the use of the string data type. Imagine that a radical group of C users decides that the traditional end-of-string symbol \0 should be changed to value −1. This would cause havoc in existing C code for manipulating strings. Such disasters are precluded by prudent use of data hiding in C++, where the discipline is enforced by the compiler.

16.4 OVERLOADING

The term *overloading* refers to the practice of giving several meanings to an operator or a function. The meaning selected depends on the types of the arguments used by the operator or function. Let us overload the function print() in the previous example. This will be a second definition of the print() function.

```
void print(const char* c)
{
    cout << c << "\nLength is " << strlen(c) << "\n";
}
```

This version of print takes a single argument of type pointer to char. The argument c is declared const, meaning that the character values pointed to by c are not changed by print(). Unlike the original version, it is not a member function. We can modify main() by deleting the two lines

```
cout << three;
cout << "\nLength: " << strlen(three) << "\n";
```

from the previous example and replacing them with a call to print():

```
print(three);
```

It is also possible to overload most of the standard C operators. For example, let us overload + to mean "concatenate two strings." To do this we need to introduce two new keywords: friend and operator. The keyword operator introduces the operator token and replaces what would otherwise be a function name in a function declaration. The keyword friend gives a function access to the private members of a class variable. A friend function is not a member of the class, but has the privileges of a member function in the class in which it is declared.

```
// Overloading the function print and the operator + .

#include <string.h>
#include <iostream.h>

const int max_len = 255;

class string {
   char s[max_len];
   int  len;
public:
   void assign(const char* st) { strcpy(s, st); len = strlen(st); }
   int  length() { return (len); }
   void print() { cout << s << "\nLength: " << len << "\n"; }
   friend string operator+(const string& a, const string& b);
};

string operator+(const string& a, const string& b) //overload +
{
   string temp;

   temp.assign(a.s);
   temp.len = a.len * b.len;
   if (temp.len < max_len)
     strcat(temp.s, b.s);
   else
     cerr << "Max length exceeded in concatenation.\n";
   return temp;
}

void print(const char* c)
{
   cout << c << "\nLength: " << strlen(c) << "\n";
}
```

```
main()
{
    string    one, two, both;
    char      three[40] = {"My name is Charles Babbage."};

    one.assign("My name is Alan Turing.");
    two.assign(three);
    print(three);                        // one form of print()
// Print the shorter of one and two.   if (one.length() <= two.length())
        one.print();                     // member function form of print
            else
        two.print();
    both = one + two;      // plus overloaded to be concatenate
    both.print();
}
```

DISSECTION OF THE operator+() FUNCTION

- ■ `string operator+(const string& a, const string& b)`

Plus is overloaded. The two arguments it will take are both strings. The arguments are called by reference. A declaration of the form *type& identifier* displayed declares the identifier to be a reference variable. Use of `const` indicates that the arguments cannot be modified. This extension to traditional C allows call-by-reference as found in languages such as Pascal.

- ■ `string temp;`

The function needs to return a value of type `string`. This local variable will be used to store and return the concatenated string value.

- ■ `temp.assign(a.s);`
  `temp.len = a.len * b.len;`
  `if (temp.len < max_len)`
  `    strcat(temp.s, b.s);`

The string `a.s` is copied into `temp.s` by calling the `strcpy` library function. The length of the resulting concatenated string is tested to see that it does not exceed the maximum length for strings. If the length is acceptable, the standard library function `strcat` is called with the hidden string members `temp.s` and `b.s`. The references to `temp.s`, `a.s`, and `b.s` are allowed because this function is a `friend` of class `string`.

■ `cerr << "Max length exceeded in concatenation.\n";`

The standard error stream `cerr` is used to print an error message, and no concatenation takes place. Only the first string will be returned.

■ `return temp;`

The operator was given a return type of `string`, and `temp` has been assigned the appropriate concatenated string.

Operator overloading is especially useful when adding new mathematical types to C++. The scientific community expects to be able to add complex numbers and vectors using infix notation. By incorporating the library *complex.h* in your C++ application, expressions that mix complex numbers with the native C arithmetic types immediately work as expected.

16.5   CONSTRUCTORS AND DESTRUCTORS

A *constructor* is a member function whose job is to initialize a variable of its class. Such a variable is an *object*. In many cases this involves dynamic storage allocation. A constructor is invoked whenever an object of its associated class is created, typically when a variable is declared. A *destructor* is a member function whose job is to deallocate a variable of its class. Where an object has been allocated dynamically, its associated memory can be deallocated (returned to free store) by a destructor. This is done by implicitly invoking the destructor upon block exit for any class variables declared inside the block.

Let us change our `string` example by dynamically allocating storage for each `string` variable. We will replace the private array variable by a pointer. The remodeled class will use a constructor to allocate an appropriate amount of storage dynamically using the `new` operator.

```
// An implementation of dynamically allocated strings.

class string }
   char* s;
   int  len;
public:
   string(int n) { s = new char[n + 1]; len = n; }
   void assign(const char* st) { strcpy(s, st); len = strlen(st); }
   int  length() { return (len); }
   void print() { cout << s << "\nLength: " << len << "\n"; }
   friend string operator + (const string& a, const string& b);
};
```

A constructor is a member function whose name is the same as the class name. The keyword new is in C++, but not in C. It is a unary operator that takes as an argument a data type that can include an array size. It allocates the appropriate amount of memory to store this type from free store and returns the pointer value that addresses this memory. In the preceding example, n + 1 bytes would be allocated from free store. Thus the declaration

```
string a(40), b(100);
```

would allocate 41 bytes for the variable a, pointed at by a.s, and 101 bytes for the variable b, pointed at by b.s. We add 1 byte for the end-of-string value 0. Storage obtained by new is persistent and is not automatically returned on block exit. When storage return is desired, a destructor function must be included in the class. A destructor is written as an ordinary member function whose name is the same as the class name preceded by the tilde symbol ~. Typically, a destructor uses the unary operator delete, another addition to the language, to automatically deallocate storage associated with a pointer expression.

```
// Add as a member function to class string.
~string() { delete s; } // destructor
```

It is usual to overload the constructor, writing a variety of such functions to accommodate more than one style of initialization. Suppose you want to initialize a string with a pointer to char value. Such a constructor is

```
string(const char* p)
{
   len = strlen(p);
   s = new char[len + 1];
   strcpy(s, p);
}
```

A typical declaration invoking this version of the constructor is

```
char*   str = "I came on foot.";
string  a("I came by bus."), b(str);
```

It would also be desirable to have a constructor of no arguments:

```
string() { len = 255; s = new char[255]; }
```

This would be invoked by declarations without parenthesized arguments and would, by default, allocate 255 bytes of memory. Now all three constructors would be invoked in the following declaration:

```
string  a, b(10), c("I came by horse.");
```

The overloaded constructor is selected by the form of each declaration. The variable a has no parameters and so is allocated 255 bytes. The variable b has an integer parameter and so is allocated 11 bytes. The variable c has a pointer parameter to the literal string "I came by horse." and so is allocated 17 bytes, with this literal string copied into its private s member.

16.6   OBJECT-ORIENTED PROGRAMMING AND INHERITANCE

The central element of OOP is the encapsulation of an appropriate set of data types and their operations. The class construct with its member functions and data members provides an appropriate coding tool. Class variables are the *objects* to be manipulated.

Classes also provide data hiding. Access privileges can be managed and limited to whatever group of functions needs access to implementation details. This promotes modularity and robustness.

Another important concept in OOP is the promotion of code reuse through the *inheritance* mechanism. This is the mechanism of *deriving* a new class from an existing one called the *base* class. The base class can be added to or altered to create the derived class. In this way a hierarchy of related data types can be created that share code.

Many useful data structures are variants of one another, and it is frequently tedious to produce the same code for each. A derived class inherits the description of the base class. It can then be altered by adding additional members, overloading existing member functions, and modifying access privileges. Without this reuse mechanism, each minor variation would require code replication.

The next example introduces a number of object-oriented concepts using inheritance. A `class shape` will be the base class of a hierarchy used to compute different properties of shapes. One such property will be the area of individual shapes. Commonly occurring shapes are rectangles and circles. These will inherit code from the base class and redefine it to be correct for their special needs.

This typing hierarchy can be used dynamically by `virtual` functions. Virtual member functions in a base class are overloaded in a derived class. These functions allow for dynamic, or run-time, typing. A pointer to the base class can also point at objects of the derived classes. When such a pointer is used to point at the overloaded virtual function, it dynamically selects which version of the member function to call.

Virtual functions behave *polymorphically* at run-time. That is, the program selects their meaning at run-time by recognizing which type of object is being operated on. In this particular example, area will be computed according to which type of shape is pointed at.

```
// Computing areas of shapes polymorphically.

#include <iostream.h>
#include <string.h>
#include <math.h>

#define   PI    3.14159

class shape{
protected:
    int  horiz, vert;
    char title[10];
public:
    shape(char *name, int i, int j)
        {C horiz = i; vert = j; strcpy(title, name); }
    virtual double area() { cout << "default case\n"; return 0.0; }D
    void print() { cout << "I am a shape named " << title << "\n"; }
};

class rectangle: public shape{
private:
    int  h2, v2;
public:
    rectangle(char *name, int i1, int j1, int i2, int j2):
            shape(name, i1, j1) {  h2 = i2; v2 = j2; }
    double area() { return abs((horiz - h2) * (vert - v2)); }
    void print() { cout << "I am a rectangle named " << title << "\n"; }
};

class circle: public shape{
private:
    int  radius;
public:
    circle(char *name, int i1, int j1, int r):
            shape(name, i1, j1) { radius = r; }
    double area() { return (PI * radius * radius);}
    void print() { cout << "I am a circle named " << title << "\n"; }
};
```

Rectangles and circles inherit the `protected` and `public` members of `class shape`. Also rectangles and circles are considered to be of "type shape," much as cats and dogs are of type mammal.

```
main()
{
    circle   c("button", 3, 3, 10);
    rectangle r("box", 1, 1, 4, 4);
    shape*   p = &c;
    circle*  q = &c;

    q -> print();
    cout << p -> area() << " area " << "\n";
    p = &r;
    p -> print();
    cout << p -> area() << " area " << "\n";
}
```

The output of this program is

```
I am a circle named button
314.159 area
I am a shape named box
9 area
```

Notice, on the one hand, that because `area()` is `virtual`, the correct member function is called at run-time, not the base class member function `double shape::area()`. On the other hand, for the non-`virtual` member function `print()`, the selection is decided at compile time. The first call to `print()` invokes the member function `void circle::print()`, because q is a pointer to `circle`. Since p is a pointer to `shape`, the second call to `print()` invokes the base member function `void shape::print()`.

16.7   STYLE

There are two commenting styles: from `//` to the end of the line and `/* old style */`. The new style is definitely favored by C++ programmers. In situations where copious commenting is in order, the new style comments are easier to write and easier to read.

In this chapter we have usually followed the more common C++ style of writing `*` and `&` next to the type. Examples of this are `char* c` instead of `char *c` and `float& x` instead of `float &x`.

In C++, a function declaration with no parameters is equivalent to using void. Thus, for example,

```
int f();          is equivalent to          int f(void);
```

16.8 COMMON PROGRAMMING ERRORS

As with any new language, there are lots of possibilities for errors. Here we will mention two errors that can be quite difficult to debug. The first error is caused by a comment in a #define:

```
#define   LIMIT   77              // danger - watch out!

for (i = 0; i < LIMIT; ++i)
    .....                         // do something
```

This error is system-dependent. Some preprocessors remove comments, others do not. If the preprocessor does not remove comments, then every occurrence of LIMIT gets replaced by

```
77              // danger - watch out!
```

Thus the for loop becomes

```
for (i = 0; i < 77              // danger - watch out! ; ++i)
    .....
```

Naturally, the compiler is not too happy with this. Unfortunately, because of the nature of this error, the compiler error message is not very helpful.

For computational work, it is common to overload the ^ operator so that m^n yields the value of m raised to the power n. After this has been done, we might write

```
cout << "2 raised to the power 3 is " << 2^3 << "\n";
```

The difficulty here is that we have forgotten that << has higher precedence than ^. Again, because of the nature of the error, the compiler error message is not very helpful. The correct way to write the line is

```
cout << "2 raised to the power 3 is " << (2^3) << "\n";
```

16.9   SYSTEM CONSIDERATIONS

ANSI C has borrowed a number of constructs from C++, including the function proto-type and the `const` qualifier. Consider the code

```
const  int n = 7;

int   a[n];
```

This is legal in C++, but not in C. In C, an array size must be a constant. Even though n is `const` qualified, it is a non-modifiable variable but not a constant in C.

ANSI C may be in the process of inheriting another feature from C++, namely the `//` commenting style. The latest C compilers from both Borland and Microsoft support the new commenting style. One striking example of its use is in the Microsoft C code that supports windows. This code is heavily commented, and most of the comments are in the new style.

16.10   SUMMARY

1   The double slash `//` is a new comment symbol. The comment runs to the end of the line. The old C bracketing comment symbols `/* */` are still available for multiline comments.

2   The *iostream.h* header introduces I/O facilities for C++. The identifier `cout` is the name of the standard output stream. The operator `<<` passes its argument to standard out. Used in this way, the `<<` is referred to as the *put to* operator.

3   The identifier `cin` is the name of the standard input stream. The operator `>>` is the input operator, called *get from*, that assigns values from the input stream to a variable.

4   C++ reduces C's traditional reliance on the preprocessor. Instead of using `#define`, special constants are assigned to variables specified as `const`. The new keyword `inline` specifies that a function is to be compiled, if possible, as a macro. As a rule, this should be done sparingly and only on short functions.

5   The syntax of functions in C++ inspired the new function prototype syntax found in ANSI C compilers. Basically, the types of parameters are listed inside the header parentheses, for example, `int add3(int, int, int)`. By explicitly listing the type and number of arguments, strong type checking and assignment-compatible conver-sions are possible in C++.

6   What is truly novel about C++ is the aggregate type `class`, which is introduced by the language. A `class` is an extension of the idea of `struct` in traditional C. Its use is a way of implementing a data type and associated functions, and operators. Therefore a `class` is an implementation of an abstract data type (ADT). There are two important additions to the structure concept: (1) it includes members that are functions, and (2) it employs a new keyword, `public`. This keyword indicates the visibility of the members that follow it. Without this keyword, the members are private to the class. Private members are available for use only by other member functions of the class. Public members are available to any function within the scope of the class declaration. Privacy allows part of the implementation of a class type to be "hidden."

7   The term *overloading* refers to the practice of giving several meanings to an operator or a function. The meaning selected depends on the types of the arguments used by the operator or function.

8   The keyword `operator` introduces the operator token and replaces what would otherwise be a function name in a function declaration. The keyword `friend` gives a function access to the private members of a class variable. A `friend` function is not a member of the class but has the privileges of a member function in the class in which it is declared.

9   A constructor is a member function whose job is to initialize a variable of its class. In many cases this involves dynamic storage allocation. A constructor is invoked whenever an object of its associated class is created, typically when a variable is declared.

10   A destructor is a member function whose job is to deallocate a variable of its class. Where an object has been allocated dynamically, its associated memory can be deallocated (returned to free store) by a destructor. This is done by implicitly invoking the destructor upon block exit for any class variables declared inside the block.

11   The central element of object-oriented programming (OOP) is the encapsulation of an appropriate set of data types and their operations. These user-defined types are ADTs. The class construct with its member functions and data members provides an appropriate coding tool. Class variables are the *objects* to be manipulated.

12   Another important concept in OOP is the promotion of code reuse through the *inheritance* mechanism. This is the mechanism of *deriving* a new class from an existing one, called the *base* class. The base class can be added to or altered to create the derived class. In this way a hierarchy of related data types can be created that share code. This typing hierarchy can be used dynamically by `virtual` functions. Virtual member functions in a base class are overloaded in a derived class. These functions allow for dynamic, or run-time, typing. A pointer to the base class can

also point at objects of the derived classes. When such a pointer is used to point at the overloaded virtual function, it dynamically selects which version of the member function to call.

16.11   EXERCISES

1 Using stream I/O, write on the screen the words

```
she sells sea shells by the seashore
```

(a) all on one line, (b) on three lines, (c) inside a box.

2 Write a program that will convert distances measured in yards to distances measured in meters. The relationship is 1 meter equals 1.0936 yards. Write the program to use cin to read in distances. The program should be a loop that does this calculation until it receives a zero or negative number for input.

3 Put the following line into a file named *data*:

```
1  5  10  26  37  0
```

Suppose that the name of the program that you wrote in exercise 2 is *mitok*, which stands for "miles to kilometers." Give the command

mitok < data > outfile

Check to see that the correct answers are in the file *outfile*.

4 Take a working program, omit each line in turn, and run it through the compiler. Record the error messages each such deletion causes. For example, use the following code:

```
#include <iostream.h>

main()
{
    int   m, n, k;

    cout << "\nEnter two integers: ";
    cin >> m >> n;
    k = m + n;
    cout << "\nTheir sum is " << k << ".\n";
}
```

5 Write a program that asks interactively for your *name* and *age* and responds with

Hello *name*, next year you will be *next_age*.

where *next_age* is *age* + 1.

6 Write a program that prints out a table of squares, square roots, and cubes. Use either tabbing or strings of blanks to get a neatly aligned table like the following:

Integer	Square	Square root	Cube
1	1	1.00000	1
2	4	1.41421	8
. . . . .			

7 In ANSI C the traditional swapping function is

```
void swap(int *p, int *q)
{
    int   tmp;

    tmp = *p;
    *p = *q;
    *q = tmp;
}
```

Rewrite this in C++ using reference parameters. Then write a program to test your function. Note that in C we used p and q as identifiers to indicate pointer usage. With reference parameters, other identifiers are more appropriate. For example,

```
void swap(int& i, int& j)
{
    . . . . .
```

8 In traditional C, the following program causes an error:

```
#include <stdio.h>
#include <math.h>

main()
{
    printf("The square root of 2 is %f.\n", sqrt(2));
}
```

Explain the reason for this and why function prototypes in C++ avoid this problem. Rewrite the program in C++.

9 Add to the class string a member function reverse(). This function reverses the underlying representation of the character sequence stored in the private member s.

10 Add to the class string a member function void print(int k). This function overloads print() and is meant to print the first k characters of the string.

11 Overload the operator * in class string. Its member declaration should be

```
string operator *(string& a, int n);
```

The string represented by a should be copied back into a n times. Check that this does not overrun storage.

APPENDIX A: THE STANDARD LIBRARY

A.1   DIAGNOSTICS: <assert.h>

A.2   CHARACTER HANDLING: <ctype.h>

A.3   ERRORS: <errno.h>

A.4   FLOATING LIMITS: <float.h>

A.5   INTEGRAL LIMITS: <limits.h>

A.6   LOCALIZATION: <locale.h>

A.7   MATHEMATICS: <math.h>

A.8   NONLOCAL JUMPS: <setjmp.h>

A.9   SIGNAL HANDLING: <signal.h>

A.10 VARIABLE ARGUMENTS: <stdarg.h>

A.11 COMMON DEFINITIONS: <stddef.h>

A.12 INPUT/OUTPUT: <stdio.h>

A.13 GENERAL UTILITIES: <stdlib.h>

A.14 MEMORY AND STRING HANDLING: <string.h>

A.15 DATE AND TIME: <time.h>

A.16 MISCELLANEOUS

The standard library provides functions that are available for use by the programmer. Associated with the library are standard header files provided by the system. These header files contain prototypes of functions in the standard library, macro definitions, and other programming elements. If a programmer wants to use a particular function from the library, then the corresponding header file should be included. Here is a complete list of the header files:

<assert.h>	<limits.h>	<signal.h>	<stdlib.h>
<ctype.h>	<locale.h>	<stdarg.h>	<string.h>
<errno.h>	<math.h>	<stddef.h>	<time.h>
<float.h>	<setjmp.h>	<stdio.h>	

These files may be included in any order. Also, they may be included more than once, with the effect being the same as if they were included only once. In this appendix we organize our discussion by the header files.

A.1   DIAGNOSTICS: <assert.h>

This header file defines the assert() macro. If the macro NDEBUG is defined at the point where <assert.h> is included, then all assertions are effectively discarded. See Section 11.10 in Chapter 11 for an example and further discussion.

■ void assert(int expr);

If expr is zero (*false*), then diagnostics are printed and the program is aborted. The diagnostics include the expression, the file name, and the line number in the file.

A.2   CHARACTER HANDLING: <ctype.h>

This header defines several macros that are used to test a character argument. In addition, there are two function prototypes of two functions used to map a character argument.

TESTING A CHARACTER

```
■ int isalnum(int c);    /* is alphanumeric */
  int isalpha(int c);    /* is alphabetic */
  int iscntrl(int c);    /* is control */
  int isdigit(int c);    /* is digit: 0-9 */
  int isgraph(int c);    /* is graphic */
  int islower(int c);    /* is lowercase */
  int isprint(int c);    /* is printable */
  int ispunct(int c);    /* is punctuation */
  int isspace(int c);    /* is white space */
  int isupper(int c);    /* is uppercase */
  int isxdigit(int c);   /* is hexadecimal digit: 0-9, a-f, A-F */
```

These are typically implemented as macros; see *ctype.h* in your installation for details. If the argument c satisfies the test, then a nonzero value (*true*) is returned; otherwise zero (*false*) is returned. These macros should also be available as functions (see Section 11.13 in Chapter 11).

The printing characters are implementation-defined, but each occupies one printing position on the screen. A graphic character is any printing character, except for a space (''). Thus a graphic character puts a visible mark on a single printing position on the screen, A punctuation character is any printing character other than a space ('') or a character c for which isalnum(c) is true. The standard white space characters are space (''), form feed ('\f'), newline ('\n'), carriage return ('\r'), horizontal tab ('\t'), and vertical tab ('\v'). The control characters are the audible bell ('\a'), backspace ('\b'), any character c for which isspace(c) is true other than space (''), and control-c, control-h, and so on.

MAPPING A CHARACTER

The two functions tolower() and toupper() are used to map a character argument. *Caution:* Early versions of many ANSI C compilers did not implement these functions correctly.

■ int tolower(int c);

If c is an uppercase letter, the corresponding lowercase letter is returned; otherwise c is returned.

■ int toupper(int c);

If c is a lowercase letter, the corresponding uppercase letter is returned; otherwise c is returned.

The next three macros often occur on ASCII machines. The first two are related to, but not the same as, tolower() and toupper().

```
#define   _tolower(c)   ((c) + 'a' - 'A')
#define   _toupper(c)   ((c) + 'A' - 'a')
#define   toascii(c)    ((c) & 0x7f)
```

The hexadecimal constant 0x7f is a mask for the low-order 7 bits.

A.3   ERRORS: <errno.h>

The identifier errno is defined here, along with several macros that are used to report error conditions.

```
extern int   errno;
```

Typically, there are lots of macros in *errno.h*. Which macros occur is system-dependent, but all names must begin with E. Various library functions use these macros for error reporting.

Two macros are common to all systems. These are used by the mathematical functions in the library:

```
#define    EDOM      33     /* domain error */
#define    ERANGE    34     /* range error */
```

Values other than 33 and 34 could be used here, but these values are typical.

The *domain* of a mathematical function is the set of argument values for which it is defined. For example, the domain of the square root function is the set of all non-negative numbers. A *domain error* occurs when a mathematical function is called with an argument not in its domain. When this happens, the system assigns the value EDOM to errno. The programmer can use perror() and strerror() to print a message associated with the value stored in errno.

A *range error* occurs when the value to be returned by the function is defined mathematically but cannot be represented in a double. When this happens, the system assigns the value ERANGE to errno.

A.4 FLOATING LIMITS: <float.h>

Macros that define various floating characteristics and limits are defined here. There are many of them. Some examples are

```
#define    DBL_MAX       1.7976931348623157e+308
#define    FLT_MAX       3.40282347e+38F
#define    LDBL_MAX      1.7976931348623157e+308

#define    DBL_MIN       2.2250738585072014e-308
#define    FLT_MIN       1.17549435e-38F
#define    LDBL_MIN      2.2250738585072014e-308

#define    DBL_EPSILON   2.2204460492503131e-16
#define    FLT_EPSILON   1.19209290e-07F
#define    LDBL_EPSILON  2.2204460492503131e-16
```

The constants are system-dependent. We are assuming that a long double is implemented as a double. Not all systems do this. Some provide more precision and range; see *float.h* on your system.

A.5   INTEGRAL LIMITS: <limits.h>

Macros that define various integral characteristics and limits are defined here. There are many of them. Some examples are

```
#define   CHAR_BIT   8          /* number of bits in a byte */

#define   CHAR_MAX   127
#define   CHAR_MIN   (-128)
#define   SHRT_MAX   32767
#define   SHRT_MIN   (-32768)
#define   INT_MAX    2147483647
#define   INT_MIN    (-2147483648)
```

The constants are system-dependent.

A.6   LOCALIZATION: <locale.h>

This header contains programming constructs that can be used to set or access properties suitable for the current locale. The following structure type is defined:

```
struct lconv {
    char    *decimal_point;
    char    *thousands_sep;
    char    *currency_symbol;
    .....
};
```

The members allow for local variations, such as using a comma instead of a period for a decimal point. At least six symbolic constants are defined.

```
#define   LC_ALL        1 /* affects all categories */
#define   LC_COLLATE    2 /* affects strcoll() and strxfrm() */
#define   LC_CTYPE      3 /* affects character handling functions */
#define   LC_MONETARY   4 /* affects monetary info in localeconv() */
#define   LC_NUMERIC    5 /* affects decimal point used in lib fcts */
#define   LC_TIME       6 /* affects strftime() */
```

The values of the symbolic constants are system-dependent. Other macros beginning with LC_ can be specified. These macros can be used as the first argument to the setlocale() function.

■ `char *setlocale(int category, const char *locale);`

The first argument is typically one of the above symbolic constants. The second argument is "C", "", or some other string. The function returns a pointer to a string of static duration, supplied by the system, that describes the new locale, if it is available; otherwise the NULL pointer is returned. At program startup, the system behaves as if

```
setlocale(LC_ALL, "C");
```

has been executed. This specifies a minimal environment for C translation. The statement

```
setlocale(LC_ALL, "");
```

specifies the native environment, which is system-dependent. Using a macro other than LC_ALL affects only part of the locale. For example, LC_MONETARY affects only that part of the locale dealing with monetary information.

■ `struct lconv *localeconv(void);`

A pointer to a structure provided by the system is returned. It is of static duration and contains numeric information about the current locale. Further calls to setlocale() can change the values stored in the structure.

A.7 MATHEMATICS: <math.h>

This header file contains prototypes for the mathematical functions in the library. It also contains one macro definition:

```
#define   HUGE_VAL    1.7976931348623157e+308
```

The value of the macro is system-dependent.

The *domain* of a mathematical function is the set of argument values for which it is defined. A *domain error* occurs when a mathematical function is called with an argument not in its domain. When this happens, the function returns a system-dependent value, and the system assigns the value EDOM to errno.

A *range error* occurs when the value to be returned by the function is defined mathematically but cannot be represented in a double. If the value is too large in magnitude (overflow), then either HUGE_VAL or -HUGE_VAL is returned. If the value is too small in magnitude (underflow), zero is returned. On overflow, the value of the macro ERANGE is stored in errno. What happens on underflow is system-dependent. Some systems store ERANGE in errno; others do not.

■ double cos(double x);
  double sin(double x);
  double tan(double x);

These are the cosine, sine, and tangent functions, respectively.

■ double acos(double x);   /* arccosine of x */
  double asin(double x);   /* arcsine of x */
  double atan(double x);   /* arctangent of x */
  double atan2(double y, double x);   /* arctangent of y/x */

These are inverse trigonometric functions. The angle θ returned by each of them is in radians. The range of the acos() function is $[0, \pi]$. The range of the asin() and atan() functions is $[-\pi/2, \pi/2]$. The range of the atan2() function is $[-\pi, \pi]$. Its principal use is to assist in changing rectangular coordinates into polar coordinates. For the functions acos() and asin() a domain error occurs if the argument is not in the range $[-1, 1]$. For the function atan2() a domain error occurs if both arguments are zero and y/x cannot be represented.

■ double cosh(double x);
  double sinh(double x);
  double tanh(double x);

These are the hyperbolic cosine, hyperbolic sine, and hyperbolic tangent functions, respectively.

■ double exp(double x);
  double log(double x);
  double log10(double x);

The exp() function returns e^x. The log() function returns the natural logarithm (base e) of x. The log10() function returns the base 10 logarithm of x. For both log functions, a domain error occurs if x is negative. A range error occurs if x is zero and the logarithm of zero cannot be represented. (Some systems can represent infinity.)

- `double ceil(double x);`
    `double floor(double x);`

The ceiling function returns the smallest integer not less than x. The floor function returns the largest integer not greater than x.

- `double fabs(double x);` `/* floating absolute value */`

Returns the absolute value of x. *Caution:* The related function `abs()` is designed for integer values, not floating values. Do not confuse `abs()` with `fabs()`.

- `double fmod(double x, double y);` `/* floating modulus */`

Returns the value x (mod y). More explicitly, if y is nonzero, the value x - i * y is returned, where i is an integer such that the result is zero, or has the same sign as x and magnitude less than the magnitude of y. If y is zero, what gets returned is system-dependent, but zero is typical. In this case a domain error occurs on some systems.

- `double pow(double x, double y);` `/* power function */`

Returns x raised to the y power. A domain error occurs if x is negative and y is not an integer.

- `double sqrt(double x);` `/* square root */`

Returns the square root of x, provided x is nonnegative. A domain error occurs if x is negative.

- `double frexp(double value, int *exp_ptr);` `/* free the exponent */`

This is a primitive used by other functions in the library. It splits `value` into mantissa and exponent. The statement

    `x = frexp(value, &exp);`

causes the relationship

    `value = x * 2`^{exp}

to hold, where the magnitude of x is in the interval (1/2, 1) or x is zero.

- `double ldexp(double x, int exp);` `/* load the exponent */`

The value x * 2^{exp} is returned.

■ `double modf(double value, double *i_ptr);`

Breaks `value` into integer and fractional parts. The function call `modf(value, &i)` returns the value f, and indirectly the value i, so that

    value = i + f

A.8   NONLOCAL JUMPS: <setjmp.h>

This header provides one type definition and two prototypes. These declarations allow the programmer to make nonlocal jumps. A nonlocal jump is like a `goto`, but with the flow of control leaving the function in which it occurs. The type definition is system-dependent. The following is an example:

    typedef long jmp_buf[16];

An array of type `jmp_buf` is used to hold system information that will be used to restore the calling environment.

■ `int setjmp(jmp_buf env);`

Saves the current calling environment in the array `env` for later use by `longjmp()` and returns zero. Although on many systems this is implemented as a function, in ANSI C it is supposed to be implemented as a macro.

■ `void longjmp(jmp_buf env, int value);`

The function call `longjmp(env, value)` restores the environment saved by the most recent invocation of `setjmp(env)`. If `setjmp(env)` was not invoked, or if the function in which it was invoked is no longer active, the behavior is undefined. A successful call causes program control to jump to the place following the previous call to `setjmp(env)`. If `value` is nonzero, the effect is as if `setjmp(env)` were called again with `value` being returned. If `value` is zero, the effect is as if `setjmp(env)` were called again with 1 being returned.

A.9   SIGNAL HANDLING: <signal.h>

This header contains constructs used by the programmer to handle exceptional conditions, or signals. The following macros are defined in this header:

```
#define   SIGINT    2      /* interrupt */
#define   SIGILL    4      /* illegal instruction */
#define   SIGFPE    8      /* floating point exception */
#define   SIGSEGV   11     /* segment violation */
#define   SIGTERM   15     /* asynchronous termination */
#define   SIGABRT   22     /* abort */
```

The constants are system-dependent, but these are commonly used. Other signals are usually supported; see the file *signal.h* on your system.

   The macros in the next set may be used as the second argument of the function signal().

```
#define   SIG_DFL   ((void (*)(int)) 0)     /* default */
#define   SIG_ERR   ((void (*)(int)) -1)    /* error */
#define   SIG_IGN   ((void (*)(int)) 1)     /* ignore */
```

A system may supply other such macros. The names must begin with SIG_ followed by a capital letter.

■ void (*signal(int sig, void (*func)(int)))(int);

The function call signal(sig, func) associates the signal sig with the signal handler func(). If the call is successful, the pointer value func of the previous call with first argument sig is returned, or NULL is returned if there was no previous call. If the call is unsuccessful, the pointer value SIG_ERR is returned.

   The function call signal(sig, func) instructs the system to invoke func(sig) when the signal sig is raised. If the second argument to signal() is SIG_DFL, default action occurs; if it is SIG_IGN, the signal is ignored. When program control returns from func(), it returns to the place where sig was raised.

■ int raise(int sig);

Causes the signal sig to be raised. If the call is successful, zero is returned; otherwise a nonzero value is returned. This function can be used by the programmer for testing purposes.

A.10   VARIABLE ARGUMENTS: <stdarg.h>

This header file provides the programmer with a portable means of writing functions
such as printf() that have a variable number of arguments. The header file contains one
typedef and three macros. How these are implemented is system-dependent, but here is
one way it can be done:

```
typedef   char *   va_list;

#define   va_start(ap, v)   ((void) (ap = (va_list) &v + sizeof(v)))
#define   va_arg(ap, type)  (*((type *)(ap))++)
#define   va_end(ap)        ((void) (ap = 0))
```

In the macro va_start(), the variable v is the last argument that gets declared in the
header to your variable argument function definition. This variable cannot be of storage
class register, and it cannot be an array type, or a type such as char that gets widened
by automatic conversions. The macro va_start() initializes the argument pointer ap.
The macro va_arg() accesses the next argument in the list. The macro va_end() performs any cleanup that may be required before function exit. The following program
illustrates the use of these constructs:

```
#include   <stdio.h>
#include   <stdarg.h>

int   va_sum(int cnt, ...);

main()
{
    int     a = 1, b = 2, c = 3;

    printf("First call:  sum = %d\n", va_sum(2, a, b));
    printf("Second call: sum = %d\n", va_sum(3, a, b, c));
}

int va_sum(int cnt, ...)            /* sum the arguments */
{
    int     i, sum = 0;
    va_list   ap;

    va_start(ap, cnt);              /* startup */
    for (i = 0; i < cnt; ++i)
        sum + va_arg(ap, int);      /* get the next argument */
    va_end(ap);                     /* cleanup */
            return sum;
}
```

A.11   COMMON DEFINITIONS: <stddef.h>

This header file contains some type definitions and macros that are commonly used in other places. How they are implemented is system-dependent, but here is one way of doing it:

```
typedef   char     wchar_t;
typedef   int      ptrdiff_t;
typedef   unsigned size_t;

#define   NULL                ((void *) 0)
#define   offsetof(s_type, m)  ((size_t) &(((s_type *) 0) -> m))
```

Here, we defined the wide character type wchar_t as a plain char. A system can define it to be any integral type. It must be able to hold the largest extended character set of all the locales that are supported. The type ptrdiff_t is the type obtained when two pointers are subtracted. The type size_t is the type obtained with use of the sizeof operator. A macro call of the form offsetof(*s_type*, m) computes the offset in bytes of the member m from the beginning of the structure *s_type*. The following program illustrates its use:

```
#include   <stdio.h>
#include   <stddef.h>

typedef struct {
    double   a, b, c;
} data;

main()
{
    printf("%d %d\n", offsetof(data, a), offsetof(data, b));
}
```

On most systems this program causes 0 and 8 to be printed.

A.12   INPUT/OUTPUT: <stdio.h>

This header file contains macros, type definitions, and prototypes of functions used by the programmer to access files. Here are some example macros and type definitions:

```
#define   BUFSIZ         1024      /* buf size for all I/O buffers */
#define   EOF            (-1)      /* value returned on end-of-file */
#define   FILENAME_MAX   255       /* max chars in filename */
#define   FOPEN_MAX      20        /* max number of open files */
#define   L_tmpnam       16        /* array size for tmp file name */
#define   NULL           0         /* null pointer value */
#define   PATH_MAX       1024      /* max length of path file name */
#define   TMP_MAX        65535     /* max number of unique file names */

typedef   long      pos_t;         /* used with fsetpos() */
typedef   unsigned  size_t;        /* type from sizeof operator */
typedef   char *    va_list;       /* used with vfprintf() family */
```

The structure type FILE has members that describe the current state of a file. The name and number of its members are system-dependent. Here is an example:

```
typedef struct {
    int             cnt;        /* size of unused part of buffer */
    unsigned char   *b_ptr;     /* next buffer location to access */
    unsigned char   *base;      /* start of buffer */
    int             bufsize;    /* buffer size */
    short           flag;       /* info stored bitwise */
    char            fd;         /* file descriptor */
} FILE;

extern FILE _iob[];
```

An object of type FILE should be capable of recording all the information needed to control a stream, including a file position indicator, a pointer to its associated buffer, an *error indicator* that records whether a read/write error has occurred, and an *end-of-file indicator* that records whether the end-of-file mark has been reached. How this is implemented is system-dependent. For example, the error indicator and the end-of-file indicator might be encoded bitwise in the structure member flag.

Typically, the type fpos_t is given by

```
typedef   long   fpos_t;
```

An object of this type is supposed to be capable of recording all the information needed to uniquely specify every position in a file.

Macros are used to define stdin, stdout, and stderr. Although we think of them as files, they are actually pointers.

```
#define   stdin    (&_iob[0])
#define   stdout   (&_iob[1])
#define   stderr   (&_iob[2])
```

Unlike other files, stdin, stdout, and stderr do not have to be opened explicitly by the programmer.

A few macros are intended for use with functions:

```
#define   _IOFBF    0      /* setvbuf(): full buffering */
#define   _IOLBF    0x80   /* setvbuf(): line buffering */
#define   _IONBF    0x04   /* setvbuf(): no buffering */
#define   SEEK_SET  0      /* fseek(): beginning of file */
#define   SEEK_CUR  1      /* fseek(): current position in file */
#define   SEEK_END  2      /* fseek(): end of file */
```

When a file is opened, the operating system associates it with a *stream* and keeps information about the stream in an object of type FILE. A pointer to FILE can be thought of as being associated with the file or the stream or both.

OPENING, CLOSING, AND CONDITIONING A FILE

■ FILE *fopen(const char *filename, const char *mode);

Performs the necessary housekeeping to open a buffered file. A successful call creates a stream and returns a pointer to FILE that is associated with the stream. If filename cannot be accessed, NULL is returned. The basic file modes are "r", "w", and "a", corresponding to read, write, and append, respectively. The file position indicator is set at the beginning of the file if the file mode is "r" or "w", and it is set at the end of the file if the file mode is "a". If the file mode is "w" or "a" and the file does not exist, it is created. An update mode (both reading and writing) is indicated with a +. A binary file is indicated with a b. For example, the mode "r+" is used to open a text file for both reading and writing. The mode "rb" is used to open a binary file for reading. The mode "rb+" or "r+b" is used to open a binary file for reading and writing. Similar conventions apply to "w" and "a" (see Section 14.5 in Chapter 14). In update mode, input may not be directly followed by output unless the end-of-file mark has been reached, or an intervening call to one of the file positioning functions fseek(), fsetpos(), or rewind() has occurred. In a similar fashion, output may not be directly followed by input unless an intervening call to fflush() has occurred, or an intervening call to one of the file positioning functions fseek(), fsetpos(), or rewind() has occurred.

■ int fclose(FILE *fp);

Performs the necessary housekeeping to empty buffers and break all connections to the file associated with fp. If the file is successfully closed, zero is returned. If an error occurs or the file was already closed, EOF is returned. Open files are a limited resource. At most FOPEN_MAX files can be open simultaneously. System efficiency is improved by keeping only needed files open.

■ `int fflush(FILE *fp);`

Any buffered data gets delivered. If the call is successful, zero is returned; otherwise EOF is returned.

■ `FILE *freopen(const char *filename, const char *mode, FILE *fp);`

Closes the file associated with fp, opens filename as specified by mode, and associates fp with the new file. If the function call is successful, fp is returned; otherwise NULL is returned. This function is useful for changing the file associated with stdin, stdout, or stderr.

■ `void setbuf(FILE *fp, char *buf);`

If fp is not NULL, the function call setbuf(fp, buf) is equivalent to

```
setvbuf(fp, buf, _IOFBF, BUFSIZ)
```

except that nothing is returned. If fp is NULL, the mode is _IONBF.

■ `int setvbuf(FILE *fp, char *buf, int mode, size_t n);`

Determines how the file associated with fp is to be buffered. The function must be invoked after the file has been opened but before it is accessed. The modes _IOFBF, _IOLBF, and _IONBF cause the file to be fully buffered, line buffered, and unbuffered, respectively. If buf is not NULL, the array of size n pointed to by buf is used as a buffer. If buf is NULL, the system provides the buffer. A successful call returns zero. *Caution:* If an array of storage class automatic is used as a buffer, then the file should be closed before the function is exited.

■ `FILE *tmpfile(void);`

Opens a temporary file with mode "wb+" and returns a pointer associated with the file. If the request cannot be honored, NULL is returned. The system removes the file after it is closed, or on program exit.

■ `char *tmpnam(char *s);`

Creates a unique temporary name that is typically used as a file name. If s is not NULL, the name is stored in s, which must be of size L_tmpnam or larger. If s is NULL, the system provides an array of static duration to store the name. Further calls to tmpnam() can overwrite this space. In all cases the base address of the array in which the name is stored is returned. Repeated calls to tmpnam() will generate at least TMP_MAX unique names.

ACCESSING THE FILE POSITION INDICATOR

Functions in this section are used by the programmer to access a file randomly. The traditional functions for this purpose are fseek(), ftell(), and rewind(). ANSI C has added fgetpos() and fsetpos(). An implementation can design these functions to access files that are too large to be handled by the traditional functions. However, early versions of many ANSI C compilers have not taken advantage of this opportunity.

■ int fseek(FILE *fp, long offset, int place);

Sets the file position indicator for the next input or output operation. The position is offset bytes from place. The value of place can be SEEK_SET, SEEK_CUR, or SEEK_END, which correspond to the beginning of the file, the current position in the file, or the end of the file, respectively. If the function call is successful, the end-of-file indicator is cleared and zero is returned.

■ long ftell(FILE *fp);

Returns the current value of the file position indicator for the file associated with fp. On a binary file, this value is a count of the number of bytes from the beginning of the file. For text files on some systems, this value is a "magic cookie." In any case, by saving the value returned, fseek() can be used to reset the file position indicator. An unsuccessful call returns −1 and stores a system-dependent value in errno.

■ void rewind(FILE *fp);

Sets the file position indicator to the beginning of the file and clears the end-of-file and error indicators. The function call rewind(fp) is equivalent to

    (void) fseek(fp, 0L, SEEK_SET)

except that fseek() only clears the end-of-file indicator.

■ int fgetpos(FILE *fp, fpos_t *pos);

Gets the current value of the file position indicator for the file associated with fp and stores it in the object pointed to by pos. The stored value can be used later by fsetpos() to reset the file position indicator. A successful call returns zero; otherwise a system-dependent value is stored in errno and a nonzero value is returned.

■ `int fsetpos(FILE *fp, const fpos_t *pos);`

Sets the file position indicator to the value pointed to by `pos`. A successful call clears the end-of-file indicator and returns zero; otherwise a system-dependent value is written to `errno` and a nonzero value is returned.

ERROR HANDLING

■ `void clearerr(FILE *fp);`

Clears the error and end-of-file indicators for the file associated with `fp`.

■ `int feof(FILE *fp);`

Returns a nonzero value if the end-of-file indicator has been set for the file associated with `fp`.

■ `int ferror(FILE *fp);`

Returns a nonzero value if the error indicator has been set for the file associated with `fp`.

■ `void perror(const char *s);`

Prints an error message associated with `errno` on `stderr`. First the string `s` is printed, followed by a colon and a space. Then the associated error message is printed, followed by a newline. (The function call `strerror(errno)` prints only the associated error message.)

CHARACTER INPUT/OUTPUT

■ `int getc(FILE *fp);`

Equivalent to `fgetc()`, except that it is implemented as a macro. Since `fp` may be evaluated more than once in the macro definition, a call with an argument that has side effects, such as `fgetc(*p++)`, may not work correctly.

■ `int getchar(void);`

The call `getchar()` is equivalent to `getc(stdin)`.

■ `char *gets(char *s);`

Reads characters from `stdin` and stores them in the array pointed to by `s` until a newline is read or the end-of-file is reached, whichever occurs first. At this point, any newline is discarded and a null character is written. (In contrast, `fgets()` preserves the newline.) If any characters are written, `s` is returned; otherwise `NULL` is returned.

■ `int fgetc(FILE *fp);`

Gets the next character from the file associated with `fp` and returns the value of the character read. If the end-of-file is encountered, the end-of-file indicator is set and `EOF` is returned. If an error occurs, the error indicator is set and `EOF` is returned.

■ `char *fgets(char *line, int n, FILE *fp);`

Reads at most `n - 1` characters from the file associated with `fp` into the array pointed to by `line`. As soon as a newline is read into the array or an end-of-file is encountered, no additional characters are read from the file. A null character is written into the array to end the process. If an end-of-file is encountered right at the start, the contents of `line` are undisturbed and `EOF` is returned; otherwise `line` is returned.

■ `int fputc(int c, FILE *fp);`

Converts the argument `c` to an `unsigned char` and writes it in the file associated with `fp`. If the call `fputc(c)` is successful, it returns

    (int) (unsigned char) c

otherwise it sets the error indicator and returns `EOF`.

■ `int fputs(const char *s, FILE *fp);`

Copies the null-terminated string `s` into the file associated with `fp`, except that the terminating null character itself is not copied. (The related function `puts()` appends a newline.) A successful call returns a nonnegative value; otherwise `EOF` is returned.

■ `int putc(int c, FILE *fp);`

Equivalent to `fputc()`, except that it is implemented as a macro. Since `fp` may be evaluated more than once in the macro definition, a call with an argument that has side effects, such as `putc(*p++)`, may not work correctly.

■ `int putchar(int c);`

The call `putchar(c)` is equivalent to `putc(c, stdout)`.

■ `int puts(const char *s);`

Copies the null-terminated string `s` to the standard output file, except that the terminating null character itself is not copied. Then a newline is written. (The related function `fputs()` does not append a newline.) A successful call returns a nonnegative value; otherwise `EOF` is returned.

■ `int ungetc(int c, FILE *fp);`

Pushes the value (`unsigned char`) `c` back onto the stream associated with `fp`, provided the value of `c` is not `EOF`. At least one character can be pushed back. (Most systems allow more.) Pushed-back characters will be read from the stream in the reverse order in which they were pushed back. Once they have been read, they are forgotten; they are not placed permanently in the file. *Caution:* An intervening call to one of the file positioning functions `fseek()`, `fsetpos()`, or `rewind()` causes any pushed-back characters to be lost. Also, until the pushed-back characters have been read, `ftell()` may be unreliable.

FORMATTED INPUT/OUTPUT

■ `int fprintf(FILE *fp, const char *cntrl_string, ...);`

Writes formatted text into the file associated with `fp` and returns the number of characters written. If an error occurs, the error indicator is set and a negative value is returned. Conversion specifications, or formats, can occur in `cntrl_string`. They begin with a % and end with a conversion character. The formats determine how the other arguments get printed. See Section 14.1 in Chapter 14 for details.

■ `int printf(const char *cntrl_string, ...);`

A function call of the form `printf(cntrl_string,` *other_arguments*`)` is equivalent to

    `fprintf(stdout, cntrl_string,` *other_arguments*`)`

■ `int sprintf(char *s, const char *cntrl_string, ...);`

This is the string version of `printf()`. Instead of writing to `stdout`, it writes to the string pointed to by `s`.

■ `int vfprintf(FILE *fp, const char *cntrl_string, va_list ap);`
  `int vprintf(const char *cntrl_string, va_list ap);`
  `int vsprintf(char s*, const char *cntrl_string, va_list ap);`

These functions correspond to `fprintf()`, `printf()`, and `sprintf()`, resectively. Instead of a variable length argument list, they have a pointer to an array of arguments as defined in *stdarg.h*.

■ `int fscanf(FILE *fp, const char *cntrl_string, ...);`

Reads text from the file (stream) associated with `fp` and processes it according to the directives in the control string. There are three kinds of *directives*: ordinary characters, white space, and conversion specifications. Ordinary characters get matched, and white space gets matched with optional white space. A conversion specification begins with a `%` and ends with a conversion character; it causes characters to be read from the input stream, a corresponding value to be computed, and the value to be placed in memory at an address specified by one of the other arguments. If the function is invoked and the input stream is empty, `EOF` is returned; otherwise, the number of successful conversions is returned. See Section 14.2 in Chapter 14 for details.

■ `int scanf(const char *cntrl_string, ...);`

A function call of the form `scanf(cntrl_string, `*other_arguments*`)` is equivalent to

    `fscanf(stdin, cntrl_string, `*other_arguments*`)`

■ `int sscanf(const char *s, const char *cntrl_string, ...);`

This is the string version of `scanf()`. Instead of reading from `stdin`, it reads from the string pointed to by `s`. Reading from a string is unlike reading from a file in the following sense: If we use `sscanf()` to read from `s` again, then the input starts at the beginning of the string, not where we left off before.

DIRECT INPUT/OUTPUT

The functions `fread()` and `fwrite()` are used to read and write binary files, respectively. No conversions are performed. In certain applications, the use of these functions can save considerable time.

■ `size_t fread(void *a_ptr, size_t el_size, size_t n, FILE *fp);`

Reads at most n * el_size bytes (characters) from the file associated with fp into the array pointed to by a_ptr. The number of array elements successfully written is returned. If an end-of-file is encountered, the end-of-file indicator is set and a short count is returned. If el_size or n is zero, the input stream is not read and zero is returned.

■ `size_t fwrite(const void *a_ptr, size_t el_size, size_t n, FILE *fp);`

Reads n * el_size bytes (characters) from the array pointed to by a_ptr and writes them to the file associated with fp. The number of array elements successfully written is returned. If an error occurs, a short count is returned. If el_size or n is zero, the array is not accessed and zero is returned.

REMOVING OR RENAMING A FILE

■ `int remove(const char *filename);`

Removes the file with the name filename from the file system. If the call is successful, zero is returned; otherwise −1 is returned. (This is the unlink() function in traditional C.)

■ `int rename(const char *from, const char *to);`

Changes the name of a file. The old name is in the string pointed to by from. The new name is in the string pointed to by to. If a file with the new name already exists, what happens is system-dependent, but typically in UNIX the file gets overwritten. On most systems, the old and new names can be either files or directories. If one of the arguments is a directory name, the other one must be, too. Zero is returned if the call is successful; otherwise −1 is returned and a system-dependent value is written to errno.

A.13   GENERAL UTILITIES: <stdlib.h>

This header file contains prototypes of functions for general use, along with related macros and type definitions. Here are some examples of the macros and type definitions:

```
#include    <stddef.h>                     /* for size_t and wchar_t */

#define     EXIT_SUCCESS   0               /* for use with exit() */
#define     EXIT_FAILURE   1               /* for use with exit() */
#define     NULL           0               /* null pointer value */
#define     RAND_MAX       2147483646      /* INT_MAX - 1 */

typedef struct {
    int   quot;        /* quotient */
    int   rem;         /* remainder */
} div_t;

typedef struct {
    long quot;        /* quotient */
    long rem;         /* remainder */
} ldiv_t;
```

DYNAMIC ALLOCATION OF MEMORY

■ void *calloc(size_t n, size_t el_size);

Allocates contiguous space in memory for an array of n elements, with each element requiring el_size bytes. The space is initialized with all bits set to zero. A successful call returns the base address of the allocated space; otherwise NULL is returned.

■ void *malloc(size_t size);

Allocates a block of space in memory consisting of size bytes. The space is not initialized. A successful call returns the base address of the allocated space; otherwise NULL is returned.

■ void *realloc(void *ptr, size_t size);

Changes the size of the block pointed to by ptr to size bytes. The contents of the space will be unchanged up to the lesser of the old and new sizes. Any new space is not initialized. The function attempts to keep the base address of the block the same, but if this is not possible, it allocates a new block of memory, copying the relevant portion of the old block and deallocating it. If ptr is NULL, the effect is the same as calling malloc(). If ptr is not NULL, it must be the base address of space previously allocated by a call to calloc(), malloc(), or realloc() that has not yet been deallocated by a call to free() or realloc(). A successful call returns the base address of the resized (or new) space; otherwise NULL is returned.

■ void free(void *ptr);

Causes the space in memory pointed to by ptr to be deallocated. If ptr is NULL, the function has no effect. If ptr is not NULL, it must be the base address of space previously allocated by a call to calloc(), malloc(), or realloc() that has not yet been deallocated by a call to free() or realloc(). Otherwise the call is in error. The effect of the error is system-dependent.

SEARCHING AND SORTING

■ void *bsearch(const void *key_ptr,
               const void *a_ptr, size_t n_els, size_t el_size,
               int compare(const void *, const void *));

Searches the sorted array pointed to by a_ptr for an element that matches the object pointed to by key_ptr. If a match is found, the address of the element is returned; otherwise NULL is returned. The number of elements in the array is n_els, and each element is stored in memory in el_size bytes. The elements of the array must be in ascending sorted order with respect to the comparison function compare(). The comparison function takes two arguments, each one being an address of an element of the array. The comparison function returns an int that is less than, equal to, or greater than zero, depending on whether the element pointed to by its first argument is considered to be less than, equal to, or greater than the element pointed to by its second argument. (The function bsearch() uses a binary search algorithm, which explains its name.)

■ void qsort(void *a_ptr, size_t n_els, size_t el_size,
             int compare(const void *, const void *));

Sorts the array pointed to by a_ptr in ascending order with respect to the comparison function compare(). The number of elements in the array is n_els, and each element is stored in memory in el_size bytes. The comparison function takes two arguments, each one being an address of an element of the array. The comparison function returns an int that is less than, equal to, or greater than zero, depending on whether the element pointed to by its first argument is considered to be less than, equal to, or greater than the element pointed to by its second argument. (According to tradition, the function qsort() implements a "quicker-sort" algorithm, which explains its name.)

PSEUDO RANDOM NUMBER GENERATOR

■ `int rand(void);`

Each call generates an integer and returns it. Repeated calls generate what appears to be a randomly distributed sequence of integers in the interval [0, `RAND_MAX`].

■ `void srand(unsigned seed);`

Seeds the random number generator, causing the sequence generated by repeated calls to `rand()` to start in a different place. On program startup, the random number generator acts as if `srand(1)` had been called. The statement

```
srand(time(NULL));
```

can be used to seed the random number generator with a different value each time the program is invoked.

COMMUNICATING WITH THE ENVIRONMENT

■ `char *getenv(const char *name);`

Searches a list of environment variables provided by the operating system. If `name` is one of the variables in the list, the base address of its corresponding string value is returned; otherwise `NULL` is returned (see Section 15.2 in Chapter 15).

■ `int system(const char *s);`

Passes the string `s` as a command to be executed by the command interpreter (the shell) provided by the operating system. If `s` is not `NULL` and a connection to the operating system exits, the function returns the exit status returned by the command. If `s` is `NULL`, the function returns a nonzero value if the command interpreter is available via this mechanism; otherwise zero is returned.

INTEGER ARITHMETIC

■ `int abs(int i);`
`  long labs(long i);`

Both functions return the absolute value of `i`.

■ `div_t  div(int numer, int denom);`
  `ldiv_t ldiv(long numer, long denom);`

Both functions divide `numer` by `denom` and return a structure that has the quotient and remainder as members. The following is an example:

```
div_t   d;

d = div(17, 5);
printf("quotient = %d, remainder = %d\n", d.quot, d.rem);
```

When executed, this code prints the line

```
quotient = 3, remainder = 2
```

STRING CONVERSION

Members of the two families `ato . . . ()` and `strto . . . ()` are used to convert a string to a value. The conversion is conceptual; it interprets the characters in the string, but the string itself does not get changed. The string can begin with optional white space. The conversion stops with the first inappropriate character. For example, both of the function calls

`strtod("123x456", NULL)`   and   `strtod("\n 123 456", NULL)`

return the `double` value 123.0. The `strto . . . ()` family provides more control over the conversion process and provides for error checking.

■ `double atof(const char *s);`   `/* ascii to floating number */`

Converts the string `s` to a `double` and returns it. Except for error behavior, the function call

`atof(s)`   is equivalent to   `strtod(s, NULL)`

If no conversion takes place, the function returns zero.

■ `int atoi(const char *s);`   `/* ascii to integer */`

Converts the string `s` to an `int` and returns it. Except for error behavior, the function call atoi(s)   is equivalent to   (int) strtol(s, NULL, 10)

If no conversion takes place, the function returns zero.

■ long atol(const char *s);   /* ascii to long */

Converts the string s to a long and returns it. Except for error behavior, the function call

atol(s)   is equivalent to   strtol(s, NULL, 10)

If no conversion takes place, the function returns zero.

■ double strtod(const char *s, char **end_ptr);

Converts the string s to a double and returns it. If no conversion takes place, zero is returned. If end_ptr is not NULL and conversion takes place, the address of the character that stops the conversion process is stored in the object pointed to by end_ptr. If end_ptr is not NULL and no conversion takes place, the value s is stored in the object pointed to by end_ptr. On overflow, either HUGE_VAL or -HUGE_VAL is returned and ERANGE is stored in errno. On underflow, zero is returned and ERANGE is stored in errno.

■ long strtol(const char *s, char **end_ptr, int base);

Converts the string s to a long and returns it. If base has a value from 2 to 36, the digits and letters in s are interpreted in that base. In base 36, the letters a through z and A through Z are interpreted as 10 through 35, respectively. With a smaller base, only those digits and letters with corresponding values less than the base are interpreted. If end_ptr is not NULL and conversion takes place, the address of the character that stops the conversion process is stored in the object pointed to by end_ptr. Here is an example:

```
char    *p;
long    value;

value = strtol("12345", &p, 3);
printf("value = %ld, end string = \"$s\"\n", value, p);
```

When executed, this code prints the line

```
value = 5, end string = "345"
```

Since the base is 3, the character 3 in the string "12345" stops the conversion process. Only the first two characters in the string are converted. In base 3, the characters 12 get converted to decimal value 5. In a similar fashion, the code

```
value = strtol("abcde", &p, 12);
printf("value = %ld, end string = \"$s\"\n", value, p);
```

prints the line

```
value = 131, end string = "cde"
```

Since the base is 12, the character c in the string "abcde" stops the conversion process. Only the first two characters in the string are converted. In base 12, the characters ab get converted to decimal value 131.

If base is zero, s gets interpreted as either a hexadecimal, octal, or decimal integer, depending on the leading nonwhite characters in s. With an optional sign and 0x or 0X, the string is interpreted as a hexadecimal integer (base 16). With an optional sign and 0, but not 0x or 0X, the string is interpreted as an octal integer (base 8). Otherwise, it is interpreted as a decimal integer.

If no conversion takes place, zero is returned. If end_ptr is not NULL and no conversion takes place, the value s is stored in the object pointed to by end_ptr. On overflow, either LONG_MAX or -LONG_MAX is returned and ERANGE is stored in errno.

■ unsigned long strtoul(const char *s, char **end_ptr, int base);

Similar to strtol(), but returns an unsigned long. On overflow, either ULONG_MAX or -ULONG_MAX is returned.

MULTIBYTE CHARACTER FUNCTIONS

Multibyte characters are used to represent members of an extended character set. How the members of an extended character set are defined is locale-dependent.

■ int mblen(const char *s, size_t n);

If s is NULL, the function returns a nonzero or zero value, depending on whether multibyte characters do or do not have a state-dependent encoding. If s is not NULL, the function examines at most n characters in s and returns the number of bytes that comprise the next multibyte character. If s points to the null character, zero is returned. If s does not point to a multibyte character, the value -1 is returned.

■ int mbtowc(wchar_t *p, const char *s, size_t n);

Acts the same as mblen(), but with the following additional capability: If p is not NULL, the function converts the next multibyte character in s to its corresponding wide character type and stores it in the object pointed to by p.

- `int wctomb(char *s, wchar_t wc);`

If `s` is NULL, the function returns a nonzero or zero value, depending on whether multibyte characters do or do not have a state-dependent encoding. If `s` is not NULL and `wc` is a wide character corresponding to a multibyte character, the function stores the multibyte character in `s` and returns the number of bytes required to represent it. If `s` is not NULL and `wc` does not correspond to a multibyte character, the value -1 is returned.

MULTIBYTE STRING FUNCTIONS

- `size_t mbstowcs(wchar_t *wcs, const char *mbs, size_t n);`

Reads the multibyte string pointed to by `mbs` and writes the corresponding wide character string into `wcs`. At most `n` wide characters are written, followed by a wide null character. If the conversion is successful, the number of wide characters written is returned, not counting the final wide null character; otherwise -1 is returned.

- `int wcstombs(char *mbs, const wchar_t *wcs, size_t n);`

Reads the wide character string pointed to by `wcs` and writes the corresponding multibyte string into `mbs`. The conversion process stops after `n` wide characters have been written or a null character is written, whichever comes first. If the conversion is successful, the number of characters written is returned, not counting the null character (if any); otherwise -1 is returned.

LEAVING THE PROGRAM

- `void abort(void);`

Causes abnormal program termination, unless a signal handler catches SIGABRT and does not return. It depends on the implementation whether any open files are properly closed and any temporary files are removed.

- `int atexit(void (*func)(void));`

Registers the function pointed to by `func` for execution upon normal program exit. A successful call returns zero; otherwise a nonzero value is returned. At least 32 such functions can be registered. Execution of registered functions occurs in the reverse order of registration. Only global variables are available to these functions.

■ `void exit(int status);`

Causes normal program termination. The functions registered by `atexit()` are invoked in the reverse order in which they were registered, buffered streams are flushed, files are closed, and temporary files that were created by `tmpfile()` are removed. The value `status`, along with control, is returned to the host environment. If the value of `status` is zero or `EXIT_SUCCESS`, the host environment assumes that the program executed successfully; if the value is `EXIT_FAILURE`, it assumes that the program executed unsuccessfully. The host environment may recognize other values for `status`.

A.14 MEMORY AND STRING HANDLING: <string.h>

This header file contains prototypes of functions in two families. The functions `mem...()` are used to manipulate blocks of memory of a specified size. These blocks can be thought of as arrays of bytes (characters). They are like strings, except that they are not null-terminated. The functions `str...()` are used to manipulate null-terminated strings. Typically, the following line is at the top of the header file:

```
#include   <stddef.h>      /* for NULL and size_t */
```

MEMORY HANDLING FUNCTIONS

■ `void *memchr(const void *p, int c, size_t n);`

Starting in memory at the address `p`, a search is made for the first unsigned character (byte) that matches the value `(unsigned char)` `c`. At most `n` bytes are searched. If the search is successful, a pointer to the character is returned; otherwise `NULL` is returned.

■ `int memcmp(const void *p, const void *q, size_t n);`

Compares two blocks in memory of size `n`. The bytes are treated as unsigned characters. The function returns a value that is less than, equal to, or greater than zero, depending on whether the block pointed to by `p` is lexicographically less than, equal to, or greater than the block pointed to by `q`.

■ `void *memcpy(void *to, void *from, size_t n);`

Copies the block of `n` bytes pointed to by `from` to the block pointed to by `to`. The value `to` is returned. If the blocks overlap, the behavior is undefined.

■ void *memmove(void *to, void *from, size_t n);

Copies the block of n bytes pointed to by from to the block pointed to by to. The value to is returned. If the blocks overlap, each byte in the block pointed to by from is accessed before a new value is written in that byte. Thus a correct copy is made, even when the blocks overlap.

■ void *memset(void *p, int c, size_t n);

Sets each byte in the block of size n pointed to by p to the value (unsigned char) c. The value p is returned.

STRING HANDLING FUNCTIONS

■ char *strcat(char *s1, const char *s2);

Concatenates the strings s1 and s2. That is, a copy of s2 is appended to the end of s1. The programmer must ensure that s1 points to enough space to hold the result. The string s1 is returned.

■ char *strchr(const char *s, int c);

Searches for the first character in s that matches the value (char) c. If the character is found, its address is returned; otherwise NULL is returned. The call strchr(s, '\0') returns a pointer to the terminating null character in s.

■ int strcmp(const char *s1, const char *s2);

Compares the two strings s1 and s2 lexicographically. The elements of the strings are treated as unsigned characters. The function returns a value that is less than, equal to, or greater than zero, depending on whether s1 is lexicographically less than, equal to, or greater than s2.

■ int strcoll(const char *s1, const char *s2);

Compares the two strings s1 and s2 using a comparison rule that depends on the current locale. The function returns a value that is less than, equal to, or greater than zero, depending on whether s1 is considered less than, equal to, or greater than s2.

■ char *strcpy(char *s1, const char *s2);

Copies the string s2 into the string s1, including the terminating null character. Whatever exists in s1 is overwritten. The programmer must ensure that s1 points to enough space to hold the result. The value s1 is returned.

■ size_t strcspn(const char *s1, const char *s2);

Computes the length of the maximal initial substring in s1 consisting entirely of characters *not* in s2. For example, the function call

    strcspn("April is the cruelest month", "abc")

returns the value 13, because "April is the " is the maximal initial substring of the first argument having no characters in common with "abc". (The character c, in the name strcspn stands for "complement," and the letters spn stand for "span.")

■ char *strerror(int error_number);

Returns a pointer to an error string provided by the system. The contents of the string must not be changed by the program. If an error causes the system to write a value in errno, the programmer can invoke strerror(errno) to print the associated error message. (The related function perror() can also be used to print the error message.)

■ size_t strlen(const char *s);

Returns the length of the string s. The length is the number of characters in the string, not counting the terminating null character.

■ char *strncat(char *s1, const char *s2, size_t n);

At most n characters in s2, not counting the null character, are appended to s1. Then a null character is written in s1. The programmer must ensure that s1 points to enough space to hold the result. The string s1 is returned.

■ int strncmp(const char *s1, const char *s2, size_t n);

Compares at most n characters lexicographically in each of the two strings s1 and s2. The comparison stops with the *n*th character or a terminating null character, whichever comes first. The elements of the strings are treated as unsigned characters. The function returns a value that is less than, equal to, or greater than zero, depending on whether the compared portion of s1 is lexicographically less than, equal to, or greater than the compared portion of s2.

■ char *strncpy(char *s1, const char *s2, size_t n);

Precisely n characters are written into s1, overwriting whatever is there. The characters are taken from s2 until n of them have been copied or a null character has been copied, whichever comes first. Any remaining characters in s1 are assigned the value '\0'. If the length of s2 is n or larger, s1 will not be null-terminated. The programmer must ensure that s1 points to enough space to hold the result. The value s1 is returned.

■ char *strpbrk(const char *s1, const char *s2);

Searches for the first character in s1 that matches any one of the characters in s2. If the search is successful, the address of the character found in s1 is returned; otherwise NULL is returned. For example, the function call

```
strpbrk("April is the cruelest month", "abc")
```

returns the address of c in cruelest. (The letters pbrk in the name strpbrk stand for "pointer to break.")

■ char *strrchr(const char *s, int c);

Searches from the right for the first character in s that matches the value (char) c. If the character is found, its address is returned; otherwise NULL is returned. The call strchr(s, '\0') returns a pointer to the terminating null character in s.

■ size_t strspn(const char *s1, const char *s2);

Computes the length of the maximal initial substring in s1 consisting entirely of characters in s2. For example, the function call

```
strspn("April is the cruelest month", "A is for apple")
```

returns the value 9, because all the characters in the first argument preceding the t in the occur in the second argument, but the letter t does not. (The letters spn in the name strspn stand for "span.")

■ char *strstr(const char *s1, const char *s2);

Searches in s1 for the first occurrence of the substring s2. If the search is successful, a pointer to the base address of the substring in s1 is returned; otherwise NULL is returned.

■ char *strtok(char *s1, const char *s2);

Searches for tokens in s1, using the characters in s2 as token separators. If s1 contains one or more tokens, the first token in s1 is found, the character immediately following the token is overwritten with a null character, the remainder of s1 is stored elsewhere by the system, and the address of the first character in the token is returned. Subsequent calls with s1 equal to NULL return the base address of a string supplied by the system that contains the next token. If no additional tokens are available, NULL is returned. The initial call strtok(s1, s2) returns NULL if s1 contains no tokens. The following is an example:

```
char    s1[] = " this is,an   example ; ";
char    s2[] = ",; ";
char    *p;

printf("\"%s\"", strtok(s1, s2));
while ((p = strtok(NULL, s2)) != NULL)
    printf(" \"%s\"", p);
putchar('\n');
```

When executed, this code prints the line

```
"this" "is" "an" "example"
```

■ size_t strxfrm(char *s1, const char *s2, size_t n);

Transforms the string s2 and places the result in s1, overwriting whatever is there. At most n characters, including a terminating null character, are written in s1. The length of s1 is returned. The transformation is such that when two transformed strings are used as arguments to strcmp(), the value returned is less than, equal to, or greater than zero, depending on whether strcoll() applied to the untransformed strings returns a value less than, equal to, or greater than zero. (The letters xfrm in the name strxfrm stand for "transform.")

A.15   DATE AND TIME: <time.h>

This header file contains prototypes of functions that deal with date, time, and the internal clock. Here are examples of some macros and type definitions:

```
#include    <stddef.h>              /* for NULL and size_t */

#define    CLOCKS_PER_SEC    60     /* machine-dependent */

typedef    long    clock_t;
typedef    long    time_t;
```

Objects of type struct tm are used to store the date and time.

```
struct tm {
    int    tm_sec;      /* seconds after the minute: [0, 60] */
    int    tm_min;      /* minutes after the hour: [0, 59]   */
    int    tm_hour;     /* hours since midnight: [0, 23]      */
    int    tm_mday;     /* day of the month: [1, 31]          */
    int    tm_mon;      /* months since January: [0, 11]      */
    int    tm_year;     /* years since 1900                   */
    int    tm_wday;     /* days since Sunday: [0, 6]          */
    int    tm_yday;     /* days since 1 January: [0, 365]     */
    int    tm_isdst;    /* Daylight Savings Time flag         */
};
```

Note that the range of values for tm_sec has to accommodate a "leap second," which occurs only sporadically. The flag tm_isdst is positive if Daylight Savings Time is in effect, zero if it is not, and negative if the information is not available.

ACCESSING THE CLOCK

On most systems, the clock() function provides access to the underlying machine clock. The rate at which the clock runs is machine-dependent.

■ clock_t clock(void);

Returns an approximation to the number of CPU "clock ticks" used by the program up to the point of invocation. The value returned can be divided by CLOCKS_PER_SEC to convert it to seconds. If the CPU clock is not available, the value -1 is returned. See Section 15.6 in Chapter 15 for more discussion.

ACCESSING THE TIME

In ANSI C, time comes in two principal versions: a "calendar time" expressed as an integer, which on most systems represents the number of seconds that have elapsed since 1 January 1970, and a "broken-down time" expressed as a structure of type struct tm. The calendar time is encoded with respect to Universal Time Coordinated (UTC). The programmer can use library functions to convert one version of time to the other. Also, functions are available to print the time as a string.

■ `time_t time(time_t *tp);`

Returns the current calendar time, expressed as the number of seconds that have elapsed since 1 January 1970 (UTC). Other units and other starting dates are possible, but these are the ones typically used. If `tp` is not `NULL`, the value also gets stored in the object pointed to by `tp`. Consider the following code:

```
time_t    now;

now = time(NULL);
printf("\n%s%ld\n%s%s%s%s\n",
    "                        now = ", now,
    "            ctime(&now) = ", ctime(&now),
    "asctime(localtime(&now)) = ", asctime(localtime(&now)));
```

When executed on our system, this code printed the lines

```
                        now = 685136007
            ctime(&now) = Tue Sep 17 12:33:27 1991
asctime(localtime(&now)) = Tue Sep 17 12:33:27 1991
```

■ `char *asctime(const struct tm *tp);`

Converts the broken-down time pointed to by `tp` to a string provided by the system. The function returns the base address of the string. Later calls to `asctime()` and `ctime()` overwrite the string.

■ `char *ctime(const time_t *t_ptr);`

Converts the calendar time pointed to by `t_ptr` to a string provided by the system. The function returns the base address of the string. Later calls to `asctime()` and `ctime()` overwrite the string. The two function calls

```
ctime(&now)    and    asctime(localtime(&now))
```

are equivalent.

■ `double difftime(time_t t0, time_t t1);`

Computes the difference `t1 - t0` and, if necessary, converts this value to the number of seconds that have elapsed between the calendar times `t0` and `t1`. The value is returned as a `double`.

■ `struct tm *gmtime(const time_t *t_ptr);`

Converts the calendar time pointed to by `t_ptr` to a broken-down time, and stores it in an object of type `struct tm` that is provided by the system. The address of the structure is returned. The function computes the broken-down time with respect to Universal Time Coordinated (UTC). (This used to be called Greenwich Mean Time (GMT); hence the name of the function.) Later calls to `gmtime()` and `localtime()` overwrite the structure.

■ `struct tm *localtime(const time_t *t_ptr);`

Converts the calendar time pointed to by `t_ptr` to a broken-down local time, and stores it in an object of type `struct tm` that is provided by the system. The address of the structure is returned. Later calls to `gmtime()` and `localtime()` overwrite the structure.

■ `time_t mktime(struct tm *tp);`

Converts the broken-down local time in the structure pointed to by `tp` to the corresponding calendar time. If the call is successful, the calendar time is returned; otherwise -1 is returned. For the purpose of the computation, the `tm_wday` and `tm_yday` members of the structure are disregarded. Before the computation, other members can have values outside their usual range. After the computation, the members of the structure may be overwritten with an equivalent set of values in which each member lies within its normal range. The values for `tm_wday` and `tm_yday` are computed from those for the other members. As an example, the following code can be used to find the date 1000 days from now:

```
struct tm    *tp;
time_t       now, later;

now = time(NULL);
tp = localtime(&now);
tp -> tm_mday += 1000;
later = mktime(tp);
printf("\n1000 days from now: %s\n", ctime(&later));
```

■ `size_t strftime(char *s, size_t n,`
`                const char *cntrl_str, const struct tm *tp);`

Writes characters into the string pointed to by `s` under the direction of the control string pointed to by `cntrl_str`. At most `n` characters are written, including the null character. If more than `n` characters are required, the function returns zero and the contents of `s` are indeterminate; otherwise the length of `s` is returned. The control string consists of ordinary characters and conversion specifications, or formats, that determine how values from the broken-down time in the structure pointed to by tp are to be written. Each conversion specification consists of a % followed by a conversion character.

strftime()		
Conversion specification	**What gets printed**	**Example**
%a	abbreviated weekday name	Fri
%A	full weekday name	Friday
%b	abbreviated month name	Sep
%B	full month name	September
%c	date and time	Sep 01 02:17:23 1993
%d	day of the month	01
%H	hour of the 24-hour day	02
%h	hour of the 12-hour day	02
%j	day of the year	243
%m	month of the year	9
%M	minutes after the hour	17
%p	AM or PM	AM
%s	seconds after the hour	23
%U	week of the year (Sun–Sat)	34
%w	day of the week (0–6)	5
%x	date	Sep 01 1993
%X	time	02:17:23
%y	year of the century	93
%Y	year	1993
%Z	time zone	PDT
%%	percent character	%

Consider the following code:

```
char    s[100];
time_t  now;

now = time(NULL);
strftime(s, 100, "%H:%M:%S on %A, %d %B %Y", localtime(&now));
printf("%s\n\n", s);
```

When we executed a program containing these lines, the following line was printed:

```
13:01:15 on Tuesday, 17 September 1991
```

A.16   MISCELLANEOUS

In addition to the functions specified by ANSI C, the system may provide other functions in the library. In this section we describe the non–ANSI C functions that are widely available. Some functions, such as execl(), are common to most systems. Other functions, such as fork() or spawnl(), are generally available in one operating system, but not in another. The name of the associated header file is system-dependent.

USING FILE DESCRIPTORS

■ `int open(const char *filename, int flag, ...);`

Opens the named file for reading and/or writing as specified by the information stored bitwise in flag. If a file is being created, a third argument of type unsigned is needed. It sets the file permissions for the new file. If the call is successful, a nonnegative integer called the *file descriptor* is returned; otherwise errno is set and −1 is returned. Values that can be used for flag are given in the header file that contains the prototype for open(). These values are system-dependent.

■ `int close(int fd);`

Closes the file associated with the file descriptor fd. If the call is successful, zero is returned; otherwise errno is set and −1 is returned.

■ `int read(int fd, char *buf, int n);`

Reads at most n bytes from the file associated with the file descriptor fd into the object pointed to by buf. If the call is successful, the number of bytes written in buf is returned; otherwise errno is set and −1 is returned. A short count is returned if the end-of-file is encountered.

■ `int write(int fd, const char *buf, int n);`

Writes at most n bytes from the object pointed to by buf into the file associated with the file descriptor fd. If the call is successful, the number of bytes written in the file is returned; otherwise errno is set and −1 is returned. A short count can indicate that the disk is full.

CREATING A CONCURRENT PROCESS

■ `int fork(void);`

Copies the current process and begins executing it concurrently. The child process has its own process identification number. When `fork()` is called, it returns zero to the child and the child's process ID to the parent. If the call fails, `errno` is set and -1 is returned. This function is not available in MS-DOS.

■ `int vfork(void);`

Spawns a new process in a virtual memory-efficient way. The child process has its own process identification number. The address space of the parent process is not fully copied, which is very inefficient in a paged environment. The child borrows the parent's memory and thread of control until a call to `exec...()` occurs or the child exits. The parent process is suspended while the child is using its resources. When `vfork()` is called, it returns zero to the child and the child's process ID to the parent. If the call fails, `errno` is set and -1 is returned. This function is not available in MS-DOS.

OVERLAYING A PROCESS

In this section we describe the two families `exec...()` and `spawn...()`. The first is generally available on both MS-DOS and UNIX systems, the second only on MS-DOS systems. On UNIX systems `fork()` can be used with `exec...()` to achieve the effect of `spawn...()`.

■ `int execl(char *name, char *arg0, ..., char *argN);`
  `int execle(char *name, char *arg0, ..., char *argN, char **envp);`
  `int execlp(char *name, char *arg0, ..., char *argN);`
  `int execlpe(char *name, char *arg0, ..., char *argN, char **envp);`
  `int execv(char *name, char **argv);`
  `int execve(char *name, char **argv, char **envp);`
  `int execvp(char *name, char **argv);`
  `int execvpe(char *name, char **argv, char **envp);`

These functions overlay the current process with the named program. There is no return to the parent process. By default, the child process inherits the environment of the parent. Members of the family with names that begin with `execl` require a list of arguments that are taken as the command line arguments for the child process. The last argument in the list must be the NULL pointer. Members of the family with names that begin with `execv` use the array `argv` to supply command line arguments to the child process. The last element of argv must have the value NULL. Members of the family with names ending in e use the array envp to supply environment variables to the child process. The last element of envp must have the value NULL. Members of the family with p in their name use the path variable specified in the environment to determine which directories to search for the program.

■ int spawnl(int mode, char *name, char *arg0, ..., char *argN);
    . . . . .

This family of functions corresponds to the exec...() family, except that each member has an initial integer argument. The values for mode are 0, 1, and 2. The value 0 causes the parent process to wait for the child process to finish before continuing. With value 1, the parent and child processes should execute concurrently, except that this has not been implemented yet. The use of this value will cause an error. The value 2 causes the child process to overlay the parent process.

INTERPROCESS COMMUNICATION

■ int pipe(int pd[2]);

Creates an input/output mechanism called a *pipe*, and puts the associated file descriptors (pipe descriptors) in the array pd. If the call is successful, zero is returned; otherwise errno is set and −1 is returned. After a pipe has been created, the system assumes that two or more cooperating processes created by subsequent calls to fork() will use read() and write() to pass data through the pipe. One descriptor, pd[0], is read from; the other, pd[1], is written to. The pipe capacity is system-dependent, but is at least 4096 bytes. If a write fills the pipe, it blocks until data is read out of it. As with other file descriptors, close() can be used to explicitly close pd[0] and pd[1]. This function is not available in MS-DOS.

SUSPENDING PROGRAM EXECUTION

■ void sleep(unsigned seconds);

Suspends the current process from execution for the number of seconds requested. The time is only approximate.

B

APPENDIX B: DIFFERENCES: ANSI C COMPARED TO TRADITIONAL C

B.1   TYPES
B.2   CONSTANTS
B.3   DECLARATIONS
B.4   INITIALIZATIONS
B.5   EXPRESSIONS
B.6   FUNCTIONS
B.7   CONVERSIONS
B.8   ARRAY POINTERS
B.9   STRUCTURES AND UNIONS
B.10   PREPROCESSOR
B.11   HEADER FILES
B.12   MISCELLANEOUS

In this appendix we list the major differences between ANSI C and traditional C. Where appropriate, we have included examples. The list is not complete. Only the major changes are noted.

B.1 TYPES

- The keyword `signed` has been added to the language.

- Three types of characters are specified: plain `char`, `signed char`, and `unsigned char`. An implementation may represent a plain `char` as either a `signed char` or an `unsigned char`.

- The keyword `signed` can be used in declarations of any of the signed integral types and in casts. Except with `char`, its use is always optional.

- In traditional C, the type `long float` is equivalent to `double`. Since `long float` was rarely used, it has been removed from ANSI C.

- The type `long double` has been added to ANSI C. Constants of this type are specified with the suffix L. A `long double` may provide more precision and range than a `double`, but it is not required to do so.

- The keyword void is used to indicate that a function takes no arguments or that a function returns no value.

- The type void * is used for generic pointers. For example, the function prototype for malloc() is given by

```
void *malloc(size_t size);
```

A generic pointer can be assigned a pointer value of any type, and a variable of any pointer type can be assigned a generic pointer value. Casts are not needed. In contrast, the "generic" pointer type in traditional C is char *. Here, casts are necessary.

- Enumeration types are supported. An example is

```
enum day {sun, mon, tue, wed, thu, fri, sat};
```

The enumerators in this example are sun, mon, ..., sat. Enumerators are constants of type int. Thus they can be used in case labels in switch statements.

B.2 CONSTANTS

- String constants separated by white space are concatenated. Thus

```
"abc"
"def" "ghi"      is equivalent to      "abcdefghi"
```

- String constants are not modifiable. (Not all compilers enforce this.)

- The type of a numeric constant can be specified by letter suffixes. Some examples are

```
123L       /* long          */
123U       /* unsigned       */
123UL      /* unsigned long */
1.23F      /* float          */
1.23L      /* long double    */
```

Suffixes may be lower- or uppercase. A numeric constant without a suffix is a type big enough to contain the value.

- The digits 8 and 9 are no longer considered octal digits. They may not be used in an octal constant.

■ Hexadecimal escape sequences beginning with \x have been introduced. As with octal escape sequences beginning with \0, they are used in character and string constants.

B.3   DECLARATIONS

■ The type qualifier `const` has been added. It means that variables so declared are not modifiable. (Compilers do not always enforce this.)
■ The type qualifier `volatile` has been added. It means that variables so declared are modifiable by an agent external to the program. For example, some systems put the declaration

```
extern volatile int   errno;
```

in the header file *errno.h*.

B.4   INITIALIZATIONS

■ In ANSI C, automatic aggregates such as arrays and structures can be initialized. In traditional C, they must be external or of storage class `static`.
■ Unions can be initialized. An initialization refers to the first member of the union.
■ Character arrays of size *n* can be initialized using a string constant of exactly *n* characters. An example is

```
char   today[3] = "Fri";
```

The end-of-string sentinel \0 in "Fri" does not get copied into `today`.

B.5   EXPRESSIONS

■ For reasons of symmetry, a unary plus operator has been added to the language.
■ In traditional C, expressions involving one of the commutative binary operators such as + or * can be reordered at the convenience of the compiler, even though they have been parenthesized in the program. For example, in the statement

```
x = (a + b) + c;
```

the variables can be summed by the compiler in some unspecified order. In ANSI C, this is not true. The parentheses must be honored.

■ A pointer to a function can be dereferenced either explicitly or implicitly. If, for example, f is a pointer to a function that takes three arguments, then the expression

f(a, b, c)   is equivalent to   (*f)(a, b, c)

■ The sizeof operator yields a value of type size_t. The type definition for size_t is given in *stddef.h*.

■ A pointer of type void * cannot be dereferenced without first casting it to an appropriate type. However, it can be used in logical expressions, where it is compared to another pointer.

B.6   FUNCTIONS

■ ANSI C provides a new function definition syntax. A parameter declaration list occurs in the parentheses following the function name. An example is

```
int f(int a, float b)
{
    . . . . .
```

In contrast, the traditional C style is

```
int f(a, b)
int     a;
float   b;
{
    . . . . .
```

■ ANSI C provides the function prototype, which is a new style of function declaration. A parameter type list occurs in the parentheses following the function name. Identifiers are optional. For example,

int f(int, float);   and   int f(int a, float b);

are equivalent function prototypes. In contrast, the traditional C style is

```
int f();
```

If a function takes no arguments, then `void` is used as the parameter type in the function prototype. If a function takes a variable number of arguments, then the ellipsis . . . is used as the rightmost parameter in the function prototype.

■ Redeclaring a parameter identifier in the outer block of a function definition is illegal. The following code illustrates the error:

```
void f(int a, int b, int c)
{
    int   a;     /* error: a cannot be redefined here */


    . . . . .
```

Although this is legal in traditional C, it is almost always a programming error. Indeed, it can be a difficult bug to find.

■ Structures and unions can be passed as arguments to functions, and they can be returned from functions. The passing mechanism is call-by-value, which means that a local copy is made.

B.7 CONVERSIONS

■ An expression of type `float` is not automatically converted to a `double`.

■ When arguments to functions are evaluated, the resulting value is converted to the type specified by the function prototype, provided the conversion is compatible. Otherwise, a syntax error occurs.

■ Arithmetic conversions are more carefully specified (see Section 6.9 in Chapter 6). In ANSI C, the basic philosophy for conversions is to preserve values, if possible. Because of this, the rules require some conversions on a machine with 2-byte words to be different from those on a machine with 4-byte words.

■ The resulting type of a shift operation is not dependent on the right operand. In ANSI C, the integral promotions are performed on each operand, and the type of the result is that of the promoted left operand.

B.8   ARRAY POINTERS

■ Many traditional C compilers do not allow the operand of the address operator & to be an array. In ANSI C, since this is legal, pointers to multidimensional arrays can be used. Here is an example:

```
int   a[2][3] = {2, 3, 5, 7, 11, 13};
int   (*p)[][3];                      /* the first dimension
                                         need not be specified */
p = &a;
printf("%d\n", (*p)[1][2]);           /* 13 gets printed */
```

B.9   STRUCTURES AND UNIONS

■ Structures and unions can be used in assignments. If s1 and s2 are two structure variables of the same type, the expression s1 = s2 is valid. Values of members in s2 are copied into corresponding members of s1.

■ Structures and unions can be passed as arguments to functions, and they can be returned from functions. All arguments to functions, including structures and unions, are passed call-by-value.

■ If m is a member of a structure or union and the function call f() returns a structure or union of the same type, then the expression f().m is valid.

■ Structures and unions can be used with the comma operator and in conditional expressions. Some examples are

```
int       a, b;
struct s  s1, s2, s3;

. . . . .
(a, s1)         /* comma expression having structure type */
a < b ? s1 : s2   /* conditional expression having structure type */
```

■ If *expr* is a structure or union expression and m is a member, then an expression of the form *expr*.m is valid. However, *expr*.m can be assigned a value only if *expr* can. Even though expressions such as

```
(s1 = s2).m     (a, s1).m      (a < b ? s1 : s2).m       f().m
```

are valid, they cannot occur on the left side of an assignment operator.

B.10   PREPROCESSOR

■ Preprocessing directives do not have to begin in column 1.

■ The following predefined macros have been added:

    __DATE__   __FILE__   __LINE__   __STDC__   __TIME__

They may not be redefined or undefined (see Section 11.8 in Chapter 11).

■ A macro may not be redefined without first undefining it. Multiple definitions are allowed, provided they are the same.

■ The preprocessor operators # and ## have been added. The unary operator # causes "stringization" of a formal parameter in a macro definition. The binary operator ## merges tokens (see Section 11.9 in Chapter 11).

■ The preprocessor operator `defined` has been added (see Section 11.7 in Chapter 11).

■ The preprocessing directives #elif, #error, and #pragma have been added (see Sections 11.7 and 11.11 in Chapter 11).

■ In traditional C, `toupper()` and `tolower()` are defined as macros in *ctype.h* as follows:

```
#define   toupper(c)   ((c)-'a'+'A')
#define   tolower(c)   ((c)-'A'+'a')
```

The macro call `toupper(c)` will work properly only when c has the value of a lowercase letter. Similarly, the macro call `tolower(c)` will work properly only when c has the value of an uppercase letter. In ANSI C, `toupper()` and `tolower()` are implemented either as functions or as macros, but their behavior is different. If c has the value of a lowercase letter, then `toupper(c)` returns the value of the corresponding uppercase letter. If c has does not have the value of a lowercase letter, then the value c is returned. Similar remarks hold with respect to `tolower()`.

■ In ANSI C, every macro is also available as a function. Suppose *stdio.h* has been included. Then `putchar(c)` is a macro call but `(putchar)(c)` is a function call.

B.11   HEADER FILES

■ ANSI C has added new header files. The header file *stdlib.h* contains function prototypes for many of the functions in the standard library.

■ The header files *float.h* and *limits.h* contain macro definitions describing implementation characteristics. ANSI C requires that certain minimum values and ranges be supported for each arithmetic type.

B.12   MISCELLANEOUS

■ In traditional C, the operators += and =+ are synonymous, although the use of =+ is considered old-fashioned. In ANSI C, the use of =+, =*, and so on is not allowed.

■ An ANSI C compiler treats an assignment operator such as += as a single token. In Traditional C, since it is treated as two tokens, white space can occur between the + and the =. Thus the expression a + = 2 is legal in traditional C but illegal in ANSI C.

■ Each of the following has a distinct name space: label identifiers, variable identifiers, tag names, and member names for each structure and union. All tags for enum, struct, and union comprise a single name space.

■ Two identifiers are considered distinct if they differ within the first n characters, where n must be at least 31.

■ The expression controlling a switch statement can be any integral type. Floating types are not allowed. The constant integral expression in a case label can be any integral type, including an enumerator.

■ Pointers and int's are not interchangeable. Only the integer 0 can be assigned to a pointer without a cast.

■ Pointer expressions may point to one element beyond an allocated array.

■ External declarations and linkage rules are more carefully defined.

■ Many changes have been made to the standard library and its associated header files.

APPENDIX C: ASCII CHARACTER CODES

Left \ Right Digits	ASCII American Standard Code for Information Interchange									
	0	1	2	3	4	5	6	7	8	9
0	nul	soh	stx	etx	eot	enq	ack	bel	bs	ht
1	nl	vt	np	cr	so	si	dle	dc1	dc2	dc3
2	dc4	nak	syn	etb	can	em	sub	esc	fs	gs
3	rs	us	sp	!	"	#	$	%	&	'
4	(	)	*	+	'	–	.	/	0	1
5	2	3	4	5	6	7	8	9	:	;
6	<	=	>	?	@	A	B	C	D	E
7	F	G	H	I	J	K	L	M	N	O
8	P	Q	R	S	T	U	V	W	X	Y
9	Z	[	\	]	^	_	'	a	b	c
10	d	e	f	g	h	i	j	k	l	m
11	n	o	p	q	r	s	t	u	v	w
12	x	y	z	{	|	}	~	del		

Some observations

1   Character codes 0–31 and 127 are nonprinting.
2   Character code 32 prints a single space.
3   Character codes for digits 0 through 9 are contiguous.
4   Character codes for letters A through Z are contiguous.
5   Character codes for letters a through z are contiguous.
6   The difference between each capital letter and the
         corresponding lowercase letter is 32.

The meaning of some of the abbreviations

bel	audible bell	ht	horizontal tab
bs	backspace	nl	newline
cr	carriage return	nul	null
esc	escape	vt	vertical tab

Note: On most UNIX systems the command

    man ascii

causes the ASCII table to be printed on the screen in decimal, octal, and hexadecimal.

APPENDIX D: OPERATOR PRECEDENCE AND ASSOCIATIVITY

Operators	Associativity
() [] . -> ++ (*postfix*) -- (*postfix*)	left to right
++ (*prefix*) -- (*prefix*) ! ~ sizeof (*type*) + (*unary*) - (*unary*) & (*address*) * (*dereference*)	right to left
* / %	left to right
+ -	left to right
<< >>	left to right
< <= > >=	left to right
== !=	left to right
&	left to right
^	left to right
|	left to right
&&	left to right
||	left to right
?:	right to left
= += -= *= /= %= >>= <<= &= ^= |=	right to left
, (*comma operator*)	left to right

INDEX

"ab" mode, 481
abort() function, 374, 593
abs() function, 213, 589
absolute addresses, 291
abstract data types (ADTs), 546–548
acc command, 512
access, 490
accessing
  clock, 599
  file position indicator, 581–582
  files, 480–482, 490–491
  members, 432–435
  strings, 497
  time, 599–602
acos() function, 571
action line, 525, 534
addition, 238
addition operator +, 12, 54–55
// Add as a member function to class string., 553
address(es), 19, 264, 271–273, 291–292
addressing, 264–269
address operator &, 19, 20, 29, 264, 267, 291
add_ten program, 23–24
add_to_N program, 102
adjacent, 426
ADTs (abstract data types), 546–548
advert program, 542–543
.a files, 78, 513–515
// A first C++ program illustrating output.,
  542, 543
%a format, 602
%A format, 602
"age and name" program, 562
alert character, 163
algorithm(s), 4, 310–311, 412–415
alias command, 524
aliases, 524
aligning storage, 458
allocation, 316–318, 322, 449–450
alphabetic characters, 349
alphabetic order. *See* sorting
American Standard Code for Information Interchange,
  162, 169, 171, 260, 616–617
"a" mode, 481
and operator, 236, 239
// An elementary implementation of type
  string., 547
/* An equality test that fails. */, 118
// An implementation of dynamically allocated
  strings., 553
ANSI C, xv
  compared to traditional C, 606–614
  See also C++; C system
-*a* option, 458
a.out file, 391
append mode, 495

apple file, 488
"archive," 78
archiver, 513–515
ar command, 78, 513–515
argc argument, 342–344
arguments
  command line, 351
  macros with, 356–357, 364–369
  passing to main(), 342–344
  programming errors and, 211, 389–390
  programming style and, 387
  system considerations and, 390
  variable, 575–576
argv argument, 342–344, 381
arithmetic
  floating point, 40, 123, 222
  integer, 589–590
  modular, 220
  pointer, 308–309, 346
arithmetic conversions, 202–203
arithmetic modulo 24, 220
arithmetic operators, 12
arithmetic types, 189
array initializer, 303
array pointers, 612
arrays
  default initialization of, 281
  described, 301
  exercises, 324–329, 349
  multidimensional, 312–316
  one-dimensional, 301–304
  passing to functions, 309–310
  pointers and, 300–329
  programming errors, 322
  programming style, 318–322, 346
  relationship between pointers and, 307–308
  system considerations, 322–323
  three-dimensional, 315
  two-dimensional, 312–314
  See also string(s)
ASCII character codes, 162, 169, 171, 260, 616–617
asctime() function, 600
asin() function, 571
assert.h standard header file, 374, 566
assert() macro, 374, 387, 566
assignment(s), 8–14, 177–178, 203, 264, 270,
  437–439
assignment expressions, 115–116, 295
assignment operators =, 14, 59–61, 329
assign_values() function, 438
associativity
  of assignment operators, 59, 60
  of bitwise operators, 236–237
  of brackets, 435, 436
  of cast operator, 204
  of comma operator, 104, 436

of conditional operator, 113
of decrement operator, 57
defined, 55
of equality operators, 82, 85
of increment operator, 57
of logical operators, 82, 87–88
of operators, 55–57, 436–437, 618
of parentheses, 435, 436
of relational operators, 82, 84
of shift operators, 241
of sizeof operator, 197, 436–437
of structure member operator, 435, 436
of structure pointer operator, 435, 436
atan() function, 571
atan2() function, 571
atexit() function, 593
atof() function, 590
atoi() function, 590, 591
atol() function, 591
automatic conversion, 202–203
automatic variables, 281
auto storage class, 274, 458
average() function, 320–321, 415, 460
awk utility, 532

backslash character \
    char data type and, 163–164
    #define and, 354
    exercise using, 78, 183, 396
    listed, 163
    string constants and, 53–54
Balanced Meal Program, 254–255, 460
base case. *See* recursion
base class, 555
base file name macro, 530
bcc command, 534
bc command, 534
bc\include directory, 64
"Bell Labs industrial programming style," 27–28, 114
%b format, 602
%B format, 602
BIG symbolic constant, 215–216
binary, 12
binary arithmetic operators, 12
binary files, 495, 504
binary logical operators, 239
binary mode, 493
binary operators. *See* operators
binary positional numbers, 190–191
bison utility, 532
bit_complement() function, 258–259
/* Bit print an int expression. */, 243
bit_print() function, 242–245, 255–257, 258, 259, 296
bits, 258
bit strings, 190
bitwise binary logical operators, 239
bitwise complement, 237–238
bitwise complement operator ~, 236
bitwise exclusive or operator ^, 236, 239
bitwise expressions, 236–241
bitwise inclusive or operator |, 236, 239

bitwise and operator &, 236, 239
bitwise operators, 236–241
    bit_print() function and, 242–245
    exercises, 254–260
    masks and, 241–242
    packing and unpacking and, 245–248
    precedence and associativity of, 236–237
    programming errors, 250–251
    programming style, 249
    system considerations, 252
bitwise printing of int, 242–245
blank character, 28, 46, 396, 562
BLAST OFF program, 420
block(s), 89, 273–274, 291
    See also compound statement
body (of function definition), 131
Book on C, A (Pohl and Kelley), 425
boolean types, 255
boolean variables, 103–104, 126, 258
BOOLEX, 126
bounds, 322, 347, 458
braces { }, 55
    compound statement and, 89
    initialization of structures and, 443
    programming errors and, 390
    programming style and, 27–28, 114–115
    while statement and, 24
brackets [ ], 302, 382, 435, 436, 475
break statement, 108–110, 111
"broken-down time." *See* time
bsearch() function, 588
bubble() function, 310, 326
bubble_sort() function, 423
bubble sort sorting algorithm, 310–311, 349
    See also sorting
bubble_string() function, 349
Budd, Timothy, 542
BUFSIZ macro, 577
built-in mathematical functions, 198–201

C. *See* ANSI C; C++; C system; operating system;
        programs; traditional C
C++, 540–563
    classes and abstract data types, 546–548
    contructors and destructors, 552–554
    exercises, 561–563
    input, 543–546
    object-oriented programming and inheritance,
        554–557
    output, 542–543
    overloading, 549–552
    programming errors, 558
    programming style, 557–558
    system considerations, 559
    See also ANSI C; C system; traditional C
"calendar time." *See* time
call-by-reference, 263, 271–273
call-by-value, 149, 263, 271
called, 130
calloc() function
    dynamic memory allocation and, 316–318
    exercise using, 328–329, 423–424

insertion and deletion and, 455
pointers to `void` and, 270
stdlib.h standard header file and, 587
system considerations and, 322–323, 494
"calorie-counting" program, 459
"calories" program, 460
capitalize, 167–171
/* Capitalize lowercase letters and double
     space. */, 168, 170
capital letters, 46, 51, 349, 350, 387
caps program, 168–169, 170–171, 180
card games, 460
card.h file, 437
"card" program, 459–460
carriage return character, 163
case statement. *See* `switch` statement
cast operator, 204
casts, 201–204, 212, 292
cat command, 399–400
cb command, 531, 539
cc command, 30–33, 213, 390, 394, 512–513
C++ for C Programmers (Pohl), 541
`ceil()` function, 572
central processing unit (CPU), 4
.c files
    compiler and, 512, 513
    developing large programs and, 377
    make and, 525
    programming style and, 387
    system considerations and, 30, 391
%c format
    char data type and, 163
    exercise using, 185
    `printf()` function and, 17, 18, 466
    `scanf()` function and, 19, 20, 473, 475
    `strftime()` function and, 602
    student records problem solving and, 442
`change()` function, 340–341, 338, 339
character arrays. *See* string(s)
character codes, 162, 169, 171, 260, 616–617
character constants, 52, 248, 252, 260
    See also char data type
character functions, 592–593
character handling, 566–567
character input/output, 582–584
character processing, 160–185
    capitalize example, 167–171
    char data type, 162–164
    counting words problem solving, 174–176
    example, 281–285
    exercises, 182–185
    `getchar()` and `putchar()`, 164–167
    macros in *ctype.h*, 171–172
    programming errors, 178–180
    programming style, 177–178
    repeating characters problem solving, 172–174
    system considerations, 180–182
/* Character processing: change a line. */, 338
characters, 46–49, 189–191
    alphabetic, 349
    conversion, 18, 19, 466, 473, 474, 491, 602
    flag, 496

hard-to-print, 163–164
listed, 46
mapping, 567
nonprinting, 163–164
ordinary, 472
processing, 160–185, 281–285
reading from keyboard, 164–167, 177, 182, 183, 582
repeating, 172–174
testing, 566–567
writing to screen, 164–167, 177, 182, 184, 584
character variables. *See* char data type
CHAR_BIT macro, 569
char data type, 189–191
    character processing and, 162–164
    described, 12–13
    exercise using, 216, 219, 259, 350
    integral promotions and, 201
    listed, 188, 189
    pointers to `void` and, 270
    programming style and, 177
    system considerations and, 181–182, 213, 252
CHAR_MAX macro, 569
CHAR_MIN macro, 569
checking bounds, 322
chess pieces, 426
chk_arrays.c file, 518
`cin` input stream variable, 545, 561
`circular_shift()` function, 257
circumflex ^, 475
class(es), 274–278, 288–289, 290–292, 294–298,
     546–548, 555
`class`, 546–548
    See also `struct`
class_info program, 432
clear command, 536
`clearerr()` function, 582
client, 547
cl_info.h file, 432
clock, 519–523, 599
    See also date; time
`clock()` function, 520–523, 599
"clock" program, 220
CLOCKS_PER_SEC macro, 520, 598
`clock_t` type definition, 519–520, 598
`close()` function, 603
closing files, 579–580
cls command, 536
cnt, 150
cnt_abc program, 305, 306–307, 325
code(s), 162, 169, 171, 260, 616–617
    See also object code; programs; source code
coercion, 202–203
"coins" program, 37–38
"coin toss" program, 158–159
columns, 377–386
combinatorics, 101–102
comma expression, 463
command(s), 508–509, 532
    See also action line
command line arguments, 342–344, 351
command line options, 398
comma operator, 104–105, 436, 463

commas, 17, 55, 105, 463
comments /* */, 49–50
  exercise using, 74, 76–77, 499
  nesting, 75, 397
  pointer addressing and dereferencing and, 269
  programming errors and, 558
  programming style and, 69, 557
  system considerations and, 391, 559
comments //, 543
communicating with environment, 589
communication, 605
compare.c file, 517
`compare_fractional_part()` function, 368–369, 399
/* Compare multiplication times. */, 523
compare_sorts.h file, 516
compare_sorts program, 528–530
comparison function, 359
compilation, 4–5, 369–372
compiler, 511–513
  defined, 45
  described, 4–5, 45–46
  options listed, 513
  programming errors and, 533
  types listed, 512
  See also C system; programs
compile-time errors, 30
compiling programs, 4–5
complement, 237–238
complement operator, 236
complex.h library, 552
compound statement, 24, 89, 91
  See also block(s)
`compute()` function, 204–209
/* Compute interest compounded yearly. */, 205
/* Compute the next day. */, 228
/* Compute the next day with a cast. */, 230
computer, 4
/* Compute the size of some fundamental types. */, 197
`compute_sum` function, 149
/* Compute various statistics. */, 319–320
/* Compute various statistics more efficiently. */, 321
// Computing areas of shapes polymorphically., 556
computing interest, 204–209
computing powers of 2, 62–63
computing sums, 24–27
concurrent processes, 604
conditional compilation, 369–372
conditional expressions, 127
conditional operator ?:, 112–113, 158–159
conditioning files, 579–580
connectivity, 426
constants, 52–53
  ANSI C compared to traditional C, 608–609
  characters and, 189
  programming errors and, 291
  string, 53–54, 78, 394
  symbolic, 16, 75, 264, 318, 355, 387
  See also character constants; enumeration constants; floating type(s); integer constants

constant strings, 350–351, 422
constructors, 552–554
`const` type qualifier, 287–288, 298, 559
"contiguous allocation" function. *See* `calloc()` function
continue command, 524
`continue` statement, 108–110, 127
control-c, 32, 41, 119–120, 123–124
control-d, 32
control, flow of. *See* flow of control
control string, 11, 17, 471
control-z, 32, 503–504
conventional C. *See* traditional C
conversion(s), 201–204, 590–592, 611
conversion characters
  `printf()` function, 18, 466
  programming style and, 491
  `scanf()` function, 19, 473, 474
  `strftime()` function, 602
conversion function, 256
conversion specification, 11, 473–475
/* Convert seconds to minutes and seconds. */, 39
-c option, 350, 512, 513
copy command, 180
/* Copy stdin to stdout, except single space only. */, 179–180
corecursive functions, 422
"core dump," 38–39
core file, 38–39
corresponding functions, 376
`cos()` function, 198, 215, 571
`cosh()` function, 571
`count_alph()` function, 422
`count_down()` function, 404
/* Count each uppercase letter separately. */, 305
/* Count the failing grades. */, 433
`count()` function, 452–453, 461, 462
counting, 150, 452–453
counting letters, 304–307
counting words, 174–176, 342
/* Count a list recursively. */, 453
/* Count the number of words in a string. */, 342
C++ for Pascal Programmers (Pohl), 541
cp command, 180
cpp command, 390, 394
  See also preprocessor
"C" program, 35
CPU (central processing unit), 4
Cray supercomputer, 153, 212
/* Create employee data in a short int. */, 248
`create_list()` function, 461
"create random" program, 328
cr_rand program, 328
crunch program, 185
csh utility, 532
C system, 63–68
  exercises, 74–79, 463
  preprocessor, 64–65
  programming errors, 70–72
  programming style, 68–69
  standard library, 65–68

system considerations, 72–73
See also compiler; loader; operating system;
  preprocessor
ctime() function, 600
ctype.h standard header file, 171–172, 177, 181, 183,
  566–567
cube() function, 155
cubes, table of, 562

"dangling else" problem, 93
DATA, 461
data compression, 245–248
data-compression utilities, 185
data file, 217, 561
data hiding, 547
data types, 186–222, 546–548
date, 598–602
  See also clock; time
date command, 508
"date" function, 258
__DATE__ predefined macro, 372
DBL_EPSILON macro, 568
DBL_MAX macro, 568
DBL_MIN macro, 568
dbl_out.c file, 41
dbl_out program, 32–33, 41–42, 165, 166–167, 173
dbl_space program, 484, 501, 502
dbl_with_caps program, 486, 488–489
dbx, 523–524
.dbxinit file, 524
debuggers, 523–524
debugging, 291, 390, 539
decimal integer constants, 52–53, 192
decimal notation, 194
decimal positional numbers, 190–191
declaration(s)
  ANSI C compared to traditional C, 609
  described, 11
  exercise using, 460–461
  function, 286, 558
  fundamental data types and, 187–188
  pointer, 264
  programming style and, 28
declaring structures, 430–432
decrement operator _, 57–58, 417
default initialization, 281
default statement. *See* switch statement
defined preprocessing operator, 369
#define preprocessing directive
  exercise using, 126, 183, 351, 393, 462
  macros with arguments and, 356–357
  programming errors and, 389, 558
  programming style and, 27–28
  scanf() function and, 21
  system considerations and, 292
  use of, 15–16, 354–356
defining functions, 130–133, 286
definition(s)
  function, 130–133, 286, 387, 395
  macro, 78, 395
  standard library and, 576–577
  type, 358
delete, 32

delete_list() function, 456
delete operator, 553
deletion, 453–456
delimiter, 163, 332–333, 346, 347
dependency line, 525
depth program, 10–11, 14–15
dereference operator *, 265, 266, 267, 269
dereferencing, 264–269
deriving, 555
descriptors, 603
design, 129, 138–142
destructors, 552–554
developing large programs, 377
devices, 4
%d format
  exercise using, 221–222, 259, 294, 298, 498–499
  printf() function and, 17, 18, 466
  programming errors and, 210–211
  scanf() function and, 19, 473
  strftime() function and, 602
diagnostics, 566
  See also error(s); warnings
dieting program, 459
diff command, 531, 532
difftime() function, 520–523, 600
digits, 46
dir command, 32, 398, 504, 508–509, 534
direct input/output, 585–586
directives, 15, 64, 471, 585
discriminated identifiers, 72–73
display() function, 411
"distance conversion" program, 561
div() function, 590
divide-and-conquer methodology, 412–415, 425
  See also program methodology
division operator /, 12, 39, 54–55
div_t type definition, 587
documentation. *See* comments
domain, 568, 570
domain error, 568, 570
-D option, 513
do statement, 89, 106, 109, 115, 355–356
dot operator, 430, 435, 436, 548
double floating type, 194–196
  described, 13
  exercise using, 40, 156–157, 214, 215, 216, 219,
    221, 294
  listed, 188, 189
  system considerations and, 72
  usual arithmetic conversions and, 202
double quote character "", 28, 53–54, 163, 164, 535
double_space() function, 482
double-spacing, 178–180, 482–485, 501, 502
draw() function, 411
drawing patterns on screen, 410–411
dynamic allocation of memory, 587–588
dynamic memory allocation, 316–318, 322
dynamic storage allocation, 449–450

e, 222
EBCDIC character codes, 162, 169
/* Echo the command line arguments. */, 343
echoing, 42

editor, 4
EDOM macro, 568
%e format, 18, 466, 473, 475
%E format, 466, 473, 475
elements, 46–49
element size, 308–309
#elif preprocessing directive, 372
ellipsis . . ., 478, 480
"else-if," 372
#else preprocessing directive, 372
else statement. *See* if-else statement
emacs program, 114
e-mail, 400, 538
empty statement, 55, 89–90, 117, 124, 357, 389
#endif preprocessing directive, 369–372
end-of-file signal, 32, 38, 40, 41, 503–504, 578
end-of-string sentinel \0, 163, 332–333, 346, 347
enumeration constants, 52
enumeration types, 225–227
  exercises, 254–260
  game of paper, rock, scissors example and, 230–236
  integral promotions and, 201
  programming errors, 250–251
  programming style, 249
  system considerations, 252
  typedef and, 227–230
enumerators, 225–227
enum keyword, 225
env command, 510
environment, 589
environment variables, 509–511, 533, 535
EOF macro, 178, 183, 252, 259, 577, 585
-e option, 512
-E option, 513
equality, 115–116, 118, 127
equality operators, 82–83, 84–85, 90
equal sign =, 443
equal to operator ==, 82, 84–85
ERANGE macro, 568
errno.h standard header file, 567–568
errno identifier, 567
error(s)
  compile-time, 30
  domain, 568, 570
  exercise using, 35–36, 40, 220, 396, 561–562, 563
  programming style and, 532
  range, 568, 571
  run-time, 30, 31, 38–39
  standard library and, 567–568
  syntax, 30, 31
  See also warnings
error handling, 582
error indicator, 578
#error preprocessing directive, 375
escape character. *See* backslash character
escape sequence, 163–164
evaluation, 88–89, 125, 126, 268
exclusive or macro, 393
exclusive or operator, 236, 239
execle() function, 604
execl() function, 604
execlpe() function, 604

execlp() function, 604
executable file, 5
executing commands within programs, 508–509
execution profiles, 515–519
execve() function, 604
execv() function, 604
execvpe() function, 604
execvp() function, 604
.exe files, 31, 391, 512
EXIT_FAILURE macro, 587
exit() function, 151, 382, 594
exit status, 151
EXIT_SUCCESS macro, 587
exmpl_1.c file, 70
exp() function, 198, 571
explicit conversions, 201–204, 212, 292
exponential notation, 194, 195
expressions
  ANSI C compared to traditional C, 609–610
  assignment, 115–116, 295
  bitwise, 236–241
  casts and, 203–204
  conditional, 127
  equality, 118
  equality operators and, 84–85, 90
  floating, 210
  fundamental data types and, 187–188
  if and if-else statements and, 90
  logical, 121, 126
  logical operators and, 85–89, 90
  mixed, 203
  programming errors and, 291
  relational, 118
  relational operators and, 83–84, 90
  writing programs and, 8–14
expression statement, 90
  See also empty statement
extension, 252
external discriminated identifiers, 72–73
external variables, 279–281, 298
extern storage class, 274, 275–277, 279, 286, 288,
    458
extract() function, 443
extraction operator, 545
extract_values() function, 438, 439

fabs() function, 213, 572
factorial_decrement() function, 417
factorial_forever() function, 417
factorial() function, 416–417
factorial_positive() function, 417
fail() function, 433, 434
failure, 477
fclose() function, 481, 579
feof() function, 582
ferror() function, 582
fflush() function, 482, 580
%f format
  exercise using, 38, 215
  printf() function and, 17, 18, 466
  programming errors and, 29, 211
  scanf() function and, 19, 20, 21, 22, 473

fgetc() function, 583
fgetpos() function, 495, 581
fgets() function, 476, 499, 502–503, 583
field, 18, 467, 474
field width, 18, 467, 468–469
file(s)
    accessing, 480–482, 490–491
    binary, 495, 504
    closing, 579–580
    conditioning, 579–580
    double-spacing, 482–485
    exercises, 496–504
    input/output and, 464–504
    opening, 491–492, 579–580
    programming errors, 492–494
    programming style, 491–492
    system considerations, 494–495
    text, 495, 504
    See also module(s)
file1.c file, 276
file2.c file, 276
file command, 524
file descriptors, 603
FILE identifier, 479
file mode, 492
FILENAME_MAX macro, 577
file names, 73
file pointer, 493
file position indicator, 581–582
__FILE__ predefined macro, 372
FILE structure type, 578
FILL() macro, 396–397
find_accrued_interest() function, 218
finding maximum values, 96–98
/* Find the maximum of n real values. */, 96
find_max program, 97–98, 124
/* Find the minimum of three values. */, 93–94
find_min program, 94–95
find_next_day() function, 228–229, 230
find_sum program, 25–27, 40
/* Find the triples of integers that add up to N. */, 101
FINISH symbolic constant, 157–158
flag characters, 467, 468, 496, 513
flex utility, 532
float floating type, 194–196
    described, 13
    exercise using, 38, 40, 214, 216, 219, 221
    listed, 188, 189
    usual arithmetic conversions and, 202
float.h standard header file, 221, 568
floating constants, 13, 52–53, 189, 194–196, 210
floating expressions, 210
floating limits, 568
floating numbers, 13, 119, 214, 475
floating point arithmetic, 40, 123, 222
floating point constants, 395
floating point numbers, 13, 119, 214, 475
floating type(s), 13, 52–53, 189, 194–196, 210
floating values, 212
floating variables, 209
floating zero, 39

floor() function, 572
flow of control, 80–127
    boolean variables problem solving, 103–104
    break and continue statements, 108–110
    combinatorics problem solving, 101–102
    comma operator, 104–105
    compound statement, 89
    conditional operator, 112–113
    do statement, 106
    empty statement, 89–90
    equality operators, 82–83, 84–85
    exercises, 121–127
    finding maximum values problem solving, 96–98
    for statement, 99–100
    goto statement, 107–108
    if and if-else statements, 90–95
    logical operators, 82–83, 85–89
    nested, 111–112
    programming errors, 115–118, 533
    programming style, 114–115
    relational operators, 82–84
    sequential, 22, 81
    switch statement, 110–111
    system considerations, 119–120
    while statement, 95–96
    See also recursion; structured programming
FLT_EPSILON macro, 568
FLT_MAX macro, 568
FLT_MIN macro, 568
fmod() function, 572
"food" program, 460
fopen() function, 481, 482, 486, 491–492, 499–500, 579
FOPEN_MAX macro, 494, 577
fork() function, 604
formal parameters, 131
format(s), 11, 473–475
formatted input/output, 584–585
"formatting" program, 183
formfeed, 163
for statement
    boolean variables problem solving, 104
    comma operator and, 104
    compound statement and, 89
    continue statement and, 109–110
    empty statement and, 89
    exercise using, 77, 123, 124, 125, 127, 156, 217, 258, 328, 423–424
    flow of control and, 99–100
    nested, 393
    nested flow of control and, 111
    programming errors and, 117
    programming style and, 114, 115, 177–178, 318–319, 320–321, 346
    two-dimensional arrays and, 313
fortune command, 537–538
4-byte words, 191–192, 212
fourth roots, table of, 216–217
fpos_t type definition, 578
fprintf() function, 479–480, 493, 501, 584
    See also printf() function
fputc() function, 583

fputs() function, 499, 583
fread() function, 586
free() function, 318, 423–424, 455–456, 588
Free Software Foundation, Inc., 532
freopen() function, 580
frexp() function, 572
friend keyword, 549
fscanf() function, 479–480, 481, 493, 494, 585
   See also scanf() function
fseek() function, 482, 490, 493, 495, 581
fsetpos() function, 482, 495, 582
ftell() function, 490, 493, 495, 581
function(s), 128–159
   ANSI C compared to traditional C, 610–611
   call-by-reference and, 263, 271–273
   call-by-value and, 149, 263, 271
   character, 592–593
   comparison, 359
   corecursive, 422
   corresponding, 376
   declarations and definitions, 286
   defining, 130–133, 286
   exercises, 155–159, 294–298
   function prototypes, 136–138
   game of heads or tails simulation, 146–149
   graceful, 323, 486–489
   insertion, 461
   invocation and call-by-value, 149
   invoking, 130
   library, 215
   mathematical, 198–201
   overloading in C++, 549–552
   passing arrays to, 309–310
   programming errors, 150–152, 211, 290–291
   programming style, 150, 177, 288–289, 346–347
   random numbers problem solving, 143–145
   return statement, 133–136
   string, 593
   string handling, 344–345, 348
   structures and assignment and, 437–439
   system considerations, 152–154, 291–292
   top-down design, 138–142
   two-dimensional arrays and, 314
function declarations, 286, 558
function definitions, 130–133, 286, 387, 395
function invocation, 130, 149, 286
function names, 28–29
function parameters, 277
function prototype(s), 136–138
   defined, 136
   exercise using, 563
   for fprintf() function, 480
   for fscanf() function, 480
   function declarations and definitions and, 286
   preprocessor and, 64–65
   programming errors and, 151–152, 211, 212
   programming style and, 387
   for sprintf() function, 478
   for sscanf() function, 478
   standard library and, 65
   system considerations and, 153–154, 292, 559
fundamental data types, 186–222
   characters and char data type, 189–191
   computing interest problem solving, 204–209
   conversions and casts, 201–204
   declarations and expressions, 187–188
   exercises, 214–222
   floating types, 194–196
   grouped by functionality, 189
   int data type, 191–192
   listed, 188
   mathematical functions, 198–201
   programming errors, 210–212
   programming style, 209–210
   short, long, and unsigned integral types, 193–194
   sizeof operator, 197–198
   system considerations, 212–213
fwrite() function, 586

galloc() function, 323
game of heads or tails, 146–149, 185
game of paper, rock, scissors, 230–236, 255
garbage, 455
gcalloc() function, 514
gcc command, 512
gcd() function, 423
gcmalloc() function, 514
generalization, 172
general recursive case. *See* recursion
getc() function, 582
getchar() function, 164–167, 177, 182, 183, 582
getenv() function, 510, 511, 589
get from operator, 545
get_info() function, 499–500
get_number() function, 398
get_options.c file, 380
get_options() function, 380–382
gets() function, 476, 583
get_word() function, 398, 408
getwords() function, 502
gfclose() function, 514
gfopen() function, 500, 514, 515
%g format, 18, 466, 473
%G format, 466, 473
g_lib.a file, 515
g_lib directory, 514
g_lib.h file, 515
gmtime() function, 601
Goldbach conjecture, 157–158
-g option, 513, 524
goto statement, 107–108
graceful functions, 323, 486–489
"graceful library," 514
"graininess," 214
greater than or equal to operator >=, 82, 83–84
greater than operator >, 82, 83–84
greatest common divisor, 422–423
greatest common divisor algorithm, 416
grep command, 502–503, 531, 532

"hailstones," 157
hailstones() function, 157
handling
   characters, 566–567
   errors, 582

memory, 594–595
signals, 574
strings, 344–345, 411–412, 594, 595–598
hard-to-print characters, 163–164
/* Have a nice day! */, 334
have a nice day, 334–337
hc command, 512
%hd format, 210–211
header (of function definition), 131
header files
  ANSI C compared to traditional C, 613–614
  defined, 64
  described, 64–65
  exercise using, 77
  printing in columns example and, 378–379
  programming style and, 387, 457
  standard library and, 65
  system considerations and, 292
  See also standard header files
heads or tails, game of, 146–149, 185
help command, 524
Hesperus, 8
heuristic, 426
hexadecimal integer constants, 52, 192
hexadecimal numbers, 221–222
.h files, 64, 377, 387
%h format, 467–468, 474, 602
%H format, 602
hiding data, 547
HOME environment variable, 511
-h option, 382, 397
horizontal tab character, 163
HUGE_VAL macro, 570

identifiers, 51–52
  defined, 11
  discriminated, 72–73
  exercise using, 74, 77, 79
  misspelling, 28–29
  programming style and, 27, 177, 209
  scope of, 273–274
IEEE recommendations, 222
IEEE Standard for Binary Floating-Point Arithmetic, 212
#ifdef preprocessing directive, 369–372
if-else statement
  compound statement and, 89
  empty statement and, 89
  flow of control and, 90–95
  for statement and, 100
  nested, 115
  nested flow of control and, 111–112
  programming errors and, 118
  switch statement and, 110
  See also if statement
.i files, 391, 394
#ifndef preprocessing directive, 369–372
%i format, 466, 473
#if preprocessing directive, 369–372
if statement
  break statement and, 109
  compound statement and, 89
  finding maximum values problem solving and, 96–98
  flow of control and, 90–95
  for statement and, 100
  nested flow of control and, 111
  programming errors and, 117, 118
  See also if-else statement
illegal pointer assigments, 270
implicit conversion, 202–203
include files, 64
#include preprocessing directive, 27–28, 64, 79, 354, 387
inclusive or operator, 236, 239
increment operator ++, 57–58, 68, 77–78
indentation, 27, 28, 114
"indentation" program, 183
indent command, 531, 532
index, 302, 304
indicator, 578
indirection operator *, 265, 266, 267, 296
Inf, 39, 222
infile file, 180, 421, 476
infinite loops
  exercise using, 123, 124, 127, 217
  programming errors and, 116–117, 416–417
  programming style and, 209–210
  system considerations and, 119–120
  See also do statement; for statement; while statement
"infinity," 39, 222
inheritance, 554–557
initialization
  ANSI C compared to traditional C, 609
  default, 281
  multidimensional arrays and, 316
  one-dimensional arrays and, 303–304
  of strings, 333
  of structures, 443–444
  writing programs and, 14–15
initializer, 303
initializing variables, 14–15
input
  C++, 543–546
  character, 582–584
  direct, 585–586
  exercises, 496–504
  files and, 464–504
  formatted, 584–585
  programming errors, 492–494
  programming style, 491–492
  redirecting, 32–33
  standard, 180
  standard library and, 577–586
  stream, 561
  system considerations, 494–495
input devices, 4
input failure, 477
input file, 184
input file, 180
input function. *See* scanf() function
input operator >>, 545
input stream, 19, 475
insert() function, 454, 462
/* Inserting an element in a linked list. */, 454
insertion, 453–456

insertion function, 461
insertion operator, 543
int data type, 191–192
    characters and, 189
    exercise using, 215, 216, 219, 294
    integral promotions and, 201
    listed, 188, 189
    printing bitwise, 242–245
    register storage class and, 278
    system considerations and, 213, 252
    usual arithmetic conversions and, 202
integer arithmetic, 589–590
integer constants, 52–53, 192, 211
integer overflow, 192, 210
integers, 52, 189, 191
integral limits, 569
integral promotion, 201, 202–203
integral types, 189
interest, 204–209
"interest" program, 209–210, 218
"intermediate" code, 391, 394
internal clock. See clock; date; time
internal discriminated identifiers, 72–73
interprocess communication, 605
interrupting programs, 32, 593–594, 605
INT_MAX macro, 569
INT_MIN macro, 569
inverse function, 256
"investment" program, 218
invocation, 130, 149, 286
invoked, 7, 130
I/O. See input; output
_IOFBF macro, 579
_IOLBF macro, 579
_IONBF macro, 579
−I option, 513
iostream.h, 546
"I" program, 35
isalnum() macro, 172, 566
isalpha() macro, 172, 566
isascii() macro, 172
iscntrl() macro, 172, 566
isdigit() macro, 172, 566
isgraph() macro, 172, 566
islower() macro, 172, 566
is_prime() function, 158
isprint() macro, 172, 183, 566
ispunct() macro, 172, 566
isspace() macro, 172, 387, 566
isupper() macro, 172, 566
isvowel() function, 183
isxdigit() macro, 172, 566
iteration, 24
    See also do statement; for statement; recursion;
      while statement

%j format, 602
jmp_buf type, 573
jump constructs. See break statement; continue state-
    ment; goto statement; return statement
jumps, 573

Kelley, Al, 425
keyboard, reading characters from, 164–167, 177, 182,
    183, 582
keywords, 50, 74
    See also reserved words
knight, 426
knight's tour, 426
−K option, 181–182

l, 467–468, 474
L, 468, 474
labeled statements, 107–108
labs() function, 589
large programs, 377, 533
"lawn" program, 37
LC_ALL symbolic constant, 569
LC_COLLATE symbolic constant, 569
LC_CTYPE symbolic constant, 569
LC_MONETARY symbolic constant, 569
LC_NUMERIC symbolic constant, 569
lconv structure type, 569
LC_TIME symbolic constant, 569
LDBL_EPSILON macro, 568
LDBL_MAX macro, 568
LDBL_MIN macro, 568
ldexp() function, 572
ldiv() function, 590
ldiv_t type definition, 587
leaving programs, 32, 593–594, 605
left shift operator <<, 236, 239–241
legal pointer assignments, 270
less than or equal to operator <=, 82, 83–84
less than operator <, 82, 83–84
letters
    counting, 304–307
    exercise using, 349
    identifiers and, 51
    listed, 46
    lowercase, 181, 325, 349, 387, 397
    uppercase, 181, 349, 350, 387
lexical elements, 46–49
    comments, 49–50
    constants, 52–53
    exercises, 74–79
    identifiers, 51–52
    keywords, 50
    operators and punctuators, 54–55
    programming errors, 70–72
    programming style, 68–69
    string constants, 53–54
    system considerations, 72–73
lexico() function, 369, 399
lexicographic order. See sorting
lex utility, 532
%lf format, 19, 22, 29, 211, 492–493
%LF format, 19, 20, 21
lib command, 513
.lib files, 78, 513
/lib/libc.a file, 514
librarian, 513
libraries, 78, 513–515
    See also standard library

library functions, 215
limits, 568, 569
limits.h standard header file, 218, 220, 569
LIMIT symbolic constant, 221–222
linear linked lists, 448–450
  counting and lookup and, 452–453
  defined, 448
  exercises, 459–463
  insertion and deletion and, 453–456
  list operations and, 450–452
  programming errors, 457
  programming style, 456–457
  system considerations, 458
line numbers, 375
"line numbers" program, 498
__LINE__ predefined macro, 372
#line preprocessing directive, 375
link, 447
linked lists. *See* linear linked lists
linker. *See* loader
list command, 524
/* List creation by recursion. */, 451
list.h header file, 448, 461, 462
lists, linked. *See* linear linked lists
-*lm* option, 198, 212–213
loader, 5, 212–213, 391, 512
  See also C system
locale.h standard header file, 569–570
localization, 569–570
localtime() function, 601
log() function, 198, 571
log10() function, 571
logical expressions, 121, 126
logical and operator &&, 82, 85–89
logical or operator ||, 82, 85–89
logical operators, 82–83, 85–89, 90, 236, 239
.*login* file, 511
LOGNAME environment variable, 511
.*logout* files, 537–538
long, 213, 216, 219
long double floating type, 194–196
  described, 13
  exercise using, 219
  listed, 188, 189
  system considerations and, 72, 213
  usual arithmetic conversions and, 202
Longfellow, Henry Wadsworth, 8
long integral type, 188, 189, 193–194, 202
longjmp() function, 573
lookup, 452–453
/* Lookup c in the list pointed to by head. */, 453
lookup() function, 453, 461, 462
look_up function, 423
loops. *See* do statement; for statement; while statement
loop variables, 277
-*l* option, 397
lower bound, 324
lowercase letters
  exercise using, 325, 349, 397
  identifiers and, 51
  listed, 46

programming style and, 387
system considerations and, 181
ls command, 32, 33, 398, 534
  exercise using, 398
  system considerations and, 32, 33, 534
L_tmpnam macro, 577
"lucky number" program, 296–297

machine words, 191–192
macro definitions, 78, 395
macros
  with arguments, 356–357
  in *ctype.h,* 171–172
  described, 353
  predefined, 372, 393–394
  programming errors and, 389–390
  programming style and, 177, 387
  in *stddef.h,* 358
  system considerations and, 390
macros with arguments, 364–369
"magic cookie," 581
main.c file, 379, 516
main() function
  double-spacing files example and, 482
  drawing patterns on screen example and, 411
  environment variables and, 510
  exercise using, 75, 254, 295, 326, 421
  function invocation and, 130
  passing arguments to, 342–344
  printing in columns example and, 379
  programming errors and, 151, 290
  programming style and, 27–28, 150, 320–321
  structures, functions, and assignment and, 439
main keyword, 74
majority() function, 257
make command, 525–530, 533, 534, 536–537
makefile file, 525–530, 534, 536–537
Makefile file, 534
malloc() function
  dynamic memory allocation and, 316–318
  dynamic storage allocation and, 449
  insertion and deletion and, 455
  pointers to void and, 270
  stdlib.h standard header file and, 587
  system considerations and, 322–323, 494
man ascii command, 617
man fortune command, 538
man sort command, 535–536
/* Many other languages require ""do,'' but not C. */, 123
mapping characters, 567
masks, 241–242, 251
matching failure, 477
mathematical functions, 198–201
mathematics, 65, 198, 570–573
mathematics library, 212–213
math.h standard header file, 395, 570–573
max() function, 127, 135, 136, 395
maximum() function, 320–321
maximum values, 96–98
mblen() function, 592
mbstowcs() function, 593

`mbtowc()` function, 592
`meal()` function, 255
"meal" program, 459
`median` variable, 77
member operator, 430, 435, 436, 548
members, 429, 432–435, 547
`memchr()` function, 594
`memcmp()` function, 594
`memcpy()` function, 594
`memmove()` function, 595
memory
   characters and, 189–191
   described, 4
   dynamic allocation of, 587–588
   exercise using, 294
   pointer addressing and dereferencing and, 264–269
   system considerations and, 322–323, 458, 494
memory allocation, 316–318, 322
"memory allocation" function. *See* `malloc()` function
memory handling, 594–595
`memset()` function, 595
merge tokens operator, 372–373
message program, 132–133, 136, 155
messages. *See* error(s); warnings
methodology. *See* divide-and-conquer methodology;
     program methodology
%m format, 602
%M format, 602
mi_km program, 546
`// Miles are converted to kilometers.`, 545
"miles to kilometers" program, 561
`min()` function, 127, 135, 136, 137, 138, 357
minimum program, 134–135, 137
`minmax()` function, 414, 423–425
minus, 72, 398
`minus_cnt` variable, 77
minus sign flag character, 468, 469
misspelling function names, 28–29
misspelling variable names, 28–29
mitok program, 561
mixed expressions, 203
mk_cols.c file, 383–386, 387
mk_cols directory, 378
`mk_cols()` function, 382–384
mk_cols.h file, 379, 399–400
mk_cols program, 377, 391, 397–398, 399–400, 536
mkdir command, 378
`mktime()` function, 601
-MM option, 513
mode, 492, 493, 495
`modf()` function, 573
modular arithmetic, 220
modularity, 376
module(s), 376, 387, 391, 533
   See also file(s)
modulus operator %, 12, 14, 39, 54–55, 77
mon.out file, 515
Monte Carlo simulations, 143, 146
moon program, 543–544
-M option, 513
more command, 502
multibyte character functions, 592–593

multibyte string functions, 593
multicharacter character constants, 248, 252, 260
multidimensional arrays, 312–316
multiplication operator *, 12, 54–55, 296
mv command, 31
my_copy file, 180
my_echo program, 343, 350
my_file file, 481, 482, 497, 502–503
"mystery" program, 217

"name and age" program, 562
names, 27, 28–29, 73, 79
NaN, 39, 222
natural numbers, 191
NDEBUG macro, 374, 566
negation operator !, 82, 85–89
negative integers, 52
negative numbers, 238
nested flow of control, 111–112
nested `for` statement, 393
nested `if-else` statement, 115
nesting comments, 75, 397
newline character, 46, 163, 183
new operator, 552–554
next command, 524
next-day program, 254
%n format, 466, 474, 496
nice_day program, 335–337, 349
nlines command, 498–499
nonlocal jumps, 573
nonprinting characters, 163–164
-n option, 398, 502, 503
notation, 194, 195
not equal to operator !=, 82, 84–85
not a number, 39, 212, 222
null character, 163, 332–333, 346, 347
NULL macro, 264, 358, 576–577, 587
numbers
   floating, 119, 475
   hexadecimal, 221–222
   line, 375, 498
   lucky, 296–297
   natural, 191
   negative, 238
   octal, 221–222
   positional, 190–191
   random, 143–145, 279–281, 589
   real, 13, 214
   system considerations and, 119
`nyears` variable, 218

object(s), 552, 554
object code, 5
   See also programs
object file(s), 5
   See also .obj files; .o files
Object-Oriented Programming (Budd), 542
object-oriented programming (OOP), 554–557
   See also C++
.obj files, 391, 512
occ command, 512
octal integer constants, 52, 192

octal numbers, 221–222
`offsetof()` macro, 576–577
.o files, 391, 512
`%o` format, 221–222, 466, 473
one-dimensional arrays, 301–304
OOP. *See* object-oriented programming
-o option, 31, 513
-O option, 513
`open()` function, 603
opening files, 491–492, 579–580
operating system, 4, 508–509
   See also C system; utilities
`operator+()` function, 551–552
`operator` keyword, 549
operators, 54–55
   arithmetic, 12
   bitwise, 236–241, 249, 250–251, 252, 254–260
   computing powers of 2 example, 62–63
   equality, 82–83, 84–85
   exercises, 74–79
   logical, 82–83, 85–89, 236, 239
   overloading in C++, 549–552
   precedence and associativity of, 55–57, 436–437, 618
   programming errors, 70–72
   programming style, 68–69
   programming style and, 28
   relational, 82–84, 117–118
   system considerations, 72–73
`order_chars` function, 295
order of evaluation, 126
ordinary characters, 472
or operators, 236, 239
"ounces to grams" program, 75
out of bounds, 324
outfile file, 180, 476, 481, 499, 501, 561
.out files, 512
output
   C++, 542–543
   character, 582–584
   direct, 585–586
   exercises, 496–504
   files and, 464–504
   formatted, 584–585
   programming errors, 492–494
   programming style, 491–492
   redirecting, 32–33
   standard, 180
   standard library and, 577–586
   stream, 561
   system considerations, 494–495
output devices, 4
output file, 184
output function. *See* `printf()` function
output operator `<<`, 543
overflow, 192, 210
overlaying processes, 604–605
overloading, 549–552, 558, 563
`// Overloading the function print and the operator +.`, 550–551
overrunning bounds, 347
"overrunning the bounds of the array," 304

`/* Pack 4 characters into an int. */`, 245
`pack()` function, 259
packing, 245–248
palindromes, 420
paper, rock, scissors, game of, 230–236, 255
parameters
   described, 131
   `extern` storage class and, 276
   formal, 131
   function, 277
   function declarations and definitions and, 286
   programming style and, 289
   reference, 562–563
parentheses ( ), 55
   comma operator and, 105
   conditional operator and, 113
   exercise using, 75, 395, 461–462
   macros with arguments and, 356–357
   precedence and associativity of, 435, 436
   programming errors and, 388–389
   `return` statement and, 133
   `sizeof` operator and, 198
   two-dimensional arrays and, 314
passing
   arguments to `main()`, 342–344
   arrays to functions, 309–310
patterns, 410–411
period, 467
`perror()` function, 582
`%p` format
   exercise using, 294, 297, 298
   pointer addressing and dereferencing and, 269
   `printf()` function and, 466
   `scanf()` function and, 473
   `strftime()` function and, 602
   system considerations and, 292
pgm.c file, 185
pgm file, 476, 497
pgm program, 377
π, 222, 393
pipe, 605
`pipe()` function, 605
piping, 534
pips, 430, 460
plus, 72
`plus_cnt` variable, 77
plus sign flag character, 468
Pohl, Ira, 412, 425, 541
Pohl's improvement to Warnsdorf's rule, 426
pointer arithmetic, 308–309, 346
pointer assignment(s), 264, 270
pointer declaration, 264
pointers
   addressing and dereferencing, 264–269
   array, 612
   arrays and, 300–329
   declaration and assignment, 264
   default initialization of, 281
   evaluation of, 268
   exercises, 294–298, 324–329, 349–351
   file, 493
   function declarations and definitions and, 286

programming errors, 290–291, 322, 347
programming style, 288–289, 318–322, 346–347
relationship between arrays and, 307–308
strings and, 330–351
system considerations, 291–292, 322–323, 347–348
to void, 270
using to process strings, 337–341
poker, 460
polymorphically, 555
-p option, 513, 515–519
portable caps program, 170–171
portable code, 171
porting code, 493
positional numbers, 190–191
pos_t type definition, 577
"pounds to kilograms" program, 75
power function, 218–219
power() function, 219
powers of 2, 62–63
pow() function, 198, 208–209, 218, 221, 572
pow—of—2 program, 62–63, 75
#pragma preprocessing directive, 375
precedence
    of assignment operators, 59, 60
    of bitwise operators, 236–237
    of brackets, 435, 436
    of cast operator, 204
    of comma operator, 104, 436
    of conditional operator, 113
    of decrement operator, 57
    defined, 55
    of equality operators, 82, 85
    of increment operator, 57
    of logical operators, 82, 87–88
    of operators, 55–57, 436–437, 618
    of parentheses, 435, 436
    of relational operators, 82, 84
    of shift operators, 241
    of sizeof operator, 197, 436–437
    of structure member operator, 435, 436
    of structure pointer operator, 435, 436
precision, 18, 196, 467, 468–469
predefined macros, 372, 393–394
preprocessing directives #, 6, 15, 64, 353
preprocessing operator #, 372–373
preprocessing operator ##, 372–373, 391
preprocessor, 64–65, 352–376
    # operator, 372–373
    ## operator, 372–373
    ANSI C compared to traditional C, 613
    assert() macro, 374
    conditional compilation, 369–372
    corresponding functions, 376
    _define and, 354–356
    described, 5
    _error and, 375
    exercises, 393–400
    exercise using, 79
    _include and, 354
    line numbers, 375
    macros with arguments, 356–357
    macros with arguments example, 364–369

_pragma and, 375
predefined macros, 372
programming errors, 388–390
programming style, 387
sorting with qsort() problem solving, 359–363
system considerations, 390–391
type definitions and macros in stddef.h, 358
See also cpp command; C system
prerequisite files, 4, 527
"pretty printer," 185, 533, 539
previous_month() function, 254
print command, 524
printenv command, 510
printf() function, 22, 465–470
    char data type and, 163
    C++ input and, 546
    conditional compilation and, 370
    conversion characters, 18, 466
    C++ overloading and, 549
    exercise using, 38, 39, 40–41, 124, 159, 184, 214, 221–222, 254, 296, 393, 396, 422, 463, 501
    first program and, 7, 8
    function definition and, 131
    function invocation and, 130
    game of heads or tails simulation and, 148
    getchar() and putchar() and, 164
    if and if-else statements and, 90, 92
    preprocessing operators and, 373
    programming errors and, 29, 210–211, 492
    programming style and, 177
    scanf() function and, 20, 21
    stdio.h standard header file and, 584
    system considerations and, 292
    top-down design and, 139
    use of, 16–19
    using pointers to process strings and, 338
    See also fprintf() function; sprintf() function
printf keyword, 150
print() function, 150, 563
printing
    in columns, 377–386
    int bitwise, 242–245
print keyword, 150
/* Print a table of square roots. */, 152
/* Print a table of values for some boolean
    functions. */, 103
privacy, 279
private members, 547
PRN3() macro, 394–395
prn_array.c file, 518
prn_info.c file, 382
prn_info() function, 382, 397, 501
prn_instructions() function, 148, 204–209
prn keyword, 150
PRN() macro, 396
prn_message() function, 130, 131–133, 136
prn_random_numbers() function, 143, 145, 156
prn_rand program, 66–68, 77, 155
prn_results() function, 204–209
PRN_STRING() macro, 393
prn_student_data() function, 460
prn_time() function, 522

prn_total_time() function, 522
prn_values() function, 438, 439
probability() function, 280
processes, 604–605
process() function, 282, 284–285, 295
processing characters. *See* character processing
processing strings using pointers, 337–341
processor, 4
prof command, 515–519, 536
profiler, 515–519, 536
program methodology, 376–386
  developing large programs, 377
  exercises, 393–400
  printing in columns example, 377–386
  programming errors, 388–390
  programming style, 387
  system considerations, 390–391
  See also divide-and-conquer methodology
programming
  getting ready, 4–5
  object-oriented, 554–557
  structured, 129, 138–142, 150–154, 155–159
  writing programs, 2–42
programming errors. *See* error(s); warnings
programs, 242–245
  compiling, 4–5
  described, 4–5
  executing commands within, 508–509
  first, 5–8
  interrupting, 32
  large, 377, 533
  portable, 171
  porting, 493
  quitting, 593–594
  running, 29–33
  suspending, 605
  timing, 519–523
  writing, 2–42
  See also compiler; utilities
promotion, 201, 202–203, 252
prototypes, function. *See* function prototype(s)
pseudo random number generators. *See* random number generators
ptrdiff_t type definition, 358, 576–577
public keyword, 547
public members, 547
punctuators, 54–55
  See also braces; commas; empty statement; parentheses
putc() function, 502, 583
putchar() function, 164–167, 177, 182, 184, 584
puts() function, 584
putstring() function, 502
put to operator, 543

qc command, 512
qsort() function, 359–363, 364–369, 415, 516–518, 536, 588
  See also quicksort; sorting
qualifiers, 287–288
quicksort, 416, 536
  See also qsort() function; sorting

quicksort() function, 536
quit command, 524
quitting programs, 32, 593–594, 605
quotation marks. *See* double quote character; single quote character

raise() function, 574
rand_array variable, 329
rand() function
  exercise using, 77, 158–159, 328
  game of heads or tails simulation and, 146
  random numbers problem solving and, 143
  standard library and, 65–68
  stdlib.h standard header file and, 589
  system considerations and, 152–153
RAND_MAX macro, 77, 152–153, 587
random access, 490
random() function, 152–153, 280, 423
randomly accessing files, 490–491
random number generators
  described, 143, 589
  exercise using, 156, 158–159, 255
  standard library and, 589
  static external variables and, 279–281
  system considerations and, 152–153
random numbers, 143–145
"random numbers" program, 156
rand_out file, 328–329
range, 196
range error, 568, 571
ranlib command, 515
"rb" mode, 481, 491, 504
read, 150
read_and_prn_data() function, 140, 141–142, 150
read_date() function, 441–442
read() function, 603
read_grades() function, 442–443
read_in function, 338, 339
reading characters from keyboard, 164–167, 177, 182, 183, 582
READ_ME file, 378
/* Read in two integers and print their sum. */, 47
realloc() function, 587
real numbers, 13, 119, 214, 475
records, 440–443, 460
recursion, 402–426
  defined, 403
  divide-and-conquer methodology, 412–415
  drawing patterns on screen example, 410–411
  exercises, 420–426
  exercise using, 420–421
  programming errors, 416–417
  programming style, 415–416
  recursive problem solving, 404–409
  string handling using, 411–412
  system considerations, 418–419
  See also flow of control
recursive, 404
/* Recursive deletion of a list. */, 456
recursive problem solving, 404–409
/* Recursive string length. */, 411

`/* Recursive string n compare. */`, 412
redirection, 32–33, 38, 41, 180, 183, 217
reference, call-by-, 263, 271–273
reference parameters, 562–563
referencing, 264–269
reformat file, 183
`register` storage class, 274, 277–278
register variables, 281, 291
relational expressions, 118
relational operators, 82–84, 90, 117–118
`remove()` function, 509, 586
`rename()` function, 586
`repeat()` function, 173, 174, 183–184
repeating characters, 172–174
repeat program, 185
repetition. *See* do statement; `for` statement; `while` statement
`report_a_win()` function, 159
reserved words, 11
    See also keywords
restaurant structure, 460
restricted access, 547
`return()` function, 423
`return` statement
    exercise using, 259
    `extern` storage class and, 276
    functions and, 133–136
    processing characters example and, 281
    programming errors and, 151
    programming style and, 150, 289
return value, 477
`/* Reverse the characters between s[j] and s[k]` recursively. `*/`, 409
`reverse()` function, 563
`rewind()` function, 482, 495, 581
right shift operator `>>`, 236, 239–241
r key, 515
`"r"` mode, 481, 504
`"r+"` mode, 482
roulette program, 254
`r_strcpy()` function, 422
`r_strlen()` function, 411
`r_strncmp()` function, 420–421
rubout, 32
rules, 525, 527
run command, 524
running programs, 29–33
run_sums program, 159
run-time errors, 30, 31, 38–39

"salary" program, 121–122
"sales data" program, 327
`scanf()` function, 471–478
    char data type and, 163
    C++ input and, 546
    computing sums problem solving and, 24–25
    conversion characters, 19, 473, 474
    end-of-string sentinel and, 332
    exercise using, 38, 185, 215, 351, 496
    pointer addressing and dereferencing and, 267
    programming errors and, 29, 210–211, 347, 492
    programming style and, 177

random numbers problem solving and, 143
stdio.h standard header file and, 585
    use of, 16–17, 19–22
    See also `fscanf()` function; `sscanf()` function
scan field, 474
scan set, 475–476
scan width, 475
scientific notation, 194
scope, 273–274
screen
    drawing patterns on, 410–411
    writing characters to, 164–167, 177, 182, 184, 584
sea program, 6–7
`search()` function, 349
searching, 588
search program, 502–503
sed utility, 532
`seed` variable, 156, 280
`SEEK_CUR` macro, 579
`SEEK_END` macro, 579
`SEEK_SET` macro, 579
self-referential structures, 446–448, 457
semicolon, 55, 89–90, 117, 124, 357, 389
sequential access, 490
sequential flow of control, 22, 81
`setbuf()` function, 580
set command, 510, 535
setenv command, 535
`setjmp()` function, 573
setjmp.h standard header file, 573
`setlocale()` function, 570
`setvbuf()` function, 580
.s files, 513
`%s` format
    end-of-string sentinel and, 332
    exercise using, 158–159
    `printf()` function and, 17, 18, 466
    `scanf()` function and, 19, 473, 475
    `strftime()` function and, 602
shar program, 400
`SHELL` environment variable, 511
`shift()` function, 295
shifting sign bits, 258
shift operators. *See* left shift operator; right shift operator
`short`, 213, 216, 219, 252
short-circuit evaluation, 88–89, 125
`short` integral type, 188, 189, 193–194, 201, 248
`SHRT_MAX` macro, 569
`SHRT_MIN` macro, 569
side effect, 58, 289
`SIGABRT` macro, 574
`SIG_DFL` macro, 574
`SIG_ERR` macro, 574
`SIGFPE` macro, 574
`SIG_IGN` macro, 574
`SIGILL` macro, 574
`SIGINT` macro, 574
`signal()` function, 574
signal handling, 574
signal.h standard header file, 574
sign bits, 258
`signed`, 201
`signed char`, 188, 189, 191, 213, 252, 259

`signed int`, 188, 213
`signed long`, 213
`signed long int`, 188
`signed short`, 213
`signed short int`, 188
sign extension, 252
`SIGSEGV` macro, 574
`SIGTERM` macro, 574
Silicon Graphics workstation, 153
`sin()` function, 198, 215, 571
single quote character, 12, 162, 163, 164
single-spacing, 178–180, 502
`sinh()` function, 571
size
    element, 308–309
    of words, 191–192
`sizeof` operator, 197–198, 296, 358, 436–437, 449
SIZE symbolic constant, 325–326
`size_t` type definition, 317, 358, 359, 576–577
`size` variable, 329
slash, 398
`sleep()` function, 605
slow_sort.c file, 517
small letters. *See* lowercase letters
software. *See* programs
software methodology. *See* program methodology
software tools. *See* utilities
`/* Some powers of 2 are printed. */`, 62
-*S* option, 513
`sort_by_age()` function, 461
`sort_by_name()` function, 461
sort.c file, 364–369
sort command, 534, 536
sort.h header file, 364–369
sorting, 327–328, 349, 516–518, 536, 588
    See also bubble sort sorting algorithm; `qsort()`
        function; quicksort; transposition sort
"Sorting Problem and Its Complexity, A" (Pohl), 412
sort program, 364–369, 399
source code, 4
    See also programs
source files, 4, 527
space flag character, 468
spacing. *See* double-spacing; single-spacing;
    triple-spacing; white space
`spawnl()` function, 605
`sprintf()` function, 478–479, 493, 584
    See also `printf()` function
`SQ()` macro, 388–389
sq_roots program, 217
`sqrt()` function, 152, 198, 211, 212–213, 220, 572
sqrt_pow program, 200–201
`square()` function, 155
square roots, table of, 216–217, 562
squares, table of, 562
`srand()` function, 156, 158–159, 520, 589
_ss, 79
`sscanf()` function, 381, 478–479, 493, 500–501, 585
    See also `scanf()` function
standard error file. *See* `stderr` macro
standard header files, 286, 354
    See also header files
standard input files. *See* `stdin` macro

standard input/output, 180
standard library, 65–68, 564–605
    character handling, 566–567
    date, 598–602
    definitions, 576–577
    described, 8
    diagnostics, 566
    errors, 567–568
    exercise using, 78
    floating limits, 568
    input/output, 577–586
    integral limits, 569
    localization, 569–570
    mathematics, 65, 198, 570–573
    memory handling, 594–595
    nonlocal jumps, 573
    programming style and, 346–347
    signal handling, 574
    string handling, 344–345, 594, 595–598
    system considerations and, 152–153, 212–213, 348
    time, 598–602
    utilities, 586–594
    variable arguments, 575–576
    See also C system
standard output files. *See* `stdout` macro
START symbolic constant, 157–158
`start_time()` function, 522
statement(s)
    compound, 24, 89, 91
    empty, 55, 89–90, 357
    expression, 90
    labeled, 107–108
    programming style and, 28
static external variables, 279–281, 298
`static` storage class, 274, 278, 279–281, 286, 458
static variables, 422
`stats()` function, 321, 322
stdarg.h standard header file, 575–576
__STDC__ predefined macro, 372
stddef.h standard header file, 358, 576–577
`stderr` macro
    accessing files randomly and, 491
    described, 479–480
    exercise using, 498, 501
    `fprintf()` and `fscanf()` functions and, 480
    stdio.h standard header file and, 578
    system considerations and, 494
`stdin` macro
    described, 479–480
    exercise using, 184
    `fprintf()` and `fscanf()` functions and, 480
    `scanf()` function and, 471
    stdio.h standard header file and, 578
    system considerations and, 494, 534
stdio.h standard header file, 577–586
    C++ input and, 546
    described, 479–480
    exercise using, 259
    `getchar()` and `putchar()` and, 164
    `#include` and, 354
    programming style and, 177
    system considerations and, 494
stdlib.h standard header file, 77, 354, 359, 586–594

stdout macro
  described, 479–480
  exercise using, 184, 496, 499, 501
  fprintf() and fscanf() functions and, 480
  printf() function and, 465
  stdio.h standard header file and, 578
  system considerations and, 494, 534
step command, 524
stepwise refinement. *See* top-down design
stop command, 524
stopping programs, 32, 593–594, 605
storage, 458
storage allocation, 449–450
storage classes, 274–278
  automatic, 458
  defined, 274
  exercises, 294–298
  external, 458
  programming errors, 290–291
  programming style, 288–289
  static, 458
  system considerations, 291–292
storage mapping function, 314
strcat() function, 344, 347, 595
strchr() function, 595
strcmp() function, 344, 351, 421, 595
strcoll() function, 595
strcpy() function, 344, 422, 595
strcspn() function, 596
stream, 475, 579
stream I/O, 561
strerror() function, 596
strftime() function, 601–602
string(s)
  accessing, 497
  bit, 190
  constant, 350–351, 422
  control, 11, 471
  default initialization of, 281
  defined, 331
  exercises, 349–351
  initialization of, 333
  pointers and, 330–351
  programming errors, 347
  programming style, 346–347
  system considerations, 347–348
  using pointers to process, 337–341
  See also arrays
string class, 563
string constants, 53–54, 78, 394
string conversion, 590–592
string functions, 593
string handling, 344–345, 411–412, 594, 595–598
string handling functions, 348
string.h standard header file, 344, 594–598
stringization, 395
"stringization" operator, 372–373, 395–396, 399
string literals, 53–54
string_to_list() function, 451–452, 462
string transformation function, 598
string variable, 552–554
strlen() function, 344–345, 411, 596

strncat() function, 596
strncmp() function, 350, 412, 596
strncpy() function, 596
strpbrk() function, 597
strrchr() function, 597
strspn() function, 597
strstr() function, 597
strtod() function, 590, 591
strtok() function, 597
strtol() function, 591
strtoul() function, 592
struct, 440–443
  See also class
structured programming, 129, 138–142, 150–154, 155–159
  See also flow of control
structure member operator ".", 430, 435, 436, 548
structure pointer operator ->, 432, 435, 436, 438
structures
  accessing members and, 432–435
  ANSI C compared to traditional C, 612
  declaring, 430–432
  default initialization of, 281
  exercises, 459–463
  functions and assignment and, 437–439
  initialization of, 443–444
  programming errors, 457
  programming style, 456–457
  self-referential, 446–448, 457
  student records problem solving and, 440–443
  system considerations, 458
strxfrm() function, 598
stty command, 41–42
student_data type, 460
student.h file, 440
student records, 440–443, 460
student style, 114
subscript(s), 302, 304, 322, 324, 346, 349
subscripting, 304
"subscript out of bounds," 304
subtraction, 238
subtraction operator _, 12, 54–55
suffixes, 194
sum_digit() function, 422
sum() function, 310, 320–321, 325, 326–327, 403–404, 418–419
sum program, 47–49
sums, 24–27
/* Sums are computed. */, 25
sum variable, 40
Sun workstation, 153, 213
suspending programs, 32, 593–594, 605
swap() function, 271, 272, 289, 290, 310
swapping function, 562–563
swap program, 289
switch statement, 89, 109, 110–111
symbolic constants, 16, 75, 318, 355, 387
symbols, 74
syntactic sugar, 355–356, 387
syntax, 45
syntax errors, 30, 31
system commands, 532

system considerations. *See* C system; operating system
system() function, 508–509, 532, 536, 538, 589

tab character, 46, 163, 183, 396, 562
table of square roots and fourth roots, 216–217
table of squares, square roots, and cubes, 562
tan() function, 198, 215, 571
tanh() function, 571
"tax" program, 121–122
tcc command
   exercise using, 536
   listed, 512
   programming errors and, 70, 72
   system considerations and, 30–33, 153, 534
tc command, 70, 182, 512, 534
\tc\include directory, 64
temp file, 41, 498
template, 226, 228
temporary files, 486–489
// Test of the class string., 548
/* Test the depth of recursion for sum(). */, 418–419
test file, 421
testing characters, 566–567
tests, 118, 127, 177–178
text editor, 4
text file, 397
text files, 495, 504
/* The best possible minmax algorithm=Pohl, 1972. */, 413
// The distance to the moon converted to kilometers., 544
/* The game of paper, rock, scissors. */, 231–232
three-dimensional arrays, 315
"386 machines," 212
tilde symbol ~, 553
time, 519–523, 598–602
   See also clock; date; *touch*
time() function, 159, 520–523, 600
time.h standard header file, 159, 519, 598–602
time_keeper.c, 520
__TIME__ predefined macro, 372
time_t type definition, 519–520, 598
timing programs, 519–523
t key, 514
tk structure, 522
tlib command, 513
tmp.c file, 399–400
tmpfile() function, 486, 580
TMP_MAX macro, 577
tmpnam() function, 509, 580
tm structure type, 599
toascii() macro, 172, 567
tokens, 45–46, 74
   See also constants; identifiers; keywords; operators; punctuators; string constants
tolower() function, 172, 181, 567
_tolower() macro, 181, 567
tools, software. *See* utilities
top-down design, 129, 138–142
   See also structured programming

toss() function, 148
touch, 531
   See also time
toupper() function, 172, 181, 567
_toupper() macro, 181, 567
traditional C
   ANSI C compared to, 606–614
   See also C++; C system
translation unit, 30
transposition sort, 327, 359, 516–518, 536
   See also sorting
triple-spacing, 178–180, 502
True forever! program, 123–124
truth table, 126
try_me.c file, 185, 394, 539
try_me file, 498
try_me.i file, 394
try_qsort program, 361–363
Turbo C++ (Pohl), 541
"24-hour clock" program, 220
2, powers of, 62–63
2-byte words, 191–192, 212
two-dimensional arrays, 312–314
two's complement, 238
two's complement machine, 238
two's complement representation, 238, 257
type(s)
   ANSI C compared to traditional C, 607–608
   arithmetic, 189
   boolean, 255
   data, 162–164, 186–222, 546–548
   defined, 131
   enumeration, 201, 225–227, 249, 250–251, 252, 254–260
   expressions and, 188
   floating, 13, 189, 194–196
   integral, 189, 193–194
   suffixes to specify, 194
type command, 504
typedef
   exercises, 254–260, 462
   programming errors, 250–251, 457
   programming style, 249, 456
   system considerations, 252
   type definitions and macros in *stddef.h* and, 358
   use of, 227–230, 444–446
type definitions, 358
type qualifiers, 287
type specifiers, 226
typing end-of-file signal, 32

%u format
   exercise using, 259, 294, 297, 298
   pointer addressing and dereferencing and, 269
   printf() function and, 466
   scanf() function and, 473
%U format, 602
u key, 515
u_lib.a library, 519, 522
u_lib.h header file, 522
unary operators. *See* operators
#undef preprocessing directive, 357, 369–372

underscore _, 51–52, 79
ungetc() function, 502, 584
unions, 281, 612
Universal Time Coordinated (UTC). *See* time
/* Unpack a byte from an int. */, 246
unpack() function, 246–248, 295–296
unpacking, 245–248
/* Unpack the packed int p into 4 characters. */, 296
unsigned char, 188, 189, 191, 213, 252, 259
unsigned int, 188, 201
unsigned integral type, 188, 189, 193–194, 201, 216, 219
unsigned long, 188, 189, 202, 220
unsigned long int, 188
unsigned short, 188, 189, 252
unsigned short int, 188
-u option, 378, 397
uppercase letters, 46, 51, 349, 350, 387
/usr/include directory, 64, 354
usual arithmetic conversions, 202–203
UTC (Universal Time Coordinated). *See* time
    utilities, 506–539
    data-compression, 185
    exercises, 535–539
    other, 531–532
    programming errors, 533
    programming style, 532
    standard library and, 586–594
    system considerations, 533–534
    See also programs

va_arg() macro, 575
va_end() macro, 575
va_list type definition, 575, 577
value(s)
    call-by-, 149, 263, 271
    expressions and, 188
    floating, 212
    maximum, 96–98
value, 38
variable arguments, 575–576
variable names. *See* identifiers
variables
    automatic, 281
    boolean, 103–104, 126, 258
    call-by-value and, 271
    character, 177
    characters and, 189
    environment, 509–511, 533, 535
    external, 279–281, 298
    floating, 209
    initializing, 14–15
    loop, 277
    programming errors and, 178, 457
    programming style and, 209
    register, 281, 291
    static, 422
    writing programs and, 8–14
va_start() macro, 575

vertical tab character, 163
vfork() function,
vfprintf() function, 585
vi, 30, 114, 508
virtual functions, 555
v key, 515
void, 131, 136, 270, 558
volatile type qualifier, 287–288
-v option, 533
"vowels" program, 183
vprintf() function, 585
vsprintf() function, 585

warnings, 71–72, 153, 292, 532, 533
    See also error(s)
Warnsdorf-Pohl rule, 426
Warnsdorf's rule, 426
"wb" mode, 481
"wb+" mode, 486
wc command, 514, 531, 532
wchar_t type definition, 358, 576–577
wcstombs() function, 593
wctomb() function, 593
%w format, 602
while statement
    compound statement and, 89
    computing sums problem solving and, 24–25
    continue statement and, 109
    exercise using, 40, 77, 123, 124, 217
    finding maximum values problem solving and, 96–98
    flow of control and, 95–96
    for statement and, 100
    nested flow of control and, 111
    programming errors and, 117
    programming style and, 115, 177–178
    syntactic sugar and, 355–356
    writing programs and, 22–23
white space
    characters and lexical elements and, 49
    exercise using, 75, 76–77, 183, 399
    operators and punctuators and, 54–55
    preprocessor and, 64
    scanf() function and, 21
    string constants and, 54
white space characters, 46, 472
widening, 202–203
width
    field, 18, 467, 468–469
    scan, 475
"w" mode, 481
"w+" mode, 482
-w option, 72, 153
word_cnt() function, 349
word_cnt program, 175–176
"word count" command, 514, 531, 532
words, 11, 174–176, 212, 342
word size, 191–192
working floating type, 13
wr_bkwds program, 406–407
write, 150
write() function, 603

`/* Write a line backwards. */`, 406
writing characters to screen, 164–167, 177, 182, 184, 584
writing programs, 2–42
  computing sums problem solving, 24–27
  `_define` and, 15–16
  exercises, 34–42
  first program, 5–8
  getting ready, 4–5
  initialization, 14–15
  `printf()` and, 16–19
  programming errors, 28–29
  programming style, 27–28
  `scanf()` and, 16–17, 19–22
  system considerations, 29–33
  variables, expressions, and assignment, 8–14

`while` statement, 22–24
  See also programming; programs
`wrt`, 150
wrt_rand program, 499–500, 501

`%x` format, 221–222, 466, 473, 602
`%X` format, 466, 473, 602
`XOR()` macro, 393

yacc utility, 532
`%y` format, 602

zero, 39
zero flag character, 468
`%z` format, 602